ARLOTTE

NORTH CAROLINA

W9-BCT-951

he Waxhaws

ncaster

Pageland   chesterfield
Jefferson

Cheraw

Society Hill

Hartsville

Darlington

PAPERBOARD MILL
GEORGETOWN

Camden

ree River

FLORENCE

TIMMONSVILLE

Pee Dee River

Little Pee Dee River

Waccamaw River

ackson

Stateburg

Sumter

Conway

CAROLINA

ort Motte

Kingstree

Myrtle Beach

Lake Marion

Brookgreen Gardens

Murrells Inlet

Eutawville

Santee River

Georgetown

Lake
Moultrie

Winyah Bay

Moncks Corner

Cooper River

to River

Ashley River

Cypress Gardens

Goose Creek

Middleton Gardens

Walterboro

Magnolia Gardens

cksonboro

CHARLESTON

Johns
Island

Sullivans Island

Fort Sumter
Morris
Island

e River

Beaufort
St. Helena Island
Marine Corps
Recruit Depot

ltonhead

COLUMBIA

SOUTH CAROLINA
Annals of Pride and Protest

REGIONS OF AMERICA

A SERIES OF BOOKS THAT DEPICT

OUR NATURAL REGIONS, THEIR HISTORY,

DEVELOPMENT AND CHARACTER.

EDITED BY CARL CARMER

SOUTH CAROLINA
Annals of Pride and Protest

by *William Francis Guess*

A REGIONS OF AMERICA BOOK

ILLUSTRATIONS AND MAPS
BY JOHN O'HARA COSGRAVE II

HARPER & BROTHERS, PUBLISHERS, NEW YORK

Grateful acknowledgment is made to Holt, Rinehart and Winston, Inc., for permission to reprint the poem "Modern Philosopher" from Carolina Chansons, by DuBose Heyward and Hervey Allen, copyright 1922 by Rinehart & Co., Inc., copyright renewed 1950 by Dorothy Heyward; to the Houghton Mifflin Company for material from A Diary from Dixie, edited by Ben Ames Williams; to Louisiana State University Press for material from Pitchfork Ben Tillman, by Francis B. Simkins; and to the University of North Carolina Press for material from The South Carolina Backcountry on the Eve of the Revolution, edited by Richard J. Hooker.

Chapter I was originally published in Harper's Magazine, December, 1957.

Contents

Contents

Acknowledgments

Most of the debts a writer incurs—those of mind and craft—he can only repay by writing well. If this book squares no such debts, I hope that it may at least signify good intent to some of my creditors. Otherwise, I wish to thank by name those people who have lent me their time and talents in recent months: Mary Katherine Kahl, who has listened and prompted with the sympathetic acuity of a loyal friend and a lively scholar; Richard Hart, of Baltimore, who has advised with a poet's perception and the wisdom of a literary elder statesman; and Mrs. Ruth Kimmerer, of Baltimore, who has worked such feats of speed and accuracy that I think of her as standing to most typists as a virtuoso to an amateur fiddler.

I have used the library facilities of several institutions—among them the State Teachers College at Towson and the Peabody Institute, of Baltimore—but none more continuously or gratefully than those of the Johns Hopkins University.

WILLIAM FRANCIS GUESS

Baltimore, Maryland

The Best Friend Of Charleston 1830   The first Locomotive built in America to run in regular service.

REFERENCE

1. Bathing House
2. White Point Garden
3. William Gibbes House
4. John Edwards House
5. William Washington House
6. George Edwards House
7. Miles Brewton (Pringle) House
8. William Ravenel House
9. Mathewes House
10. First Baptist Church
11. First Scotch Presbyterian Church
12. South Carolina Society Hall
13. St. Michael's Church
14. Post Office
15. Horry House
16. Izard Houses
17. Mills House
18. City Hall
19. City Hospital
20. St. Andrew's Hall
21. Unitarian Church
22. St. John's Lutheran Church
23. Circular Church
24. Powder Magazine
25. St. Philip's Church
26. Slave Market
27. Chisholm's Mills
28. College of Charleston
29. The Citadel
30. South Carolina R.R. Depot
31. North Eastern R.R. Depot
32. Ship Yards
33. Mt. Pleasant Ferry
34. Custom House

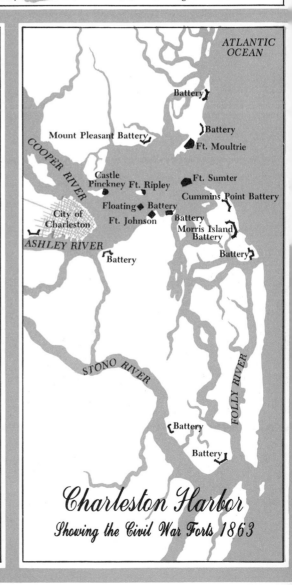

Charleston Harbor
Showing the Civil War Forts 1863

Cowpens ■

■Kings Mountain

Caesars Head

York •
•Paris Mountain ★ SPARTANBURG   ROCK HILL ★

★ GREENVILLE

Walhalla •

Clemson •   Union •   • Chester
        • Pendleton

        • Anderson

                        • Laurens   Winnsboro •

Due West •   • Newberry

Abbeville •   • Greenwood   Saluda River   Broad River

GEORGIA   Lake Murray

                • Willington   COLUMBIA ★

                                                    SOUTH
                • Edgefield   Co
                • Trenton   North Fork Edisto River

                • Graniteville • Aiken   South Fork Edisto River
AUGUSTA ★   Orangeb
        • North Augusta
        (Hamburg)
                                            Bamberg •
                                            • Barnwell

                        Savannah River Plant
                        Atomic Energy Commission

                                    Savannah River

                                                    Yema

BOONE HALL PLANTATION HOUSE

                                    SAVANNAH

CHARLOTTE

NORTH CAROLINA

The Waxhaws

Lancaster

Cheraw

Society Hill

Lynches River

Hartsville

LAMAR

Darlington

Camden

Wateree River

FLORENCE

OLANTA

rt Jackson

Stateburg

Sumter

CAROLINA

Fort Motte

Pee Dee River

Little Pee Dee River

Conway

Waccamaw River

Kingstree

Myrtle Beach

Lake Marion

Brookgreen Gardens

Murrells Inlet

Eutawville

Santec River

Georgetown

Lake Moultrie

Winyah Bay

Moncks Corner

Cooper River

disto River

Ashley River

Cypress Gardens

Goose Creek

Middleton Gardens

Walterboro

Magnolia Gardens

Jacksonboro

CHARLESTON

Johns Island

Sullivans Island

Fort Sumter

Morris Island

ahee River

Beaufort

St. Helena Island

Marine Corps Recruit Depot

ound

Hiltonhead

PAPERBOARD M
GEORGETOWN

O. D

COLUMBIA

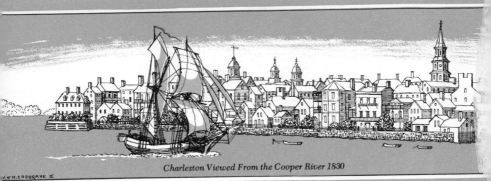

Charleston Viewed From the Cooper River 1830

J.O'H. COSGRAVE II

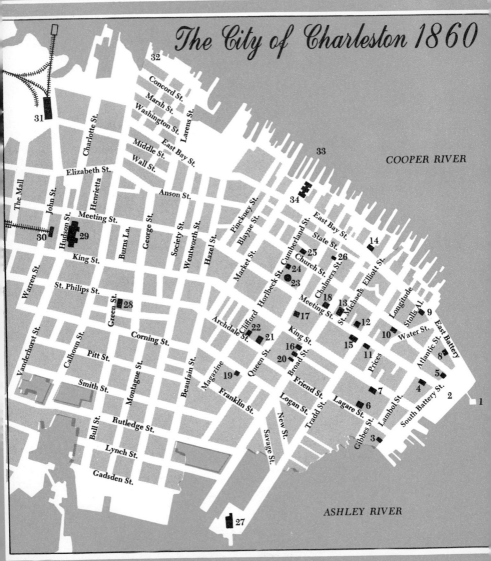

The City of Charleston 1860

COOPER RIVER

ASHLEY RIVER

32

Concord St.
Marsh St.
Washington St.
Larens St.
East Bay St.
Middle St.
Wall St.

31

Charlotte St.
Elizabeth St.
Henrietta
Meeting St.

The Mall

John St.
Hudson St.

30   29

King St.

Warren St.

St. Philips St.

Burns La.
George St.
Society St.
Wentworth St.
Hazel St.
Anson St.

Green St.   28

Vanderhorst St.

Corning St.

Calhoun St.
Pitt St.

Smith St.

Magazine

Beaufain St.

Montague St.

Bull St.

Rutledge St.

Lynch St.

Gadsden St.

Franklin St.

19

Archdale St.   22
        21

Clifford
Horlbeck St.

New St.

Savage St.

27

Pinckney St.
Blayne St.

Market St.

Cumberland St.
State St.
Church St.

34

25   26

24
23

18   13

17

16
20

King St.

Queen St.
Broad St.

Friend St.

Logan St.

Tradd St.

33

East Bay St.

14

Chalmers St.

St. Michael & Elliot St.

12

15

11

10

Longitude

Stolls Al.

9

Water St.

Prices

7

6

Lagare St.

Gibbes St.   3

Lambol St.

Atlantic St.

East Battery

8

5

4

South Battery St.

2

1

SOUTH CAROLINA
Annals of Pride and Protest

A Personal Prologue

A young Carolinian on leave from an overseas appointment stung from my paternal grandmother one summer afternoon the tart reflection, "I wonder we had the gumption to bring *you* forth, my boy."

Though in part she was only asserting her matriarchal privilege of trimming swaggerers down to fit their breeches, she was also declaring a principle so bred in the bone that I doubt she ever phrased it—allegiance to one's own. Her sense of one's own—her own, that is, and by *force majeure* ours—comprehended all blood kin, the state of South Carolina and her native land, The South. It stopped short of her nation, I fear, which she regarded—having come to girlhood under the Confederate Stars and Bars—as a kind of nation-in-law. (During World War I she simply would not hear of the government's deciding how much sugar she could have: she wanted it by the barrel and got it.)

Often while writing my account of our state I have recalled the verbal hickory switch my grandmother wielded that afternoon and the certitudes that moved her. At skeptic turns I have felt a bit like an outcast from the court of her affections, as though for some childish indecorum I had been denied the pantry where cold waffles and blackberry jelly awaited the midmorning pinch. Not that she ever committed that enormity, I hasten to add, being as tender of our gullets as she was careful of our pieties.

But I have also recalled that impious—and impish—young man as he popped in and out through the coming years. The fact that he did pop in for a month or two every second year scarcely imports a disaffected heart. Though he never curbed his irreverent tongue —except, I presume, during his courtesy calls on our matriarch— he buoyantly renewed his ties of blood and friendship, making the rounds of his kin, joining the ten-o'clock musters at the drugstore and swapping reminiscences at the Fourth of July barbecue on the Edisto. I believe he also anticipated retiring thereabouts as a gentleman farmer. Circumstances took him elsewhere, but when he died not long ago, he was buried, surely by his own direction, among the dead of his town and countryside. I doubt that he could have rested well anywhere but in the sandy gray soil of middle South Carolina under a clean brown spread of pine needles.

Ultimately I expect to lie not far away, within the iron-fenced plot, if there's room, where our clan gathers under spiring Lebanon cedars to return the earth its own. I can't imagine a friendlier place to sleep, encircled as it is by family woods and pasture, in sight of my father's birthplace (from the roof at least, for our country lies as flat, they used to say, as the palm of your hand) and not half a mile distant from the graves of my ante bellum forebears. They lie, incidentally, on a Negro college campus, though by commercial accident rather than philanthropic design. A cash offer for the land outweighed someone's filial sentiment, I gather, some- one not unlike the kinsman who in my own time glibly rationalized his plowing up an earlier and very neglected family graveyard. "On Judgment Day," he said, "I'd just as soon come up in a clean cotton field as in a brier patch."

Lest scoffers think I dare not return to South Carolina until I'm safely dead—a tricksy Virginian has recommended that as the only prudent course for a man who would prod the ghosts of all those Secession fire-eaters—let me say that I expect to go as often as I can. Usually I can and do go twice a year, at Christmastime and in late summer. Spending Christmas "at home" might seem an inescapable gesture, but choosing to pass the dog days in South Carolina might well suggest a more than dutiful leaning. It would, I think, to a good many devout South Carolinians, those, for ex- ample, who as I arrive are making their annual escape to the North Carolina mountains. August in South Carolina is—well, as an inspired Negro cook once complained, it's "humilifying." If I could pick my time, I'd go in October, a season of pine-winy after-noons and smoky twilights and crisp evenings, as much a season of renewal after the withering heat as May in Vermont after the dead-ening cold. In late summer what strength you don't lose to the elements you spend batting and blowing at the gnats that dance about your eyes the moment you set foot out of doors.

No, that's not strictly true. There's strength left for talking. Or perhaps the weather and the gnats drain us of the urge to exert anything but our vocal cords. At any rate when our clan gathers in the dog days—observing by instinct, for all I know, the old cotton-country habit of renewing neighborhood and kinship ties while the crop "makes"—we do little more strenuous than wag our tongues. We rock on the piazza and talk, and as we talk, restoring the souls of our hearts with communion, we restore the souls of our stomachs with boiled peanuts and scuppernong grapes. Late afternoons we may adjourn to the banks of the Edisto River and renew old acquaintance under the moss-hung trees where our Methodist grandsires held camp meeting every August and where the generation of my youth danced barefooted all summer long. The camp houses have bathrooms now and electric stoves, but the kids still dance barefoot as before and the river flows cold and black and unpolluted by industrial waste.

The main thread of our talk is the family. Whatever subjects we discuss or stories we tell our drift is always toward preserving the legend of our collective being. Telling each other of "what is past, or passing, or to come," we affirm our sense of continuity. We keep up the spirit, in effect, of the charge that rang through all our child-hood ventures, "Remember who you are!"

For all its retrospective bias our talk is not a litany of lustrous names and deeds. Ours is scarcely a resonant Carolina name. We have our illusions and pretenses, but we do not humor ourselves, for instance, with the image of grandfather standing sword to sword with General Beauregard at Charleston in 1861. If he ever stood in Beauregard's presence, he very likely stood at attention, for, as we freely admit, he was a private soldier attending a coastal gun. We also admit that he started pretty much from scratch after the war, using his several hundred patrimonial acres so wisely that he was able to increase his holdings to several thousand. We would insist, however, that whether or not he was gently born, he was a gentleman, that is, a man of lenient disposition and firm character.

Grandfather's service at Charleston typifies our connection with South Carolina's "holy city," which is much in our talk. We have always felt ourselves after a fashion loyally attendant. Until fairly recent times, of course, we were economically attendant. My grandparents made semiannual excursions there—journeying the seventy miles by way of the old Charleston-Hamburg railway, which abutted our land—to market cotton and to lay in goods for the house and the plantation commissary. Kerrison's (department store), the Citadel Square Baptist Church and the St. John's Hotel were names my grandmother spoke with veneration. Not surprisingly, she packed her sons off in turn to The Citadel.

To me as a boy Charleston was a fabled place. Taken there on a ritual visit at the age of nine or ten, I was stricken with wonder. It was partially the wonder of any child's encountering the ocean and staying in a big hotel for the first time in his life, but it was also a wonder of the special place, with its vestiges of the past, of my past as consciously a Carolinian. Gazing out from St. Michael's spire across the palm-lined Battery to the dim shape of Fort Sumter in the harbor, I felt very solemn, as though flags waved and a band played "Dixie."

Though our legend has its grave chapters, we are not a grimly high-toned tribe, and our talk is full of laughter. (If, as a Southern writer has remarked, blue Charleston blood precludes a sense of humor, then ours must be more red than blue. Which may explain why a Charlestonian with a name like a flying pennon once addressed me, "Sir, you don't take South Carolina seriously," and why I refrained from answering, "Sir, I don't take it solemnly.") We are seldom a dull company. Not that we are inveterately facetious or whimsical, God forbid. But we do manifest a fairly continuous sense of the human comedy and a healthy fear of boring each other to death. Few subjects are wholly sacred with us, as witness the exchange that took place between an aunt and her portly husband on the brink of his joining the Baptist Church (by total immersion): "Honey," she said—by her own account—"you'll never make it. For a man of your bulk they need locks like the Panama Canal. And besides, you know good and well that preacher's got but one arm to his name. I'm scared he'll drown you." To which he countered, "Now, baby, just put your mind at rest. If that one-armed preacher can push me down, by God I can get up myself."

Since our characteristic laughter is deeply infectious—to each other at least—and one comic reminiscence invariably leads to a dozen more, the sound of our family gatherings often threatens to wake the dead. Almost literally on occasion when we have lingered in the cemetery after a funeral. Our high spirit at those times does not confess a lack of feeling for the dead, as the dead themselves have surely known, but one of my grandmother's kinsmen thought it betrayed such a lack of propriety that he excused himself from mortuary attendance in our quarter. "The last Guess funeral I went to," he snorted, "turned out a damned picnic."

What I've said thus far would imply that my roots all run in the plantation country of my father's family. Yet I am equally rooted in the cotton-mill-town upcountry, the country of my mother's Scotch-Irish Presbyterian family. And not merely by inheritance. From the age of four I grew up in my mother's old home—we were transplanted after my father's death—more or less under the thumb of a tall, calm, firm-willed grandmother (still the indubitable mistress of herself and sphere at ninety) who lived by the Calvinist presumption of duty as the first law of life.

Though born into the Presbyterian Church, my mother's people were Calvinists by experience as much as by indoctrination. As farmers or even as medical doctors in the lean red-clay hills of Chester and York counties they found slim evidence that God was likely to favor any man who didn't work like the devil. Even the closest application to the land yielded no columned mansions, and exhausting rounds of the sick often yielded nothing but hay. My great-uncle John was heard to remark late one summer that if he didn't stop taking horse feed "on account" the old mare would grow too fat to pull the buggy and he to "pore" to carry his satchel. Shortly thereafter he ordered a delinquent patient to haul his wagonload of fodder back home and return with a sack of potatoes. "I'm no jackass," he barked. His bark, of course, was worse than his bite, and whether he got the sack of potatoes or not, he would have hitched up in the middle of the night if the poor man had come in distress over a sick child. "That's what the Lord put me here for," he might have said if he had ever thought to explain, "and hard work never killed a man yet." (He doctored for nearly sixty years, by the way, and died of old age.) In attitude he was not unlike my grandfather, who habitually made his calls after dark because "People don't worry over sickness in the daytime; they get scared and need a doctor at night."

The character of my mother's family—and of Scotch-Irish Presbyterians in general, I suspect—was never so epitomized as by my mother herself when she threw off a seizure of nerves one fall and resumed her job at the local high school, announcing that she might have a breakdown if she could afford it. She used "afford" in a fairly literal sense: she had children to support. But she used it also in a moral sense: she could not shift her burden onto other shoulders, however convenient or willing.

Though in some respects the family exotic—more imaginative and volatile than the rest—she nonetheless typified the clan persuasion to hard work as the means to grace, if not the reason for living. Always up with the sun, she rose to no day more brightly than that on which she had "a thousand things to do." With puerile cynicism we used to think she meant a thousand things for us to do, but she surpassed all our efforts combined. On a spring Saturday, for example, she might gather the vegetables, weed her perennial borders, make a chocolate cake (beating the fudge icing by hand), add a round or so to the rug she was presently crocheting, fly off in midafternoon to a club meeting, then fly home at twilight to whip up waffles for the current flock of Winthrop (College) girls making our house a second home. I trust no one sizes her up as a drudge or for that matter anything but a lady. She drew the proper lines. Never, that is, unthinkably never, did she hang out the wash or kill a chicken.

If my mother did not bequeath me her passionate energy, she did infect me with some of her curiosity about people and about the past. Having a literary and antiquarian bent, she came to serve the family in a casual way as archivist and annalist, a function we almost unavoidably shared: our living-room desk constituted her filing cabinet and the floor her worktable. On pleasant Sunday afternoons she often enlisted our aid in what we called "ancestor hunting," which meant tramping around in country graveyards and rubbing chalk on the stones to brighten their faded legends.

My mother was fond of certain ante bellum letters in her collection that showed a skeptical and even scornful turn of mind. These derived from what she called "the brainiest branch of the family," who in the 1850's let fly at the Secession movement. They rated its prophets as demagogues or as fools ablaze with their own Vesuvian rant. Farmers and medical practitioners, doubtless as familiar with a plow handle as their slaves, these ancestors kept the cool heads of enlightened self-interest. If they did not scruple at slavery, they did at risking war for coastal slaveowners. Secession rallies in their own district presented the spectacle of "all the jackasses in the county" cavorting and braying at the whip of their masters. Of course, when the frenzy erupted in war, as they knew in their bones it would, they fought. They took the line, I suppose, of the Greenville Unionist leader B. F. Perry that if one's state persisted in "going to the devil," first affections demanded that one go along.

It these were not Carolinians of the great romantic tradition, they were nonetheless Carolinians of what I think an honorable tradition. They had good hard sense in their heads and good warm blood in their veins. There was no doubt of my mother's pride in springing from such a breed nor of her expectation that we would justify the heritage, most unequivocally by using our brains to shine at school.

In my day at school, incidentally, one could shine by using voice as well as brains, using it, that is, in the antique Southern mode. A big event of the spring session was an oratorical contest, in which I assailed my fellow students for at least three years with the question, "Shall the Statue of Lee Stand in the Hall of Fame?" It was undoubtedly the subject rather than my skill that brought me to their notice, but at any rate the United Daughters of the Confederacy invited me on a grave-decorating junket one Saturday in May, and in half a dozen country cemeteries I addressed that ringing question to a company of tombstones while my sponsors stood by with clasped hands and eyes reverently downcast.

Influences were not so much of the graveyard persuasion as I seem to imply. We lived, after all, in a fairly bustling cotton-mill town, or city, as the voice of progress insisted. Yet our very engines of progress, the cotton mills themselves, recalled the old plantation order. Each had a village for workers, a company store and a more or less fatherly autocrat in command. One of my uncles was a mill superintendent, and his relation to the "hands" was pretty much that of an overseer—a kindly overseer, for he was a very mild-tempered man. Rank and status were symbolically reaffirmed every Christmas when workers assembled with their families around a lighted tree and received gifts of fruit and toys from my uncle's hands under the obliging gaze of their mutual captain.

The cotton-mill villagers, with their bony frames, their slow mountain ways and their mountain twang—usually muffled by a wad of snuff—were a breed apart; and except for my mother's sympathetic association with them as a teacher I would have regarded them as not quite human. As a child of six or seven I often went along to the night school (literacy class, we'd call it now) she taught at one of the villages rimming the town, and I can still see her bending over those earnest overalled and ginghamed figures as they awkwardly traced out their names and see their faces take light from hers as they made a final triumphant stroke. She gave a Christmas party for them once at our house, and they gave her in great pride and diffidence a huge metal object new to our experience —a kind of urn with a flaring notched shelf from which depended at least two dozen spoons. Though it never occurred to me before —and I'm sure it never did to my mother or her "pupils"—the gift strikes me now as transparently appropriate: she was the sugar bowl and they were the spoons.

It goes almost without saying, I think, that my mother's sympathies went out to Negroes, both as men and women who served us and as a troubled race. Now I don't mean that she was merely tactful enough to say "colored people" instead of "nigra" and generous enough to weed out the clothes closets in their behalf. Though she did not, of course, treat them as equals, she did recognize their separate identities. She acted as though they had natures, not simply a common nature. Furthermore, she behaved as though they deserved more than they got. As she paid them off, for instance, she would often remark, "I do wish it were more."

Growing up in a lean time, I thought she was only deploring the state of her purse, but later I came to see that she was apologizing by indirection for their status. Her conscience was admitting that in spite of the good will on both sides they couldn't help giving so much for so little. However fetching the Carolina myth of a chosen dependency, she knew they had not exactly chosen the life of handouts and hand-me-downs.

Not long ago she confessed her pleasure of late in seeing Negroes have things they never had before. "Some people resent it, you know, as though it's sinful for them to ride in a new automobile instead of a wreck." And then she recalled suddenly her childhood devotion to her nurse, "Aunt" Betsy, who was still attached to the family when I came along. "Every Monday morning," she said, " 'Aunt' Betsy would fill with indignation as she stood on our back porch and saw a gang of Negroes led from the town jail to answer in court for their weekend misdemeanors. 'Done nothing white folks ain't do,' she would mutter. 'But nigger has to pay for his frolic. Ain't no justice for us po' niggers, honey. No justice in this world.' And you know I would reach my hand into hers and grieve for 'us po' niggers' with all my heart and soul."

The pathos did not prevent my mother's speaking with a note of complacency. A devoted "Aunt" Betsy is, after all, a token of what we think of but seldom refer to as background. Not that she is at pains to convince herself that we have it but that habitually she speaks of certain things, as we all do, with a conscious presumption of their social value. Most often, I suppose, it is of Negroes that we presume, since they traditionally have made or attended what has made, the great Carolina social value. One might deplore the ancestral war for slavery but not without first making it known that one's ancestors owned slaves to war about.

As a youngster I was quite aware of Negro dependents as a social endowment. Their swarming presence was not unrelated, I'm sure, to my preference for my grandmother Guess's "Big House" plantation world over the town neighborhood sphere of my mother's family. A more ingenuous reason for the choice was that one meant play and the other work. One meant running loose and the other meant buckling down to books and backyard chores. Squads of Negroes smiled on all our goings and comings, all our capricious enterprises, fostering the matriarchal illusion of knightly, if not princely, rank. I shall never again feel as grand as I did on occasion at the age of twelve, passing on horseback down "the line" (the row of Negro cabins fronting our sandy access road) and taking, as I fancied, the obeisance of my adoring servitors.

The "Cap'n" of our plantation—my father's younger brother—called it "the place" and himself a farmer. But he was not far removed in spirit from the ante bellum master of a cotton domain. Even in dress, for he wore the traditional planter's black and white, though the tie was a bow instead of a string and the hat a snap-brim. He governed his principality from the back of a Tennessee walking horse or, since he was not consciously out of tune with his age, from the driver's seat of a Model T Ford. His fate was to have been born and molded, dedicated, as it were—to a role—to a whole way of living—that was barely tenable when he assumed it from his father. A tough and resilient nature has brought him through unembittered at the attritions of time and circumstance, the failure of cotton as a stable money crop, the drifting away of his tenants and retainers; but he falls nostalgic now and then as he gazes off to partially idle fields. In such moods he has been heard to say—not without a smile, of course—that when the last wagon-load of "nigras" rolls off "the place" he'd just as soon swing along. In my reconstructed mind I know that the changes he regrets are long past due, but in the unreconstructed reaches of my heart I know exactly how he feels.

I

The Incurable Aristocrats

When Thomas R. Waring, Jr., opposes school desegregation before a national audience—which he has done on television and in print —he performs a high symbolic office. For he speaks not merely as one Southerner who commands a hearing in New York but as editor of the venerable *News and Courier* in the city of Charleston in the state of South Carolina. He speaks, in other words, as a hereditary guardian of the Southern ethos from the city that touched off the guns of disaffection in 1861 and from the state that walked out of the Union to lead the South towards Appomattox.

Mr. Waring's footing as a spokesman, however, suggests more than mythic or poetic congruity. It declares that the voice of South Carolina speaks the quintessential mind of the South, that after ninety-four years of "reconstruction" the state of John C. Calhoun still exemplifies the Southern compulsion to kick at the traces of the national will.

If South Carolina has not led the region since 1865, she has unfailingly typified the restive Southern temper. As she figured centrally in the discords of Reconstruction, so she has figured symptomatically in the murmurous prologue to and the clamorous aftermath of the 1954 Supreme Court assault on the "separate but equal" doctrine. Though the ruling arose from cases in several states, the South Carolina suit was joined with it in the public mind, and the Clarendon County school district at issue, with its preponderance of Negro children, posed conditions most vocally at the root of white alarm. Countering the decree by anticipation, South Carolina set a pattern for her neighbor states: At the nod of her prestigious governor, former U. S. Supreme Court Justice James F. Byrnes, she "abolished" her public school system by constitutional surgery.

When the Truman civil rights program loomed in 1948, South Carolina not unexpectedly offered her governor—J. Strom Thurmond—to galvanize the South as leader of a States' Rights party. Though even the candidate scarcely imagined spurring a horse to the White House in a jet-plane age, his home constituency—plus a few million neighbors—bet on his chances. Six years later they raised him to the U. S. Senate on a write-in vote, protesting a local Democratic party maneuver but also endorsing him as a spokesman of dissent.

Meanwhile voters had followed Thurmond's defection to Eisenhower in such numbers that the state all but lost its Democratic virtue in 1952 (and again in 1956). Few, of course, joined the Republican party. They had small reason to, they would claim, having chosen it as a lesser evil. In truth, however—aside from the fact that only Democrats count in local elections—they shrank from a tag still linked in the racial mind with carpetbaggers.

Recent political turns all betray the same old distrust of the federal power that moved John C. Calhoun to lead the state to Nullification (of the protective tariff schedules) in 1832. Now, as it was then, the bone of contention, is the Negro. While Calhoun the dialectician argued state rights to the nation, Calhoun the cotton planter named slavery as the root issue. So today, while a calm Thomas Waring deplores a sociological reading of the constitution, less tempered voices speak out against racial equality. If the Negro—as slave or citizen—has not caused the trouble, the mildest national concern over his status has troubled every cause. (The first great modern student of slavery, Ulrich B. Phillips, oversimplified perhaps, but he did not go far wrong in deducing white supremacy as the "central theme" of Southern history.) Certainly any move to empower the Negro touches South Carolinians to the quick. When Byrnes, for example, threatened to shut down the public schools in 1954, he struck outsiders as belying the commitments of his long and distinguished Washington career; but to South Carolinians he only proved that his heart had always been in the right place.

Byrnes' gesture, in fact, was only one sign of a general "retreat from reason" that a young South Carolina editor noted as he regretfully cut his appeal for moderation on the school issue. Federal District Judge J. Waties Waring—Thomas R. Waring's uncle—took risks the editor could not afford to incur when he decided in 1947 and 1948 the Negro's rights to join the South Carolina Democratic party and to vote in its primary election. Cold-shouldered by his own patrician kin and kind in Charleston, he was treated to noisy harassments by the not-so-gently born. Of retirement age in 1952, Judge Waring left Charleston for New York, having compounded his affront by siding with the petitioners in the Clarendon school case.

Judge Waring is not the only eminent South Carolinian in recent years to go against the grain. Last year, for example, J. McBride Dabbs, a one-time professor at Coker College (in Hartsville), still residing in his native Pee Dee section, offered in *The Southern Heritage* a fairly sharp review of the state's racial policy. No doubt he lost friends thereby, and if he had been teaching in a state college when the book appeared he might have lost his job. At least one professor has been expelled from the University of South Carolina for voicing like sentiments.

All these excursions and alarms imply a fixation on the Negro as *bête noire.* The very Carolinians who induce them, however, would and do often swear deep affection for "our colored people." If love and hate are the two faces of a coin, then the Carolinians do not, as their critics suppose, knowingly talk from both sides of the mouth at once. They really do love the black man as much as they fear him. Or at any rate they muse on smiling presences of field and kitchen as often as they imagine red-eyed bucks prowling in the night. Felicitous images consort more naturally, it is true, with memories or visions of the past than with the current scene. Every South Carolinian of even middling status commemorates some old fond master and servant relation, calling golden scenes to mind that often have their semblance in the yellowing pages of a family album: a grave young squire in the saddle, for example, and a beaming Booker T. perched behind; or perhaps the winsome black face of a Lady Belle peeking around the flounces of Little Missy's bridal organza. In the grip of such memories the Carolinian loses for the moment or the hour his fright of the Negro as schoolmate or equal at the polls.

The fondness, in other words, presupposes caste lines. The leisured status of white desire still argues a race meant to be "hewers of wood and drawers of water." It argues complementary rights and duties. Even at this remove few South Carolinians would protest Henry Adams' judgment of Southerners (from those he knew at Harvard before the Civil War), as masterful, charming and uncerebral. They value a commanding presence more than a searching mind; they like to think of themselves, in fact, as born and bred commanders. They claim, for instance, that Negroes served best under white Southern officers in both World Wars, that lazy black boys responded to nothing so well as the clement Southern hand in the iron glove.

In the commonest terms of the relations, however, a lady can't preside over the pots and pans, and somebody must. South Carolina girls are still brought up to that irreducible view of ladyhood. It is yet possible in their world to assume the station on an outlay of twelve dollars a week, and all who can, do. If ladyhood survives by exploitation, the sense of it does not oppress any more than humanly it ever does. An occasional bow to conscience will do. "But they're such children," a lady can say. "What in heaven's name would they do without us? Why, Elvira dresses every bit as good as I do. And no wonder; she can beg the gladdest rags I own right off my back." Or she can wryly disclose the abuse she takes from Ella Mae: "Lord, Miss Maggie, you don't have to tell me what a fool I is. I wouldn't of been working for you seventeen years if I wasn't."

If self-vindication is a frequent note in the casual commentary on the Negro, so is appreciation of his responses to the blunt facts of life. A nursemaid's advice to her fretful charge will pass down through the generations of one family, because no one ever put a naked truth plainer or better: "Honey, you has to learn to want and not git." So probably will the sighing utterance of a widowed Negro cook: "Jake ain't been very good to me, and Jake ain't live wid me very much, but chillun is chillun, and a piece o' man is better'n no man a'tall."

Figured in piazza dialogues as workhorse, child or rustic wit, the Negro is similarly portrayed in South Carolina literature, past and present, even that which shows him in habitats more or less free of white intrusion. For all their compassion, DuBose Heyward and Julia Peterkin—the state's most significant modern novelists—do not explore the tragedy of white and black lives simultaneously entwined and divided.

Black and white relations are paradoxically simpler and more complex than they look from a distance. Fundamentally, black is black and white is white, and never the twain shall meet as social equals. They do meet, however, in ways that blur the caste distinctions. Some whites, for example, patronize black doctors and dentists. Admittedly, they do save face—with the doctors' helpless complicity, of course—by waiting in rooms sacred to their color.

By his confinement to a servant caste the Negro promotes an equality among whites that the aristocratic spirit would seem to discourage. Historically, the Negro afforded a pretension to exalted rank so general that by 1850 owners of a dozen slaves were apt to claim descent from William the Conqueror. His potential unruliness, however—as ante bellum slave or postwar peasant—induced a kind of alliance between whites that tended, along with other factors, to blur class lines, though such demagogues as "Pitchfork Ben" Tillman used him (in the 1880's) as a wedge to estrange poor whites from their "bloated" aristocratic captains. Still united by the creed of color and divided by the myth of blood (as well as the usual appurtenances of money), white Carolinians snoot each other by standards so publicly indistinct and hotly nourished in the bosom of the family that a Blue Book compiler would retire from any quarter in psychic if not epidermic tatters.

That a genuine aristocracy once existed both legend and history affirm, and certain French and English names—Ravenel, Rutledge, Pinckney, Middleton, Legaré, for instance—strike astral bells in the minds of all South Carolinians. But these, of course, belong to Charleston, not merely the state's but one of the nation's sanctuaries of gentility. They have historic national connections, moreover—with the early Congresses, with the Declaration of Independence, with the Revolution. Other names reverberate in South Carolina, but few so far and wide; and clans entered in the Charleston peerage abide here and there in the old plantation country up and down the coast.

Desirable as it is to have sprung from pedigreed Charleston seed, all pedigrees do not by any means originate in Charleston. Gentry has flourished from plain seed in every soil. It has often acquired or kept its bloom by inward grace, so to speak, having few outward signs of glory. Though claimants do not find them strictly necessary, suggestive trappings help: a high-boned visage for the living-room mantel, a coat of arms or two, a scattering of crested silver goblets on the sideboard. These may be, of course, authentic family relics, but no one who mattered would ask. The genealogical craze has no doubt subsided of late, but at least one member of any self-respecting family can put a ready hand to old Aunt Mamie's bloodline tickets to the D.A.R. or the Colonial Dames. Facts are scarcely to the point, though, in tribal converse, which takes its cue from Dr. Johnson's remark that no man speaks on oath in a lapidary inscription. Such talk, with its lyric burden of vanished grandeurs, has been heard so often by nearly all grown Carolinians that they would have understood a wry old codger's saying the womenfolk owed a monument to William Tecumseh Sherman: He meant that in burning down the houses the Yankee scourge had freed them to build mansions of glory every afternoon.

Claims to high birth are so usual in South Carolina that to admit belonging to the middle class is to admit that you just don't belong. Consigning a company of his own bourgeois kind (by American standards) to the bourgeoisie, a "Yankeeized" native has been told, "Speak for yourself, my good man, speak for yourself!" Certain that blood, like murder, will always out in the end, they aphorize when marital choices are at stake, "Better a bad egg from a good nest than a good egg from a bad nest." They enjoy flaunting their names in a public pinch, rather scorning precincts where their names don't signify. "When a low bastard of a cop flags me down in New York," a nameflaunter once complained, "I'm sunk."

Blood-conscious Carolinians stoop to their putative inferiors so graciously that a stranger might be pardoned for wondering who was stooping. They do it in part, no doubt, from an atavistic sense of *noblesse oblige* but in greater part, surely, from a rueful sense of pressures long active within if not built into the social complex.

When Mary Boykin Chesnut—whose husband represented South Carolina in the U.S. Senate at the outbreak of the Civil War—sighed that the vote was a mighty leveler, she voiced for our time as well as her own the rearguard patrician quarrel with the Jacksonian faith.

Since 1865, however—and down to the very recent past—South Carolinians have fallen to a mightier leveler than the ballot for the "shiftless" white man or its denial to the "shifty" black: hard poverty. The war and Reconstruction toppled the old planter gentry from their perches, and if they never reascended they at least had the comfort of seeing the eyries remain deserted. For more than half a century life for nearly all Carolinians was a matter of declining or unimproving fortunes. Some Romanly stoic matrons may have sat in decaying halls and "dined off cabbage from a rosewood table," but more often than not they swapped the tables for cabbage and abandoned the halls to the wind and the rain.

The children of ruined families went to free schools and public colleges, when they got to college at all. In close quarters and in competition with their inferiors, they learned human as well as textbook lessons, often acquiring sympathies unknown to their elders, but—and this is a very salient "but"—they taught lessons as well. Their manners and tastes at least softened the Gothic utilitarianism enthroned in the educational factories of the late nineteenth century. Though Pitchfork Ben Tillman (as governor in the 1890's) conceived the first—and only—state college for women (Winthrop) as a seminary for kitchen economists and primer-level schoolmarms, it soon erased the "normal and industrial" stamp and ducked the "teachers' college" stamp to become a liberal arts institution. If the transformation was not effected by demand of penniless gentleladies, it was brought about through the cultural influence of their class and kind. Poor as Job's turkey "Debe's" Winthrop daughters might be—"Debe" was the founding president, Dr. David Bancroft Johnson—yet surely they were no less deserving of the arts and sciences than young ladies to the north, who looked upon "the normal" as a kind of intellectual beauty parlor for servant girls.

Actually, Winthrop set no precedent in educating ladies at the taxpayers' expense: she followed more or less the course marked out by the state's first collegiate institution on its founding, the

South Carolina College (now the University), which unapologeti-
cally served a classic gentlemanly fare. When the legislature finally
acted in 1801 to repair the century-old omission of higher learning,
the members conceived the handiwork as their Oxford, a pedagogic
servant of the ruling orders. It was shaped and kept—partially by
high admission standards—a patrician citadel, a fact of which the
lower orders were not unaware.

If the university has not maintained the classic curriculum of its
youth, it has kept the reputation for high jinks that frisky and bib-
ulous young squires brought it in its youth. Strait-laced parents
are inclined to loose their sons in the presumably drier pastures
of Calvinist Erskine, Methodist Wofford or Baptist Furman, just
as their ancestors founded these institutions to offset the "godless"
teachings of "the College."

Though gentle Carolinians have normally and quite unashamedly
sat with hoi polloi in public classrooms, higher incomes in the past
twenty years or so have turned their fancies to select private
academic groves of Virginia and beyond. This propensity, especially
the drift to stylish boarding schools, is only one sign of a fast-
spreading keep-up-with-the-Jonses mania rather at odds with aristocratic self-assurance. (Another sign is the rash of coming-out balls
in towns where boys and girls have frequented easygoing neighborhood circles from birth and "society" has foregathered in municipally
owned country clubs.) A few South Carolinians have always gone
north to school—just as a few colonials went to Oxford—but they
have never gained the advantage thereby in Columbia or even in
Charleston that a Groton-Harvard background supposedly yields in
the metropolitan East. Prep schools for boys, moreover, if not
tea-pouring seminaries for girls, were regarded in the not very
distant past more as halls of detention than of learning.

If South Carolinians have defended their claims to patrician
rank against the equalizing assaults of war, poverty and the American
dollar, they have done it with a noticeable lack of social fret and
strain. They are a gregarious and informal tribe, though they cling
to certain forms long passé or never in vogue elsewhere, the practice
of "sirring" and "ma'aming" one's elders, for instance, a practice
outsiders had better not interpret as earnest of a servile soul.

Loving society, in the eighteenth-century usage, Carolinians have worked at—perhaps indulged a weakness for—the social art of conversation, lamented as defunct in our time. A visiting listener might judge they only like to talk and talk too much—understandably enough, since it does often appear that they vie for the conversational lead like hens for a choice grubworm. Many have reputations as "a great talker," and when two get together, as often happens, the result can be mutual exhaustion: as two have frequently sighed about each other, "I declare I just love to see her, but Lord-a-mercy she does wear me out."

Their talk is local and primarily anecdotal, but at its comic best and in its concern with the vagaries of life rather than the value of things it is agreeably redolent of the eighteenth century. Leafing through the annals of local idiosyncrasy, the talkers often evoke characters not unworthy of a Congreve. In happy collaboration they will shape a portrait, for instance of "Miss" Gussie Whitfield, who as a Gold Star mother on the battlefield of Verdun, heard a Yankee voice repine, "Oh, that General Sherman had been here to save us from that terrible defeat!" At which the stern Confederate daughter in Miss Gussie parted company once and for all with the plaintive American mother. "Madame," she scathed, "how dare you mention that scoundrel's name in my presence? He marched through the South burning and pillaging; he marched across our plantation burning and stealing. He is not still marching, madame, but he is still burning. I thank you not to speak to me again on this trip."

With equal facility the talkers might conjure up the character of "Miss" Drucie Laird, who, laid up in her canopied four-poster with a touch of arthritis, was mirrored to an unexpected visitor in an adjacent room frantically rouging her cheeks, squirming out of a rumpled sack into a bed jacket of cerulian crepe de chine, leaping back to her pillows, opening Mr. Freeman's *Robert E. Lee* and then at last inquiring, "Did someone call? I must have been dozing."

Again they summon the shade of Mr. Fitzhugh Watts, one of God's impatient men, who, if he had lived in a dueling age, would have haunted the grounds but, as things were, dissipated his ire in reckless speed, twisting a Packard around every telephone pole in the county, so the legend went. He boasted that he never blew his horn but once, and anything that didn't move out of his way he sent flying.

If these figures scarcely invite emulation, they might well draw a tip of the hat; for they were all passionate natures, and any show of passion seems not altogether contemptible in an age of meek adjustments to the group. Mr. Fitzhugh trespassed on his neighbor's rights, but he had the daring to risk his neck as well as theirs; Miss Gussie was intolerant of her neighbors, but neither fear nor favor ever curbed her tongue; and Miss Drucie, though she fooled her neighbors a bit, offered for their steady contemplation a fine-wrought image of ladyhood, a cunning work of art.

Speaking from a South Carolina background in *I Came Out of the Eighteenth Century*, the educator John Rice said that while teaching in Nebraska he resolved never to cross the Mississippi River again but once, in going back east: he judged Midwestern society as irredeemably flat, having missed the leavening of aristocratic values. If he was not speaking of such values as Miss Drucie embodied, he was speaking of the impulse she represented. He had come to see in Nebraska the difference between a people whose inspiration derived from William Jennings Bryan or the sisterhood of the Eastern Star and a people whose aspirations reached, if only in retrospect, to such a scholar-gentleman as John C. Calhoun, who had himself looked to models of aristrocratic dignity and cultivation.

Though it may be idle to claim that patrician standards animate the present socal culture, it would be wrong to count them utterly extinct. Archaic they assuredly are but not yet obsolescent. They often survive, of course, at the level of farce, in the impulse, for example, that moves a soda-pop heir to flaunt a coat of arms in iron at the entrance to his "estate," a piece of ostentation, one should fairly add, matched by new-rich Carolinians at nearly every stage of history. More worthily, many still assume that the aristocratic principle of who you are, if not superior to that of what you are, transcends at least the standard of what you have. Fewer perhaps, but enough to make a difference, maintain the now un-American right to flout the local mores or, worse, stand off from the crowd.

Though the aristocratic tradition survives in none too consequential ways, it does find tonic exemplification in the life and works of an occasional figure like Mary C. Simms Oliphant. Tirelessly serving the memory of her novelist grandfather, William Gilmore Simms, she makes some odd gestures, as when a few years ago she marked the hundredth anniversay of a Simms magazine piece by inviting the descendants of the writer's slaves to an old-time Christmas fete at Woodlands, the Simms plantation in Bamberg County. (The response to her gesture was no less odd than the gesture itself, around a hundred Negroes lending themselves to her charade, some from as far away in space and spirit as New York's Harlem.) Such whimsical devotions, however, are more than balanced by Mrs. Oliphant's scholarly exertions, her sixteen-year effort, for example, at searching out (in libraries and private collections both here and abroad) the William Gilmore Simms letters, now published by the University of South Carolina Press and affording a documentary feast to students of ante bellum Dixie.

Living much in the past, Mrs. Oliphant—whose appearance recalls an oval-framed planter's lady by Thomas Sully—lives also very much in the present, or, more accurately perhaps, she is simultaneously and passionately at home in both. She circulates in bustling upcountry Greenville from an antique home base, the city's oldest dwelling, which she bought and restored some years ago as much from civic pride, it would seem, as from her antiquarian bent. Repairing to Woodlands at intervals, she concerns herself as much with the conservation of its fields and woods as with the preservation of its ante bellum lineaments. (Actually, the mansion house is a post bellum structure, built up from a wing that survived two wartime burnings.) In the bright studio-library of her Greenville home or in the somber drawing room at Woodlands she teaches the values of the aristocratic tradition by simply being what she is, a lady and a scholar, though she never misses a chance to expound these values from a domestic or a public dais.

Believing that the present needs the past to mitigate the fevers of materialism, she could certainly find no present mode of life more needful than that of Greenville, where conversations tick off new-made millionaires and new-risen palaces on suburban Paris Mountain. (The mountain overlooks, by the way, Furman University's new multimillion-dollar campus, which speaks not only of money but of the Baptist disposition to give till it hurts.) Industrial tycoons are nothing new to Greenville, however: large cotton mills have operated there since the late nineteenth century.

If the current industrial boom—giving the state more than a

thousand new manufactories in the past fourteen years—has not altered the character of Greenville, it has whipped up a good many languid towns to the Greenville pace, more to the gratification of Main Street, by the way, than to the joy of magnolia-shaded piazza circles. Factory payrolls set cash registers atune, but the spenders themselves often jangle the old social nerves, crowding schools, churches and golf courses, often demanding enlargement of venerable facilities. When the prospect of a new industry arises, however, the piazza murmurs are scarcely heard beneath the clamor of Main Street: Carolina merchants and bankers are as hot after the main chance as the state's official promoters.

The new industrial prosperity may not only increase the number of Cadillacs and columns—it may, if the right leadership appears, work public benefits the state has never been able to afford. It might, for example, help raise the standards of higher education: in a state lacking first-rate graduate school facilities they undeniably need a boost. Some moves are already being made in that direction—at least opulent buildings are rising on public campuses—but professorial pay does not yet invite, and buildings do not make learning.

The new money may also keep more of the ambitious young at home than have stayed in years past, counteracting the northward lure that has steadily drawn off Carolina brains since the Civil War. (It has long been a commonplace that New York is full of bright and prospering Southerners.) The feeling that all great prospects lie beyond is still so general that a young Ivy League Ph.D., for example, finds that he must justify teaching at his Carolina alma mater to himself as well as to his Northern friends.

Whatever changes the industrial boom has worked or promises to work, it has thus far scarcely affected the Negro's status. Segregation laws keep blacks firmly out of the mills or at least admit them only in a menial capacity. The shutout is nothing new, but expanding possibilities have meant increasing frustration and departure from the state. Actually, the ratio of blacks to whites has declined steadily since 1880, from 60 per cent to 38 per cent in 1950.

The Negro may not get his share of factory jobs, but he does get, as South Carolinians now like to boast, more than his share of the educational tax dollar. Since the drive started in 1951 to back up the "separate but equal" claim, more than half of the well over a hundred millions allocated for buildings has gone into schools for Negroes, which have sprung up all over the state.

Negro teachers had been given pay equal to whites a few years earlier, or, to be exact, they had been given the chance to earn equal pay by measuring up to the same criteria. Salaries were geared to various qualifications, including the letter grades (A to D) teachers made on a compulsory examination. The latter criterion was designed both to help Negroes and to gratify whites. On the whole it serves the dual purpose: Some Negroes make higher salaries, but whites make generally higher scores. Some whites, however, draw low grades, and that is a rub.

The situation typifies Carolina's approach to her chief problem. Her thought running in traditional rounds—along inherited wires, so to speak—she wastes a good deal of energy in maneuvers. In their hearts many Carolinians know this to be true, and it makes them defensive. They can bridle at the blandest criticism, especially from a native. Yankees they try to excuse as heretics by birth and training.

The holier-than-thou preachments Carolinians have taken from the rest of the nation in the past century and a quarter have not helped. In addition, many have defensive mechanisms peculiar to their class and clime. They have had to reconcile all their lives the unreconcilable states of poverty and pride. In their own world, it is true, shabbiness almost equated with birth and breeding: if the paint was peeling from the columns and the Buick had come to voting age, who at any rate dared cast the first stone? They were not, however, oblivious to a world beyond, and entering it, as they did sometimes, they felt painfully diminished, as though they drove rattletrap buggies in a vast procession of chauffeured limousines. The trains going north led to opportunity, but they also led to the reproach of Northern opulence.

Oddly enough, however, what Carolinians did have—pride of being—gave them distinction, set them apart and not infrequently paid off in a world ostensibly scornful of patrician airs. Their ingratiating manners assisted, of course, as did their pleasant dialect with its flattened vowels and neglected consonants. ("Any civilized man should know," a Carolinian once rebuked his Yankeefied cousin, "that 'river' is pronounced 'rivuh.'") Taken all together these qualities, when they don't infuriate, are very likely to seduce. They can be as fatally irresistible in men as in women, so both Northern women and men will testify. The one word that names what they have—Hollywood-soiled but inevitable—is "glamour."

If distinctive ways derive from a special kind of life, the life has a local habitation, and—terrestrial emanations aside—a people belongs to a land. Actually South Carolina is two lands: the north-western plateau natives call the upcountry and the coastal plain they call the low country. (Sometimes they distinguish the intermediate region from the others as the sandhills.) The two are technically set apart by a fall line that bisects the state a hundred miles inland from the Atlantic, though proper low country to a proper low-countryman hugs the shore, scarcely reaching beyond the tidal sway in coastal rivers.

The upcountry presents typically vistas of long cedar-greened hills, ochreous fields and swirling terra-cotta rivers. Settled largely by Scotch-Irishmen emigrating from Pennsylvania through the Valley of Virginia in the mid-1700's, it became a land of small farms, unpainted homesteads and austere Presbyterian meeting houses—a character modified but never entirely transformed by the spread of cotton, slavery and aristocratic pretension from the coast after the Revolution and the rise of cotton mills after the Civil War. The low country, by contrast, presents, typically, vistas of flat, gray fields, rivers stained black by water-loving cypress, and clusters of moss-draped live oaks and long-leaf pines. Settled primarily by Englishmen and West Indian English, it became a land of extensive plantations, manor houses and Anglican churches in the neoclassic mode. Through the ravages of war and the death in turn of its three great fortune-making crops (four, counting slavery)—indigo, sea-island cotton and rice—it has kept the semblance of its original character. Owing to a twentieth-century invasion of Northern millionaires, in fact, its manor houses gleam as perhaps never in the days of their authentic majesty.

Though the essentially hard-driving, more or less puritanical spirit of the upcountry has long dominated South Carolina, the low country holds a special place in most Carolina affections as the source and museum of a leisured culture they all look backward to through rose-colored glasses. Though they may not agree with Ludwig Lewisohn that Charleston, the heart and soul of the low country, is all of South Carolina that matters, they cannot resist its antique charm nor the afterglow lingering there of two defiant historic transactions for which the nation will always remember their state—secession and the opening shot of the Civil War.

II

A Lordly Enterprise

South Carolina is the only state in the Union (except her stepsister
state to the north) that looks back to a native order of hereditary
nobles. For half a century, from 1670 to the royal eviction of the
lords proprietors, men of title—landgraves and caciques—owned
vast baronies along the coastal rivers and creeks. As a light on the
state's course from province to sovereign commonwealth to not
always devoted satrapy of Washington, this fact often suggests feudal
origins: Conceived and reared in the shrunken lap of the Middle
Ages, so the notion runs, the state grew up in scorn of its democratic
colonial cousins. Early Carolinians, however, were antipathetic to
the local institution of nobility, legally sidestepping the body of laws
that gave it force. Pondering this fact, one might conclude that
landgraves and moss-draped baronies were foppish vanities denied,
like corkscrewing Stuart wigs cast off for the cropped heads of
Puritanism.

Actually, neither deduction is warranted, neither image fits. The
first ignores the profit-seeking drive of Restoration London and the
shrewdness of Anthony Ashley Cooper, the Restoration Londoner
who shaped the colony. The second makes improbable levelers of
the *bourgeois gentilhommes* who settled Lord Ashley's grandiose
republic.

Despite its feudal complexion Lord Ashley's plan for Carolina
envisioned a timocracy, a state where rule and rank derive from
property; not a feudality, where property and rank derive from a
heaven-sent ruler. Though formal rank scarcely caught on, the timo-

27

cratic idea took such firm hold that it gripped South Carolina for a hundred and ninety-five years, until it was dislodged more or less by force of arms. Dr. William Watts Ball, late editor of the Charleston *News and Courier,* spoke at least a partial truth when he complained (in *The State That Forgot*) that South Carolina enjoyed aristocratic good health until the Carpetbag constitution of 1868 "injected the deadly and foreign poison of democracy."

Pioneer Carolinians were men of a kind with Ashley Cooper. When they flouted his lordship and company, they sought not to prove that all men were equal but that *they* were as good as London nabobs. Initially glad to accept Lord Ashley's titles as badges of their self-esteem, they disclaimed them at last as base coin—not cast at the royal mint—and as a kind of symbolic compliance in quitrent claims on their lands. Learning to feel baronial on their baronies, the Carolinians quickly lost all sense of tenantry.

The landlords were to begin with, however, a very lordly crew for commoners to oppose. More or less in the order of their favor at the court of Charles II they were, first, the Earl of Clarendon, Lord High Chancellor and father-in-law of the King's brother; and General George Monck, Duke of Albemarle, so close to the throne that the diarist Samuel Pepys noted him pretasting the King's food at the coronation banquet. Somewhat lesser figures were the moneyed Earl of Craven, companion to the King's aunt; John, Lord Berkeley, governor of the royal household in exile; and Sir George Carteret, the richest man in England, who had taken the fleeing Charles to his arms on Jersey Island in 1649. These five had been chosen as a kind of front office to impress the King. Needy himself and attached to such costly baubles as Lady Castlemaine, Charles was hard to impress with the wants of lesser subjects. The real promoters of Carolina, more distant from the royal breast, had dressed their enterprise with care. Sir Peter Colleton, a sometime Barbadian planter, first harbored the scheme of exploiting the lands between Virginia and Spanish Florida to relieve crowded Barbados and make himself a fortune. He then broached it to Lord Ashley, Chancellor of the Exchequer, and Sir William Berkeley, Governor of Virginia.

As expected, Charles did not succumb at once. But such lofty claims on his gratitude swayed him at last to the point of granting these eight men as lords proprietors a domain far vaster than he or they could have known. It extended between the 36th and 31st parallels and swept from sea to sea. A second charter annulling an old one of his father's pushed the boundaries to Virginia on the north and to a point below St. Augustine in Spanish-claimed and -guarded Florida.

After several colonizing efforts had petered out, Lord Ashley (later Earl of Shaftesbury) took the lead of what was essentially a landholding company. With aid from John Locke, the philosopher, he first drew up the Fundamental Constitutions, often derided as a child of feudal fancy and theoretic muddle. In Locke's defense it serves to recall that his political spirit authored the Declaration of Independence and that nothing in this admittedly baroque Carolina plan jarred with his later defense of individual rights—the rights of private property. Also, whatever medieval vapors hung in Ashley Cooper's mind, they did not prevent his founding the Whig, or middle-class, party to block Tory stringencies. That noble was tough in head and limb. He kept Cromwell and Stuart favor and scurried about minding his fortunes for twenty-four years with a gold drainage tube protruding from his liver, inserted by his friend and private doctor, John Locke.

In 1669 the two busied themselves at Exeter House in London with the Constitutions, which projected a government "agreeable to the Monarchy under which we live" and avoiding "a numerous democracy." Since the royal charter had granted powers of the palatinate of Durham (given to Maryland and Maine proprietors as well), a princely office created as a bulwark against the Scots, the document fixed the eldest proprietor as palatine and created highfalutin offices for the other seven. Assuming the chartered right of giving titles of honor different in style from the home variety, it created two noble classes, landgraves and caciques. The first term was borrowed from the Germans, and the second from the Indians. (The associative stigma of feathered headdresses and war paint may partially explain why caciques have been less in genealogical vogue than landgraves.) From landgraves in the colony the Palatine would name a deputy, if no one higher in the fixed order of precedence was on the ground. In practice this meant that governing deputies sailed to the province direct from hasty rites of ennoblement: Few colonials were titled, and proprietors were scarcely drawn to the wilds from a London warming up after the Puritan freeze, offering perhaps an evening's choice between *'Tis Pity She's a Whore* at the Salisbury Court playhouse and *All's Lost by Lust* at the Red Bull.

To bear up the structure the province would be divided into counties, seigniories, baronies, colonies or precincts, and manors, each except the manor to embrace 12,000 acres. The proprietors with their seigniories and the frontier peers with their baronies would have two-fifths of the land and the people three-fifths. Estates would be tenanted by "leetmen" (a leet was a manor court in feudal England), who would voluntarily bind themselves and their issue forever to the land. From what prehistoric glooms these were to emerge the Constitutions do not say, though not unreasonably Ashley Cooper must have counted on the poor's being always with us. There was a lure of land-use privileges to catch villeins but so feeble that General Edward McCrady, late nineteenth-century historian of South Carolina, inquires, "Could the framers of this instrument . . . suppose that for the rental of these few acres upon marriage, freemen would have thus enslaved themselves?" The General defended slavery in the Civil War, but no doubt he entertained the Greek ideal of freedom, not incompatible with servitude for "natural born" slaves.

As far as the records show no freeman ever did thus enslave himself, but many did indenture themselves to like status for a certain term. And some paid feudal quitrents, though not enough to please milords, who thought in terms of small emerald isles instead of green seas of wilderness into which a laggard taxpayer could vanish.

The Constitutions assumed black slavery, providing that freemen should rule absolutely their bondsmen "of what opinion or religion soever." The intent here was to quash the tender notion that Christians could not hold Christians in bondage, a notion, by the way, which a few pious slaveowners took so much to heart that they strove to keep their blacks in pagan ignorance. Ashley Cooper, it may be added, had money out in the slave trade.

Though like the charter the Constitution assumed the Established Church, they gave freedom of worship, allowing church privileges to "any seven or more persons agreeing in any religion." Lord Ashley thus appealed to orthodox and Puritan. He wanted colonists, and he had an eye to what dissenting New England traders had accomplished in codfish and rum.

Government would, of course, rest on property, the man of largest acreage having the loudest voice and those with less than 500 acres barred from any share at all. The local parliament would have the right only to accept or turn down laws offered by a proprietary instrument called the Grand Council.

As Lord Ashley reasoned, the proprietors would replace the crown in Carolina affairs, and the nobles would stand for the peerage at home, though in winning titles by merit they would spur the general. Prospering planters and merchants would acquire manors and enter the ranks of the gentry. That expectation was prophetic. If Carolinians did not vie for synthetic titles, they did for lands and slaves.

In approving these laws for their colony the proprietors did not reckon on the potential of one clause in the royal charter—in those of Maryland, Maine and Pennsylvania as well—which a historian of early America judges of "momentous importance": laws were to be made and taxes levied with the advice and consent of colonial freemen. The clause gave Carolinians status as property-owning Englishmen. It gave them a weapon of dissent, and they used it. The proprietors might speak as from the throne, but they did not wear the crown. They could order, suggest and cajole, but the colonists stood on their chartered right in refusing to legalize the Constitutions and in demanding a larger share in government.

Making immediate plans for a settlement at Port Royal in their domain, the proprietors in 1669 pooled funds and bought three ships, the *Carolina*, the *Port Royal* and the *Albemarle*. They, or their agents, recruited passengers in London, and arranged for others to be picked up in Ireland, Barbados and Bermuda. The party that came ashore a few months later from the *Carolina* was no doubt typical: sixty-two were servants, seventeen were masters and thirteen were unbound persons without servants. The chances are that most of the native English were Londoners and that the masters were of the trading middle class, a sprinkling from well-to-do families. David Duncan Wallace, the most recent historian of South Carolina, says that letters reflect good educations for some, and "several aptly nailed a point with a Latin phrase." Commenting that the list shows names later to shine in South Carolina, he adds that several appearing as "servants" were "much above the servant class . . . really near relatives of their 'masters,'" who took this means of increasing their land allotment. Patently no gentle family can have sprung from a snuffling Piccadilly bootblack or a gamy stableboy from the Dog Tavern. A name Wallace may have been shielding is that of Barnaby Bull, rated as servant of Step (Stephen) Bull, later a deputy for Lord Ashley, sire and grandsire of able lieutenant governors. The family trace their origin to the Bulls of Sheldon Hall in Warwickshire and are jealous of their name, now shared by a German clan who put an Anglicizing "l" in place of the original "h" in Buhl. A blooded English Bull is apt to restore the "h" with the reminder that "Those are not our Bulls."

To serve until Ashley Cooper's blueprint for a landlord's utopia could be effected, the temporary governor Joseph West carried along some fairly tight instructions. There was to be a ruling council of the Governor and ten men, half proprietary deputies and half elected freemen. Every freeman was to have a small parcel of land and a like amount for every servant, slave or member of his family. They were to throw up a fort, leave the Indians alone, and above all settle in towns. Scattered about like Virginians on their tobacco holdings, they would not raise crops of hungry consumers, Lord Ashley feared, to buy the crops from great estates. Furthermore, only controlled ports could be made to pay in revenue. Virginia planters had a distressing habit of shipping direct from their plantation docks.

A healthy supply of food and goods for the Indian trade were loaded as well as a royal gift of twelve cannon. In Barbados the Governor was to pick up seeds and plants—cotton, indigo, cane, grape, and olive—and carry them in tubs of earth. In short, Ashley Cooper had seen well to the venture, and in result there was nothing of Captain John Smith's "starving time" in Jamestown. There was to be little profit either, but that he failed to foresee. One can only wonder that he expected more from adventurers across the Atlantic than the token gift of twelve cedar planks Sir John Yeamans sent "as the first fruits of that glorious province."

A hurricane wrecked the *Albemarle* at Barbados, and storms and losses attended the rest of the hop-skip voyage through the Caribbean. At one stop the expedition took on Dr. Henry Woodward, who was to do wonders for the colony in making Indian friends. He was already something of a wonder himself, having voluntarily dropped from an earlier expedition to visit the Indians at Port Royal, escaped from a Spanish prison at St. Augustine, doctored a privateering crew and survived shipwreck in a hurricane. But he leaves no trail of the swashbuckler. Fearless he must have been, but otherwise his nature seems to have blended the qualities of loyal lieutenant, scholar, naturalist and man of good will. As proprietary agent he helped divert the southwest Indian trade (in the present Georgia) from Spain to South Carolina, and he is thought to have spread the famous Carolina Gold rice.

At Bermuda Sir John Yeamans, who was charged with naming a governor and had come along from Barbados, chose Colonel William Sayle, "a man of no great sufficiency yet the ablest I could meet with." The colonists grumbled at sailing under a graybeard of eighty, but the old Puritan's pluck and colonial experience were to serve them reasonably well. Stranger than the clamor against him is the old man's taking the job, lamenting separation from the "Godly society" and "faithfull ministry" of Mr. Sampson Bond, in the parting from whom there was "nothing in all this world soe grievous to my spirit." He brought slaves but no kith and kin. Only an "elected" Calvinist saint would have put himself out to such distress of soul and body. In the colony he tried almost at once, naturally, to stop profanation of the Sabbath.

At Port Royal, which proprietary orders had fixed as the colonizing site, the "freemen" elected five of their number to form with the Governor and five proprietors' deputies a council of rule. With all those "servants" humbly standing by, this was no democratic procedure. It far from matched the Mayflower Pilgrims in their "covenant" to obey laws they would afterward make. But it was better than the squabblings of "poor gentlemen, tradesmen, serving-men, libertines and such like" at Jamestown, Virginia, in 1607.

Turned away from Port Royal by the persuasive Indian caciques of Kiawah, the colonists sailed a day's journey northward, entering what is now Charleston harbor in late April, 1670. When a strayed ship arrived a month later, the first South Carolinians made about 148 in total number. The "South" and "North" had not come into use, of course, and the two regions were one in the charter, but even so the colonists at Kiawah (lands bordering the river to be known as the Ashley) were not the first Carolinians. Squatters had already filtered in from Virginia to settle on the coast of the present North Carolina.

A protected townsite was chosen on the western bank of the Ashley, nearly opposite the present fortress-like buildings of The Citadel, the South Carolina Military College. The colonists called their town Albemarle Point in honor of the Palatine, the Duke of Albemarle, but the proprietors christened it Charles Town for their royal sire. The name passed a decade later to the present site of Charleston, a form adopted after the Revolution.

Only four months after they landed the colonists met frightening signs that they were settled in the "very chaps of the Spaniards." Happily warned by Dr. Woodward's Indian friends at Port Royal, they readied the cannon to drive off a Spanish fleet appearing in the harbor, but the attackers withdrew. Why, no one knows, except that Spain's imperial blood had cooled. Not that peace dawned forever in that moment. Both were to pay out their enmities for decades in Indian warpaths and settler scalps; and the Spanish made a bloody pounce in 1684 at Port Royal, where a malarial Scotch band tried miserably to plant their Covenanter faith.

But after the Spanish departed in 1670 the colonists felt safe for a time, surrounded as they were by helpful Indians. The ailing Governor Sayle did the best he could, wisely reserving a new townsite on the neck of land between the Ashley and Cooper rivers and naming the Quaker tradesman West to succeed him.

Several months before his death Sayle wrote Lord Ashley that the colony wanted provisions, which no doubt would be supplied, but "there is *one thing* which lyes very heavy upon us, the want of a Godly and orthodox minist'r." That no divine had come out with the colonists indicates as much as any other single fact the spirit of Ashley Cooper's Carolina. Not godlessness, for the Constitutions had forbidden any freeman holding lands who "doth not acknowledge a God, and that God is publicly and solemnly to be worshiped." Rather a spirit of rationalism or deism, a faith stripped clean to accord with Newton's clockworks universe and his God the high clockmaker. It was a faith unsympathetic to clerical tutorage and above all sympathetic to what a later age would call the rights of private enterprise, the rights of businessmen to invest and exploit without any meddling from church or state. It was the leading faith, by the way, of the aristocratic merchants and planters who made the American Revolution and insisted on separating politics from religion.

Deism, like the Protestant movement, grew inseparably with the rise of urban or middle-class capitalism in Europe. And all the American colonies were born from the urges of capitalism. Both the first English colony at Jamestown, Virginia, and the settlement at Charles Town, almost the last, were planted in the countinghouses of London. To the burgher lords of these houses both Sir Walter Raleigh and Ashley Cooper spoke as to equals.

A native historian, St. Julien Ravenel Childs, has shown the difference between middle-class and feudal enterprises in comparing Ashley Cooper's Carolina with a sixteenth-century Spanish settlement on Parris Island, now a United States Marine base near Beaufort, South Carolina. The Spanish colony ran communistically like a medieval manor, yielding profits only of prestige and glory to crown and cross. Peasant colonists worked the ground to feed themselves, the career soldiers on guard for Philip II and the Jesuits preaching to heathen Indians. In Carolina, on the contrary, men planted or traded for profit, guarded the colony themselves and let the Indians die unsaved.

Of that Carolina, with its landgraves and baronies, we might say that little survived. But if history is a slow evolution rather than a series of abrupt stops and starts, impulses lived as well as splendid names affixed to tracts of land like Hobcaw Barony, on Winyah Bay, Bernard Baruch's restoration of a proprietary estate. Shown in fiction as living a century after the colony was founded, William Gilmore Simms' old planter lord, Colonel Sinclair, had his counterparts in life. He had earned his rank whipping the Cherokee Indians for king and colony, and he sat now on his barony nursing his gout, growing indigo for the London market, cursing the rebels who threatened his profitable loyalties and flourishing his gold-headed cane at tenant whites like *Mister* Pete Blodgit whining at his door. His equally imperious slave lieutenant sizes him up as a "gentleman what don't blieb berry much in de rights ob poor buckrah [poor whites]."

III

Revenues and Rebels

In the winter of 1671 a newcomer to the settlement on the Ashley advised the proprietors by letter that "though the Governor [Sayle] is crazy yet if there were a wise Council, or three or four men of reason, *planters,* who knew what did belong to settle a country, it would be to the good of the country and their Lordship's interests." Obviously a planter himself, this self-appointed counselor was also a gentleman of Barbados, one of a sizable pioneering company only a few weeks away from that overcrowded sugar island in the West Indies. Doubtless he spoke their collective mind, for they were old colonial hands, bred to the gainful uses of slavery and the swagger of a master caste. They were primed, in other words, to rule the Carolina roost.

Since they also came in force enough to double their lordship's original tenantry, the Barbadians had a fairly irresistible advantage. Individually shrewd and brash, they were also clannish. They wasted no more time in staking out choice lands than they did in voting each other to elective office. Bestriding the province, they made it seem an outpost of Caribbean empire.

Considering the time, the latitude and the proprietary motives, Carolina was possibly fated to go the way of Negro slavery and a one-crop agricultural system. If not, if another way lay open, the Barbadians closed it off. Rooting themselves and their social and economic order, they made it certain that whoever came afterwards would conform or perish.

The Barbadians were, of course, English to the bone, not Spanish-

American. Middle class by origin, they had acquired patrician airs if not aristocratic patents through membership in an island squirearchy that had everything "requisite to pomp and luxury," as a contemporary British historian observed, citing an Egyptian plenitude of human livestock. At least one Barbadian emigrant to Carolina, Sir John Yeamans, was a bona fide knight of the realm, though not to the English manor born, it would seem, judging from Mrs. Ravenel's remark (in *Charleston, the Place and the People*) that "the old people" used to shrug off his kind as " 'only-badian Baronets.' "

Though they brought a fervid addiction to slavery, the Barbadians did not introduce the first slaves into the colony. For what it is worth that honor belongs to Governor Sayle, who stepped ashore with John Senior, Elizabeth and John Junior in his train. (If this nameless pioneer family survived, a good many blacks have Carolina bloodlines incontestably as long as any white.) The Barbadians did, however, introduce a legal conception of slavery less humane than any other American colony would know. As they shaped it, the Carolina code ordered punishment for killing slaves but otherwise left the blacks pretty much to the master's caprice.

Wanting absolute control of their own slaves, the Barbadians nonetheless favored ready help from their neighbors in a pinch, and they foisted on Carolina the military system by which their home island curbed insurrectionary tempers in the cane fields. Under this dispensation every white male was a part-time soldier, willy-nilly obliging the master class; every big landowner took his turn as militia "captain" or "colonel"; and the high sheriff kept the peace in the guise of a provost marshal. These forms accompanied slavery wherever it spread, favoring if not causing the growth of a martial strain in the Southern character. Indubitably they fixed the Southern habit, as McCrady says, of awarding military titles to local bigwigs in preference to such handles as "judge" and "squire." The habit persisted generally in South Carolina until recent years, dying out along with swallowtail coats, gold-headed canes and senatorial coiffures. It survives at present only among the thinning ranks of conscious (perhaps self-conscious) gentlemen. If any white man feels awe of his betters these days he doesn't advertise it with a deferential

"cap'n." Even Negroes, in fact, are stingy with the titles they used
to dispense in fawning profusion.

The Barbadians imported one cultural value they would have
spurned as either cultural or valuable, the Gullah (or coastal Negro)
dialect, which has made two or three literary reputations in Carolina.
(A high-pitched jabber, Gullah defies all but salt-water ears, sounding
in crude approximation like this: "Enty-maa-teh-yuh-nah-fah-say-
nahtin?" which means in literal translation, "Ain't ma tell you not
for say nothing?") At least the Charleston annalist Samuel Gaillard
Stoney plausibly claims that it first developed on the West Indian
plantations, "from peasant dialects of English bondsmen . . .
mouthed into shape by the negroes." In fixing a plebeian origin
Mr. Stoney implies a gap between the speech of high and low that in
fact does not exist. The vulgate may be a poor relation to gentle
speech in any given region, but it is related. Gullah sounds find
echoes on the best Charleston piazzas, and a Charlestonian at old St.
Michael's in Bridgetown, Barbados, or, for that matter, at the
Myrtlebank hotel in Kingston, Jamaica, can hear the family talking.
They all say "Jamay-uhca," and their beloved rice they call "raw-
ece." (Sound rapidly to get the proper effect: nobody drawls in
Barbados or Charleston.)

In other respects any old Caribbean town might remind the
Charleston visitor of home, displaying similar wrought-iron balconies
and walled gardens and exuding smells reminiscent of "heavy salt,
pluff mud, oleanders and drains," as the Charleston novelist Josephine Pinckney renders the native aroma. Certainly the weathered
and tinted stucco would jog the memory, for Carolina's one sure
heritage from Spanish America was the practice of building or
overlaying in "tabby," made of seashells partly burned to lime and
partly crushed.

Social, economic, cultural and political influences, then, all
seeped into Carolina from Barbados. On the side of politics Landgrave Yeamans seized the governorship from Sayle's appointee
Joseph West in 1671 on the basis of his title. None too happy at the
coup, the proprietors admitted the landgrave's rank made him "preferred to any Commoner." Yeamans stood almost supreme as head
of the Grand Council, which made judicial as well as executive

decisions and drew up measures for the twenty-member Parliament to vote on.

With Yeamans' death three years later, the proprietors neatly solved the problem of skill versus rank by naming West governor and raising him to landgrave at one stroke. The Quaker tradesman led ably, for one thing extracting funds from stingy London, but he was unseated for dabbling in the Indian slave traffic. The proprietors had forbidden Indian enslavement but had later condoned it as a way of "encouraging the soldiers." In other words, the military took their pay in captives which they sold to the West Indies. Since red men were apt to be "morose" under the lash and sluggish at felling timber in the swamps, the sale was never brisk in Carolina marts.

The Indians were more gainful as deer hunters and tanners than as captives. This fact, which the proprietors knew and sharp colonists saw instantaneously, caused more bad blood perhaps than governmental disputes. The proprietors wanted the Indian trade for themselves, and otherwise they "earnestly desired" rent-paying growers of such produce as olives, oranges and wine grapes, which England hungered for, could not grow herself and for which she unbalanced her trade. Though oranges were grown and exported, the climate was scarcely suitable for tropical fruits, as the colonists felt in their bones the first winter when ice formed an inch thick. Cattle flourished, but the proprietors refused to send any more at one point— English meadows were full of cattle. Colonists tried a variety of crops—cotton, tobacco, peas, barley, and indigo—but the easy money lay in bartering with the Indians, trinkets for deerskins. The trade was so gainful that skins became shortly the chief export—fifty years later running second only to rice—and it was so extensive that traders led their pack mules northwestward to the Blue Ridge Mountains and southwestward to cross trails with the French spreading trinkets and gunpowder from Mobile, on the Gulf. As a result Charles Town shortly became the mouth of a vast trading funnel and the only important port town south of Philadelphia.

Laying out the new town, occupied about 1680 under West, Sir John Yeamans must have followed some of Lord Ashley's expansive orders, for a London visitor noted the regularity of its "capacious streets" and sites reserved for public structures. On one of these St.

Philip's, the first church building in the province, soon arose of black cypress on a brick foundation. The merits of the townsite had caused a good deal of transatlantic bickering. With the ignorance that distance lent to his view, Lord Ashley kept insisting on high ground to men who could only stand twenty feet above sea level by scaling a pine tree. Opposing the new site at first, he finally gave in at reports of "distempers" among colonists at the old town.

If these distempers were malaria, as one study plausibly infers, then the Carolina summer and autumn curse was first at hand. As diseases go, it is not a prime killer, but anyone who has burned, shivered and vomited through its seizures will understand why for two hundred years it was a subject of apprehension, misapprehension and periodic flight for the well-to-do. Of course it does not inhere in the climate or the swamps, and the parasites that caused it probably swam to Carolina in the blood of colonists from London: the Indians were free of it and so were the settlers from Barbados. But since the bug-carrying mosquito likes muggy weather and underbrush, malaria will surely break out anew where infected people gather with others near steaming swamps. One uninfected man alone will not take it, because the vehicular mosquito sticks close to her damp lairs.

Unfeeling history concludes that in the long view malaria did not affect Carolina's development: in spite of chills, fever and sometimes death, men cleared the swamps, planted the rice and whacked away at the Indians. True, full-blooded Negroes with their relative immunity, or in clinical terms "their extraordinary tolerance for the parasite," did much of the pioneering work. But anyone who would know the human atmosphere of low-country Carolina early and late must visualize men, women and children recurrently taking to their beds in the dog days or dragging around with liverish faces. As someone expressed it in a slightly later day, Carolina was a paradise in the spring, a hell in the summer and a hospital in the fall. Peruvian bark (quinine)—from the cinchona tree in the Andes— was already known as a specific in the late seventeenth century, but no one had as yet discovered effective dosages nor, it may be added, the gelatin capsule to shield the mouth from its scouring, scalding bitterness.

As Charles Town rose on its permanent site, the first of several

French immigrant parties sailed in from England. Called Huguenots
—the word joins a reformer's name, Hugues, with another meaning
companion—they were as dourly Calvinistic as the Boston theocrats.
Many of their persuasion had fled across the Channel to England
in Charles I's day, and now the tribe was flying again as Catholic
enmity sharpened for the kill—the revocation in 1685 of the tolerat-
ing Edict of Nantes. Though England gave asylum, the post-
Restoration mood there was scarcely clement: after all, Huguenot
brothers in heresy—Puritans—had beheaded the present King's
father at Whitehall Palace. Under the circumstances Carolina seemed
a God-appointed haven. Lord Ashley's free-worship clause guaranteed
safety; and the proprietor himself, aware of the Huguenot wine-
and silk-making genius, pledged a glad welcome in his republic.

The welcome was not as glad as he would have liked—then as now
men looked askance at strangers "jabbering" another tongue—but
suspicion quickly wore off as the enterprising Huguenots took root
on the land and plied their needed crafts in Charles Town. Increase
of worldly goods naturally recommended their sons and daughters
for marriage, and soon they were mixing their blood with the lustiest
Barbadian. One step more—conversion from their grim heretic faith
to the King's religion—and they were ready to share the reins of
power.

Since the vote was reserved to Anglicans, it would seem that
Huguenots were less than earnest converts. Perhaps so, but considering the austerities of Calvinism, it might have been well for the
colony that they felt obliged to shift allegiance. At least they never
emulated their spiritual cousins in Massachusetts to hang witches
amid the Spanish moss.

These Frenchmen, the majority arriving in the 1680's and 1690's,
were predominantly middle class. Their group biographer cries up
the noble few, like the St. Juliens de Malacre, but a scholar of that
blood remarks that though some Huguenots came from families
"recently ennobled . . . socially and by occupation all were bourgeois." Wallace says they were generally aristocratic in "worth rather
than blood." Some brought money and some only the clothes on
their backs. Many artisans fled one jump ahead of the ecclesiastical
bloodhounds, leaving behind even the tools of their trade. The first
shipload to land in Charles Town, however, must have left with

ample warning, for they packed along silkworm eggs to hatch out and spin their fibers in the New World. Unhappily, the worms emerged at sea and died for want of mulberry leaves.

Whatever they brought of blood or substance, the Huguenots did not pause to weep their outcast fate. Trusting in God but relying on themselves like all good Calvinists—and Frenchmen—they set to work, some at crafts in Charles Town, most on the land. A good few struck out up the coast and founded homesteads on the Santee River, fifty miles from town and a universe removed from neat provincial France.

Coastal legendry inclines to gloze the fact of a pioneering plunge into the swamps with a good sharp ax as the chief family treasure. It scarcely magnifies, for example, such an image as the Santee pioneer Judith Manigault was herself not the least ashamed to post abroad: "I have been six months together without tasting bread, working the ground like a slave; and I have even passed three and four years without tasting it when I wanted it." Mythmakers scarcely pass up the fact, by contrast, that Judith's merchant son built one of the great fortunes in colonial America.

The quick-rooting Huguenots ultimately joined with Barbadians against English Dissenters in quarrels leading to the formal estab-lishment of the Anglican Church. Dissenters had come in number along with the French and for almost identical reasons. Persecutions fell on them in waves after the Restoration, as English Cavaliers paid back the Cromwell mischief with Cromwell's Hebraic rigor. Both exiled for their faith—and a like faith at that—Dissenters and Huguenots had every good reason, it would seem, to hang together. Since they didn't, we can only assume the Huguenots reasoned in French: they calculated the profit and the loss, that is, and clove to the Barbadian party.

Members of each group—Anglicans, Huguenots and Dissenters—naturally hung together at first, and the three counties defined in 1685 took on religious complexions: Berkeley (the Charles Town region) became an Anglican stronghold, Colleton (southwest of town) was a Dissenter refuge, and Craven (to the north) belonged to the French. The Barbadians on Goose Creek understandably formed the earliest Anglican congregation outside the town. Also quite naturally their stuccoed church evokes the West Indies; and the pride of a planter ruling class is still reflected there in scutcheons on tablets, in at least one fine heraldic memorial and in the hatchment of Ralph Izard—very likely the only one in the state—rich Revolutionary dabbler in diplomacy.

Goose Creekers, of course, gave weight to the Barbadian element as it warred with the proprietors in the decade before 1700.

At one point this aggressive clan joined with the proprietor Seth Sothell (then resident in Charles Town) to oust a governor who had, among other caprices, fined a preacher for a sermon he disliked. Sothell was at best, however, only a focus for grievances, having been expelled from the Albemarle colony (North Carolina) for a season of outrageous misrule.

Squabbles between the colonists and their management were not surprising in view of the risky distance from England and the whimsical choice of governors. No Caesar to begin with, Sothell did not help matters at Albemarle by arriving three years overdue, though, of course, he could scarcely help the delay—he was captured enroute by Algerine pirates. Those who arrived on schedule often had little to recommend them but their favor with a noble patron. Arrogant with borrowed power, they were no match for slave-driving planters and hustling traders.

Also, management worsened as the overlords died off: by 1684 seven of the original company had gone, Ashley Cooper among them, and their shares had passed by inheritance or sale to minors and nondescripts.

Replacing Sothell in 1691—he had ruled surprisingly well—the proprietors tried to unify their province by naming a governor of all Carolina and empowering him to rule at Albemarle by deputy. Neither he nor later governors, however, could bind the colonies together. They remained distinct. North Carolinians stayed under the proprietary thumb a decade longer than the Charles Town settlers, until 1728, the year Virginia's ducal Willam Byrd fixed them in lasting caricature as sluggards of Lubberland, an early version of Dogpatch. In mild weather, he says, the men lean upon the cornfield fence and "gravely consider whether they had best go and take a Small Heat at the Hough but generally find reasons to put it off till another time."

Many South Carolinians, including the Secession fusileer Robert

Barnwell Rhett (born Smith), descend from one of those governors of North and South Carolina, Landgrave Thomas Smith. Of the peppery Goose Creek tribe but loyal to the masters, he gained with his commission 48,000 acres of land. Already well-to-do, he had just recently acquired 12,000 acres at the altar by uniting with the widow of Jan Van Arrsens, Seigneur de Weirnhoudt, who had led a small company of Hollanders to Carolina. Medway, the widow's house of "homemade" brick on Back River, has stood from 1686 to hold its present distinction as the oldest dwelling of record in the state. Governor Smith's alliance and the manner in which his acres grew, though both legal and above reproach, illustrate vividly how ruling classes come to rule. The road is from wealth to prestige to power. Though often in our ironies we forget that founders of aristocracy need character and some vision of the common welfare, it is none-theless true that wealth comes first.

Before he died in office within the year he had figured to London the central shortcoming of its rule, writing that it was "impossible to settle the country except a Proprietor himself was sent over with full power to heal grievances." Taking sound American advice for once, they sent the Quaker John Archdale, "being in the nature of a Proprietor," and he managed to relieve some of the major pains. He approved acts to fix land tenure and to adjust rentals, involuntarily erecting a kind of Magna Charta for the province, since these measures embodied the principle that London could not overrule the Assembly without its consent.

The arrival in 1699 of a royal collector of customs signified the crown's growing envy of proprietary expectations. No more in favor with the Carolinians than the landlords, whom he accused of winking at illicit trade, he nonetheless by his presence nourished the local grudge against the proprietors. Grumbling at the presence of this crown interloper, the proprietors bestirred themselves and dispatched a chief justice and an attorney general as an earnest of legal rectitude.

Nicholas Trott, the attorney general, intriguing behind the scenes for the next two decades, kept gossip tongues wagging. At times he was figured as the bastard son of Lord Shaftesbury; at others a knavish governor of the Bahamas (actually a cousin). Indisputably a self-seeker, Trott was neither a rogue nor a dolt, so Wallace concludes. He drew up a notable code of laws, indited legal treatises and worked at a Hebrew text of the Bible. In failing to make his witchcraft charges stick on a luckless woman, he also unwittingly kept the state from that New England department of shame.

Anglicans and Dissenters fought through the first years of the new century. When the Goose Creek Indian trader James Moore unseated a Dissenter governor on a legal technicality, the next elections brought accusations mindful of the latter-day notion that Charleston in a tight spot blithely votes the graveyard. But Dissenters had more and even juster reasons to rail when the next governor, Sir Nathaniel Johnson, hounded them from the Assembly and tried legally to keep them out. Though he failed in that, he did manage to establish the Church of England through an act which not only set up parishes but made them civil subdivisions, a status they kept in the low country until 1865. Control of local affairs thus passed to the church vestry and wardens, chosen by taxpaying adherents of the King's faith.

"Our public enemies"—the Spanish and French—as well as "our domestic foes"—Sir Nathaniel's style for Dissenters—made trouble during those first years of the new century. While still governor, James Moore bolstered Queen Anne in her war with France and Spain by leading an expedition to Florida and burning St. Augustine. Four years later Colonel William Rhett drove a French fleet from Charles Town harbor, and the next year Captain Thomas Nairne aimed to wipe out the French at Mobile with an Indian force, thus diverting the rich Mississippi trade to the Cooper River docks. It was a bold and likely scheme, but a rumored French attack by sea called him home, only to go to jail on a public charge that hid a private grudge: Nairne as Indian agent had stopped a gubernatorial son-in-law's enslavement of friendly tribesmen.

The snake in the grass, Thomas Broughton, had traded so fruitfully in human flesh and other commodities that by 1714 he was ready to build his "castle" Mulberry on the Cooper River, the one surviving monument to the first big wave of Carolina wealth. "The most elaborate residence to be seen in the colonies at the time," by a recent critical review of the nation's architecture, it is less imposing than artful. Attaching four Jacobean towers to the corners of a typical parish country house, Broughton achieved a whimsical effect, as though he took his own pretensions with a grain of humor. At any rate he shaped a felicitious work of domestic art, proving, if nothing else, that in feeding their own vanity the buccaneers do often please the world.

Though Mulberry's pseudo-military towers were designed purely for ornament, the house did serve as a fortress soon after it was built, fitly enough against the very Indians Broughton had preyed on to build it. Under the alert rule of Governor Charles Craven the colony had scarcely put down the Tuscaroras to the north when the Yemassees to the south leaped murderously on the settlers in their domain. Not unexpectedly, for the wise and humane had long warned of the whirlwind such men as Broughton were sowing for the colony to reap. Before the outbreak was quelled the harvest amounted to hundreds of dead settlers and soldiers. In addition, military expenses had virtually cleaned out the province treasury.

The Yemassee war inspired Carolina's ante bellum romancer William Gilmore Simms to write the one fictional account of the vanishing Indian that rivals Fenimore Cooper's battered classic *The Last of the Mohicans*. The only Simms work now read at all— by other than literary historians—*The Yemassee* sharply actualizes the Indian fate where Cooper transforms it to heroic myth. Simms' rum-soaked Occonestoga, scheming to sell his tribal lands to the English, may well be a truer symbol than the sacrificial Mohican Uncas. Facing the death of his soul by exile from the tribe, Occonestoga is poetically saved for the happy valley—by a tomahawk blow from his mother—but his end is closer to the pitiable reality than the last Mohican's noble leap into eternity for the sake of a maiden's virtue.

Patching things up with the Indians by 1717, the colony turned to deal with the pirates feeding on her trade as they roamed back and forth between their lairs in the West Indies and along the North Carolina coast. She made a quick and thorough job of it, virtually settling the pirate hash for all time by hanging forty-nine cutthroats in a single month of 1718.

Despite the losses in the Yemassee war, the colony had riches to lure the hungriest Caribbean sharks: Adding a thousand slaves annually to her work force, keeping the pack mules jogging along the trails to the back country, the colony supplied large fleets with cargo to England and the Northern colonies. As the flow increased, so, of course, did the picaroons. Unchecked, they got so bold at last that Blackbeard on one occasion rounded up eight or nine ships in the Charles Town harbor and demanded a chest of medicines from shore as the price of his departure.

Goaded beyond endurance, Governor Robert Johnson stopped crying to indifferent London for help and sent Colonel William Rhett to sea as vice-admiral of a makeshift fleet of war. Rhett caught Stede Bonnet, the gentleman buccaneer from Barbados, in North Carolina's Cape Fear River, subdued him in a nine-hour pistol fight—both vessels were grounded—and sailed on the rising tide with his quarry in tow. As the Bonnet gang stood trial in Charles Town, Governor Johnson hooked a second notorious brigand, Richard Worley, just outside the harbor.

A good many Charles Town squires welcomed the ingratiating Bonnet rather as a cousin in distress than a prize neck for the noose. They pleaded his cause in court with tearful zeal, begging mercy for one so palpably "a man of honor, a man of fortune, and one that had a liberal education." Unmoved, the attorney general ventured that such graces might well be taken as "aggravations of his crime." Equally unbeguiled, the Chief Justice (Nicholas Trott) declared for the gallows. The sanctimonious Trott, however, could not miss a chance to moralize. He suspected that Bonnet had wandered from the straight and narrow rather because than in spite of his education: dabbling in "*Polite* Literature; and the vain Philosophy of the Times," the man had blinked the true purpose of all studies, "a serious Search after the *Law* and *Will* of God."

Bonnet's deportment in the face of death tended to confirm the judge's imputation. He whined and whimpered like the wronged maiden of a courtly romance, throwing himself at the Governor's feet and beseeching the "tender bowells of pity and compassion." Clutching at the pen, he promised to "mourn all my Days in Sackcloth and Ashes to work out Confident hopes of my Salvation." He might have swallowed his fright and left a reputation for courage as well as criminality, for he touched none but unofficial hearts. Trott's sentence was duly carried out.

Having thrown off their pirate oppressors, the Carolinians were ready for a showdown with proprietary rule, which they had come to regard as a kind of piracy in decay, more nuisance than menace. The opportunity arose with the proprietors' veto in 1718 of more than a dozen Assembly laws, many touching sensitive and vital spots. Among other things their actions nullified a new scheme for parish representation; removed the Assembly's right to elect the provincial treasurer and denied the use of Yemassee Indian lands to encourage immigration. They also ordered the governor to dissolve the Assembly and have another elected on the old plan.

The Governor and Council sent an emissary to London, but he failed to gain a willing, much less a sympathetic, proprietary ear. The Assembly of 1719, then, backed by the sworn "lives and fortunes" of leading colonists, refused to accept the vetoes and asked the Governor to "hold the reins . . . for the King till his Majesty's pleasure be known." Johnson dissolved the Assembly, but the members sat tight and proclaimed a new governor to represent the King. Very slow in nodding to this show of fealty, the King did not send a proconsul for several months, leaving time for disruptive scuffles and quarrels between proprietary and royalist factions.

To name specific grievances is not to suggest that these alone undid the proprietors. They were only telltale marks of decay within and pressures without. In 1719 no original proprietor still lived, and heirs were as little engrossed in Carolina affairs as stockholders in a profit-losing company. About the only dividends they got were sinecures for a few indigent cousins and sons-in-law. The Palatine, Lord John Carteret, grandson of the first proprietor of his name, had weightier matters on his mind. When the provincial emissary called in 1719, he was readying to assume his first diplomatic post on the Continent and simply waved the boresome colonial away. By virtue of such indifference, authority had devolved for many years more or less on the clerk of the board.

The Board of Trade and Plantations, a crown agency, applied the major pressure from without. It had long wanted to scrap such anomalies as Carolina presented—a private empire within the Empire—and manage all colonies alike. Though the proprietary charters had furthered the most up-to-date brand of bourgeois enterprise, they had after all exhumed a feudal principle dead in England since the thirteenth century, that of subleasing lands given in vassalage. The pirate raids had demonstrated, if demonstration was needed, the vacuity of the feudal bond: the vassals were having their throats cut, so to speak, while their liege lords pooh-poohed the peril at an ocean's remove.

The Carolina ruling class, however, was thinking and acting far ahead of the Board of Trade and Plantations. By 1719 they were losing their immigrant identities as Barbadians, French Huguenots and English Dissenters: they were born Carolinians now, many of the third generation. Though aristocratic by desire they were middle class by origin and a hard-driving middle class in fact. If their fathers had ever fancied the vassal relation, *they* fancied nothing so much as a moneyed independence.

IV

"Carolina Gold"

*Sending a barrel of Carolina rice to an English school in mid-*eighteenth century, Eliza Lucas Pinckney wrote the headmaster that her sons—the future generals Thomas and Charles Cotesworth— "love it boild dry to eat with their meat instead of bread."

The English genius for reducing any edible to a sodden lump makes it doubtful that they got it "boild dry." If not, they must have groaned to their mother across the Atlantic, little gentlemen though they were and bred to endure. For on the Carolina coast rice was— and still is—not only the common staple but a sacred food as well, a daily sign and pledge of clan continuity. Not to have it at all might grieve the stomach; but not to have it steaming hot and dry—each grain apart—would surely lacerate the soul.

In Eliza Pinckney's time rice was an economic bulwark as well as an object of culinary and social piety! For most of the crown rule years—from 1719 to 1776—it joined with indigo to afford the colony's chief wealth among planters and Charles Town merchants. It came first to afford the steady income a landed ruling class needs to perpetuate its rule. Without it, or at least without a crop suited to swampy lands, black chain-gang labor and the world's hunger, the Barbadian sugar system imported to Carolina might have withered to a semblance of farming patterns in Pennsylvania.

With rice assured as a money crop, Carolina planters raced each other to extend their domains, driving homesteaders back from the coast to pellagrous futility in the pinelands. The crop then became such a vested interest—along with slaves and later indigo—that it largely swayed votes in the Commons Assembly, thwarting the wise solution of three interlocking colonial problems: Indian hostility, the ravenous importation of blacks and the needs of back-country settlers.

Like the silky-fibered sea-island cotton of a later day, rice was a blue-blood crop. Or so it came to be as the generations prospered and joined their blood and rice fields in marriage. Rice planters were born but never made; and their mystique of the calling suggests that they grew it in filial piety alone, much as the old Chinese coveted official rank to please the ancestral shades. Whatever their motives, surely no moneygrubber ever wrote such a graceful valedictory to his livelihood as the fifth-generation Carolina rice planter Duncan Clinch Heyward in his *Seed from Madagascar*.

The book is almost an apologia for his backsliding from the faith. Holding on against ruinous storms and competition from other sections, Governor Heyward stood nearly alone as a Carolina grower when he sold out to "Northern capitalists" just prior to World War I. For this act, he said, he had often fancied his great-grandfather Nathanial gazing down in stern reproof from the portrait over his dining-room mantel. He might have felt even sharper reproof from Nathaniel's father, Daniel, the first rice planter of the line, who left nearly a thousand slaves at his death during the Revolution. Even *his* father, Thomas the second, might have censured the birthright sale, for he had taken up Yemassee lands after 1715 to become the first Heyward planter.

Though Heywards did not establish the crop, the Governor claims descent from the man tradition regards as the founding father— Dr. Henry Woodward. He supposedly planted, around 1685, the first seed of the Carolina Gold variety—named for the tawny color of its husk—which gave the province's rice such renown that Louisiana and Texas growers still market their crops as "Carolina rice." He sowed, in other words, the "seed from Madagascar," less than a bushel he got by way of a New England sea captain from that island off the eastern coast of Africa.

The proprietors had urged rice growing from the start, and it was tried in the early years, but the Madagascar seed, improved methods and slave labor made it a golden crop. It was first grown in the inland swamps, which were easy to clear and by a system of dams and wooden gates could be flooded and drained at intervals. In mid-eighteenth century, with an ample corps of slaves on hand, planters switched to the thickly timbered swamps bordering the fresh-water rivers. Here they used tidal pressure to back the river water over the fields.

One gets some idea of what this swamp-clearing work entailed by raking for crabs in the Carolina coastal marshes, sinking up to the knees in the alluvial slime the natives call pluff mud, from the blue-gray puffs or pluffs it sends boiling smokily up into the water when disturbed. As a Negro fisherman once advised, "When you crab in the marsh, you keeps one knee bent," meaning that a man's pause to scratch a sand-fly bite can sink him down toward a muddy grave. Add to this hazard the menace of alligators, which abounded in the early days, and water moccasins, which still do, and the bloodthirstiest mosquitoes in creation.

After the trees and underbrush were out, the tides did some of man's labor, forcing the water over the fields to nourish the young rice plants and kill the weeds and grass; but there was plenty left to do, from burning the old year's stubble in the spring to flailing the grains from the stalk and then husking the grain with wooden mortar and pestle. Tide-driven pounding mills husked the rice on some plantations, but not till after the Revolution did any marked relief appear for the drudging Negroes. The blessing came in the shape of an English millwright, Jonathan Lucas, who was providentially cast up by shipwreck near the mouth of the Santee River to devise the first efficient machinery for pounding and cleaning rice.

Rice developed almost steadily as a money crop through the eighteenth century—exports rose from 300 tons in 1770 to 35,000 around 1775—thriving especially after 1730 when Parliament allowed the planter to ship direct to Europe and thus evade tribute to British middlemen. This act helped to ease a decade's distempers, partially resulting from the clashes with proprietary rule that brought on royal control. Neither the first royal governor, General Sir Francis Nicholson, nor his native successor, President of the Governor's Council Arthur Middleton, soothed many ruffled feathers in their terms.

No man had less of the calming touch than Sir Francis, who as recent governor of Maryland had taken so hard a lady's choice of another suitor that he threatened to slit the throats of her bridegroom, the licensing magistrate and the parson who sealed the match. He was equally violent in the service of "our Holy Mother the Church of England," ramming through Commons a bill forcing members to swear on the Bible, thus barring Dissenters, who were so skittish of rituals that they would only swear by holding up their hands. Nicholson also raised tempers through his tangle with the old pirate-fighter Colonel Rhett. As customs controller and owner of a wharf and married to a merchant wife, Madam Sarah, Rhett stood in a position that not even a saint could hold without envy or suspicion, and he was anything but a saint. When Nicholson accused him before the Council of smuggling, he brazenly returned the compliment and went to jail rather than pay the fine clapped on for slander. But the Governor was cheated of his aim to prosecute on assorted charges when "old Rhett died of an apoplex," as Sir Francis wrote to London, leaving behind a reputation so contradictory that one historian can only string out the adjectives, "greedy, violent, vulgar, lawless, brave, impulsive, generous."

Other than popping off at fellow combustibles, Nicholson shored up the colony's defenses against the Spanish and French, building (in present Georgia) the first in the English chain of frontier forts.

After he left, but in line with his warnings of the Indian peril, Carolina officials quit their shifty game of playing the Creeks off against the Cherokees and invited the tribal chieftains to peace-making feasts in Charles Town. The gesture paid off, but not nearly so much, oddly enough, as an extraofficial mission to the Cherokees a few years later—in 1730—by a somewhat balmy Scottish baronet, Sir Alexander Cumings. The mission was so private, in fact, that Charles Town had no wind of it until the "conqueror" marched down from the Appalachians with news of a "conquest" straight out of *Don Quixote*.

Sir Alexander had sailed to Carolina supposedly on a tip from his wife, who foresaw his Cherokee apotheosis in a dream. More prosaically, as a Royal Society member he wanted to collect minerals and medicinal herbs. Learning that French proselytes had been among the Cherokees for two years, he determined to subdue them for his king. Armed with pistols and a "Sword under a Great Coat," and backed by convenient eruptions of thunder and lightning, he stalked into the chieftains' house at Keowee and to the awe of Carolina traders commanded all to kneel and drink to his Britannic Majesty.

Intoxicated by their compliance, he persuaded the chiefs to call the towns in for a great feast day and a ceremonious surrender of possum-hair crowns to him as viceregal deputy of King George. He then shepherded a party of seven ambassadorial Cherokees to London, presented them at court and saw them through a heady season of public appearances. They feasted with merchants trading to Carolina, had their portraits painted and drew admiring crowds when they "took the Air in St. James Park, habited in rich Garments laced with gold, presented to them by his Majesty." And finally, awed by the pomp of court and the power of maneuvering troops, they signed an agreement with the Lords of Trade to fight English enemies and to welcome English settlers. With imperial magnanimity milords granted them civil rights: an Englishman killing a Cherokee would be punished under British law and a Cherokee killing an Englishman also would be punished under British law.

Pacific Cherokees were a godsend to Charles Town, for their hostility had helped threaten the colony with economic ruin. Indian war costs had been met so freely with unbacked currency that from 1710 till 1725 the relative value of provincial money to sterling declined perilously. Creditor merchants began urging a dam across the rising river of paper, to the anger of indebted planters who were fearful that the dam would maroon them on the sands of bankruptcy. Sir Francis Nicholson's successor, Arthur Middleton, was caught between the factions. Obeying a London order to halt inflation, he faced a total breach between Council and Commons and finally an armed band of planters in Charles Town. The planters howled that merchant skinflints in London pulled the strings of Carolina government, and their local agents joined the Council in hurling back charges of treason. A governmental deadlock rather than open civil war resulted, and Governor Robert Johnson, arriving in 1730, needed all his skill to break it.

During Governor Johnson's term a newly beneficent mood in London touched off a stampede for land in which buccaneers drove settlers off their holdings like rabbits. On the advice of British merchants the King had offered to forgive quitrent arrears if the Assembly would legally insure future payments in cash instead of rice and potatoes. The royal bargain also allowed the colony to delay retiring the paper money and use the funds thereby freed to help poor Protestant settlers. The landowning Assembly leaped at the offer as a chance to confirm the old proprietary patents, which London courts had nullified, stipulating in their act that land titles must be registered within eighteen months.

Both Johnson and the King were thus trapped in a bargain they never made. Though a London veto was in order, the King was induced to let well enough alone, and well enough turned into a legalized root-hog-or-die race for the lushest coastal acres.

Much of the land granted by the old patents was not only unclaimed but unlocated. Many a landowner could show, that is, grandfather's title to 50,000 unspecific acres. With a reason now to pin them down, he did the humanly greedy thing: he claimed as fair a domain as he could mark with tree blazes before some fast-riding neighbor beat him to it. The poor farmers who had staked out their legal claims of 50 acres per head within the new domains were out of luck.

The popular imagination tends to figure the English kings as robbers of the people, snatching the bread and meat from cottage tables. In fact, the kings often tried to save the common man's bread and meat from the robber barons of the kingdom. Presumably in 1731, for instance, George II would have parceled out Carolina lands to the landless, but his London advisers on colonial affairs, the Lords of Trade, persuaded otherwise. After all, they represented the British merchants, who stood to gain from fattening Carolina planters.

The planters, moreover, could fend pretty well for themselves. Controlling the Commons House of Assembly, they virtually ran the colony, holding the right to vote governmental expenses. The crown-appointed governor and Council, the latter functioning as an upper legislative house, could make little headway without funds.

For arbitrary exercise of power the planter Commons could match a monarch any day. They could and did, for instance, jail men on such picayune charges as maligning them in tavern gossip. While Commons sat, moreover, the accused had no redress from confinement in what one observer called a "Close and Stinking Gaol," so crowded that when a prisoner "was suffocated by the Heat of . . . Summer—and . . . a Coffin was sent for the Corps, there was no room to admit it, till some wretches lay down, and made their wretched Carcasses, a Table to lay the Coffin on."

Not surprisingly, the land-hungry, penny-pinching Commons showed little enthusiasm for Governor Johnson's plan to encourage white immigration from abroad. They generally admitted the wisdom of balancing the population—then about 15,000 whites to some 30,000 Negroes—and throwing a protective ring of settlers around the coastal lands. But when it came to spending money to execute the plan they felt inclined to let tomorrow take care of itself. Johnson's proposal would mean hauling settlers at colony expense and giving them tools and food for a year.

The Commons did at last give token support, enough to finance a few settlements in the back-country portions of the coastal plain fifty to a hundred miles from Charles Town. As for the rest of the land made available in Johnson's new-settler townships, they and other planters grabbed it, having an eye to their own welfare if not the colony's safety.

During the same period settlers pushed on without inducement to the tidal rice lands along the Waccamaw River seventy miles or so north of Charles Town. Here those stock genealogical figures, pioneering brothers, planted in the 1730's the Allston name, which sprouted so abundantly that at one time or another the tribe owned nearly every plantation on the river for twenty miles. Traveling northward from his Charles Town visit in 1773, the Boston merchant Josiah Quincy Jr. stopped for the night with a second-generation Allston planter, Joseph, "a Gentleman of immense income all of his own acquisition." A few years earlier he had "begun the world with only five negroes—has now five plantations with an hundred slaves on each." No doubt Joseph had bestirred himself, but his father and uncle had started with no mean grant of land, at least 6,500 acres.

Settlers on the coastal plain back of Charles Town fell into the established pattern. The stronger and cannier engrossed the richest lands and bought slaves. Soon they were vaunting the blueness of their blood and vying with coastal barons in despising their "shiftless" neighbors, as often as not a set of puny or luckless cousins. A latter-day descendant of Orangeburg pioneers once snorted of a branch of her family tree that she wasn't "kin to a soul by that trashy name, dead or alive." She was kin, nonetheless, sunk though that name might be in po'-whitedom. Indeed, her ancestors had probably helped sink it.

Poor whites, in other words, were as much a by-product of somebody's greed and good fortune as they were victims of their lack of sense and grit. With land, a few slaves and a little pull with his neighbors a planter was in a fair way to getting more land, more slaves and a seat in Commons. In the course of his acquisitive progress he might unsettle a dozen homesteading families, who would trudge to fallow acres inland and there root for a living. "Poor and spiritless peasants," Josiah Quincy called them, but they lacked the protections that sustained the lowliest peasant under feudalism. Pariahs of the body politic, they slouched away their lives, hooking strings of catfish now and then, scratching listlessly at a corn patch between bouts of fever and spawning children to endure the same dreary lives.

Poor whites were not the issue of an immemorially scurvy stock, as legend would have it. If they came of indentured servants, as the legend further declares, so have a number of Carolinians who could hold their heads very high in meeting. All we indubitably know of indentured servants, so one historian says, is that they landed dirt poor. Otherwise they wouldn't have come in bondage. Whatever blood they carried in their veins, however, it was gentle enough not to curdle the best in the colony, for it mixed with the best.

Though she characterized the whole people as generally "hospitable and honest," Eliza Lucas (Pinckney)—recently arrived from the West Indies—distinguished two Carolina classes in a 1742 letter to England: the "better sort," having a "polite gentile behaviour," and the "poorer sort," who were "the most indolent people in the world or they could never be so wretched in so plentiful a country as this." The observation shows that the social waters had well settled by mid-century, but it also implies that Eliza Lucas never doubted the dogma of the fortunate: that misfortune is always and forever the wages of misbehavior. She saw no connection between the poverty of her poor neighbors and the growing ostentation of such Ashley River friends as the Middletons of Middleton Place and the Draytons of Drayton Hall. Judgments aside, however, she was unfailingly kind. Between her duties as plantation mistress, her social appearances and the private discipline of reading Vergil and John Locke she gave legal advice to the "poorer sort," who lacked the time and money for visits to a Charles Town lawyer.

Eliza Lucas spent at least one of her social days at Drayton Hall, one of the great country houses of the time and still an eminent Georgian pile, though it misses the double flankers or wings that once relieved its central mass. The only Ashley River mansion now left of three that survived Sherman's fires in 1865, it was built around 1738 by a member of the Governor's Council, John Drayton, the third generation in Carolina of lusty Barbadians. On the day of Eliza's visit its huge entrance hall and its grand second-story dining room were open to all the gentry thereabouts to celebrate Mr. Drayton's dynastic alliance with a Middleton from a few miles upriver.

Though Miss Lucas offers no details of the "festal day," her biographer, Mrs. St. Julien Ravenel, works up a pretty picture. She tells us that the ladies arrived in dresses of brocade, taffeta or lute-string, wearing slippers to match with "heels even higher and more unnatural than our own."

> *Their unhappy bodies were, we regret to state, laced out of all shape till they looked like pegs. . . . 'Tis true that in the back of the saque, covered by the Watteau plait of the court train, there is a laced piece. By pulling a bobbin, instant relaxation may be obtained, but then how many hours must have passed when the bobbin could not be pulled!*

"Gay would be the feast," the table presenting every delicacy from venison and terrapin to syllabubs and puddings. And, since "these were not blue ribbon days," the company would have "washed down their dinners with copious draughts of good Madeira":

> *The dinner over, the ladies withdrew, and before very long the scraping of the fiddles would call the gentlemen to the dance —pretty, graceful dances, the minuet, stately and gracious, which opened the ball; and the country dance, forerunner of our Virginia Reel, in which everyone old and young joined.*

> *Gay, joyous old days, enjoyed alike by master and man, by*
> *mistress and maid, when the feast begun in the hall was con-*
> *tinued in the servants' quarters, and the negroes without took*
> *up the dance, and footed gayly in the piazzas and the lawn.*

If there were many such "festal days," Eliza Lucas must have declined invitations. For, though still under twenty at the time, she virtually managed the Lucas plantation on the Ashepoo River. Her father, Major Lucas, having settled the family in Carolina with the hope of improving his wife's health, had left Eliza in charge when he returned to his British Army duties in the West Indies. Experimenting there in the early 1740's with the indigo plant and the process of converting it into dye, she founded by example a Carolina industry second only to rice in the eighteenth century. Since a colonial supply would help England put off the expensive flow of dyes from France, indigo was profitable almost at once, and in a few years it made fortunes for many of her fellow coastal planters. Exporting a few pounds in 1744, the colony was sending abroad just before the Revolution over a million pounds a year.

Thriving in dry, sandy soil, indigo perfectly complemented the swamp-growing rice as a low-country crop. Raised together they promoted a stretch-out of slaves as well as land, a fact the prudent Scots Governor James Glen did not fail to note in his 1749 *Description of South Carolina*: "the Labour attending *Indigo* being over in the Summer Months, those who were employed in it may afterwards manufacture Rice, in the ensuing Part of the Year, when it becomes most laborious; and after doing all this, they will have some Time to spare for sawing *Lumber,* and making *Hogshead* and other *Staves,* to supply the *Sugar-Colonies*." In its fairly brief harvesttime indigo alone required a good deal of arms and backs, as we read between the lines of this slave memory of its cultivation for home use:

> . . . *it growed just like wheat. When it got ripe, they gathered*
> *it, an we would put it in a barrel and let it soak 'bout a week,*
> *then we would take the indigo stems out and squeeze all the*
> *juice out of 'em and put the juice back in the barrel and let it*
> *stand 'nother week, then we just stirred and stirred one whole*
> *day. We let it set three or four days, then drained the water*
> *off and left the settlings, and the settlings was blueing just like*

*we have these days. We cut ours in little blocks, and we dyed
clothes with it too.*

Indigo made in that fashion was no doubt a crude product, for it
took a practiced eye and hand to turn out lumps of dye in competition with the expert French. In her first attempts Eliza Lucas had
skilled help from a man her father had sent up from Montserrat, but
in an excess of loyalty to his indigo-making island he deliberately
spoiled the results, much as a jealous cook adds the pinch of flour
that ruins the cake. Eliza Lucas found him out, however, made a
satisfactory product and passed on the recipe to her neighbors.

In letters written at the time of her indigo experiments Eliza Lucas
reported that she was teaching "two black girls" to read. Though
she does not say how they got on, the effort itself shows that she did
not, like many Carolinians of a later day, think all Negroes hopeless
numskulls. Actually, in Miss Lucas' day it was not unusual to take
some mental capacity for granted; and until a nineteenth-century
law forbade it, many conscientious ladies summoned the yard pick-
aninnies for a morning spell at the primer.

Under less compulsion to rationalize a "barbarous" system to a
"civilized" world, eighteenth-century Carolinians took a far more
realistic view of the Negro and of slavery than their descendants in
the nineteenth. On the whole they saw the institution for what it
was, a means of breaking a luckless "savage" people to gainful domestic use. Having no prophets to sanctify their motives, they sometimes doubted their moral position and granted the Negro a quite
normal human aspiration to freedom.

In short, they theorized less about slavery than they worried about
the problems it daily—and nightly—presented. They reasonably
judged blacks as "domestic enemies," having fairly good cause to
rise up and murder their masters in bed. They were very plausibly
concerned also about the disproportion of blacks to whites—almost
two to one by mid-century.

Their concern was not frequently justified in blood. A large group
of slaves rebelled on the Stono River in 1739, for instance, stole guns
and killed twenty-one whites. The next morning they marched
toward Florida—and Spanish promises of freedom—killing and
burning as they went. Lieutenant Governor William Bull discovered

the uprising on his way to Charles Town from the south and sent militia after the mutineers. Executions promptly followed.

A government committee reported afterwards that "every breast was filled with concern. . . . With regret we bewailed our peculiar case that we could not enjoy the benefit of peace like the rest of mankind, and that our industry should be the means of taking from us all the sweets of life." Regardless of the tone, this scarcely anticipates pre-Civil War defensiveness. "Our peculiar case" does not refer to slavery as such but to Carolina's slave-won prosperity, which the Spanish envied so much that they worked to subvert the slaves.

We may smile ironically at the committee's high-flown expression of alarm: "Evil brought home to us within our very doors awakened the attention of the most unthinking." Suspending moral judgment for a moment, however, we might spare a tinge of compassion for the Carolina planter and his family, living miles from a white neighbor and surrounded day and night by fifty to a hundred "domestic enemies." At night especially—when the blacks retired to the plantation "street" or "the quarters"—they withdrew into a separateness as haunting in its silence as in its eruptions of anger or gaiety. For they were violent in their loves and pleasures. Many were fresh from Africa, "unseasoned," as the saying went, moodier and more liable to outbursts than old hands, broken to the hoe and whip.

The early slaves did show a fairly savage temper, though it stemmed perhaps as much from the conditions of their enslavement as from their "wild" African natures. Wrenched from their very human and natural place in the world as members of a tribe, they had been tied up and shipped across the sea like pigs for the slaughter, then dumped out on a foreign shore to endure life as beasts of burden. Often they had as little in common with each other—attuned to different tribal ways and speaking dissimilar dialects—as with the whites who bought and used their brawn. As slaves they had to absorb a new culture or rather two cultures, the white man's and the hand-me-downs their fellow bondsmen had made their own. No wonder they slashed each other's throats now and then or brandished an ax at a master's pate. No wonder, too, whites lay abed and shivered, hearing voices babble to the climax of a long eerie wail of fatality. Many living Carolinians have heard that kind of wail and then listened for the flesh-crawling scratch on the back screen door, rousing them from bed to find an old Lizzie holding the blood in at her throat with her bare hands.

Recognizing but loath to admit the inhumanity by which they prospered, many slaveholders took comfort in the saving grace to heathens of dwelling in a Christian land. Others assuaged their consciences by freeing their slaves for an exceptional service or by willing freedom to their house servants. No one claimed, as before the Civil War, that blacks were too thickheaded to grasp the boon of freedom or too blissful in their bondage to want it. The merchant-planter and Revolutionary statesman Henry Laurens certainly recognized the longing when he offered a Negro the bargain of his family's liberty if he died from an experimental smallpox vaccination. The slave leaped at the bargain, by the way, and died from the vaccination; and Laurens, to his honor, paid off with manumission for the man's children.

Even so a plantation mistress was probably reporting actual fact when she wrote after her husband's death that "several of [his slaves] would willingly have given up their own lives, to have had his spared to their children . . . so sensible were they of their great misfortunes; many of them now say they would rather serve his children than be free." In a world of masters the kind are surely preferable to the cruel.

If affections grew a little on both sides, the chief white emotion in the mid-1700's was still alarm at the Negro's sheer strength in numbers. It rose so high after the 1739 uprising that the government revised the slave code, not to strengthen but to soften its rigors. The revised code of 1740, which forbade crippling physical abuse and a working day of more than fifteen hours, remained on the books until 1865. If the code enjoined leniency of a sort, it nonetheless left the slave to the casual mercies of drumhead justice. As Josiah Quincy was shocked to learn in Charles Town, "any two justices and three freeholders might and very often did *instanter* upon view of complaint try a negro for any crime, and might and did often award execution of death, issue their warrant and it was done forthwith." Worse yet, "to *steal* a negro was death, but to *kill him* was only fineable."

Urgent as the slave problem continued to be, the colony met other difficulties in the thirties and forties: Spanish thrusts at the newly

planted Georgia colony to the south and Cherokee Indian trucu-
lence to the northwest. Of these and others the wavering Cherokees
required, but seldom got in its wisest form, the chief public attention for the twenty years before 1761, when a scorched-earth campaign reduced them to beggary. The Cherokees had always inclined
to the English, as their salaams to Sir Alexander Cumings implied.
But trader chicanery, French enticements and above all the whims
of Charles Town and British policy kept them restless.

Used to the stately amusements of a Drayton Hall, coastal gentlemen found it hard to admit that they lived on the edge of a huge
and troubled frontier. As dispensers of public money in Commons
they balked, for instance, at building forts which the Indians pleaded
for as a shield against the Franco-Indian enemies in the Ohio Valley.

While they eschewed both the journey toward the hills and the
plaguesome Cherokee question, at least one curious and determined
man rode the trail up from Charles Town and forced the colony's
attention. And no Scots Don Quixote this time with cloak and sword
but a Saxon stripped of all but theories and fellow feeling. If the
planter Commons had known what the "little ugly man," Christian Gottlieb Priber, was up to when he landed from France in 1734
they would have locked him up. For he was that most scandalous of
all phenomena to middle-class probity, a social philosopher bent on
putting his theories to the test. Perhaps he kept his plans secret, but
he did stop in the city long enough to sell his belongings through the
Gazette: "cloaths, wiggs, spaterdashes [leggings] of fine holland,
shoes, boots, guns, pistols, powder, a silver repeating watch, a sword
with a silver hilt." Of the trappings of civilization he kept only paper,
pen and ink, and a trunkful of books. With these he set out to work
a communistic republic, a "Kingdom of Paradise" in the southern
Appalachians.

Before long traders were noting that he "ate, drank, slept, danced,
dressed and painted with the Indians." They had good reason to
note, for he taught his companions the use of weights and measures,
doing more to arm them against foxy traders than agents had accomplished in thirty years. He also taught them to regard the English
along with the French as intruders on their natural rights. Essaying
the role of prime minister under the Tellico headman as Cherokee
emperor, he soon wielded influence enough to propose "a confedera-

tion among all the Southern Indians" for their joint defense against white nations. A pure communism would then follow: no man would own property, every citizen would dispose his labor for the common good, women would have equal status with men, and free love would replace the galling yoke of wedlock. This ideal republic would embrace all who sought its blessings, of whatever race, creed or color. It would open the gate to "Criminals, Debtors, and Slaves, who would fly hither from Justice or from their Masters."

Trader howls finally echoed along the grapevine to Charles Town and a police detail was posted northward to capture this ideological threat to peace and cupidity. Georgia agents anticipated the Carolinians, however, and in 1743 dragged him off to jail at Fredericka, where he spent the few remaining years of his life discoursing to sundry gentlemen of the town on matters scarcely dreamt of in their philosophies. To one of these he remarked like a true Socratic, "It is folly to repine at one's lot in life. My mind soars above misfortunes."

James Glen, in many respects the ablest colonial governor, arrived in Charles Town the year of Priber's arrest and imprisonment. With the Anglo-French contest for North America approaching a climax, he needed all his Scotch vigor and decisiveness to deal with a problem which steadily worsened under French incitement and English neglect. He seems to have had a kind of Rooseveltian gusto for rough-riding in the back country, but he could scarcely have avoided spending most of his official energies on the Cherokees during his long term—until 1756.

In a 1746 tour of the back country at the head of a "greater body than has ever been seen in this part of the world at once," he settled disputes among the small Indian tribes and got promises from the Creeks and Cherokees to stand off the French. The next year he made the first South Carolina purchase of Cherokee lands, promising in return to build forts in their territory. But, for several costly years a stingy Commons and London indifference combined to delay making good his promise. Though Glen himself supervised the building of one fort, the other was not erected until after he had left the colony. His last important act of diplomacy was to secure for the King overlordship of the 360,000-square-mile Cherokee domain for some $300 worth of presents.

If Governor Glen hit it off with the Indians—he sometimes gave visiting chieftains bed and board in his Charles Town home—he had his troubles with the jealous Commons and Council oligarchs. The Lords of Trade backed him in resisting inroads upon the royal prerogative, but the Commons could play dog in the manger with funds and appoint officials he could not touch.

In spite of their quarrels, however, even the Commons came to appreciate his success with the Indians. In modern eyes, however, he added perhaps the "brightest jewels" to his own crown by standing up almost alone for the wretched French Acadians who were forcibly exiled from their island homes off the coast of Canada and dumped helpless on the Charles Town docks. Feeling a pity that lesser men did not share, he kept badgering Council and Assembly to give them food and shelter. They were confined at first, and a report that some had escaped to rob a plantation house on the Santee did not lessen the general contempt for them as enemy French. Glen managed to get a little help for them, but under his less humane successor, Governor Lyttelton, most of them were "manacled with irons and dragged out of Charles Town to be 'distributed' in the parishes."

Governor Glen's friendship with the Cherokees did not suffice to keep them from the French. In 1759 they rose against the Carolinians, murdered some traders in their midst and laid siege to a Carolina fort. The chances of making peace were bungled when an Indian embassy to Charles Town was seized after it had been granted safe passage. A force sent into the Appalachians the next year failed to subdue the now fully aroused nation, and it took a much larger force to crush the will to fight in 1761. Towns and growing crops were fired and Indian families driven into the high mountains to starve. A resulting treaty laid down flinty terms which the Indians could only submit to, among others that no Cherokee could venture more than forty miles below the fort on the Little Tennessee.

With all North America virtually secured to Britain by the Anglo-French treaty of Paris in 1763, London inaugurated a policy that would soothe the red man but ultimately madden land-hungry whites. At a congress in Augusta, Georgia, the Creeks were promised that white settlements would extend only as they had agreed, and the Cherokees were guaranteed protection from swindlers by the exclusion of all private traders from their nation.

The year of the Cherokee defeat and the Indian congress was fateful in the history of the world. It saw a vast portion of the earth's surface change from French to British hands and the last great barrier to the American West fall before adventurous Eastern colonists. The final shrinkage of the Indian's lands and the killing assault on his way of life had begun in earnest. Henceforth Indian sovereignty would be a myth. The Catawbas of upper South Carolina pathetically symbolize the attrition. Once roaming the whole length of the river which bears their name, they agreed in 1763 to a 15-mile-square holding, diminished in modern times to a 625-acre tract in York county, on land "so po'," as a politician once exclaimed, "it takes three God-damned peas to grow—one to push, one to pull and one to come up."

The coastal planters could now shrug off more or less for good the tax-eating Indian nuisance. They were shortly to find, however, that not even Indians would so grate upon their devotions to pleasure, profit and the snug forms of the Anglican Church as the hard-bitten Scotch-Irish Presbyterians now kicking up the dust of the Great Philadelphia Wagon Road down through the Valley of Virginia to back-country Carolina.

V

"All Your Artillery ... an Hiccory Switch"

"You call us a Pack of Beggars—" the Commons leader John Rutledge was rudely assailed in 1770, "Pray Sir look back to your own Origin? . . . step back only to the beginning of this Century—What then was Carolina? What Charlestown? What the then Settlers (Your Ancestors)—Even such as We now are."

Thus improbably an English gentleman curate spoke the temper of the Carolina back country on the eve of the Revolution. Failing to drive a frontier "Herd of Wild Enthusiastic sectaries" toward the Established Church, the Rev. Charles Woodmason had become at last the spokesman of their discontent at scornful Charles Town. The settlers could have found no better mouthpiece, for he was one of God's angry men, and they were largely Presbyterian Scotch-Irish, a tough and angry race.

There were Swiss and Welsh and Germans in the back country, too—all equally astray in their Baptist and Lutheran heresies—but the Scotch-Irish prevailed. They had led the columns swarming into piedmont South Carolina after 1761 to double the colony's population in little more than a decade. Between 1763 and 1775 the number of people living above the fall line rose from 22,000 to 83,000, forming not only half the total population but three fourths of the colony's whites.

The taunting shot at John Rutledge was only one in a series Mr. Woodmason fired at Charles Town in his efforts to rouse concern for the civil, religious and judicial needs of the back-country settlers. Most of the broadsides he composed as scribe and adviser for the

68

Regulator movement, a frontier rebellion against coastal neglect. Getting no civil privileges in return for their taxes, back settlers organized to ride against the heedless squires of Charles Town if need be. But first they would track down the cattle thieves and marauders who were terrorizing the hill country in the absence of police authority and local courts.

The Regulator uprising brought partial results. Chronically nervous of the slave "enemy" in their own actual back yards, provincial rulers saw the peril of a bolder enemy in the colony's back yard and at least provided courts for seven points outside the city. The bitterness remained, however, to impede the Revolutionary cause a few years later: many a back-settler counted the land-granting King a truer friend than tidal aristocrats. When independence failed to bring hillmen a just representation in the Assembly, the bitterness continued; it remained, in fact, until carpetbaggers imported to South Carolina the "foreign poison of democracy" after the Civil War.

Settlement of the South Carolina back country came as the final stage of a great southward migration from Pennsylvania. Moving to the lure of cheap lands, Germans and Scotch-Irish invaded in turn western Maryland, the Valley of Virginia and piedmont Carolina, North and South. By 1800 the settlements extended along a 600-mile corridor from the Mason-Dixon line to the Savannah River. More akin to one another than the Chesapeake Bay or Ashley River barons, these uplanders formed a southern tail, as one historian puts it, of Greater Pennsylvania. Though increasingly subject to influences from coastal seats of power, they kept generally the hard-working, plain-living character of their cousins in the Conestoga Valley. Even in modern times upcountry South Carolina—its manufactures overriding a small-farm economy—has more in common with Pennsylvania than the names of three adjoining counties: Lancaster, Chester and York.

Some back-country immigrants came directly from Pennsylvania in the 1760's, but most joined the procession in Virginia and North Carolina, loading the washpot and the corn-shuck mattresses on the family wagon and striking out for greener pastures. The Pettigrew family's 28-year pilgrimage from northern Ireland to Long Cane River in Abbeville District typifies the racial wanderlust. James

Pettigrew, the first of the line in America, landed at New Castle, Pennsylvania, in 1740. As a filial scribe takes care to explain, James "had a good classical and general education" and "In Philadelphia he knew the prominent men of the day, Dr. Franklin among others." Refusing Dr. Franklin's advice that he study medicine, he "obtained a tract of 300 acres" in western Pennsylvania. "Well-established" when the French and Indian War broke out, he sold his land after Braddock's defeat in 1755 and moved to Virginia. Uprooting his family again after three years, he settled in North Carolina, stopping there until rumors of Arcadia enticed him to the trail again in 1768. After four years on Long Cane Creek, in South Carolina, he moved again, but this time only a mile or so down the trail. That his family sank their New World roots at last probably testifies more to a stubborn wifely foot than to his own heart's fulfillment. For he was manifestly a true pioneer, always dreaming of the paradisal valleys beyond the hills. His spiritual descendants would light out for Alabama in the early nineteenth century, and *their* descendants would push on to California. Some would perhaps live out their days, like John Steinbeck's old pioneer, in the fixed desolation of that moment when they stared out across the Pacific and knew the marvelous journey had ended.

Some Scotch-Irish have claimed Huguenot descent—James Pettigrew's eminent grandson James Louis changed his name to Petigru on that assumption—but, as their names imply, they are essentially Scotsmen. Originally Scotch yeoman farmers, they were transported in the early 1700's to Ulster, in northern Ireland, to pit their flinty Presbyterianism against Irish popery. They dug into the Irish soil so briskly that soon their cattle and wool were undercutting English landlords; and the British government, which had paternally sponsored their migration, turned on them with a series of prohibitive tariffs. Along with the native Irish they sank then into the hopeless misery that moved Jonathan Swift to dip his pen in gall and advance his "Modest Proposal" for economic redemption: the raising of children as meat for English tables.

Swiftean indignation, if not satiric genius, informed the Rev. Mr. Woodmason's portrayal of the back-country populace as "A Cargo of fifty Thousand Prime Slaves" in an "Advertisement" he "posted up" at the Charles Town Exchange. Knowing that bona fide slave advertisements were "posted up" in Charles Town, we find the device much less effective than Swift's outrageous proposal. Eighteenth-century Carolinians, however, dealing comfortably in heathen black flesh, must have squirmed at the vision of Christian white skins on the auction block. For Mr. Woodmason claims his mock notice gave "Great Offence to the Senators," causing "many who before were indifferent to Things for to interest themselves in behalf of the People."

The man who conceived this pasquinade affords as much irony as anything he wrote in the back country cause. In the first place, he was no gospel shouter in homespun breeches but a gentleman curate who wore the full canonicals. An offshoot of British gentry, he had known social and official favor in Charles Town, where by 1765 he had become "the principal acting Magistrate" and, in his own words, "ev'ry ones favriter." Previously he had lived for more than a decade the life of a planter-merchant north of the city, owning slaves and inveterately holding church and civil offices.

He seems to have hungered for public office. In fact, his quest of one—that of distributor under the hated 1765 Stamp Act terms—may have precipitated his taking holy orders. Not that he ran from disfavor to the bosom of the church, for he emerged from the Stamp Act turmoil with his justiceship intact. Actually he turned his back on a lucrative post to become, after taking orders in London, a starveling itinerant minister in the back-country parish of St. Mark's. In doing so he risked the "Laughter of Fools" and the dismay of his friends, for no one suspected apparently a genuine zeal for the church or knew that for years he had privately entreated England for ministers to save back-country Anglicans from being "trodden under foot by the Herd of Sectaries."

Perhaps apostolic fervor alone could have wrenched a middle-aged gentleman from Charles Town ease and plunged him into the literally and figuratively churning waters of the back country. On one cold February Sunday, for instance, "the Wind blowing very sharply at N.E. and Ground Cover'd with Ice," he was unable to cross a swollen stream until a "Bold Man brought a very large strong and High Horse," carrying first his saddle and baggage to the opposite bank:

> *The Women then stript me Naked, and gave Him my Cloaths which he carried on his Head in like Manner—They put their aprons around me—and when he returned, I got behind Him, and the Horse carried us both over very safe—but I never trembled more in my Life. The People placed themselves at Places below, to take me up if I slipt off, or that the Horse sank under me. The Man afterward brought over my Horse—but I was almost stiff and torpid with the Cold.*

A few weeks later as he proceeded "along the Line across the Province baptizing all the Way," he lost himself in the rain amidst the cattle tracks and winding paths and was unable to "procure Guides for money." He rode to and fro till night came,

> *when got to the Cabbin of a poor old Dutch Woman, who inform'd me that I was got into the Waxaw Distric among a Tribe of Presbyterians. . . . She had no Refreshments. Not a Grain of Corn for the Horse. . . . She dry'd my Cloaths, and I sat up all Night by the Fire, quite tired and spent, having not made what could be called a meal for some days—Nothing but Indian Corn Meal to be had Bacon and Eggs in some Places— No Butter, Rice, or Milk—As for Tea and Coffee they know it not. These people are all from Ireland, and live wholly on butter, Milk Clabber and what in England is given to the Hogs and Dogs.*

The compassion Mr. Woodmason came to feel for the back settlers and his exertions in their behalf are astonishing in the light of his contempt for their heresies. Though he hated all the sectarian tribes, he reserved his blackest bile for the Scotch-Irish. "The worst vermin on Earth," they applied the "perverse persecuting Spirit" of Presbyterianism more violently "here than in Scotland." It was dangerous to live "among such a Sett of Vile unaccountable Wretches," he claimed, for "if they cannot cheat, rob, defraud or injure You in Your Goods—they will belye, defame, lessen . . . the most valuable person breathing, not of their Communion."

The Scotch-Irish did little to sweeten Mr. Woodmason's disposition. In fact, if he did not overstate the case, they used every trick in the backwoods bag to thwart his ministry and humiliate his person. He was obliged to cut his sermon short and dismiss the communicants on one occasion because the Presbyterians had "hir'd a band of rude fellows to come to Service who brought with them 57 Dogs (for I counted them) which . . . they set fighting." He said it was vain to bring such ruffians to law, since they hadn't a shilling between them and it would take a year's salary to send them to Charles Town for trial. And besides "as all the Magistrates are Presbyterians, I could not get a Warrant—if I got Warrants as the Constables are Presbyterians likewise, I could not get them serv'd—If serv'd, the Guard would let them escape."

On another occasion he appeared at Fishing Creek to find that the loyal churchmen had responded the Sunday before to a fake notice of his coming. Resolving to "search into this Presbyterian Trick," he found at the bottom of it one "John Gaston a Justice of the Peace among these Presbyterians," who wanted to "have a laugh at the Church People." This thorn in Mr. Woodmason's flesh, by the way, who had "set up to marry People" against the province laws, sired a numerous progeny to carry the Gaston name to places of dignity and distinction in South Carolina and other Southern states.

To the Baptists, however, Mr. Woodmason charges baudier—if not more vexing—japeries. Two miscreants of that unholy persuasion once entered the "House where I was when in Bed—stealing my Gown—putting it on—and then visiting a Woman in Bed, and getting to bed to her, and making her give out next day, that the Parson came to Bed to her."

Much as he wished to blame his tribulations on the heretics, Mr. Woodmason admitted suffering the most infernal trick at the hands of his own parishioners. On his arrival at St. Mark's, he reported to an English friend, the vestry advised him to marry, a duty he declined on the candid grounds of his "Incapacity for Nuptial Rites" (having some years before sustained a delicate injury in a fall from a horse). When the vestry took his explanation as a joke, he proceeded to court

two Ladies, and fairly told my Case—who declared they chose not to live as married Nuns—I then desired the Vestry to look out for Me—Our Vestry Sir consists of 9 persons, all related too, and under controul of one Man. This Person nam'd a Relation

> *of his—A Girl of about 28—Handsome and Agreeable—she received my Addresses—and we were engaged—But very luckily, in Interim, I learn'd, that my Fair One, had had a Lying in in Virginia before her Settlement here—and had no Nuns flesh about her—On which I dropp'd Affairs.*

If such bamboozlements were not a commonplace of American frontier life—how Mark Twain's Mississippi rubes would have hooted at putting it over a crusty old parson—we might judge Mr. Woodmason something of a paranoiac. He was undoubtedly telling the truth, but what he told was scarcely the whole truth about the backwoods settlers. Writing normally for English friends or church officials, he wished to startle the first and impress the second with the need for more civilizing servants of the church. He dwelt, that is, on the aberrations of frontier life, passing over the dull respectabilities.

He reports meeting now and then, however, with "serious and Religious persons," as at Sandy River, where the service was performed before 500 persons "with as much pomp as if at St. Paul's." Or he characterizes a family as "neat decent People," who took care of his horse and gave him milk and "a fowl broil'd—the 1st fresh Meat had tasted for some time." At this home he preached to a gathering of the "best drest, and well behav'd sensible religious People that have met with in these parts." And Samaritans did appear, as he testifies, when he fell by the wayside: Captain Dougharty, for instance, who "with his People ventur'd their Lives" to carry him across a swollen creek on fallen trees and then brought him ill with pleurisy to his loyal merchant friend Joseph Kershaw at Pine Tree Hill (Camden).

Either Mr. Woodmason did not see or refused to admit the sobering mercies that flowed from Presbyterian and Baptist communions. By 1759 at least five fully organized churches of these sects were smoothing out the social and moral crudities in widely separated regions. The Waxhaw Presbyterian church, for example, worked a strong influence through the efforts of its minister in the sixties, the Rev. William Richardson, an Englishman educated at the University of Glasgow.

He was too enlightened for his flock, though, Mr. Woodmason surmised, and went to his death a victim of Presbyterian fanaticism, or, as he puts it, "A Martyr to the persecuting Spirit that Distinguishes Superstition and Enthusiasm from Reason and Religion." Found dead in his study kneeling in the attitude of prayer and with a bridle around his neck, Mr. Richardson was hastily buried without mention of the bridle, an omission the church elders decided upon, they later claimed, to shield the church's name from the stain of suicide. The news leaked, however, and whispers against his wife, by then remarried, forced exhumation of the body a year later and a ghoulish test of her innocence—she had to touch the skull and withdraw her finger unspotted with blood. Her doing so may have convinced the watchers that her husband had taken his own life, though it seems odd that no one inquired how a man could hang himself in a kneeling position. Mr. Woodmason, of course, inquired—in a private memorandum—suggested murder and named the murderer —the widow's brother, embittered at the minister's reading formal prayers to his family after the presbyters had denied their use in church.

If murder seems an extravagant reaction to the minister's offense, it is well to recall that conflicting notions as to what tunes to sing in church have at least caused congregations to split and new sects to arise. Passion in such matters may be, in fact, a measure of religious zeal, though, as Mr. Woodmason believed, it might well connote cultural poverty.

Dissenter though he was, the Rev. Dr. Richardson had enjoyed Mr. Woodmason's respect as well as sympathy. He too was an English-born patrician and with his Master of Arts degree a more educated man than the planter-merchant turned missioner. By virtue of his ecclesiastical standing, in fact, the Waxhaw church was the only back-country pastorate of his time having a full Gospel ordinance. As a learned man, Dr. Richardson awed the frontier with "literary evenings" in his two-story manse, which with its library was one of the sights of the Waxhaw country.

Though other Waxhaw houses scarcely matched the manse's splendor, some were roomy enough to shelter large families in comfort and receive necessitous kin. James Crawford offered the refuge of such a house as this to his just-widowed sister-in-law, Elizabeth Jackson, who bore there in 1767 her third child, Andrew, the seventh president of the United States. Or so General Jackson himself later claimed, though some scholars have insisted he was born at the nearby farmstead of another uncle and thus in North rather than South Carolina. Jackson clearly thought himself a native South Carolinian, but it doesn't much matter whether he had the facts straight or not. It does signify, however, that in parading on a national scale the virtues and vices of the Scotch-Irish Presbyterian back countryman he became a genuine popular hero.

Many Waxhaw settlers traded at the market town of Camden, a three- or four-day wagon journey to the south. They could and did reduce the bulk of their produce and make the long haul more profitable by having their grain refined into whisky at public stills, such as the one operated by Andrew Jackson's uncle James Crawford. They swapped the whisky for farm tools and household needs with merchants like Joseph Kershaw, Mr. Woodmason's Samaritan friend at Camden, who dispensed it by the gourdful or shipped it in barrels on his wagons to Charles Town. Along with the whisky went quantities of hemp, tobacco, flour, indigo, cattle and hogs. The Kershaw goods joined caravans rolling toward Charles Town from the whole back country at the rate of some 3000 four-horse wagons a year.

Though he found solace at Camden, Mr. Woodmason also found raucous Presbyterians and so much sin that he named it a "little Sodom." Even the good Mr. Kershaw, who often "poured Wine and Oil into my Wounds," was a party to the carnal intrigues exposed in his "Letter to John Chesnut" and the complementary "Burlesque Sermon," which reveals the curate as a frontier combination of John the Baptist and the ribald eighteenth-century writer Laurence Sterne. If the letter ever reached the hands of John Chesnut—a backwoods hustler busy founding a rich and prideful Carolina clan—it's a wonder Mr. Woodmason's head was not brought in on a platter for the gratification of "Mother Chesnut," the chief object of his scarifying pen. (She was accused of trafficking in her daughter's flesh to improve the family's meager fortunes.)

The lewd note undoubtedly commends these pieces to modern readers, though not that alone. They offer something we vainly seek in most colonial records—the sense of flesh and blood. They show our forebears *au naturel,* so to speak, before successive generations had clothed them in the stately garments of their own vanity. They would certainly have intrigued one South Carolina lady who came afterwards to bear the Chesnut name, Mary Boykin Chesnut—she married John's grandson—whose Civil War diary pokes holes in the operatic sets of the Confederacy.

In the midst of his strictures on the "Carriage and Manners, as well as Morals of these wild Peoples" Mr. Woodmason's eyes sometimes wander in helpless admiration, or perhaps in carnal envy. Remarking what "a Great Novelty" one of his backwoods congregations would appear to a Londoner, he describes the men as wearing only "a thin Shirt and pair of Breeches . . . barelegged and barefooted" and the women as "bareheaded, barelegged and barefoot with only a thin Shift and under Petticoat," a minimal costume the summer heat made them loath to increase. And then in the guise of further reproach he goes on to image the "Young Women" in "a most uncommon Practice, which I cannot break them off":

> They draw their Shift as tight as possible to the Body, and pin it close, to show the roundness of their Breasts, and slender Waists (for they are generally finely shaped) and draw their Petticoat close to their Hips to shew the fineness of their Limbs— so that they might as well be in Puri Naturalibus—Indeed Naked, without Ceremony—Rubbing themselves and their hair with Bears Oil and tying it up behind in a Bunch like the Indians.

One doubts his hoping "to bring about a Reformation."

Mr. Woodmason's vignette of the back-country girls certainly explains why he found "not a Cabbin but has 10 or 12 Young Children in it." He noted that when "the Boys are 18 and Girls 14 they marry —so that in many Cabbins You will see 10 or 15 Children. Children and Grand Children of one Size—and the mother looking as Young as the Daughter. Yet these Poor People enjoy Good Health." Among such vigorous and fruitful dissenters no wonder the curate despaired of saving the back country for mother church. And we may join him in his consternation at the following scene, but we suspect he was enviously bedazzled, as we are, by the wild joie de vivre:

> Here [at Flatt Creek] I found a vast Body of People assembled —Such a Medley! such a mixed Multitude of all Classes and Complexions I never saw. . . . I was a Great Curiosity to them

—And they were as great Oddities to me. After Service they went to Revelling Drinking Singing Dancing and Whoring—and most of the Company were drunk before I quitted the Spot— They were as rude in their Manners as the Common Savages, and hardly a degree removed from them. Their Dresses almost as loose and Naked as the Indians . . . I could not conceive from whence this vast Body could swarm—But this Country contains ten times the Number of Persons beyond my Apprehension.

As if such daylight jubilees were not sufficient "to multiply Subjects for the King in this frontier country," New Light Baptist Love Feasts notoriously served the purpose by night. In one of his sermons Mr. Woodmason "excoriated these pious agencies of lewdness and immorality," to which

much Liquor is privately carried and deposited on the Roads, and in Bye Paths and Places. The Assignations made on Sundays at the Singing Clubs, are here realized. And it is no wonder that Things are as they are, when many Young Persons have 3. 4. 5. 6. Miles to walk home in the dark Night, with Convoy, thro' the Woods? Or staying perhaps all Night at some Cabbin (as on Sunday Nights) and sleeping together either doubly or promiscuously? Or a Girl being Mounted by a Person to be carried home, and any wheres.

At least some contemporaries who visited the back country bear out Mr. Woodmason's general view, though admittedly English gentlemen like himself with an eye to a London audience. His comment that "thro' want of Ministers to marry and thro' the licentiousness of the People, many hundreds live in Concubinage—swopping their wives as Cattel," is matched by Governor James Glen's reproach of certain back-country parents who took "so much care in raising a Litter of Piggs, their Children are equally naked and full as Nasty, The Parents . . . come together without any previous ceremony, and it is not to be wondered at that the Offspring of such loose Embraces should be little looked after." From a parish south of Charles Town a curate reported that many brides appeared noticeably and quite shamelessly pregnant at the altar.

To offset these unflattering glances we have the verdict of a modern Carolina scholar, who is impressed with the back settlers' "integrity [and] their goodly heritage of ideas and customs." Though social anarchy was a constant threat, the absence of church establishment promised a freer and more democratic society than most had ever known before.

With his ingrained belief in firm social controls, Mr. Woodmason saw primarily the threat of anarchy and to counter it embraced a militant social gospel far ahead of his time. He saw that religion alone—certainly one middle-aged parson alone—could not civilize a wilderness. The motley frontiersmen needed help from Charles Town and weren't getting it. By his account, in fact, some coastal bigwigs blandly denied there were more than "a thousand People in the Back Country." They needed not only churches and ministers but courts of law and schools and roads. They needed voting places less than a hundred miles away and a reasonable number of seats in Commons.

In his growing awareness of these needs Mr. Woodmason turned from denunciation of the vigilante Regulators movement to a fierce and articulate championship. He guided the Regulator campaign and formulated its demands of Charles Town.

The lawless Regulator movement arose as an answer to lawlessness and official indifference. Rogues and robbers swarmed into the back country with honest pioneers and for years preyed almost at will on isolated settlers. As Woodmason tirelessly named their depredations, they stole cattle and horses, broke up cowpens, burned houses, turned families naked into the woods, plundered stores, "ravished" married women, "deflowered" virgins and committed other "unheard of Cruelties." He reports that they sometimes "put Irons in the Fire" and burned "the flesh of Persons to make confess where they conceal'd Money"; and on one occasion "They carried off about twenty of the finest Girls of the Country into the Woods with them—and kept them for many Months, as their Concubines in Common among them—till they grew past Shame—and never could be brought back to a life of Vertue."

The settlers lacked even a handy means of bringing their tormentors to justice. Except for the minor jurisdiction of the magistrates, there was only one law court in the province, at Charles Town. The time and expense of going to court themselves, much less what it cost to haul prisoners and witnesses to the coast, forced victims to suffer in silence or retaliate on their own. Since the outlaws rode in gangs, a lone settler thought twice before he dared do more than curse his luck.

Not even his curses were heard in Charles Town, for he had practically no voice in the Commons House. Technically, back settlers lived within parishes and had the right to vote, but since the original parish lines had been extended only a short way from the coast, they actually wandered "in the Mazes of Supposition." After establishing his legal residence, the intrepid voter could then ride a hundred miles or so to mark his ballot at the parish church. To transact any public business, even to obtain land warrants, the settler "must trudge" to Charles Town, an imposition that made one planter wish the Assembly "would lay a tax on urine and ordure as Augustus did—and then ev'ry one when he needed, would go to C.T. to evacuate."

One of two officials sympathized with the back-country plight and tried to help, notably Lieutenant Governor Bull, an able and intelligent native South Carolinian with a high sense of civic duty. In 1765 he urged the Assembly to establish a court system, and he would undoubtedly have pacified the Regulators with far less damage to the body politic if a bumbling governor, Lord Charles Montagu, had not arrived from England the next year. Officiating thereafter only in Montagu's absences, he did what he could to undo the governor's damage.

The Regulator campaign began in the spring of 1767 with the spontaneous pursuit of robber gangs by a number of neighborhood posses. Many of these posses soon joined together, apparently, for the following autumn rumors came to Charles Town of an assemblage which had not only "burnt the Houses of some Persons . . . Reputed to be Harbourers of Horse Thieves" but talked of "Coming to Charleston to make some Complaints." When the Governor asked the Assembly soon afterward for legislation to "suppress these licentious Spirits," both houses voted sentiments of anxiety. But they were jolted into more than routine alarm when in November Woodmason's "Remonstrance" was put into their hands.

This detailed protest and petition, signed by four Wateree planters in the name of 4,000 settlers and more than hinting a back-country invasion of Charles Town, brought quick results. Within four days an Assembly committee reported in favor of a court system, a vagrancy act and two companies of soldiers for three months to "Suppress and prevent disturbances" in the back parts. Some months later the Assembly also passed a court act but included provisions, so the back country thought, to ensure its disallowance in London.

Manned by Regulators, the Assembly-granted companies went off in pursuit of the outlaw gangs but, as they did, Charles Town officials arrested other Regulators for having previously taken the law into their own hands. Construed as a stab in the back, these arrests produced in the back country a "Plan of Regulation," which not only asserted the right to punish marauders but denied jurisdiction to the Charles Town court. Soon afterwards Regulators blocked and turned back two arresting parties from the coast. Mutinous as these actions were, the Regulators shortly carried their defiance to the ultimate point and refused to pay their taxes. They stood on the timely and embarrassing grounds that taxation without representation was tyranny.

Weighing back-country strength against low-country weakness, Lieutenant Governor Bull, in charge during Montagu's absence, concluded sensibly that moderation if not appeasement was in order. As he wrote to London, the only soldiery available to suppress the uprisers were coastal whites, who had their hands full in keeping order among the "numerous domestic enemy . . . thick sown in our plantations." Besides, the Regulators were not "idle vagabonds . . . the mere dregs of mankind," but "mostly the tenants of His Majesty's, landholders, though poor." He believed that under the circumstances the "only method of quieting their minds is the treating them with moderation . . . and their grievances with reasonable redress."

Responsive to Bull's lenient hand, the Regulators surveyed parish lines and marched peaceably on the polls in the October, 1768, elections to name some of their candidates to the Assembly. But the soon-returning Governor Montagu broke the shaky truce by sending to arrest accused Regulators a shady back-country character with an outlaw rabble in his train. This affront stirred up such a back-country commotion that, as Woodmason said, "The people were about to march downward and destroy all the Plantations of these Gentlemen whom they thought in the Plot—And it was with difficulty they were restrain'd—They may thank the Writer of the Remonstrance for keeping them Still."

At this point the Regulators named a delegacy, including Woodmason, to appeal directly to the King and Parliament, but Woodmason refused, and the mission to London did not materialize. However, Woodmason did renew the literary attack with his satiric "Advertisement" to be posted in the Charles Town Exchange:

To Be disposed off
On the Congaree, Saludy, Savanah, Wateree, and Broad Rivers
A Cargo of
Fifty Thousand Prime Slaves
(Remarkably healthy, and free from the Small Pox)
Lately imported from Great Britain, Ireland, and the Northern
Colonies
In the Good Ship
CAROLINA
George Rex, Master,
In a short passage of Ten Years— . . . Credit will be given
till—Public Good be preffer'd to Private Interest—
N.B. The above Slaves are sold for no fault—But they being
stript of their Property by Thieves and Vagabonds—Plunder'd
of their Effects according to Law, by Mercenary Demagogues
—and given up as a Prey to Vagrants and Outlaws, for to have
their Throats out—Their Estates rifled their families ruin'd
—. . . And not having any Courts of Justice where to lodge
Complaints—Or proper Magistrates to whom to seek Redress
or Injuries—Or Rulers to notice their Grievances—Nor any
Places for Public Worship wherein to implore the Divine Pro-
tection against, and Deliverance from these and other Evils,
renders it absolutely necessary for the above Sale taking Place—
Public Spirit—Love of Country—Religion—Humanity—
Charity Patriotism, and such Old-Coin, will be taken in Payment

Whether this did more than nettle a few Charles Town tempers no one knows. It did that, certainly. At least Woodmason's letter to John Rutledge represents that gentleman as chiding the back inhabitants for impertinence in calling themselves slaves, "When no People on Earth are in so great a State of freedom." Probably other circumstances won the day for the back country, and not the least of those the Regulator troops that stood off the deputized rowdies on their mission.

At any rate, the crisis passed with the Assembly's passage and crown approval a few months later of a circuit court act, which Governor Montagu had himself finally urged and which he carried with him to London on retiring from the province. Back in the executive chair, Lieutenant Governor Bull was able to heal many wounds by pardoning Regulators still under indictment for usurping the law and by restoring others to the magistracy and to their militia posts.

Courthouses and jails to be built under the Circuit Court Act went up slowly, and it was not until the fall of 1772 that the first back country courts actually went into session. Suspicions on both sides were noticeably allayed when circuiting lawyers and judges rubbed shoulders with backwoods clients and petitioners. Lieutenant Governor Bull reported that the legal travelers returned to Charles Town "astonished with the View of a Fine Country, of whose Value and Importance they had before had very Inadequate Ideas." And echoing the Rev. Mr. Woodmason, who had already left the province ill and discouraged, he said they were "highly satisfied with the . . . general Conduct of the Inhabitants,—who in those Parts where they are termed in a great Measure uncivilized, only want good Schools and School Masters, Churches and Ministers, and fit Magistrates to render them as valuable a People as any upon Earth."

A few months before he left South Carolina to serve a parish in Virginia Mr. Woodmason stood up at St. Mark's and passed a benediction on the Regulator movement in a sermon also prophesying the back-country fight still ahead. He praised the Regulators for their restraint: "You might have had recourse to Arms," he said, "and obtain'd by Forces what You could not by 20 Years Entreaty and Supplication Tho' You only demanded Your Birth Rights and Privileges as Britons and Free Men." Then he added in a phrase that not only graces the movement but attests the curate's metaphoric power, "But all your artillery was an Hiccory Switch."

Though Mr. Woodmason did not suggest it, the peaceful issue of the conflict was due as much to governmental impotence as to back-country moderation: Charles Town would undoubtedly have sent a shooting force against the Regulators, as Governor Tryon had against the North Carolina vigilantes, if the slave threat could have been left unattended on the coast.

Mr. Woodmason did suggest, however, that rights as yet ungranted and not apt to be forthcoming might "oblige You in a few Years to recommence *Busy Bodies*." He referred specifically to "a proper Representation in the General Assembly [which] you may depend on being debarred of for as long as possible." You have long been Ruled," he warned, "by a *Junto* of Your fellow Subjects, and been under an *Aristocratic* Government instead of a *Royal* and *Free*: And this *Junto*, as it has alway[s] had the Lead in All Public Affairs, will still hold fast the Rod, and make it prove to you a Rod of Iron, if not timely prevented . . ."

VI

London of the Southern Coast

"*Speak O Ye Charlestown Gentry,*" *the Rev. Mr. Woodmason once* exhorted from a back-country pulpit, "who go in Scarlet and fine Linen and fare sumptuously ev'ry day. Speak O Ye overgrown Planters, who wallow in Luxury, Ease and Plenty."

The curate was begging aid at this point for the "Swarms of Orphans, and other Pauper vagrant vagabond Children" who roamed the frontier. Though no Charles Town gentry sat to listen, he addressed them rhetorically to dramatize their power of speaking, if not from the heart, which he doubted was full of charity, certainly from the purse, which he had no doubt was full of money.

Actually the Charles Town squires often gave to local charities with plutocratic largess. But Mr. Woodmason did not exaggerate their addiction to private and public luxury. When he sermonized in 1770, Charles Town had fully earned its repute as a small London of the Southern coast. For Josiah Quincy, arriving from Boston in 1773, it surpassed in "grandeur, splendour of buildings, decorations, equipages . . . commerce, shipping" all he had ever seen or expected to see in America; and on quitting a round of entertainment he judged a bit sourly that "State, magnificence and ostentation, the natural attendants of riches, are conspicuous among this people: the number and subjection of their slaves tend this way."

Before he took up the cudgels for the back country, Charles Woodmason himself had sung the city's praises in heroic couplets for the London *Gentlemen's Mazagine*:

> *What! tho' a second Carthage here we raise,*
> *A late attempt, the work of modern days,*
> *Here Drayton's seat and Middleton's is found,*
> *Delightful villas! be they long renown'd.*
> *Domes, temples, bridges, rise in distant views,*
> *And sumptuous palaces the sight amuse.*

With a 1770 population of around 11,000, more than half Negroes, Charles Town stood fourth in size of colonial cities. But as the social and legislative magnet for rice barons up and down the coast, as the trading focus of a vast interior domain and as the only sizable port below Philadelphia, it seemed to the natives like the mistress of an empire.

Oddly enough, however, it had no corporate existence as a city but was ruled by the planter Commons Assembly. Though fitful and often niggardly in their aldermanic duties, the members were scarcely absentee lords. For they usually owned and dwelt seasonally in town houses no less commodious than their country seats, and they shared power with a few town merchants.

Scarcely a merchant belonged to the governing class, however, who had not turned some of his profits into watery acres and slaves. For at least by the century's end it was socially wise to command a plantation regardless of how many docks and warehouses one commanded. The big merchants—factors for British houses—escaped the stigma of "trade," but even so they gravitated to the land, usually at length removing altogether from the countinghouse. Giving further hostages to repute, they sent their sons to the Inns of Court in London, from which they returned with planters' sons to form a ruling planter-lawyer combine.

Henry Laurens, who as a South Carolina delegate presided over the Continental Congress in 1777-78, typified the planting merchants who could marry their daughters to Middletons and Pinckneys. And John Rutledge, first president of the Republic of South Carolina in 1776, best typified perhaps the planting lawyers who came to wield power and to marry each other's sisters or mercantile heiresses. The son of an immigrant Huguenot saddler, Laurens went into business after serving an apprenticeship abroad and made enough money during the fifties and sixties to buy eight or ten plantations. John

Rutledge, the son of a landed heiress, became a Charles Town barrister after studying at the Middle Temple and with Laurens' patronage rose shortly to play a key Commons role in the prologue to revolution.

Laurens wrote in 1750 that the planters were "full of money," and in 1769 he reported during a supervisory stay at Mepkin Plantation (near Moncks Corner) that he was "fixing a new overseer (the old one having grown rich and set up for himself)." That the overseer could set up for himself does not mean that his son could set up to a Pinckney, but if he doubled his capital in a year or two, as many did, his daughters could seen catch the sons of lesser squires. A moneyed father was not the least of a bride's attractions in colonial Carolina, as the Gazette artlessly proclaimed in lauding a wife as "endowed with all agreeable Accomplishments, and a Fortune of £15,000."

The Charles Town oligarchs not only rebuilt their town after a sweeping fire in 1740 but tried to bear out its pretension as the British Empire's second city. In the next quarter century they graced it with most of the public and private buildings that survive to manifest its currently antique and profitable Georgian demeanor. Wrought iron, stucco and tiered piazzas suggest a Franco-Spanish origin, but basically the old quarter, nestling between the convergent Ashley and Cooper rivers, takes its line from the London Sir Christopher Wren reconstructed after the Great Fire of 1666. Both dwellings and public structures were copied after, or adapted from, London models.

Around 1750 the local Commons voted funds for two buildings —a State House and a second parish church, St. Michael's—which swelled civic pride and staggered visiting colonials. British travelers, recalling the domed splendor of St. Paul's or the expansive grace of Hampton Court, might have spurned these provincial essays. If they knew their London, however, they should have prized St. Michael's as a meet reminder of St. Martin's-in-the-Fields, though whether they noted the likeness or not they should have felt at home in a town setting so faithfully neoclassic.

Straight off the boat from Liverpool, a visitor could scarcely have known that St. Michael's topped every other American church on its completion in 1761, quite justifying provincial wonder. Though the State House, which rose simultaneously, long ago burned down, St. Michael's still points its tiered white spire above the city to speak more eloquently of the past and more poignantly of home to a home-coming native than any other landmark on the low-country horizon.

St. Philip's, the city's first parish church, raises a not dissimilar steeple a few blocks away, but the building dates only from 1835, its early eighteenth-century predecessor on the site having succumbed to one of the fires that along with cannonades, hurricanes and earthquakes have periodically ravaged Charleston. Though St. Philip's may once have claimed ascendancy, St. Michael's queens it today on the strength of age and parish bloodlines. (An irreverent South Carolinian has said that "one rests in its graveyard in the peace that comes to those who live among the best and the knowledge that any other paradise is bound to be a comedown."). Actually they both approximate Mandarin family shrines, which the living generation must keep in good repair but not necessarily repair to more than once a year. They may have been achieving that status by 1773, for Josiah Quincy noted a small congregation at St. Philip's, "though this former part of the day is the most full." Small or not, it made too much cheerful noise to suit his Puritan humor:

> *A young scarcely-bearded boy read prayers, with the most gay, indifferent and gallant air imaginable: very few men and no women stand in singing-time. A very elegant piece of modern declamatory composition was decently delivered by another clergyman by way of sermon. . . . Having heard a young church-parson very coxcomically advance a few days before, that no sermon ought to exceed twenty-five minutes, I had the curiosity to see by my watch whether our clerical instructor was of the same sentiment, and found he shortened the space above seven and one-half minutes. It was very common in prayer as well as sermon-time to see gentlemen conversing together. In short . . . I could not help remarking in the time of it, that here was not, certainly "solemn mockery."*

Opened for use in 1771, the Exchange and Assembly Room undoubtedly impressed the arriving visitor more than any other Charles Town building. With its tall ornamental columns fronting the Cooper River, it made for Mr. Quincy "a most noble appearance." It impressed Mr. Woodmason, however, as a sinful extravagance, partially intended as it was to supply a *"Ballroom for the ladies."* Considerably altered by earthquake and the simplifying hand of menders, it still stands at the foot of Broad Street.

Even less excusable to Mr. Woodmason was the Assembly's voting £1000 for a marble statue of William Pitt in gratitude for Stamp Act repeal: money spent "just to humour a few Noisey Bell weathers and Swaggerers, who bellow for Liberty, while they have already more than they make good use off." Made by Joseph Wilton in England, it was set in the crossing of Broad and Meeting streets on July 5, 1770—the first statue of a public man to be raised in the American colonies. At least South Carolina historians make that claim, pointing out that New York did not erect her Pitt statue until 1773. A New York antiquary, however, lately pushed the date back to September, 1770, all but calling the South Carolina hand—which suggests, if nothing else, that "firsts" are apt to slip and slide under the nimblest historical foot.

In the twenty-five years before the Revolution Charlestonians housed themselves in a style befitting their civic aspirations. Though none built mansions quite on the London scale, they aimed at Palladian pomp, and within the limits of local craftsmanship they achieved results as agreeable as the colony could show.

The typical house was city Georgian in all but its relation to the street and in the number and extent of its piazzas. As an early writer put it, the houses "stand sidewaies backward into their yards, and only endwaies with their gables towards the street." Tiered piazzas, that is, fronted on cooling semitropic gardens and faced generally south to ward off the midday sun and catch the southwest evening breeze. According to their one- or two-room width these were called "single" or "double" houses. Fanlighted Georgian entrances were set in the walled end of the first-floor piazzas, but similar doorways opened from the piazzas to a central hall.

Though these practices lent Charles Town's architecture a distinctive cast, the most imposing late eighteenth-century house faces the street in the usual Georgian manner. This is a square brick dwelling on lower King Street built in the 1760's by the wealthy merchant Miles Brewton. A recent critic judges it the "finest architectural achievement of the city" and adds that "its interior carving and its two-story portico set a standard of dignity unrivaled in the colonies." Josiah Quincy was impressed—even a bit scandalized —at its rumored cost, £8,000. He enjoyed the Brewton cuisine, however, especially "the richest wines I ever tasted," and he eyed the furnishings with awe if not approbation: "azure blue window curtains, rich blue paper with gilt, mashee borders, most elegant pictures, excessive grand and costly looking glasses etc."

Skirting ingratitude, Quincy conveys nonetheless his New England reverence of the means to luxury at odds with his Puritan mistrust of the luxury itself. He approves Miles Brewton's standing as a "gentleman of very large fortune" but morally suspects the use to which he puts his God-given bounty. We don't how how Miles Brewton felt, but his establishment and his table imply that he liked money chiefly for what it would buy. The two men are perfectly symbolic. Their descendants would oppose each other from a variety of motives, but these antithetic responses to life would infuse all their differences. When Josiah Quincy referred to Carolina's black population as "vile slaves," he meant consciously that slavery was a vile practice, a denial of inborn human rights, but he instinctively felt, as did Yankees of a later day, that it was an instrument of idleness and vain display.

It is presumed that Ezra Waite, "Civil Architect, House-builder in general, and Carver, from London," designed the Brewton house, since he crossly denied reports to the contrary in the *South Carolina Gazette and Country Journal,* begging

> leave to do himself justice in this public manner, and assure all gentlemen, that he the said Waite, did construct every individual part and drawed the same at large for the joiners to work by, and conducted the execution thereof. Any man that can prove to the contrary, the said Waite promises to pay him One Hundred Guineas, as witness my hand, this 22nd day of August, 1769.

A few other notable dwellings of the period still stand, including the Huger house on Meeting Street, which sheltered for a few unhappy months in 1775 the last royal governor and his wife, Lord and Lady William Campbell. When she arrived in June, the

Governor's lady was actually returning to her native place. Born Sarah Izard, she had been married—as "a young lady esteemed one of the most considerable fortunes in the province"—to the "fourth son to his present Grace the Duke of Argyle," so the *Gazette* explained, then commander of "his majesty's ship the Nightingale."

Lady Campbell probably enjoyed few of Charles Town's normally extravagant bows and curtsies. In the first place, the colony was intractably at odds with England and, in the second and more telling place, she was after all, however sublime her marriage portion, a local product. Mrs. Ravenel represents female society as wondering whether she'd be "natural and agreeable as Lady Charles (the wife of Governor Montagu) had been" or somewhat airish in her titled incarnation. Since prophetesses are no more honored in their own country than prophets, one can easily guess what they made up their minds to expect and how they planned to behave. Why they'd no more "Ladyship Sally Izard" than "curtsy to old black Sally in my Negro Yard!" Nonetheless—such is parish fervor—they would have resented derogation of Lady Campbell from abroad. To an alien critic they would doubtless have declared her "good enough for any lord and too good for most."

But when highness arrived from abroad, no paradoxical feelings strove in their bosoms. They could bow in singlehearted deference to such a presence as "Sophia Carolina Mathilda, Marchioness de Waldegrave, own sister to the queen," whose arrival the *Gazette* announced in July, 1772. Bedecked with jewels and flashing the Queen's picture, this lady made a kind of royal progress through the city's haughtiest drawing rooms, holding out promised commissions and offices with the right hand as she borrowed with the left. Finally, running out of hostesses and shrewdly guessing the tenor of "public Conversation," she departed to the north, leaving her benefactors to the snickers of the *Gazette*, which suggested that "THE KNOWING ONES are sometimes taken in." Their humiliation was complete when a letter from Maryland described the traveling eminence as a runaway convict servant, who had been deported to the colonies for thieving from a maid of honor to the Queen. Before her Charles Town splash she had been exposed in the newspapers of nearly every colonial city. Nevertheless, she went from triumph to triumph, escaping Charles Town to conquer in turn New York,

Philadelphia, Boston, Newport and smaller towns between. A Boston printer exclaimed that she was "the most surprizing genius of the female sex that was ever obliged to visit America. What an improvement on Moll Flanders!"

It would be intriguing to have Eliza Pinckney's estimate of the fake marchioness, for she had waited upon royalty in England when she crossed with her husband at mid-century to put their sons in school. She doesn't say why she persevered in seeking audience with the widowed Princess of Wales, whom she found not receiving on her first attempt. Certainly her small Harriott's present of three Carolina birds for Princess Augusta sounds pretextual, and between the lines of her letter we discern the usual gratification at the accomplished fact: she had been to court! Though she tries to sound casual, she betrays herself in the remark that after a few minutes she "could converse with as much ease with [the Princess] as with almost any of my acquaintance, such was her condescension and her affable engaging manner." They talked among other things of wet nurses, the Princess inquiring if she suckled her children. "Princess Augusta was surprised at the suckling blacks [slave wet nurses in Carolina]; the Princess stroked Harriott's cheek, said it made no alteration in the complexion and paid her the compliment of being very fair and pretty."

If Mrs. Pinckney seems unduly worshipful as an American, it is well to recall that she was a royal subject. One of her compatriots, however, the vain, rich and splenetic Ralph Izard, who much preferred London to Charles Town, refused to pay his respects at court, because he would not "bow the knee . . . to mortal man."

Peter Manigault, son of the wealthy merchant Gabriel and grandson of the pioneer Judith, learned gratifyingly of Mrs. Pinckney's social coup when he traveled from his Temple lodgings to call on the family at Richmond, "which by the Bye was no small Compliment, as it cost me seven Shillings in Chaise Hire." As he reported to his mother in Charles Town, he found the Pinckney's occupying "a furnished House in Craven Street at £120 a Year, which is a Tip-Top Rent," and expressing "great Satisfaction with regard to the Civility they have been received with by every body. They have made many Acquaintances, among which the most considerable is that with princess of Wales." He also makes it plain which of

the Pinckneys was most caught up in the London flurry: "The Coll°
sticks to his Resolution of continuing but three Years in England;
and I believe all that his Lady will be able to say, will not put
honest Carolina out of his Head."

Like the prudent but aspiring burgher's son that he was, Peter
himself strove to cut a decently ample figure abroad without seeming to presume on the ample fortune at home. Wishing to set up
as a gentleman law student after his cramped residence with a London tutor, he hoped that his father would "allow me handsome
Lodgings, fit for a Person of my Condition; & a Servant to wait
upon me." The indulgence was scarcely granted, though, before he
was having to counter tales of a haughty—and by implication wastrel
—conduct that buzzed across the ocean to Charles Town and settled
in the paternal ear. He couldn't name the slanderer, but he would
guess it to be

> somebody, whom I did not chuse to wade through the Mire
> with to see Lions in the Tower; Or who knows that it is not
> somebody that I refused to sit with in the Pit of the Play-house,
> to have Tobacco spit upon me out of the One Shilling Gallery;
> but chose to go into the Boxes, because that is the proper
> place for Gentlemen to be seen in; Or perhaps the mighty
> Affront was, that I did not accompany some of my honest
> Country-Men to an Ordinary where they dined for three pence
> half penny, a head & had their Shirts washed into the Bargain.
> . . . Be the Cause of this Report what it will, notwithstand
> the Clamours of nonsensical people, I am determined to keep
> the best Company I can get into, & to do nothing inelegant,
> whatever unpolite people may say of my Proceedings.

Peter Manigault's stay abroad signifies a tie with England that
Carolinians have thought unique for the colonies. Though historians have proved that an equal number of travelers set out from
the northern ports, Charleston still savors the colonial boast that a
man who had not been to England made as odd a sight locally as
the man in New York or Boston who had.

Carolinians, though, seem to have led the fashionable spring and
summer exodus to Newport. At least so many voyaged to that Rhode
Island resort in the twenty years before the Revolution that it

acquired a name as "the Carolina hospital." Newporters doubtless felt some misgivings about this label: the Carolinians not only came to improve their health, but they often sickened and died of the malaria they had traveled north to escape. Planters who couldn't afford the Newport junket or who didn't feel up to the seven- to sixteen-day coastal voyage repaired from the country to the safer air and the gayer society of Charles Town, where they stayed usually from May until the first frost in late October or early November. Offering fewer lairs for anopheline mosquitoes, the city was of course much healthier than the rice swamps.

Travel undoubtedly broadened the gentry's vision, just as London schooling gave their sons opportunities they could scarcely have found anywhere in the colonies. But if a disposition to see the larger world reflects only credit, the habit of seeking education abroad confesses not only cultural ambition but the colony's failure to provide it at home. It further confesses a ruling-class indifference to the aspirations of poor young men who couldn't buy passage to London much less afford Peter Manigault's "handsome Lodgings."

A few Carolinians—Henry Laurens, for insance—felt the reproach of having to send their children abroad "for A B C and a little Latin," as he overstated the case, and some felt shame at having no college a hundred years after the colony's founding. Most of the other colonies had thriving collegiate institutions, the Boston Puritans having built theirs at Cambridge only sixteen years after they landed. Carolinians who spoke up for adequate schools and especially for a college in the decades before the Revolution did not fail to point up the humiliating contrast. And when a *Gazette* correspondent inquired why the colony could not imitate "so successful an example," a "Native" replied that the rich did not favor an institution "which might deprive their sons of the only advantage of being distinguished among their Countrymen": if they had small learning to show, they could at least flaunt the privilege of having gone far off to get it.

Actually legislative proposals for a college were made in the sixties and seventies but were killed in polemic skirmishes over such questions as the Stamp Act. The most determined effort was made in 1770, when large handouts to solicitors from Northern colleges roused public opinion to the realization that charity not only should but very well could start at home. Flying in the face of patrician prophecy that "learning would become cheap and too common, and every man would be for giving his son an education," Lieutenant Governor Bull urged and John Rutledge introduced a Commons bill which would have made Charles Town, had it passed, "the center of the first broadly conceived experiment in public education in America"—a free school system with a college at its head.

On the strength, however, that Commons would shortly hear and approve, a few well-to-do merchants and planters and, surprisingly enough, one cabinetmaker left bequests for an endowment fund. These donations enable the college of Charleston to claim 1770 as a founding date, though a charter was not issued until 1785 and a standard collegiate course was not offered until well into the nineteenth century. Gaining city support in the 1830's, it established grounds for its claim to be the first municipal college in the United States. Or at least its one-time claim. That distinction lost its savor a few years ago when in fear of legalistic Negro taxpayers the college retreated to the sanctity of private white control.

Carolinians were rich enough and had been for several decades to build a college without Commons subsidy: only the social atmosphere can explain the failure. In the first place, land and slaves were so prized as a means to status that few young men discerned the use of Plato and Aristotle. Even those who schooled abroad seldom liberalized their minds at Oxford and Cambridge but sought at the Inns of Court the practical training they could work as a Charles Town bootstrap and pocket-liner. Josiah Quincy observed in this regard that since the province laws were unavailable in book form, "No wonder their lawyers make from £2000 to £3000 sterling a year! The rule of action altogether unknown to the people." The pulpit attracted no sedulous young men in Charles Town by contrast with New England, where the Calvinist demand for a learned clergy moved the early founding of colleges and their devoted nurture. One historian puts the cart before the horse in suggesting that the absence of a college explains the Carolina disrelish for holy orders. More logically, disrelish for a profitless career helps explain the failure to start a college, since, moreover, the colony could allure no end of shabby-genteel curates from England.

English curates offered much of the schooling colonial Charles Town did afford. Under Society for the Preservation of the Gospel auspices, a succession of clerics came out from the 1730's on to conduct the Free School, free, that is, to a dozen public scholarship holders. Teachers drew a living from the province treasury, but otherwise the school ran on fees and donations. The boys were administered the usual gentlemanly tonic of Latin and Greek though not in such salutary or killing doses as their counterparts at Eton or Harrow. Most came from the lesser squirearchy, and the masters led them appropriately down the not too thorny paths of bourgeois virtue and politesse.

Under impetus from Commissary Alexander Garden (Anglican bishop's deputy), the S.P.G. also underwrote a school for Negroes, which for two decades at mid-century annually taught about sixty slave children their A B C's. The commissary envisoned the school as a gospel propagator, which would return its pupils to their home plantation zealous to pass on their learning. Slaves comprised "a Nation within a Nation," he declared, laboring and conversing "almost wholly within themselves, so that if once their children could but read the Bible to them . . . this would bring in at least a Dawn of the blessed Light." With society funds he bought two likely boys to train as teachers and solicited gifts to build a schoolhouse. The good work ceased in the early sixties when one pedagogue died and the other "turned out profligate"—since the S.P.G. had invested too meagerly in slaves "to keep up the stock," no more were available.

Various good-will agencies sponsored primer schooling for poor white children, but these did not, of course, fill the need as well as New England's tax-supported system. Even the Carolinians who wrought these charities were not convinced that education was the first of human blessings, scarcely needful at any rate to every urchin and ragtaggle. Those who could buy it for their young bought in decent moderation, since they were not disposed to breed a race of scholars and theologues. A few country squires employed tutors, but Charles Town was so near that it did just as well to board the children at one of the numerous small private schools that sprang up from the 1730's on.

Eighteenth-century Charlestonians harbored a London passion

for the theater. Though they had welcomed actors for irregular seasonal performances from 1735 on, they outdid themselves and all other American townsmen in a 1773-74 season, when David Douglass presented the best of the London repertoire—seventy-seven plays, farces and operas—in a newly constructed playhouse. Douglass had given Charlestonians in 1766 their first taste of comic opera done in the Covent Garden style when he returned from England with new-painted scenery and "very eminent performers." His exertions helped stimulate a winter social whirl so lively that Mr. Woodmason scolded: "While these Provincials were roaring out against the Stamp Act . . . they were rioting in . . . Balls—Concerts —Assemblies—Private Dances—Cards—Dice—Turtle Feasts—Above all—a Playhouse was supported and carried on. These People took from £60 to £100 Sterling, every other Night, for Months together."

Charles Town's first permanent theater building (probably burned in 1740) had opened thirty years before with a performance of Farquhar's comedy *The Recruiting Officer*. The same play marked the completion in 1937 of the Dock Street Theater, an eighteenth-century playhouse built on the reputed site of the first. In keeping with ancestral custom a prologue was written locally for the occasion—by the Charleston novelist DuBose Heyward. If it lacked the satiric point of an epilogue for Otway's tragedy *The Orphan*, which had opened the city's first dramatic season in 1735, Mr. Heyward was scarcely at fault. He could only strike a gracefully antiquarian note, lacking the early versifier's incentive to set Boston's grisly diversions against the civilized amusements of Charles Town:

> *Nor real Virtue blames the pleasing Strife,*
> *To blend Amusement with the Shades of Life;*
> *Wise, innocent, serene, she smiles at Ease,*
> *Nor hanging Witches, nor abjuring Plays.*

Fashionables no doubt loved the seeing and being seen as much as instrumental harmonies, but they nonetheless encouraged a good deal of musical activity. Though occasional concerts were played during the first half of the century, more elaborate and regular performances came with the founding in 1762 of the St. Cecilia Society, named for music's patron saint. According to "Rules" published a decade later, 120 gentlemen paid £25 each annually for the privilege of hearing the music along with as many female relations as their own discretion permitted. The managers sought to attract virtuosi, advertising liberal stipends in journals to the north.

Whether the St. Cecilia had acquired by 1773 its awful repute as a social fortress no contemporary bothers to say, but Josiah Quincy, who attended a concert on a guest ticket, had to pass more than routine inspection before gaining the silken assemblage. At the gates to the concert house he was met by a "Constable with his staff," who inspected the ticket and passed him on to "a white waiter, who directs me to a third, to whom I delivered my ticket and was conducted in."

Though in 1822 the St. Cecilia exchanged concert listening for dining and dancing, it has carried on steadily since its founding: "Only in the sixties, as during the Revolution," Mrs. Ravenel explains, "all the men being in the field, and the city under fire, it was necessarily interrupted." Blooded Charlestonians still dance and sup together at its ceremonious functions—minus those who have breached propriety by marital divorce—guarding the privilege with invisible knives that glint only in the searchlight of parvenu ambition. In *Mamba's Daughters* DuBose Heyward tells of a wealthy newcomer's disarming the male guardians with a neat flip of the business wrist after his wife had tearfully abandoned her teatime assaults on the dowagers. Mrs. Ravenel, writing at an earlier date, suggests that the gates do open to admit the alien, though the way to this triumph suggests the perilous search for the Holy Grail. A local youth, she says, is almost perfunctorily elected if his sires or "any of his immediate kindred" have belonged, though

> blackballs . . . have fallen, when the applicant was a notoriously unworthy scion of his family tree. If a new resident, or of a family recently brought into notice, there will be inquiry, perhaps hesitation, and a good backing will be desirable. But if he be of character and standing calculated to make his membership acceptable to the Society, he will be elected—unless he has some adversary; then he may fail. The presenter of such a one will make careful examination into public feeling before subjecting his friend to mortification; and will withhold the letter if in doubt. When a man is elected, the names of the

ladies of his household are at once put upon "the list" and
remain there forever. Only death or removal from the city erases
them,—change of fortune affects them not at all. "To be dropped
from the St. Cecilia" is an awful possibility sometimes hinted
at, but which (as far as known) has never come to pass.

Though Charlestonians patronized the theater and the concert
hall, the diversion closest to their hearts was probably horse racing.
As early as 1734 they had occasional meets at the York Course,
where in the forties races were run almost monthly. In 1754 Thomas
Nightingale from Yorkshire opened the New Market Course within
a mile of the city and started the famous "Charlestown Races."
Founded a few years later, the Carolina Jockey Club sponsored the
running of three great feature races for purses as high as £1,000.
Though such stable owners as the Draytons, the Middletons and the
Ravenels naturally dominated the sport, people of all classes turned
out for the races and for the cockfights often staked between heats.
Both gentlemen and "mechanicks" also frequented Charles Town
cock mains.

The general addiction to such sports drew occasional censure
from evangelic scourgers like the Rev. George Whitefield and the
native Quaker Sophia Hume or from a *Gazette* correspondent like
"Margery Distaff," who wrote, "There is not one night in the week
in which they [the men] are not engaged with some club or other
at the *tavern*, where they *injure their fortunes* by GAMING in various
ways, and *impair their healths* by the intemperate use of spiritous
liquors, and keeping late hours, or rather spending whole nights,
sometimes, in these disgraceful and ruinous practices." The Franco-
American essayist J. Hector St. John de Crèvecœur, who visited
Charles Town in the 1760's, mused that "the rays of their sun seems
to urge them irresistibly to dissipation and pleasure."

A race so given to amusements would obviously neglect the values
of reading, thinking and writing. Busy spending the margin of
profit they had come so lately to enjoy, they had, of course, scant
time for these solitary diversions. Moreover, they were so imbued
with mercenary pieties that they scarcely dreamt of different philosophies. They scarcely apprehended, that is, the spirit of learning for
learning's sake, a spirit that Americans early and late, it is only

fair to add, have feebly espoused. Charlestonians read, of course, the well-to-do owned a hundred books or so, and a group of men established in 1748 the Library Society, which owned by 1770 a 2,000-book collection. Of the thirteen founders, by the way, only two were planters; burghers, not squires, promoted the Carolina literary culture, as Carl Bridenbaugh, the historian of colonial cities, observes.

Utility largely dictated their reading and their study. Though untypical perhaps in his stern application to private and public business, John Rutledge sounds a not uncommon note in urging his brother Edward to pursue the useful in his study abroad. Busily shaping his own career at thirty, he recalls the prototypic American on the make, Benjamin Franklin, and reminds us that bourgeois ambition was not incompatible with a leisure-class manner. John suggests a steady sense of purpose in turning aside for the graces. The theater entertains, he says, but it may also impart a graceful turn of speech. The literary classics have their noble beauties, but "a good private tutor" can point them out quickly "and make you in six months at your age better acquainted with them than a boy at school in seven or eight years." He advises reading English history but enjoins discrimination between the instructive and the merely "curious." Finally he suggests writing down aphorisms in a commonplace book: "Lord Bacon did not think this beneath him" and "Bacon you know is my favorite." No doubt he also admired Polonius' charge to Laertes, for his parting advice echoes it, "Let your dress be plain, always in the city and elsewhere, except when it is necessary that it should be otherwise, and your behavior rather grave."

Since the newspaper by its very function reflects bourgeois interests and tastes, it is not surprising that Charles Town claimed several, but it is creditable that they "attained as high a standard as any in the colonies," especially the Timothys' *South Carolina Gazette,* which began in 1732. Compared with Northern craftsmen, however, Charles Town printers could expect a small sale of other works they published. In fact, they could find few original works to publish.

Eighteenth-century Carolinians made few contributions to science, but Charles Town could claim one significant figure, Dr. Alexander

Garden, who corresponded on botanical subjects with European scientists and won membership in learned societies in America and abroad. He roamed the Carolina swamps and fields in search of specimens and sent drawings of his finds to London. His name survives in the gardenia, the fragrant white flower which older Carolinians prefer to call the Cape jessamine.

Dr. Garden often despaired at the general neglect of scientific and scholarly interests in Charles Town, and the Rev. Alexander Hewatt concluded that the Carolina society had "not advanced beyond that period in which men are distinguished more by their external than internal accomplishments." He found that "beauty, figure, agility and strength form the principal distinctions among them, especially in the country" and that they were "chiefly known by the number of their slaves, the value of their annual produce, or extent of their landed estates."

Having reached the extreme limits of the plutocratic stage, the Carolina gentry lacked as yet the collective political wisdom and the vision of the common wealth that marks a matured aristocracy. As bosses of the Commons House of Assembly they selfishly denied local government to town and country, giving cause for Mr. Woodmason's febrile complaint that not "one real disinterested public spirited Person, devoid of Party and Self Interest, ever yet appear'd in this country." And in their drive for wealth and distinction they partially justified another critic's strictures: "Every Tradesman is a Merchant, every Merchant is a Gentleman, and every Gentleman one of the Noblesse. We are a Country of Gentry, *Populous generosum*: We have no such Thing as a common People among us: Between Vanity and Fashion, the Species is utterly destroyed. . . . The better Sort of Gentry, who can aim no higher, plunge themselves into Debt and Dependance, to preserve their Rank."

Pushing this society may have been and conspicuously wasteful in its gestures, but in Charles Town it shaped in its houses and its churches images of classic beauty; and even its dress, its manners and its public pleasures reflected some vision of grace that diamond-studded vulgarians of a later day never knew: one cannot imagine such a race building vast shrines to their greed in Pittsburgh Gothic or collecting bankrupt Italian titles to hang on the family tree. For they looked to an aristocratic mode that guided their taste and posed a dignified and ethical standard for their means of making and spending money. They did not, of course, conceive the mode—they imported it from abroad as they imported their wines and their music. But they had the good sense to know the first-rate and the genuine. They had the only leisure-class society of colonial America, as Carl Bridenbaugh has said, but if they lived for the "unbought graces of life"—pleasure, charm, polish—they left the agreeable memory of not having lived for bread alone.

VII

Preamble to a Furious Cannonade

At midnight of October 23, 1765, a Charles Town mob roused Henry Laurens from bed demanding the stamps just in from London to effect Parliament's levy on all paper used in the American colonies. Disguised in "soot, sailors habits, slouch hats &ca," the men searched the wealthy merchant's house, brushing off his word that he had no "connection with stamps" and his pleas for respect of his wife, "a poor sick woman far gone with child," who appeared "shrieking and wringing her hands."

Laurens, of course, did not have the stamps, as the intruders were finally convinced, though they failed to extort from him either "A Bible Oath" or the avowal " 'May God disinherit me from the Kingdom of Heaven' if I knew where [they] were." He had, in fact, as little reason to hide the stamps as any other man in the Carolina Commons, which unanimously opposed their use. The stamps were secreted at Fort Johnson, but rumor not unnaturally pointed to Laurens, who had condemned raids on stamp officers' houses as "burglary and robbery."

Like most of his class north and south, Laurens was perplexed at the turn of events: he resented Parliament's hand in the province till, but as a favored merchant son he hated to jostle the fatherly crown. Since refusing to use the stamps would involve propertied men "in the utmost confusion," would, indeed, "prove our ruin and destruction," he reasonably wished to "show a graceful obedience to the law until we can procure its annihilation in a constitutional way." A man so honest with himself not unreasonably sus-

105

pected the rioters of wanting to hold off paying their debts. Behind the assault on his premises he also divined "the cloven foot of a certain malicious villain," his one-time merchant friend Christopher Gadsden, whose running with the underdogs Laurens could only regard as treason to the master kind.

Whether or not Gadsden set the pack on Laurens, he was the acknowledged leader of the Charles Town radicals, skilled workmen for the most part—bricklayers, shipwrights, blacksmiths—who owned a house and lot and voted for Commons members but scarcely presumed to stand for office. But he was no more the arrant leveler than Henry Laurens: he decried far-off tyranny from a dais of local privilege.

Son of an Englishman, schooled in London and prospering under the crown, Gadsden had as good reason as Laurens to show "a graceful obedience" to Parliament. Having stood in the middle of a long quarrel between Commons and Governor Thomas Boone, though, he had more reason to balk. In 1762 the Governor had dissolved Commons on grounds of a picayune illegality in Gadsden's election, breeching what might be called squatters' rights to the local polls. When a two-year hail of polemic shot failed to budge the Governor, Commons petitioned his ejection and circulated at home and abroad a lengthy indictment. As a parting shot they put Boone on the boat to England without his pay, honoring the £7,000 claim only at the King's request.

Though he loudly bore the brunt of the quarrel, Gadsden himself was not an issue. Boone's request for a tighter election law had met a curt rebuff from Commons, so historians account for the row, and he determined to cut this prideful body down to size. But in view of his initial repute with the oligarchs as a former Carolina resident and landowner, it seems likely that Boone added social insult to political injury. It seems very likely that he compromised himself by flaunting a mistress after his wife's abrupt departure for England with the children.

The Governor is known to have departed the colony with another man's wife, a woman "of some prominence," so Wallace allows. Whether he installed her in his drawing room before he left is problematic but plausible. At least such an event would have racked Charles Town's proper bourgeois soul as nothing else could.

John Rutledge's biographer Richard Barry tells poetic if not factual truth when he says the Governor sprang his paramour on the unsuspecting Commons chieftains and their wives. Invited to dine, they found the woman in shameless command of the Governor's dinner table and his humor. Since he answered to the King alone, the men could not rebuke his effrontery, but their ladies could and did rebuke his unlawful "lady." They never laid eyes on her again. If she swam into view, they didn't "see."

As the Charles Town rulers saw it,

> *Their Governor could have but one lady and that lady must be his wife. If this was lese majesty, let him make the most of it. If divorce was in the air no one ever mentioned it. Divorce was not only unheard of; it was unthinkable. The South Carolinians were like the Mongolian tribe which had no knowledge of marital infidelity and consequently no word with which to express adultery.*

When Barry wrote in 1942, divorce was still legally unthinkable. It was not unthought of, however, and just-across-the-line Augusta, Georgia, enjoyed a lively trade with restless South Carolina mates. Not until 1945 was divorce permissible at home.

Though Boone undoubtedly touched the rebel quick in Christopher Gadsden, he raised no obstacle the Carolina politicians had not previously vaulted or slid around. They had dealt with highhanded royal governors before. But the Stamp Act posed new and disconcerting threats, political and economic. It signified Parliament's intention of usurping powers the local Commons had held inviolate by long custom, if not by law. Worse, it seemed to warn that merchants and planters must always conform their girth to the same old tributary breeches.

With the lesser irritants of knavish and often dull-witted crown functionaries, these passes at self-rule and prosperity so fretted the Carolinians for a decade that at last they turned in despairing wrath and fought. As hereditary, if untitled, lords of great domains, they could not bow to an upstart British Commons, but they grieved at quitting the British realm, where nobles properly bowed to their sire.

South Carolina broke with England in more painful deliberation, perhaps, than any other colony. Unlike the merchant aristocrats of the North, who yielded to clamorous middle classes, her rulers had little to fear from Charles Town's handful of mechanic voters and nothing to fear from the back country, which looked rather to the King as a benefactor. When they heard radicalism in the Commons House, they heard it roll in Ciceronian periods from Christopher Gadsden, a pillar of that select club, where men "conversed, lolled and chatted much like a friendly jovial society," as Josiah Quincy observed.

By sending Gadsden to the Stamp Act Congress in New York— October, 1765—the membership appeared to endorse his view that the British Constitution's guarantees of self-rule made the local Commons equal with Parliament. Most probably did not guess, though, how close Gadsden came to the Massachusetts rebels, already bypassing the Constitution and appealing to God as the author of human rights. They showed a radical bent also in choosing Thomas Lynch, a wealthy planter who embraced the Gadsden heresy, if he seldom preached so loud and long. But as the third delegate and a kind of tamer for the two old lions they chose the young conservative lawyer John Rutledge, who had returned only five years back from the Inns of Court.

Gadsden tirelessly exhorted the Congress to ask only the King for redress and ignore the House of Commons, which had trifled with colonial petitions. But Congress refused his defiant counsels and adopted the politic Rutledge strategy of addressing King, Lords and Commons. Though in their address to Commons Americans first dogmatized "no taxation without representation," they did it with a by-your-leave, so to speak.

Repealing the Stamp Act next spring, Parliament warned rebellious Americans that it could legislate for the colonies as it chose. Gadsden in turn warned his Charles Town following of this Damoclean sword at a rally under the moss-hung branches of a great live oak, afterwards famous as the Liberty Tree. It was such an eyesore to the British, incidentally, that during the war they tore it limb from limb and burned the limbs.

In an access of relief and gratitude the Assembly commissioned the William Pitt statue, showing less tact, however, than New York's legislators, who ordered George III as well as Pitt memorialized in stone. In fact, no one arose even to second William Wragg, of St. John's Parish, in his motion to honor the King instead of Mr. Pitt.

But anxieties for the future stirred beneath the surface and not only in such agitated spirits as Gadsden: Henry Laurens, for instance, was glad to have the act repealed, "though I know not what cause to ascribe it to, nor am I clear about the durability of our present seeming happiness." His happiness, at least, was to flee a year later when he clashed with the admiralty courts over prosecutions against his coastwise ships. Despite his proven innocence in court, he was gouged of fees by a crown-appointed judge acting simultaneously as paid lawyer for the accusing customs officer. Exposing this outrage in a pamphlet widely circulated in England, Laurens also pointed out the inequities of trade. He figured Americans as captive producers for Britain and captive customers for British merchants. He styled himself pointedly as one "whose heart bleeds" at the idea of a falling away from the Empire, which he would wish to "perpetuate . . . great and inviolate to latest times."

Within the next few years Charles Town's recoil from a series of London arrogations underscored Laurens' warning note. Following the New York and Massachusetts lead, Commons defied the billeting act, refusing to pay British troop expenses. They argued, of course, from the principle basic to almost every colonial difference with England: as a self-governing body they could and would decline obligations they had not made. They next joined with other colonial assemblies in protesting the 1767 Townshend law taxing such imports as glass, paper and tea.

In the fall of 1768 Gadsden's faction drank toasts around the Liberty Tree to "the glorious ninety-two anti-rescinders of Massachusetts Bay"—the Boston Assembly had voted 92 to 17 not to withdraw its Townshend Act protest—and adjourned to back up their fire-eating candidates at the polls. Of the three available seats, however, they took only one, for Gadsden himself. The libertarian flurry swept up so few voters that two moderates, Henry Laurens and Charles Pinckney, easily won the other places.

Enthusiasts had more luck the next summer in getting names for an Association pledging nonimportation of British goods until the revenue acts were repealed. Nonimportation, that is, of all but certain necessities like tools, cloth for slave wear, powder, lead and shot.

Planters could keep on planting, workmen working, and the soldiery could prime for slave unrest. No wonder the merchant howled. It looked as though the patriots had nudged him up to the sacrificial altar.

Nonetheless, tradesmen joined with planters and mechanics in a General Committee to enforce the Association. Gadsden probably thought up the class representation to make it appear that all three "estates of the realm" were one in disaffection. But at least one member of the planting estate scorned the implied fraternity. William Henry Drayton, Oxford-trained nephew of Lieutenant Governor Bull, sneered in the *Gazette* that an educated man did not consult on public affairs

> *with men who never were in any way to study, or to advise upon any points, but rules how to cut up a beast in the market . . . cobble an old shoe . . . or to build a necessary house. Nature never intended such men should be profound politicians or able statesmen, and unless a man makes a proper use of his reading, he is but upon a level with those who never did read. From which reasoning I conclude that in point of knowledge all the members of the committee are upon a level with each other. A learned body of statesmen truly!*

It was not the first time the young crown votary had struck at the patriots. Hopping mad at the Association's proscription of non-signers, he wrote that no power could accuse of sedition but "the *voice* of the *legislature,* and no person but a *traitor or a madman* would think of any other." The reference was plainly to Gadsden who, he further declared, should be lodged in the madhouse and kept there, at least during the change and full of the moon, at public expense. Gadsden, of course, gave insult for insult, bearing down on the conceit and folly of youth. In their reply the mechanics did not rise above the sophomoric level of their betters: they suggested that his wife's fortune rather than his own merit saved Drayton from driving a dung cart.

Every bit as haughty as Drayton but standing to his colors with becoming calm, the planter William Wragg shrugged at seeing his name fixed to a handbill as a nonsigner. It redounded to his honor, if anything, showing him "as one upon whom neither fear, interest, or the . . . desire . . . of swimming with the stream could operate" to sway his judgment. Lacking all resources but "what a plantation affords," he would "endure everything" rather than submit to the humors of "men not having authority."

Drayton's fire was to shift so abruptly in the revolutionary wind of the next few years that in 1775 as chairman of the Provincial Congress' Secret Committee he would help tar and feather men— of low station—who spoke out against the patriot cause. William Wragg, who remained like Balaam unable to speak anything but what the Lord put in his mouth, enjoyed a highborn immunity, but he was packed off to his barony in malarial summer when he declined swearing enmity to the King. Finally, permitted to sail for England, he was shipwrecked and drowned.

Nonimportation fervor petered out within the year but not before a poor widow, hauled up for her trading sins, artfully claimed that she had as much right to use goods ordered before the Association as Lawyer John Rutledge did to keep his carriage horses recently bought from England. Though such inequities lent their weight, merchant discontent probably carried the 1770 vote to break the agreement. Gadsden maneuvered and Lynch wept, but Charles Town was ready for business.

However, resistance had been solid enough throughout the colonies to win the point in London, which not long afterwards removed all duties except that on tea, which the King insisted upon "to try the matter with the Americans." And even that tax was so reduced that tea came cheaper in America than in England. But the principle was still at stake, and in May, 1771, Gadsden led his boys under the Liberty Tree in a resolve not to import tea while the duty remained.

Later that summer one of Gadsden's Liberty Boys quickened drowsy tempers by killing a crown functionary in a hasty tavern duel. The victim, something more than a British ne'er-do-well, was Peter Delancey, his Majesty's postmaster general of the Southern District of North America, scion of the New York Delanceys, one of the richest and most powerful families in the colonies. He was married to a daughter of the South Carolina squirearchy, and his sister was married to Ralph Izard, of the Charles Town and Goose Creek Izards, another very rich and tony American clan.

Having shot Delancey without witnesses, Haley could scarcely claim exemption from the law as a duelist, and he was tried for murder, with John Rutledge as his chief defender. The quarrel had started, it came out, with Dr. Haley's drunken boast that some of Charles Town's wealthiest men were hot American patriots, while Northern moneybags swung to the royal coattails. Delancey drunkenly pronounced him a liar, Haley challenged, Delancey accepted, and together they reeled upstairs to shoot it out.

When Attorney General Leigh sermonized the royalist jury at length on the infractions of the Liberty Boys, that "unprincipled rabble which defies law and order and the decency of our Beloved Majesty," it looked as though Dr. Haley would swing for his politics. But John Rutledge (by Richard Barry's plausible account) with his cannier grasp of the legal and human fundamentals, skirted politics altogether and gravely expounded the antique right of self-defense. In simple truth, Dr. Haley had acted to preserve his honor in the gentleman's way. Delancey had, of course, accepted the challenge to his honor in the gentleman's way. The gentlemen jurors nodded their heads: momentarily, but quite long enough, they saw the rabble-rouser transfigured. Dr. Haley was safe.

The Carolina historian David Ramsay, recalling the scene from memory, according to Barry, wrote that "When Rutledge spoke it was as if he transported us, by some magic to an ancient place, far removed from all the feeling of the day. We were all like little boys, listening to a revered headmaster, whose words were eagerly absorbed, so that they might be forever treasured." In print, he said, the words would seem "cold with logic, and dry with facts," but the lawyer spoke with such feeling that "everyone was filled with indescribable pathos."

Ramsay notes here a manifestation of the quality in John Rutledge that led his fellow oligarchs to entrust him with the state during the war. He was not only begging for his client's neck—he was apparently speaking from the depths of his own Anglo-Carolinian pieties. He spoke seldom for a public man, and what remains in print does not, as Ramsay noted, burn with rhetorical fire. But his thoughtful hearers all remarked on his eloquence, derived, it would seem, from intensity of belief in the common faith. Believing what he said, he said what men of his class felt in their bones as gospel truth.

At the time of the Haley trial and for several years thereafter the Carolina Commons argued with London its right to spend the public money without a nod from Governor or Council. The question arose when it appropriated a sum to aid the English reformer John Wilkes in his ten-year free-speech battle with the crown. Since Wilkes had offended with a newspaper attack on a George III utterance from the throne, his Majesty boggled at this philanthropy. He ordered the Governor and Council to disallow the payment and to quash any tax bill putting money to such an odious use. Doggedly reciting the constitutional formula that usage equals right, Commons stuck at sharing the purse strings. Governor and Council in turn stuck at dealing with Commons. Public business rather languished after that.

Finally in 1775—four years later—Council yielded to a sizzling public temper largely raised by one of its own members, William Henry Drayton, who had come full circle to match Gadsden in apostasy. Drayton initially defected from personal pique. Named an assistant judge as well as a Council member by his uncle Lieutenant Governor Bull, he might be ignominiously bumped by some London nincompoop with a friend at court. In protesting, however, as he did from the bench, he spoke for the blocked ambitions of many young and able Carolinians.

Council concessions in 1775 mattered little in the face of an extra-legal Provincial Congress already in virtual power. The Congress evolved from a 1773 mass meeting at the Exchange to dispose of the tea just in from England. The meeting resolved to have no truck with imposed tea, and merchants agreed not to receive the current lot. Carolinians at this point behaved more like pennywise Bostonians than pennywise Bostonians had at a similar juncture. They abstained from dumping good merchandise in the harbor. Instead, customs officers quietly stored the tea in the Exchange basement. Though a libertarian gang did manage to impress and sink one later shipment, several more lots arrived in peace and found their way to storage. A few years later Carolinians took reward of their prudence when they sold the tea to meet war expenses.

When blockaded Boston called on Charles Town in 1774 to stop all traffic with England, the sharply divided response signified that crown loyalty had not yet withered on the Southern vine. In a series of general meetings conflict centered on the election of delegates to a general American (the First Continental) Congress. Moderates wanted to limit delegates and radicals to let them go all the way with Boston, which flatly denied Parliament's authority. The radicals rushed in voters to elect their old war horses, Lynch and Gadsden, and a third younger man, Edward Rutledge. Conservatives, however, more than balanced the scales with John Rutledge and Henry Middleton, the lord of "Middleton Place" and married to one of the few authentic ladies in the colony, Lady Mary, daughter of the Earl of Cromartie.

Lest the vision arise, however, of two murderous factions sailing off to cut each other's throats in Philadelphia, it may be well to pause for a genealogical briefing. The radical Edward Rutledge was John's brother and had served under the elder's tutelage almost from birth; furthermore, Edward was married to Henry Middleton's daughter Henrietta; and the Rutledges had a family link with Gadsden through their brother Andrew, married to the old man's daughter Elizabeth.

The Rutledge wives and Mrs. Middleton went along on the junket, as did a retinue of body servants. The party took over a floor of Philadelphia's chief tavern and sauced politics with lighter diversions. Though the ladies did not tipple, the gentlemen improved their idle hours with a new French drink, the julep, which John Rutledge's man learned from the public-room barman downstairs.

Teetotaling Christopher Gadsden may have repaired off duty to his ideological mentor, Sam Adams, the prime *agent provocateur* in the colonies. He certainly joined Adams in forcing the delegates to a radical position: the Congress wound up pledging the colonies not to trade with England and putting "the immutable laws of nature" before the English Constitution as the source of American rights. Conservatives had, of course, wished to avert "the laws of nature," which would mean turning their backs on the British realm and marching toward the equalitarian kingdom of God. Rankling at the outcome, the great Philadelphia merchant Joseph Galloway saw the move as a triumph of bankrupts, "overwhelmed in debt to the British merchants" over "men of loyal principles," who "possessed the greatest fortunes in America."

Though he lost the major battles, John Rutledge did not forget his duty to the ruling class at home. Pointing out that New England traded lightly and his own state heavily in the articles under ban, he got rice exempted from the agreement. The nontrading plan looked to him suspiciously like a scheme "among the flour colonies" to push their product at the expense of rice. He thought it "not unreasonable for me to say that if we are to bear burdens in the cause of America they should be as equal as possible." The delegates could not squirm around his logic, of course, and surrendered the point.

Back in Charles Town, however, Rutledge had to defend his action against wrathful indigo planters at the January, 1775, meeting of the first Provincial Congress. To appease them required a form of economic control which ironically they were all trying to escape: commissioners would claim a third of the rice crop brought to market, sell it and buy indigo and other produce. In moderate accord, delegates then re-elected John Rutledge and company for the Second Continental Congress and adjourned.

But they were mistaken if they thought that George III and his merchants were going to take the Philadelphia impertinence in silent regret. April brought news to the contrary: Parliament had granted forces to execute the revenue laws in America. Stung to the realization that England meant war, the Charles Town patriots seized powder magazines and arms from the State House, then appeared in Commons next day to disclaim all knowledge of the deeds to the Governor.

When echoes reached the city shortly afterwards from "the shot heard round the world"—the battle of Concord in Massachusetts—the Congress went briskly to work. It ordered troops raised, formed an Association to "be ready to sacrifice our lives and fortunes against every foe," ordered refusers of this vow sharply dealt with, created a Council of Safety to act in Congress' name, and authorized a million pounds paper currency to meet expenses. Then pushing the situation to the last reaches of anomaly, patriot legislators met in the Commons House of his Majesty's government and voted the funds to usurp his Majesty's rule. It was their last act, naturally, on behalf of his Majesty.

As joint Congress and Council head the patriots chose Henry

Laurens, who had just come back from overseas somewhat more dis-
gruntled with King and Parliament than in 1771, when he closed
out his business and departed to put his sons in school. He did not
return, however, shouting defiance. Though he had removed his sons
from wicked England to upright Switzerland and had lingered there
himself to admire the workings of that Calvinist republic, he still
fancied a legal salve for American sores. Himself bred to the Calvinist faith in hard work and the rule of rich and godly men, he feared
civil discord and, above all, underdogs on the prowl. But he had a
brave eye for necessity, and when he saw independence at last as a
necessary end he pledged his fortune to the cause, bore uncomplain-
ingly a year's imprisonment in the Tower of London—he was
captured en route to Holland on a government mission—and in the
"blessed sunshine of peace" thanked God that he had a son "who
dared to die [for] his country."

Expressing his dilemma in 1775, Laurens probably spoke for his
class when he wrote his brother in England: "God deliver us from
Kingly, ministerial and popular tyranny." He was resolved "to hazard all [his] estate rather than submit to . . . those brethren . . . on
your side of the water," but he shrank from "forcing . . . consciences,"
as the Congress had done in coercing men to sign the Association.
Even as Congress president Laurens would not sign without first declaring himself a King's man and disavowing the impeachment of
nonsigners. Anticipating the charge of inconsistency, he said that the
enemies he swore to resist were also the King's enemies, "fellow subjects" who had "misinformed" his Majesty. Among those enemies he
refused to include Carolinians who would not sign for conscience's
sake but whom he knew to be "friends to all America."

Laurens naturally deplored the tar and feathers young patriots
smeared on men daring to question the new-laid dogma, that is,
men without fortune or name to keep bully-boys at a distance. He
also deplored violence against the Negroes, many of whom were
hustled to prison for parroting the cry of "Liberty." One free Negro,
a harbor pilot, was hanged and burned, despite Governor Campbell's efforts to save him, on the hearsay testimony that he stood
ready to guide British warships across the bar.

Revolutions run a violent course. They do not issue, as Henry
Laurens seemed to imply, in the legal maneuvers of a court of equity.

He and his fellow moderates were blinking the crass fact that his Majesty scorned their distinctions of loyalty. When Americans traded shot with British troops at Concord, George III cried rebellion. When Carolina's turn came to fire in "self-defense," he would still cry rebellion. A few men like William Henry Drayton saw plainly in the spring of 1775 that the King would not deny Charles Town the test, and he nagged at the colony to meet it with a stout rebel arm. Work on the harbor fortifications lagged and militia companies drilled understrength as the Council of Safety argued what to do and how much to spend. A firm voice was needed, and Drayton as a Council member was ready to supply it.

Figuring back-country loyalism as a serious drag on the colony's defensive muscle, Drayton rode toward the hills in July with a troop of soldiers and a preacher to explain the quarrel with England. It was no easy mission. A coastal planter himself and no doubt publishing his caste with a salt-water brogue, shining boots and a blooded mount, Drayton must have personified arrogant Charles Town to the back settlers. The likes of him had shrugged off their pleas for law and order in the back country, taxing them all the while without a sign of representation. The King at least had granted land, which was more than Charles Town had ever bothered to do. Who minded a piddling tax on tea? Surely the high and mighty could scrounge an extra penny here and there for the King.

Not all the back-countrymen, of course, leaned to the crown. Some readily signed the Congress Association, though not enough to suit Drayton, who resorted to highhanded threats and stratagems, so the back country complained. He crossed words with several churlish tribes and ordered a number of arrests. Instead of justifying the quarrel with the King, in fact, he seems to have picked a fight.

In the fall of 1775, at Ninety Six, South Carolinians—coastal militia ranged against back-country irregulars—spilled each other's blood in the first real battle of the Revolution. For a family squabble the clash involved a sizable number of men. Initially 500 patriots dug in around the Ninety Six courthouse to stand off nearly 2,000 Tories. Shortly, however, 3,000 militiamen arrived on the scene to overwhelm the Tories in a couple of days, capturing most of their leaders. Casualties were light on both sides.

The large force Congress put in the field undoubtedly awed the back country, but arms alone would scarcely have dented flinty Scotch-Irish minds. Those who yielded to Charles Town after the Ninety Six battle did so only as the Council of Safety freed their captains from seizure and gave their bailiwick a larger voice in Congress. Some, of course, never yielded at all.

Charles Town oligarchs might conciliate the back country in a pinch, but they swore no vows of equality and fraternity. Adopting the first state constitution in the spring of 1776, they kept the existing apportionment for the lower house: 138 for the low country and 64 for the more populous north. They also resisted Christopher Gadsden's urgings that they strike for independence, being content to justify their government as a stopgap "until an accommodation of the unhappy differences . . . can be obtained (an event which, though traduced and treated as rebels, we still earnestly desire)." They not only resisted the old Lion of Liberty (now senior colonel in the South Carolina forces), they resented his loud irreverencies. For he was taking his text at this point from Paine's *Common Sense*. Returning from the Continental Congress to assume his military post, he had brought along to laggard Charles Town that stirring impeachment of kings—and ruling classes. Gadsden thundered, no doubt, that "government, even in its best state, is but a necessary evil," that the "palaces of kings are built upon the ruins of the bowers of paradise." This would have seemed at best a maudlin proposition to men bent not so much on undermining the King's rule as on shoring up their own. If he thundered a corollary Paine proposition—that "one honest man" was worth more "to society, and in the sight of God, than all the crowned ruffians that ever lived"—they probably jeered aloud. For that was to insinuate that Gadsden's mechanic rabble was fit to consort with rice planters.

Not surprisingly, they failed to vote Gadsden an office. As president they chose John Rutledge and as vice-president Henry Laurens, both of whom still wanted to patch up the quarrel with England. Still officially a delegate to the Continental Congress, Rutledge had returned a few months earlier to attend his legal and planting affairs, knowing full well that weightier business was afoot in Charles Town than in Philadelphia. Charles Town was a seat of government and a source of power. Philadelphia offered by contrast a forum, where men risked boring each other to death. For no central colonial government as yet existed. The delegates could "suggest," but they lacked the usual screws for enforcing suggestions. They levied no taxes and paid out no money.

The Continental Congress did, however, plan as best it could a joint defense of the colonies. Anticipating a British attack to the south early in 1776, it ordered Major General Charles Lee in command of a newly erected Southern Department. Uncertain as to where the blow would fall, Lee went to Charles Town early in June, arriving almost on the dot with a British fleet comprising nine warships and more than thirty troop transports.

He found President Rutledge manning a command post as chief of the South Carolina forces, pushing work on the harbor fortifications and posting militiamen as they came in from neighboring parishes and, significantly, from the upcountry as well. (One of Andrew Jackson's uncles, Captain Robert Crawford, led a company down from the Waxhaws, 200 miles away.) Having marched with British and European armies and not exactly hiding his past from colonials, Lee brought confidence to the frightened city. He also brought a dictatorial manner, offending Carolina gentlemen as he snapped them around in blazing June. So Rutledge had to order that Lee was "to be obeyed." The President, however, reserved the ultimate power of decision or at least the right to argue with the General. On the critical point, for instance, of whether to man the half-built fort on Sullivan's Island (its guns commanding the harbor from the north) or to abandon it, as Lee insisted, and defend the mainland, Rutledge argued and won his case. He did more than argue. He sent the following message to Colonel William Moultrie:

> *Genl. Lee wishes you to evacuate the Fort, you will not do so without an order from me.*
> *I will cut off my right hand sooner than write it.*

Lee thought the fort "could not hold out half an hour," and in theory he was right. Accident alone upheld the President.

In leisurely eighteenth-century fashion the British waited five days to begin the battle. On June 9 Sir Henry Clinton landed troops on Long Island (now the Isle of Palms) just north of Sullivan's. But there he stalled and there he stayed, unable to cross the body of water between the islands: boats ran aground on the shallows, and wading soldiers plumped into seven-foot holes. Sir Henry's force of between two and three thousand men could only dig into the sand among the myrtle thickets and fire across the water at the South Carolinians and Continentals behind their palmetto-log emplacements. To Admiral Sir Peter Parker, then, was left "the glory of being defeated alone."

Taking more than two weeks to ready his fleet for action, Sir Peter finally moved in on the 28th and started a "furious and incessant cannonade" against the Sullivan's Island fort, under command of Colonel William Moultrie. Enough metal was thrown at the fort to blast it to pieces, but incredibly it held together and its guns returned the British fire all through the day and into the evening. The secret of its strength lay, of course, in its palmetto-log construction. Used because they grew thickly on the island, the spongy palmettos absorbed the shot. Though they quivered under simultaneous broadsides from three and four ships, the walls stood fast. When the flagstaff was cut away at one point, Sergeant William Jasper, of the 2nd South Carolina Regiment, climbed out through an embrasure and at the risk of his life remounted the blue flag with its white crescent and its bold emblazonment of "Liberty." It takes nothing away from his heroism to wonder if he had refreshed himself from the grog-laden fire buckets which Colonel Moultrie said were passed along the platform, remarking that he "never had a more agreeable draught than that which I took out of one of those buckets." What with the June heat and the smoke and roar of cannon the defenders had, Moultrie concluded, "a very honorable situation, but a very unpleasant one."

The Carolinians did heavy damage to the fleet, but a stroke of luck brought the advantage they needed to dissuade the British. It also vindicated the President's decision. Three of the British ships, swinging around to enfilade the fort, grounded on a shoal and, sitting there as targets to the shore guns and obstructions to the rest of the fleet, ignominiously helped the rebels to victory. By nine o'clock all firing had stopped, and Sir Peter withdrew his battered fleet under cover of night, leaving not only Charles Town but the entire South free of danger for more than two years.

The province's last royal governor, Lord William Campbell, who had been urging the attack on Charles Town ever since his humiliating flight the previous September, sailed off with injuries that were to cause his death two years later. He lay wounded among 131 of his fellows. The British had 64 men killed outright, by contrast with the Americans, who lost only 12 and counted 25 wounded.

It must have been hard for Colonel Gadsden to stand his tame Fort Johnson watch while guns boomed across the harbor, but he could doubly rejoice—in vindication no less than victory. A day's gunfire had probably worked more conversions to the independence cause than his oratorical volleys had wrought in a decade. With Carolinians lying dead, who would dare insist that George III cared a straw for all the weaseling colonial pledges of loyalty?

Certainly the battle encouraged Charles Town to rejoice when news came in August of the Declaration of Independence. It must also have prepared the Assembly for unanimity in hailing the establishment of "free and independent States" as an event "which every friend to justice and humanity must not only hold justifiable . . . but equally rejoice in, as the only security against . . . oppression and the most promising source of future liberty and safety."

One battle, however, could not root out Carolina's filial piety. She had quarreled with her mother country, but always in the spirit of loyal opposition. Not a few Carolinians must have felt as Henry Laurens did when the news reached Charles Town of the signing in Philadelphia. "I wept that day," he later wrote, "as I had done for the melancholy catastrophe which caused me to put on black clothes—the death of a son, and felt much more pain."

British identity would remain so deeply rooted in John Rutledge that two years later he would resign the presidency rather than agree to a new Carolina constitution that severed the final tie. He must have seemed at the time to act in paradox and to speak in riddles, but his remarks suggest that he was thinking impossibly ahead of his time. He believed reunion with Britain "as desirable now as it ever was" but hoped nonetheless for "a peace which will secure the sovereignty and independence of America." He may have spoken in simple perplexity of feeling: wanting to be a free Carolinian, he yet wanted to remain a loyal Briton. But it sounds as though he had pondered a kind of union that would not come to pass until the twentieth century in the British Commonwealth of Nations.

VIII

"Not Too Ragged to Fight"

Sometime during the afternoon of May 12, 1780, General Sir Henry Clinton arrived with his red-coated staff at the Miles Brewton mansion on lower King Street. Uninvited, he was probably not unexpected. For the widowed Rebecca Brewton Motte, who had lived there since the loss of her brother and family at sea in 1775, had no doubt been warned of his approach by a scouting slave. Otherwise she would simply have guessed that the conqueror of Charles Town would choose its stateliest dwelling for his quarters.

Though Mrs. Motte devoutly confessed the patriot faith, she greeted her enemy guests with a smile and perhaps a bit of a curtsy. A gentle mien might bring out their gentle best, and she did after all have three young daughters tucked away under the sun-baked garret roof. As a charming hostess she might also in time charm from her guests some useful intelligence for nearby patriot forces.

If Mrs. Motte did anticipate playing the spy, it was well for her morale that she could not know how victorious the British really were. In taking Charles Town after a month's siege they had consummated their drive to crush armed resistance in the Southern colonies. General Benjamin Lincoln's surrender of the garrison that morning—which historians account "one of the greatest disasters suffered by the Americans during the whole war"—had meant losing the only sizable force in the Southern Department and the last remaining warships.

Sir Henry Clinton capped his triumph by sending militiamen home as prisoners on parole, free of all restraint so long as they hoed a neutral row. Though he made prisoners of the whole Charles Town citizenry, he gave simultaneous parole and sent them also about their normal business. His lenient course made such quick friends that when he shortly offered similar terms to all who submitted, militia grounded their muskets at various points throughout the state.

From this auspicious beginning Sir Henry might well have gone on to lead South Carolina back along the road to full crown allegiance. In the first place, many Carolinians—of those who cared one way or another—rejoiced at Charles Town's fall as the removal of a lawless barrier from the King's own highway. And the rest apparently did not put on sackcloth and ashes. Given peace at the price of going back home to sow and reap and sell, they could swallow a fair amount of gall.

Initially perhaps the least rebellious of the colonies, South Carolina had barely glimpsed the malignant face of war, suffering few of the wounds that harden the soul. If the battle of Sullivan's Island had blunted some of the keenest hopes for reconciliation, it had not united the body politic in defiance. As a spur to the American cause, it was a triumph too easily won, leaving a self-contented mood that no event would ruffle for more than two years.

In fact, after driving off the British fleet in the summer of 1776 the colony enjoyed a long interlude of peace and profit. Military forces moved to put down the restive Cherokee Indians that summer and fall, and they forayed briefly against the British in Georgia the following year, but otherwise they languished in garrison. That is, those whom the state could induce to serve on the pay they got in declining local currency. Farmer and planter soldiers (militiamen subject to emergency call) found it more gainful to repine at home. They could sell every scrap they could raise in Charles Town, where, as a contemporary observed, trading fortunes were never made so quickly. Wagons hauled north what ships brought from Europe or what legal piracy garnered from British ships passing nearby.

During this period the General Assembly drafted and voted a Constitution that asserted the rights of a free people to govern themselves, so alarming the Anglophilic President Rutledge that he resigned his office. He claimed objection to certain "democratic" innovations but significantly did not oppose the more radical move to disestablish the Anglican Church. Other conservatives demurred at this Gadsdenian measure, but the legislature unanimously concluded to exempt dissenters from fiscal genuflection at the King's altars.

Charles Town's season of safety ended in late 1778 when the British captured Savannah, Georgia, less than a hundred miles down the coast, obviously aiming to drive northward. A frantic plea for help to the Continental Congress yielded a miniscule force and the advice that South Carolina and Georgia should arm 3,000 slaves, offering freedom if they served to the end of the war. Congress would foot the bill. Though George Washington took a dim view of the scheme, pointing out that the British, with more arms at their disposal, might readily improve on the example, both Henry Laurens and William Henry Drayton endorsed it, and Laurens' son Lieutenant Colonel John Laurens was commissioned to carry the plan to Charles Town. An eager emancipationist himself, John Laurens hoped to raise and command a black regiment, declaring it would be "my duty and my pride to transform the timid slave into a firm defender of liberty & render him worthy to enjoy it himself." But Carolina slaveholders harbored no such knightly dedications, and they hotly rebuffed the young colonel when he argued his case to the legislature.

Encouraging his son in defeat, Henry Laurens wrote that it was "a great task . . . to persuade rich men to part . . . with the very source of their wealth." Though he had blinked that unhappy truth, the younger man was not meeting it for the first time in his life. In fact, he had not too long since written his father that Southerners invariably quibbled about slavery; "but it was easy to perceive that they considered only their own advantage. . . . Indeed when driven from anything else, they generally exclaimed: Without slaves how is it possible for us to be rich?"

Declining to arm her black "domestic enemy," South Carolina, with Tarheel assistance, gave General Lincoln troops enough to try an invasion of Georgia in April, 1779. As Lincoln crossed the Savannah River and marched toward Augusta, however, the British General Augustine Prevost crossed from the opposite shore and headed toward Charles Town, meeting only token objection from General William Moultrie as he retreated northward. But where the hero of Fort Sullivan failed to block the British drive, avarice providentially delayed it. Prevost's men could not resist calling at plantation houses along the way to seek out coin, jewelry and silver plate. While they dawdled to loot, Charles Town threw up defenses to the south and assembled enough troops from the countryside to dissuade Prevost from immediate attack. Instead he deployed his army before the freshly turned earthworks and called for surrender.

Governor Rutledge (re-elected to the office he had formerly held as president) offered to give up the city on condition that the harbor and the rest of the state be regarded as neutral until the end of the war. What moved him no one precisely knows. Even at this unlikely juncture he might have been courting the British crown. That inveterate jumper at conclusions, Christopher Gadsden, believed so, for he leaped up with the charge of treason to the American cause. Rutledge may have thought to save the state from ruin, but it is possible he was only stalling for time, hoping to immobilize Prevost until General Lincoln could arrive from Georgia.

Prevost declined, however, to treat with anyone but General Moultrie, whose answer that "We will fight it out," along with the threat from Lincoln, prompted a British removal to John's Island. After Lincoln attacked him there in June, Prevost withdrew his army in boats along the sea islands to Beaufort.

Ramsay's remark that soon after Lincoln's attack the impatient militia "generally returned to their homes" suggests one good reason why the British were able to subdue Charles Town and the rest of the state less than a year later. The militiamen came and went as they pleased, spurning all authority, since it could only punish with a small fine for insubordination and a few months' sentence to the Continental lines for desertion. The militia were so jealous of their personal freedom that they would risk losing it for life rather than cede it for an hour. Under the stress of imminent siege in February, 1780, for instance, the legislature eagerly handed Governor Rutledge almost every power of government except the one he most needed— the right to "subject the militia to articles of war." He could not, in other words, hold the death sentence over the heads of fractious or fickle citizen soldiers.

In arming Rutledge with unusual but temporary powers the Assembly acted from warnings of a peril to Charles Town that could

scarcely have been overdrawn. For Sir Henry Clinton was not chanc-
ing the prize a second time: he sailed up the coast from Savannah
with ninety transports and fourteen fighting ships in his train. The
fleet put 6,000 men ashore on John's Island. In the next few weeks
Clinton encircled the city without snapping a trigger, for General
Lincoln, instead of posting approach defenses, had chosen to huddle
his 5,000 troops behind breastworks on the peninsula. This arrange-
ment was doubtless easier on a gouty and rheumatic general need-
ing two orderlies to stretch a tunic across his splendid belly, but it
was fatal to Charles Town. Lincoln did try to keep a way open to
the north by sending mounted troops to the head of Cooper River,
but Clinton's hard-riding chief of dragoons, Banastre Tarleton,
routed this force in April. After that Clinton could make his kill at
leisure, though he had hung fire so long already that he seemed to
hope the defenders would collapse from nervous exhaustion.

When Clinton's ranks moved to within yards of the defending
lines on the peninsula, Lincoln wanted to evacuate or sue for terms,
but Lieutenant Governor Gadsden and his Council bellowed damna-
tion on both alternatives. One councilor raged that the townspeople
would burn their boats and join the British in pursuit if the American troops tried to get away. Acting on his own, Lincoln offered
surrender, but Clinton, of course, rejected his naïve (or nervy) condition that both the army and the American ships in the harbor be
allowed to retire from the scene.

Negotiations were carried on intermittently, however, until May
9, when the fortifications erupted in a cannonade, which the British
thunderously answered. A mere outburst of sound and fury, the
exchange left the British unmoved and brought unnecessary damage
on the city. After a night of horror, when it seemed to Moultrie
"as if the stars were falling to the earth," the townsmen were ready
to submit on any terms.

This was the Revolution, then, as Carolina had known it when
Clinton presumed with a heel-clicking bow on Mrs. Motte's hospitality and allayed fears with his bounteous reprieves. Only a strip
of coast had felt the gouges of a plundering army. The rest of the
state had scarcely seen a redcoat, much less seen cattle led away or
corn fired in the fields. Charles Town itself, though damaged, did not

by any means lie a smoking ruin. Shops were open, food was coming
in from the neighborhood, and wholesale merchants rubbed their
hands at the prospect of resuming trade with England. Even the
soldiery took heart at the mildness of their captors. The Continental
officers were a bit crowded in their camp at Haddrell's Point, but
they could entertain their families and apparently they did not go
thirsty, for they incited their guards to a stricter watch when they
drank too many toasts at a July 4 dinner. Aboard the prison ships
anchored in the harbor, private soldiers doubtless lacked for Madeira,
but they had plenty of bread and molasses, for the British hoped
to sweeten them up for an invitation to fight for the King.

On June 3 Sir Henry Clinton wrecked any chance he might have
had of winning South Carolina back to the crown: he canceled all
paroles, except those of the Charles Town citizenry and garrison,
and outlawed all who failed to swear British allegiance by June 20.
Allegiance implied shouldering a musket for the British, an onerous
prospect, as Clinton surely knew. But his duty was to restore to the
King his rightful subjects as well as to crush rebellion: the logic
of loyalty permitted no man to stand idly neutral while his fellow
subjects fought a war. Admitting his initial error, Clinton published
a rectifying order. Then, deputizing Lord Cornwallis, he sailed north,
sure that he had pacified a province, free of any notion that he had
roused it from lethargy instead.

William Gilmore Simms' Revolutionary novel *The Partisans* opens
with the reading of Clinton's order to the people of a garrison village
near Charles Town. Among the crowd are Major Singleton, who is
secretly recruiting a troop for Francis Marion's partisan regiment,
and a simplehearted youth, whom he has already induced to tear up
his British "protection." The stripling can't understand why it
pleases the major to "listen to such villainy as this," but, of course,
the major is pleased at his companion's displeasure. As he later
explains, the British action is a "grand one for our cause: it must
bring out . . . those who skulked for safety into contracts, measuring
honor by acres, and counting their duty to their country by the value
of their crops." Though "with us in spirit . . . they thought to avoid
danger, while they believe themselves unable to serve us by their
risk." Now, compelled to fight, they must choose between the

British and their friends and neighbors, even their own blood kin. He counts on their pride and parochial affections, of course, to dictate the choice.

His uncle Colonel Walton, of "The Oaks," is one of the honorables he knows the proclamation will incite, but he makes doubly sure. When the colonel asks after the crops at his nephew's place on the Santee, Singleton replies, "Such as the storm leaves us, good uncle. The tories have been sowing fire in my fields, and left it to ripen in lieu of corn and provender." Distressed for his nephew, the colonel is naturally concerned for his own fields. With heavy irony Singleton offers a safe course of action:

> *"Fear not for 'The Oaks,' uncle, so long as you keep cool, submit, swear freely, and subscribe humbly. Send now and then a trim present of venison and turkey to the captain's quarters, and occasionally volunteer to hang a poor countryman, who loves war to the knife better than degradation in a foreign chain. There can be no difficulty in keeping 'The Oaks,' uncle, if you only continue to keep your temper."*

The colonel soon pledges himself to valor, needless to say, more readily perhaps than some of his counterparts did in life but from a spirit not untypical of the actual planter gentry.

Before calling at The Oaks Singleton had led his recruits in their first enterprise, ambushing a party of Tory dragoons on the hunt for a patriot farmer named Frampton, who had killed one of their men. Having found his wife beaten to death in reprisal, Frampton had brought her body to the partisan hideout in the cypress swamps and sat holding her hand through the night and wildly cursing her murderers. After the ambush he had crept into the hut where a wounded Tory prisoner lay groaning and driven a knife into his heart. The unwounded prisoners had escaped a similar fate by joining the partisan ranks.

In these initial pages of his novel Simms accounts for the rise and draws the essential lines of the civil warfare that bloodied the Carolina woods and swamps for two years after the fall of Charles Town. British regulars and Continentals clashed in the major battles, but in numberless small encounters South Carolinians fought each other, waging perhaps the most savage warfare of the Revolution. Simms lays the killing of a wounded prisoner to a virtual madman, but as William Dobein James recalls in his memoir of General Francis Marion, prisoners had about as much chance of saving their skins as a treed possum.

British troops sent to occupy and subdue the rest of the state after Charles Town's fall added injury to Clinton's insult. The quickest in applying fire and sword to the countryside was Tarleton, the flinthearted twenty-six-year-old lieutenant colonel who forayed out of Camden, where Lord Rawdon commanded the chief interior post. On the march up from the coast in late May, Cornwallis had sent him in pursuit of Colonel Abraham Buford, then retiring to North Carolina after failing to reach Charles Town before the surrender. When Tarleton overtook and speedily overwhelmed his prey in the Waxhaws, Buford hoisted a white flag and ordered his men to ground arms. But Tarleton let his troops fall on the unarmed Americans or declined to intervene as they ranged the field slashing the fallen wounded. When they finally wearied of the slaughter, 113 of Buford's men lay dead and 200 wounded. Tarleton lost a bare handful. Whatever he gained for his chief by this exploit, he certainly gained an infamous name for himself. From that time on, when Carolinians gave "Tarleton's quarter" to a helpless redcoat, they finished him off.

On the horse-killing ride after Buford, Tarleton paused long enough for his men to ransack and burn the plantation of Thomas Sumter, thus rousing up a scrappy veteran soldier who in leading the back-country Scotch-Irish would prove, as Cornwallis said, "the greatest plague in this country." If Tarleton would never regret the provocation, he would come to respect the adversary it put in the field. At least he would concede the justice of his *nom de guerre*— the Carolina Gamecock.

Tradition claims that Sumter, warned by a neighbor, departed a few hours before Tarleton's dragoons reined up in his front yard, but he must have stayed close enough to learn of the pillage, for it is said to have "roused the spirit of the lion" and sent him roaring off in search of troops to lead. He may even have gnashed his teeth in a nearby thicket as his invalid wife was carried out of the house in her chair and the house set afire.

Though Sumter could hear the Charles Town guns on still days, he had abstained from the fight, perhaps thinking the British would fail again as in '76. He had campaigned for two years after Fort Moultrie, however, against the Cherokees and against the British in Georgia.

Riding into the Cherokee mountains in the fall of 1776, Sumter crossed trails he had traveled fifteen years earlier on an expedition from his native Virginia. In a sense, too, he betrayed old friendships. For in 1761 he had conducted three Cherokees to London for an audience with the King. Decked out in scarlet knee breeches and jackets, Sumter's charges rivaled the splash Sir Alexander Cumings' Cherokee vassals had made thirty-two years before. Sergeant Sumter might well have displayed his wards to better advantage than the Scottish baronet, for he is said to have found gold pickings among the coins thrown by gentlemen sightseers. The frontier soldier came home, a contemporary reported, "a changed and elegant man," in dress, at least, for he strutted through Williamsburg in scarlet and gold lace.

He had returned by way of Charles Town, traversing as he rode to the Cherokee nation the region he was to settle in a year later when he fled imprisonment for debt in Virginia. Here—in the Carolina middle country—he would vigorously court fortune and fame, first courting a well-to-do widow.

Having goaded Sumter to action, Tarleton just missed capturing Governor Rutledge a few hours later. In fleeing Charles Town Rutledge had traveled no farther than Camden, perhaps hoping to establish a makeshift capital thereabouts or lingering to scout British intentions before riding on to safety in North Carolina. At any rate he was stopping the night of May 28 just above Camden at the plantation of a well-known loyalist, Colonel Henry Rugely. It seems an odd roof to have sought, but the colonel was a Carolina gentleman. No doubt he and the Governor had sipped a glass together in Charles Town during the colonel's trading career. The Governor's trust was not misplaced, apparently, for Rugely routed him from bed and wished him Godspeed when news came of Tarleton's approach.

As Rutledge carried the civil government to North Carolina exile, Sumter was recruiting men east of the Catawba River, where a volunteer band had voted him their general. He swelled his ranks considerably by striking the first successful blow against the British since the Charles Town surrender, routing a sizable force under a Tarleton legionnaire. Though he shortly afterwards failed to dislodge the enemy from their strong position at Hanging Rock, in the present Lancaster County, Sumter inflicted so many casualties and nabbed so many horses and guns that he was not far wrong in thinking he had won a signal victory. It might have been more signal, though, if his men had not all flopped down in the British camp to engage with captured bottles. Loath to engage the enemy with a stupified soldiery, the General withdrew, remarking that it wasn't good "to pursue a victory too far."

While Sumter hardened opposition to Tarleton along the Catawba, partisans were gathering west of the Pee Dee River to fight back at the vandalizing Tory Major James Wemyss. To organize their resistance Governor Rutledge sent Francis Marion, then a lieutenant colonel in the Continental lines but later to be a Carolina militia brigadier. Unknown to the men who received him on Lynch's Creek in early August, the swarthy little figure in scarlet coat and leather cap was soon to command both their trust in his fighting skill and their esteem for his character. If his *nom de guerre*—the Swamp Fox—suggests the wily tactics he necessarily devised to operate in swamp country with an outnumbered force, it also implies his compassion for his troops. As General Peter Horry is represented as saying in Parson Weems', panegyric of Marion, "he steadily pursued the warfare most *safe* for *us,* and most fatal to our enemies." Striking usually from the woods, he drew quick blood and faded back into the woods as the enemy recovered and disposed itself to battle.

Though still on active duty at the time, Marion was, like Sumter, missing from Charles Town when the city fell. From his plantation home, Pond Bluff, on the Santee, he too could hear the siege guns, but he had come home on orders to nurse an ankle sprain acquired, so the legend goes, when violating an old Charles Town custom, hospitality by *force majeure,* so to speak. A grave and temperate man, he did not appreciate his host's locking the door until guests had done full justice to his wine cellar. Decamping through a window, Marion incurred his first wound in four years of active duty. Having sweated through the cannonade at Fort Moultrie in '76, he had served continuously with state troops thereafter.

A day or two after his arrival on Lynch's Creek Marion led his partisan "army" to disperse a body of Tories at Britton's Neck, using for the first time, so Major William James reports, the maneuver which so endeared him to his own men and so disconcerted the orthodox British military: seeing his force outnumbered, he feigned retreat, then disposed his sharpshooters in the woods to ambush the unsuspecting Tories. Having served with Marion as a boy of fourteen, Major James recalls this action, and, in fact, every move the General made, with awe, as though he had marched with Charlemagne against the Saracens in Spain. And yet he seems to reflect accurately the idolatry Marion inspired in all his men. Any one of them, probably, would have thought it "an honor," as the young James did on one occasion, "to be invited to dine with the General" (in place of his father, then absent from the camp). Somehow in his wooden phrases James conveys the impression that he sat like a cup-bearer in the circle of the gods:

> *The dinner was set before the company by the general's servant, Oscar, partly on a pine log, and partly on the ground; it was lean beef, without salt, and sweet potatoes. The author had left a small pot of boiled hominy in his camp, and requested leave of his host to send for it; and the proposal was acquiesced in gladly. The hominy had salt in it [salt was a very scarce commodity during the Revolution], and proved, although eaten out out of the pot, a most acceptable repast. The general said but little, and that was chiefly what a son would be most likely to be gratified by, in the praise of his father. They had nothing to drink but bad water; and all the company appeared to be rather grave.*

With Sumter and Marion harassing the British, the time was propitious for Continental forces to strike for recovery of the state by knocking out Cornwallis' post at Camden. But Congress, without bothering to consult Washington, sent forth to galvanize the effort their martial favorite, General Horatio Gates, who at Saratoga, as Parson Weems expresses it, "got his temples stuck round with laurels as thick as a May-day queen with gaudy flowers." Shrugging off a friend's advice that he take care "lest your Northern laurels turn to Southern willows," Gates galloped down to North Carolina, took ceremonious command from the able Baron de Kalb, and then, ignoring all cautions, force-marched half-sick and hungry troops to what has been called "the most disastrous defeat ever inflicted on an American army." Poorly disposed for an attack on Camden the night of August 15, Gates' army met instead a sudden British onslaught which so confused and terrified the Americans that thousands of men and officers—the center and the left wing of the attacking line —threw down their muskets and ran "raving along the roads and by-paths towards the north." Leading the frightened pack was General Gates, astride the fastest horse in the army, not relaxing his spurs until he reached Charlotte, sixty miles away. The right wing alone held the field, Maryland and Delaware Continentals under General Mordecai Gist and de Kalb. They fought a hand-to-hand battle for more than an hour, finally giving way at the sweep of Tarleton's cavalry. The Americans lost two-thirds of their 3,000-man force in killed, wounded and captured.

Tarleton followed up the Camden triumph by falling on Sumter, in careless rest on Fishing Creek, collaring 300 men and nearly a thousand horses. Sumter himself, caught lying in the shade of a wagon, leaped to his mount and fled, minus coat, hat and saddle. The fiasco did not lower his stock, however, for a considerable force gathered around him in Charlotte a few days later.

At this point Cornwallis faced no strong opposition in the state, but he encountered the hazards of summer fever, sniping partisans and growing ire among the people. In haste to finish the job of pacification, he now effected a scourge that alienated all but the most fanatic loyalists or craven moneybags. He ordered the gallows for every man who had deserted redcoat for patriot ranks, rigorous punishment for those who had broken parole and jail for those who had refused to bear arms for the King. Hangings began at once, and numbers were clapped in jail. In line with these measures Cornwallis banished sixty-three prominent Carolinians to St. Augustine, Florida, on vague charges of stirring up rebellion. They remained there until exchanged for British prisoners some months later, Christopher Gadsden sitting alone in jail rather than take parole from captors he judged blackguards for carting him out of Charles Town.

An order sequestering all rebel property brought Cornwallis in

September tardy felicitations on his Camden victory from 164 prudently "loyal inhabitants of Charles Town," but otherwise it only added one more link in the chain of explosives the British were laying for their own blowup. Cornwallis intended it, of course, as a final link in the chain of subjugation, and he confidently moved his army north to subdue and yoke rebellious Tarheels—and even Virginians—in like fashion. He planned a three-column drive: his main army in the center, Tarleton sweeping up the coast in his right, and Major Patrick Ferguson, already operating in the back country, striking northward in the shadow of the western mountains.

Cornwallis himself ran into trouble at Charlotte, but Ferguson met worse trouble in the foothills, the threatened descent of 3,000 "overmountain men" (from across the Blue Ridge), riled up at his braggart demand that they stop opposing the King or take the consequences: he would march over the mountains himself, hang their leaders and desolate their country. As brave an officer as the British had in the field, Ferguson nonetheless saw that he could not stand to this boast against a force three times larger than his, and he kited for Charlotte. Under their colonels—Shelby, McDowell, Sevier, Campbell and Cleveland—acting more or less as a democratic council of command, the mountaineers followed close on his trail, armed with tomahawks, scalping knives and their long lethal Deckhard rifles. They were not so much an army as a voluntary band of proud and resourceful freemen gathering like Scotch clansmen to head off invasion. As Major James says:

> Gunpowder they had already learnt to prepare from the saltpetre in their caves, and lead they dug out of their mines. Dried venison satisfied their hunger, pure water slaked their thirst, and at the side of a rock they enjoyed comfortable repose. Armed with rifles, sure to hit the white speck on the target, at the distance of one hundred paces, or to decapitate the wild turkey on the top of the tallest pine—these were indeed a formidable band.

They caught up with the fleeing Tories on October 7 at King's Mountain, a rocky and wooded outlying spur of the Blue Ridge in the present York County, where Ferguson had encamped with the reported gasconade that "he was on King's Mountain, that he was king of that mountain and that God Almighty could not drive him from it." He did occupy a position of extraordinary natural strength, but the attack came as a surprise, it was mounted and sustained with driving force, and the thickly wooded slopes gave such protective cover that the assaulting frontiersmen were able to shoot in safety as they scrambled from tree to tree. As the rebels gained the crest and dashed out onto the open plateau, Ferguson exhorted his men to the bayonet and drove them back, but they only dropped down into the fringes of the woods and picked off the unprotected Tories with their rifles. Caught in a ring of sharpshooters, the Tories could see that they were whipped, but Ferguson would not give up. Twice he cut down white flags with his own sword, and to an officer who begged him to stop the carnage he snorted that he "would never surrender to such banditti." But at last, admitting that the battle was lost, he tried to cut a way through the ring of his enemies and caught a volley of shots that toppled him from his horse. He died with one foot caught in his stirrup.

A white flag went up immediately, but it was some time before the mountaineers ceased fire, partially, as Colonel Shelby reported, because men ignorant of events came on shooting up the slopes and because "some who had heard that at Buford's defeat, the British had refused quarters . . . were willing to follow that bad example." No doubt many a Tory died with the shout of "Tarleton's quarter" ringing in his ears.

Nearly 700 Tories fell into rebel hands, all Americans. In fact, everybody on the mountain, dead or alive, was American except Major Ferguson, a regular in the British Army. Tory casualties were 157 killed and 163 wounded so badly that they had to be left on the field. The patriots lost 28 killed and 62 wounded. The battle had lasted perhaps an hour. Both victor and vanquished spent the night on the field "amid the dead and the groans of the dying, who had neither surgical aid nor water to quench their thirst."

The dead were buried next day but, as one soldier wrote, insufficiently, being

> *thrown into convenient piles and covered with old logs, the*
> *bark of old trees and rocks, yet not so as to secure them from*
> *becoming a prey to the beasts of the forest, or the vultures of*

the air; and the wolves [later] became so plenty, that it was
dangerous for anyone to be out at night for several miles around.
Also the hogs in the neighborhood gathered into the place to
devour the flesh of men. . . . *Half of the dogs in the country were*
said to be mad and were put to death. I saw myself in passing the
place, a few weeks after, all parts of the human frame.

The victory at King's Mountain turned the tide of war in the
South. It frosted Cornwallis' hopes for the conquest of North Carolina and sent him back along his now muddy path to encamp at
Winnsboro, his army worn out with partisan harassments and racked
with fever. It meant a campaign to retake South Carolina, with fewer
loyalists to count on and more snipers on his flanks. For King's
Mountain had veered the weathercocks from the crown and embold-
ened timid patriots. Ten days after the battle Sumter was rumored
chasing Tarleton with thousands in his train.

The rumor was more wish than fact, though after his capture of
the notorious Major Wemyss in November Sumter's force did increase to a thousand. Shortly afterwards he gave Tarleton a sharp
blow, incurring a wound, however, that disabled him for weeks.
Hearing that he was "speechless, and . . . past all hopes," Cornwallis
rejoiced to be rid of his "greatest plague" and wished—to Lord
Rawdon—that "your friend Marion was as quiet." The joy was premature. By no means gasping his last, Sumter needed only time—
though hardly as much as he took. Sometimes compared to Ajax,
he was at this stage playing Achilles, sulking in his tent because the
new Southern Department commander, General Nathanael Greene,
had assigned a Continental brigadier, Daniel Morgan, to join him
for a mission west of the Catawba. A militia brigadier, Sumter would
automatically take second place. The Gamecock's hackles were also
up at Continental slurs on militia, Greene having said (by letter) that
"partisan strokes in war are like the garnish of a table," useful but
affording "no substantial national security." He also insinuated that
Sumter's motives were not of the purest, writing that "Plunder and
depradation prevails, so in every quarter I am [afraid] all this
Country will be laid waste. Most people appear to be in pursuit of
private gain or personal glory."

While the peevish Sumter nursed his wounds, Greene marched

to camp at Cheraw with half the Continental force then at Charlotte, and Morgan set out with the balance to operate west of the Catawba. At Winnsboro Cornwallis acted instantly to counter the threat, sending a force to Camden and another under Tarleton to find Morgan and "push him to the utmost." He himself would lead the main army into North Carolina to intercept and destroy the remains of Morgan's force, which he expected to run from Tarleton.

Maneuvered into a stand at Cowpens, near the Broad River just south of the North Carolina line, Morgan scored on January 17 a triumph that heartened the whole country. He chose an unlikely spot for the battle—a fairly open plain ideal for Tarleton's cavalry and with a swollen river behind—offering the churlish justification later that he needed a swollen river at his back to keep the militia from running away. But he disposed his troops so well that he was able to repulse a British force that outnumbered his two to one, thoroughly drubbing and routing the ineffable Tarleton for the first time in his American career. As he raced toward Cornwallis with the news, Tarleton left three fourths of his thousand men captured, killed or wounded.

Both Congress and the states passed out rewards and honors to the officers responsible for the coup. And well they might, for the battle though "small in scale" was "momentous in result." It cleared the way for Greene's campaign of "dazzling shiftiness," a campaign that led his opponent by "an unbroken chain of consequences to the catastrophe at Yorktown" and American independence.

Emerging from his tent of disaffection in February, Sumter led an unsuccessful foray against British posts on the Congaree, failing partially because too few men would or could leave spring plowing to join in the action. Since his followers got no pay in the field, except in pickings from the enemy or from hapless Tory farms along the road, and since they left their families helpless when they rode off to fight, they were pardonably spasmodic in answering the call to arms. To correct this deficiency Sumter tried substituting controlled plunder for random pillage. He would seize loyalist property for the state, in other words, and pay the military therefrom on a scale adjusted to the value of Negroes, the range to run from one slave per private to three and a half per lieutenant colonel. A bold remedy, surely, and it sounded feasible, but it only spurred patriots and Tories to worse eye-for-eye rapacities and attracted muckworms to the ranks.

While Sumter was operating ineffectually along the Congaree, Marion was giving the British a run in the country south, having aid from Virginian Colonel Henry Lee's crack Legion. To the north Greene was losing battles but slowly winning a war by attrition. Bowing to Lord Rawdon at Camden, he did such damage and raised such a scare that Rawdon decided to evacuate. His departure from that strategic point marked the beginning of the end for the British in South Carolina.

In May, Sumter and Marion justified Rawdon's fears by knocking out the British posts between Camden and Charles Town. The action at one of these—Fort Motte, Mrs. Rebecca Motte's stockaded plantation house on the south bank of the Congaree—gave the lady herself a second chance to prove her devotion to the American cause. Her first chance had materialized after all: she had kept up a lively correspondence with General Marion from Charleston by means of her slave women, who could pass unsuspiciously through the lines with a basket of yams on their turbaned heads. Perhaps fearing that her guests would at last smell a rat, however, she had begged passage through the lines herself, only to greet another troupe of enemy guests on the Congaree. This time she had to vacate her mansion and shelter in a nearby farmhouse.

There she entertained Colonel Lee while his men readied a siege position to the north of Fort Motte. (General Marion was to advance from the east.) If Lee's manners were as stately as the prose of his *Memoirs*, the "rustic abode" must have borrowed for a term the atmosphere of a London palace:

> *Nor was the attention of this amiable lady confined to that class of war which never fail to attract attention. While her richly-spread table presented with taste and fashion all the luxuries of her opulent country, and her sideboard offered without reserve the best wines of Europe—antiquated relics of happier days—her active benevolence found its way to the sick and the wounded; cherishing with softest kindness infirmity and misfortune, converting despair into hope, and nursing debility into strength.*

As far as the reader is concerned, Lee might as well have been in London, for no vulgar detail mars the Johnsonian grandeur of his generality. Alas for the social historian, most eighteenth-century observers effused the same pomposities.

When Lord Rawdon arrived from Camden, Marion and Lee decided to hasten the assault by firing the "fort" with bow and arrow in the Indian manner. They adopted this plan reluctantly, hating to destroy the property of such a generous partisan, one, moreover, whose "only marriageable daughter was the wife of Major [Thomas] Pinckney, an officer in the South Carolina line . . . now a prisoner with the enemy." However, when the "embarrassed officer" broke the news to "this exemplary lady," she "instantly gave relief to his agitated feelings" by declaring that she was "gratified with the opportunity of contributing to the good of her country, and that she should view the approaching scene with delight." More than that, "seeing accidentally the bows and arrows which had been prepared," she sent for Lee and offered him some arrows "imported from India," which she thought "better adapted for the object."

Shot at the roof of the house, the arrows kindled a blaze in the dry shingles; and when soldiers tried to put it out, they were driven in by shots from Marion's fieldpiece. Realizing they were trapped, the British waved a white flag, and rebels and redcoats fraternized in dousing the flames. Then the officers fraternized at Mrs. Motte's "sumptuous" table, "soothing in the sweets of social intercourse the ire which the preceding conflict had engendered." The hostess presided with such impartial affability that, as Colonel Lee observed, no one could have told from her manner which was friend and which foe. The Americans were so at ease with the world by the pudding that they paroled their dinner companions to join Lord Rawdon on his retreat to Charles Town.

In the next few weeks the British vacated their remaining posts or surrendered them to Greene, Sumter, Marion or the third partisan chief, General Andrew Pickens. After the battle of Eutaw Springs, in fact, on September 8 (1781), the British were pretty well bottled up in Charles Town.

At Eutaw Springs, the last important battle in South Carolina—in the deep South, actually—the major state forces and their leaders (except Sumter, whose brigade fought under Pickens) joined with

Greene to engage the main British Army, now under Lord Rawdon's successor, Colonel Alexander Stewart. Greene's immediate purpose was to keep Stewart from marching north in aid of Cornwallis, squeezed on the Chesapeake Bay between Lafayette and Washington. Though Greene did head Stewart off and send him back to the coast, he just missed a victory that might have ended war in the state. As it turned out, however, Charles Town remained in British hands, and bitter contention raged for a year after Cornwallis' Yorktown surrender.

The armies that met at Eutaw Springs, on the Santee a few miles from Marion's plantation, Pond Bluff, matched each other fairly in strength—about 2,000 men apiece—and experience. Most had previously campaigned with the other side, for by the close of the war, as Greene said, "we fought the enemy with British soldiers; and they fought us with those of America." After a morning's clash, which Greene called "the most obstinate I ever saw," the redcoats gave ground and "had it not been for one of those little incidents which frequently happen in the progress of war, we should have taken the whole British army." Greene's "little incident" hides another wholesale patriot drunk. It was a steamy day, the boys were dry as a cornplowing mule, and they understandably found the enemy's bivouac tents more alluring than his spore. Their officers, accordingly, soon found themselves chasing redcoats with solitary pluck. Wheeling back to invite assistance, they found the boys, "utterly unmanageable," as one of them wrote, a trifle more bluntly than Greene. They had discovered in the British camp many "objects to tempt a thirsty, naked, and fatigued soldiery." Greene decided, as Sumter had on a like occasion, that one shouldn't "pursue a victory too far." Ordering a retreat, he led an exhausted and rum-soaked army toward the High Hills of Santee, leaving 139 dead on the field. Holding their Eutaw Springs position for the moment as nominal victors, the British counted much heavier losses.

Though Greene's army was too weak and poorly supplied to move toward the coast for some weeks, its presence in the state and the baleful news of Cornwallis' surrender in November, 1781, kept the British in edgy Charles Town confinement. Their immobility afforded patriots in some districts the first open season on Tories, who, of course, took to the swamps and struck back with knives and fire-brands in the night.

Nonetheless, Governor Rutledge, who had arrived at Greene's camp in August, decided to restore civil government and to that end ordered elections for legislators to meet in January, 1782, at the village of Jacksonborough, south of Charles Town. He also reorganized the state militia, falling in with Greene's plea that they be dismounted and parted from their horses for the sake of his dragoons and supply wagons. When the order was not enforced against Marion, Sumter took it as a personal cut. As he well knew, it arose less from Greene's need than from his odious notion that horses too readily sped militia from the battle scene with loads of plunder. Already disaffected, Sumter hung on for a time, but he had little heart for footslogging missions and in February, 1782, resigned from duty.

Along with most of the other military leaders, Sumter was elected to the legislature that met on schedule at Jacksonborough, under protection of Greene's army. There he was forced to hear, if not join in singing, hosannahs to "the great and gallant General Greene," whose "achievements in this State . . . will engrave his name in indelible characters on the heart of every friend to this country." Though Marion, Pickens and himself were only "deserving of the highest commendation," Greene was found deserving of an estate worth 10,000 guineas sterling value.

After praising its friends the legislature swore ruin to its foes, acting to banish from the state and confiscate the property of the most unregenerate Tories and to amerce the estates of others. A few men opposed this vindictive course, Christopher Gadsden for one, who in pleading for moderation in the name of charity distinguished himself more perhaps than he ever had in exhorting to violence in the name of freedom. He argued that the Confiscation Bill not only condemned men without hearing or trial but smacked of inquisitorial barbarities. Many estates were confiscated, nonetheless, most to be restored in time by the courts and the legislature.

Though the British Commons voted to stop the war on February 27, Charles Town remained in enemy hands for ten months longer, while peace commissioners talked in Paris. Encamped on the Ashley a dozen miles from the city, General Greene's army waited through spring, summer and fall, battling malaria and the vapors of inaction and grumbling at Congress' failure to send supplies. Greene complained to the President in March that "not a rag of clothing had come from the northward," that three hundred men were minus arms and a thousand "so naked . . . that they can only be put on duty in case of desperate necessity." He did not blame South Carolina for his plight. She gave what she could, but the foragings and plunderings of two years had left her little to give. For Greene's men she had only rice, a diet that might content the Carolina swamp fighter but only whetted the Continental soldier's appetite for beef and potatoes.

Returning to the state from his exile at British hands, General Moultrie made a "dull, melancholy, dreary ride" in September from Winyah Bay to Greene's camp through the woods of a country he "had been accustomed to see abound with live-stock and wild fowl of every kind" but which he now found "destitute of all." He observes that

> *not the vestiges of horses, cattle, hogs, or deer etc., were to be found. The squirrels and birds of every kind were totally destroyed. The dragoons told me that on their scouts no living creature was to be seen except now and then a few camp scavengers [turkey buzzards], picking the bones of some unfortunate fellows who had been shot or cut down and left in the woods above ground.*

On the journey he stopped off for the night at his own plantation, where,

> *as soon as the negroes discovered that I was of the party, there was immediately a general alarm and an outcry . . . that, "Massa was come! Massa was come!" and they were running from every part with great joy to see me. I stood in the piazza to see them. They gazed at me with astonishment, and every one came and took me by the hand, saying, "God bless you, Massa! I'm glad to see you, Massa!" and every now and then some one or other would come out with a "Ky!" and the old Africans joined in a war-song in their own language of "Welcome the war home."*

. . . The tears stole from my eyes and ran down my cheeks. . . .
I then possessed about two hundred slaves, and not one of them
left me during the war, although they had had great offers;
nay, some were carried down to work on the British lines, yet
they always contrived to make their escape and return home.

But moved as he was by the welcome from his slaves, the old war-
rior did not feel the ultimate joy in his coming home until he
marched with Greene's army into Charles Town on December 14,
as the British General Leslie loaded his troops, his train of depend-
ent Carolina Tories and his captive blacks aboard a fleet drawn up
in the harbor. Symbolically at least, Moultrie returned as deliverer
of a city he had been powerless to save in 1780, restoring it to the
proud state of independence he had helped it maintain in 1776. No
wonder he could "never forget the happy day," the elation at seeing
"the balconies, the doors and windows crowded with the patriotick
fair, the aged citizens and others congratulating us on our return
home, saying 'God bless you, gentlemen,'—'You are welcome, gentlemen.' " He does not vaunt himself, but he understandably enjoys
appearing as an "instrument of releasing his friends and fellow-
citizens from captivity."

For Moultrie only one regret marred the exultations of that day—
the absence from the procession of the men who had fought with
Marion and Sumter and Pickens. They were thought

too irregular, too ragged of raiment to share this triumph! They
were not too ragged to fight, only too ragged for show. It was a
most ungenerous and ungrateful exclusion from the scene of the
very men to whom the best part of the grand result was due!
They were disbanded here and there in swamp and thicket,
wherever the moment found them; disbanded without pay or
praise, naked, starving, having the world before them, but los-
ing from that moment all their customary guides but Providence!

Actually it was not any official shame of their ragged state that
denied them the triumph but apprehension of their temper. Governor Mathews and the Council feared that the sight of escaping Tories
might arouse partisan fury and turn a peaceful evacuation—pledged
on both sides—into a bloody free-for-all.

For the people of Charles Town one note was sadly missing from the jubilant sounds that echoed through the battered city all afternoon and half the night: the bells of St. Michael's. They had been dismounted and shipped off to England as a British officer's "perquisite." They had hung in the white spire for less than twenty years, but they had rung so often in those eventful years that they had come to speak for the city in her moment's of fulfillment or of loss. But perhaps the empty spire represented more appropriately than joyful bells the Carolina condition after more than two years of nightmarish wastage and killing.

IX

Tides of White and Black

When President George Washington arrived for a state visit in the spring of 1791, Charleston had regained her symbolic voice and her accustomed economic strength. Back home from England, the bells of St. Michael's rang out in welcome. Restored in fortune, the citizenry gave a weeklong salute to the national patriarch.

Washington attested Charleston's recovery from the dislocations of war when he sized up "The Inhabitants" as "wealthy—Gay & hospitable." He also attested his inveterately patrician caste of mind. Since he had not seen butchers' wives attended through the street by footmen in scarlet livery, he obviously meant inhabitants who counted—Rutledges, Pinckneys, Draytons, for instance, names that graced his Federalist party councils.

He might well have written "too hospitable," since they accorded him every known show of veneration, parading him daily through the streets, toasting him endlessly at formal dinners, dancing ceremoniously before him at balls and applauding him at musicales. From the time he arrived at Haddrell's Point in a "12-oared barge rowed by 12 American Captains of Ships, most elegantly dressed," until his carriage rolled south across the Ashley River attended by "the principal gentlemen of the city," he scarcely had a moment alone to remove those famously ill-fitting teeth.

Washington first received the embrace of South Carolina's coastal gentry when he arrived from the north at Clifton, Colonel William Alston's seat on the Waccamaw River, near Georgetown. His hostess in the "large, new, and elegantly furnished" manor house was the second Mrs. Alston, who as Mary Motte had crouched in the Brewton house garret while young British officers pined and tippled below. Though a truly magisterial discretion guided the President's journalizing pen, permitting no tribute to her charms, he must have been enraptured, for he granted her a lively utterance: he said that her husband's rice fields, then green with young shoots and glittering in the April sunshine, "looked like fairyland."

Approaching Charleston, the President turned off the highroad to breakfast at Hampton plantation with Mrs. Daniel Horry, widowed sister of Washington's friends Charles Cotesworth and Thomas Pinckney. The now venerable Eliza Lucas Pinckney made "her last public appearance," as her biographer phrases it, when she stood with her daughter between the columns of Hampton's new white portico to greet the visitor. (She may have curtsied as she once had to royalty, though as a Charleston lady mused in pondering the question, "She was a Southern lady, remember, and a Pinckney at that.")

Though housed alone by choice—wishing to avoid the appearance of favoritism—Washington was officially the Charleston guest of Governor Charles Pinckney, who may already have embraced the Jeffersonian heresies that would assure him Republican leadership in the state and ensure him lasting disrepute as a traitor to his Federalist class. No doubt, though, the two men got on well enough. Washington had a royal contempt for politics, and recollections of Philadelphia in 1787 would serve the uses of stately intercourse. Moreover, the Governor yielded nothing socially to a Washington, as the Carolina gentry would sadly have to remember through the coming years. Not even the epithet "Blackguard Charlie" could muddy the blue of his Pinckney blood or sever his cousinly bond with the immaculate brothers Charles Cotesworth and Thomas.

Washington's Diary suggests that the man behind the monumental front was unusually susceptible at fifty-nine or that Charleston's gentlewomen were as decorative as legend insists. Noting an afternoon call at his quarters by "a great number of the most respectable ladies of Charleston," he counts it an honor "as flattering as it was singular." At a "very elegant dancing Assembly" the same evening he apparently spent the hours in happy assessment, for he recorded exactly 256 "elegantly dressed & handsome ladies." But next evening's concert yielded "at least 400 ladies the number and appearance of wch. exceeded any thing of the kind I had ever seen." These are lyric outbursts for what is surely the most laconic diary on American record. Perhaps we must conclude that if the Father of His Country had a roving eye, Charleston gave it very pleasant excuses to rove. Or at least her women had the means to drape themselves in the costliest of lace and satin concealments and the art to brighten their malarial complexions.

Washington interrupted the festivities at midweek to examine the battle lines for the campaign of 1780, winding up "satisfied that the Defence [of Charleston] was noble and honorable" but "taken upon wrong principles and impolitic." Inspecting Fort Moultrie on another day, he found nothing to blame, as old General Moultrie himself re-enacted the triumph of 1776.

Traveling south from Charleston toward Savannah, the President stopped off at Mulberry Grove plantation in Georgia to ask General Greene's widow "how she did." He probably knew that she did rather poorly: Her debt-ridden husband had sold the estate given him by the state of South Carolina, and now she feared losing Georgia's bounty, her present home. Poor in a rich way, however, she still afforded summers in the North. Returning from her fever-season hegira in 1792, she would fall in with a young man whose stay under her roof would almost literally touch off a world revolution. The young man, of course, was Eli Whitney, who at Mulberry saw the need for a machine to separate upland cotton from its seed and invented one on the spot. A year later he began to manufacture and sell cotton gins faster than he could turn them out in his Connecticut works.

As an effect of Whitney's tinkering a white tide would spread in a few years through the South Carolina back country, drawing after it a black tide of Negro slaves. But these tides were yet to roll as Washington turned back from Georgia and jogged through the middle country to Columbia, seeing no glimmers of fairyland. In fact, he passed the whole distance from Augusta through "a pine barren of the worst sort, being hilly as well as poor"; and he found the new-laid capital on the Congaree River "an uncleared wood, with very few houses in it, and those all wooden ones." He ate dinner in a "commodious . . . but unfinished" State House with "a number of

Gentlemen and Ladies of the Town . . . & Country round about, to the amt. of more than 150, of which 50 or 60 were of the latter." What ignominy for Columbia's colonial dames—to survive in the record as neither "elegantly dressed" nor even "handsome" but just latterly. They might have seemed a bit rustic, of course, though more likely the old gentleman was played out.

There was yet one more spate of Carolina adulation to endure, however. Half a day's ride to the north the President was greeted by Mr. Woodmason's old merchant friend, Colonel Joseph Kershaw, who as Camden's intendant gave "a welcome, though less splendid, yet not less sincere," than any he had received. The colonel asked that

> *Almighty God long preserve a life so beloved, and make the future as happy as the past has been illustrious; and at the close of a life rendered thus illustrious, may you greet on the happy shores of blissful immortality, the kindred spirits of those heroes and patriots, who have in all ages past been distinguished as the guardians of liberty and the fathers of their country.*

Banqueting the gentry that evening in Washington's honor, Colonel John Chesnut signified his arrival at the summit of fortune's hill. If future Kershaws would not forget his ragtaggle start in their ancestral country store, future Chesnuts could recall that he was suitably housed to entertain a president. Morever, they could point to a Gilbert Stuart likeness as incontrovertible proof of his Revolutionary note and his patrician mien. From the painted evidence he might have been blood brother to Washington. In Gilbert Stuart's generalizing neoclassic eye, of course, so he was. The painter drew all the old American heroes as types, variations, so to speak, on the archetypal Washington.

Taking the path of General Gates's frantic sprint north from Camden, the President could have wound through the Carolina upcountry in a doze, that is, if the wheels did not jounce him from his seat at every turn along the rocky, red-clay road. There were no towns lying in ambush with ponderous greetings and massive dinners. In fact, there was scarcely a tavern at which he might have found hog and hominy and a corn-shuck mattress for the night.

To the east of this route, however, and far to the west toward the

Blue Ridge villages were springing up around country stores, and settlers were clearing more land for wheat, corn and tobacco. With county divisions and county courts, back-countrymen no longer wandered in a judicial and political wilderness. Having fought for self-government against the crown, they were now demanding and getting more self-government from the low-country oligarchs. Pressure from their elected spokesmen had partially determined, in fact, removal of the capital from Charleston to its present site, approximately the geographic center of the state.

Though back-countrymen had won the battle for a new capital site in 1786, they had to fight it all over again at the Constitutional Convention in May, 1790. In the second scrap they were forced to grant Charleston an equal claim on the chief state officers and agree to hold the Governor in rude Columbia for legislative terms only. They tried but failed to change the basis of legislative representation from wealth (counted in slaves as well as land) to population: the slave-rich lowland planters were resolved to keep a firmer grip on the state than men they judged better qualified to grip the plow.

Actually upcountrymen fought harder for the capital than for additional seats, showing more pride of precinct than concern for needy voters. Delegates themselves, of course, scarcely felt the pinch of deprivation. Owning lands and chattel enough to mingle with coastal oligarchs, they readily borrowed the oligarchic frame of mind. Certainly they were property-minded enough not to shy at the silent premise of the Constitution, that government should approximate the function of a royal gamekeeper, scaring off peasant poachers.

Enthroning property, the Constitution makers also decreed a hierarchy of the propertied. They so reduced the assets demanded of candidates for office in 1778, however, that a few starchy old captains of the ship of state bellowed mutiny. The scale required five hundred acres and ten Negroes for admission to the lower house and double these amounts for entrance to the Senate. To approach the ballot box a man had to own fifty acres or a town lot, and once there he could vote for legislators alone. The General Assembly chose almost every functionary from the Governor down to county tax collectors.

Two years before—in the spring of 1788—many of the same delegates had met to debate the Federal Constitution, which no less favored the rich and well-to-do. Though too weak to block ratification, upcountry members voted no almost to a man, following the lead of such blunt tongues as General Sumter and the tough old Indian killer Patrick Calhoun. They balked, however, not so much in zeal for the common man as in fear of uncommon national power. Having battled for their voice in Carolina counsels, they were understandably jealous. They held out, then, for "states' rights," prophetically sounding an alarm the coastal gentry would raise a few decades later. In that anxious time sons of coastal nationalists would ironically hail as their high priest and defender a son of old Patrick, who had ridden to Charleston in 1769 as the first backwoodsmen to invade the aristocratic Commons and now rejected a Constitution aristocrats had made.

Among the strenuous pleaders for ratification was Charles Pinckney, whose immodest claims to having written the Constitution probably helped deny him the credit he deserved. As a delegate from South Carolina—along with John Rutledge, Charles Cotesworth Pinckney and Pierce Butler—he submitted a "draught" containing about half the provisions ultimately adopted at Philadelphia. Taking its cue from contemporary silence on the matter, history has slighted his contribution. His colleagues may not have known what use had been made of his "draught," though they might very well have meant to punish him for breaking the vow of secrecy they all swore: they had felt, apparently, as Jefferson did about the Declaration, that it should appear as a creation of the American mind. Certain patriarchs might have tended also to minimize the abilities of a cockerel—the thirty-year-old Pinckney was next to the youngest delegate—who crowed too loud on and off the floor.

Pinckney has not lacked for South Carolina champions, however, any more than in his own time he lacked for passionate followers. In a state where political fervors are handed down with land grants from the King, his name still evokes a halo or a forked tail, as the case may be. There are South Carolinians today who can tell you only one thing about the Constitution of the United States, that Charles Pinckney assuredly wrote it.

Scarcely anyone ever claims that John Rutledge wrote it, though as chairman of the Committee on Details (a body of five men who actually drafted the document) he had a better chance than Charles

Pinckney to decide its form and content. But, unlike Pinckney, he never made any claims for himself. Nor for anyone else apparently. In fact, he seems to have honored his oath of secrecy down to the grave.

In view of South Carolina's later crusade for states' rights, it may seem odd that her ruling class espoused centralism in 1788. At both junctures, of course, they served their own interests. In 1788 they feared the newly assertive democracy at home rather than Northern threats to their welfare. Slavery was not in question, and in every other respect they saw eye to eye with Yankee factory- and shipowners. As large-scale planters they produced for a world market, and they knew that a strong central government was essential to overseas trade. In addition, South Carolina's Revolutionary delegates to Congress had learned that a loose confederation could not stand the strain of war.

The men who carried the vote to strengthen the central power in 1788 (Federalists by national party alignment) faced increasing opposition in the coming years from Jefferson's disciples (Republicans), who favored individual and states' rights. By 1800, in fact, the tide flowed powerfully enough to sweep Federalists from control of the legislature and thus deny Charles Cotesworth Pinckney the vote for vice-president of the United States in that year and the vote for president in 1804 and 1808. For these stabs to the heart of a Carolina Galahad the old aristocrats never forgave Charles Pinckney, who had defected from Federalism out of pique, they said, when a coveted diplomatic post went to his cousin Thomas. Republican follies did not shake them half so much as a Pinckney's betrayal of a Pinckney. The tenor of C. C. Pinckney's political thought—and the measure of his *noblesse oblige*—may be gauged, by the way, from his proposal to the Constitutional Convention in Philadelphia that "no salary should be allowed" to senators. "This branch," he said, "was meant to represent wealth; it ought to be composed of persons of wealth."

Though Republicans professed an antiaristocratic bias, they longed not so much to abolish the old ruling class as to gain the inner circle. Besides Charles Pinckney, the party leadership comprised such back-country arrivistes as General Sumter and his old cavalry colonel Wade Hampton. Of frontier cabin origins, these men not only had proved their mettle in war but in staking out vast domains they had won the same right to public sway as coastal nationalists were born to.

These men did not, of course, construe their politics as merely a leg up in the world for themselves. Like Jefferson, they avowed the welfare of the common man, the social and material promise of frontier America. The chance to raise his own Monticello must be kept open, they believed, to every ragtag plowboy of sense and energy. And, like Jefferson, they saw the chief threat to this chance not in estate as a source of power to deserving men but in the guarantee of estate and power to their not always deserving sons.

Jeffersonian Republicans wanted to make America safe for free enterprise. They saw little danger from enterprising men, any more than latter-day Republicans have wanted to see that economic license may fatten the few and starve the crowd. The danger lay rather in America's perpetuating a rotten European polity with its hereditary autocrats and nobles. Titles of themselves did not signify. Given scope, a president could tyrannize with regal severity; and generations of exalted citizens could plant lordly heels on the yeoman's neck.

Since in the largely agrarian America of 1800, finance capitalism had barely shown its undemocratic hand, Jeffersonians concentrated their fire on the monarchial and "aristocratical" tendencies in America's planter-merchant ruling class. They accused both Washington and John Adams of aspiring to kingship and their Federalist cohorts as rapturously anticipating a coronation. Congressman Sumter (the old General), for instance, mulishly withheld any public sign of what might be construed as the tribute due a monarch. A contemporary reports his behavior thus at a Philadelphia theater where President Adams was expected:

> *A clapping of hands commenced, and one Fitzhugh called out in a loud voice, asking why the general did not clap? A second rumor arose, and a second demand was made upon this venerable veteran. At the same time, Fitzhugh attempted to seize his hands, and force him to clap. General Sumter represented that there was no mutual acquaintance to justify such freedoms . . . and asked if the latter knew who he was? "Oh, damn you, we know you, and all your party," replied the royal-*

ist. "I hope in six months time, to see you all banished from the country." . . . At last Mr. Adams did appear. Fitzhugh then attempted to snatch off General Sumter's hat, asking why, like the rest of the company, he did not uncover?

The writer adds that the General found out the popinjay's name and called next day at his lodging only to find that "Fitzhugh was gone." Absence was no doubt in this case the better part of valor. It would have been risky that morning, if not fatal, to be caught at home by the ruffled Gamecock of the Revolution.

Thwarting monarchism was not the General's only postwar occupation. With an eye to resale he bought numerous tracts of unclaimed land he had spied out on his upcountry campaigns, amassing more than a hundred thousand acres in Camden District at the state's giveaway price of ten cents an acre. The General also founded a potential state capital, which he hopefully named Stateburg. He built a store and a hotel, laid out a racecourse and encouraged the Baptist divine Richard Furman in starting a seminary of learning "presided over by a gentleman of European experience and classical attainments."

In short, General Sumter measured up to the gentlemen of the coast. And whatever prejudice he had against born patricians, he must have swallowed in 1802 when Thomas Jr. married a French marquis's daughter, Natalie de Lage de Volude, who had fled to New York from democratic upheavals at home. He probably took the news in better grace than the bride's mother, who, as General Gates wrote from Paris, where young Sumter was secretary of legation, "is a furious royalist and will not hear of her daughter's being married to a republican." If she had known of his two illegitimate children (whom his father and mother reared as their own) she might have thought him a man of at least royal indiscretions.

General Sumter's martial and political comrade Wade Hampton took a similar course after the war, buying up huge tracts of South Carolina land at the ten-cent giveaway price and speculating further in the notorious Yazoo grants, obtained by fraud from the Georgia legislature. But Hampton far outstripped the General in driving purpose and in business acumen. While Sumter was scratching around to pay his debts, Hampton was piling up such phenomenal

wealth that within twenty years of his start he would be reputed the
richest man in America. Probably the first South Carolina planter
to use Whitney's cotton gin, he was raising a $90,000 crop by 1799;
and in 1811 he added more than $100,000 a year to his income by
purchasing a great sugar estate on the Mississippi.

The two men emerged from almost identical frontier origins.
Wade Hampton also came from Virginia, settling a few years before the Revolution in what is now Spartanburg. As a young man
there in 1776 he came home one afternoon to find only smoldering
ashes and butchered flesh: in his absence Cherokee raiders had struck,
murdering the whole family except three younger brothers who also
happened to be away at the time. Calling neighbors to their help,
the four Hamptons paid back the score in Cherokee blood and then
left the region, Wade to distinguish himself soon afterwards as a
partisan fighter. Like Sumter, he married auspiciously, acquiring
through his union with Mrs. Martha Epps Howell the Richland
District estate which remained for generations a ducal Hampton
seat.

In their public character both Thomas Sumter and Wade Hampton made distinctive marks in the state and to a lesser extent in the
nation. But in their private exploits and speculations they were far
from unique. They had their counterparts by the hundreds throughout the back country, operating on a smaller scale perhaps but
equally charged with frontier sap and avidity.

Whatever their motives, such men powerfully stimulated the back
country. Their promotions—of towns, bridges, roads and canals—
furthered trade, opened remote sections to civilizing influences from
the coast and above all brought frontiersmen together. Communi-
ties formed and spokesmen arose to chorus alarming suspicions of
the low-country slave economy. Behind these spokesmen lay an ever-
increasing potential of enmity.

Parish fear of this potential largely determined the founding in
1801 of the South Carolina College (later the University of South
Carolina), the state's first authentic collegiate institution and perhaps the first in the nation to receive adequate public support. In
proposing the college to the legislature Governor John Drayton
tactfully stressed the general welfare, but he did not fail to suggest
the need of sectional fraternity, which was no doubt uppermost in

his mind. Off the floor he might have put the case as plainly as the
Charleston lawyer Henry W. DeSaussure, who said, "We of the lower
country knew that the power of the State was thence forward to be
in the upper country, and we desired our future rulers to be educated men." His measure of education included, we may take it, a
Roman reverence for slavery—a grace that back country louts might
well gain by intercourse with salt-water squirelings if not straight
out from Cicero and Demosthenes.

Nonetheless, parish squires served their state handsomely in plump-
ing for a college and in voting money to build and run it. (The
North Carolina legislature, by contrast, gave the infant university
at Chapel Hill $10,000 and told it to get along as best it could.) If
back country legislators did not howl the project down, neither did
they talk it up. Largely self-taught and self-made, they thought others
might well follow their example. And since they spoke for a fairly
hard-bitten race of bear hunters and cornshuckers, they shied at
spending tax money on fripperies. Of back-country origin himself,
James L. Petigru explained the sectional qualms thus in his fiftieth
anniversary speech to the college:

> . . . the pittance wrung from the hand of reluctant poverty, it
> was said, was to be lavished on the education of the rich . . .
> there was then no provision for education by means of Free
> Schools. It was hard that the rich should be assisted by the pub-
> lic treasury in giving their sons an education suitable to their
> station in life; while the children of the poor were taught at
> their own expense.

Petigru also claimed that the college came into being as the last
will and testament of the expiring Federalist party. Since Federalists
had lost control of the legislature, however, they obviously borrowed
voting strength from Republicans, who as Jefferson's disciples should
have venerated learning. In any event the General Assembly not
only voted good intentions—it chose trustees and put money in their
hands. They in turn hastened to buy land in Columbia, put up a
building and engage a faculty. By January, 1805, they were ready for
students.

If the college was not a Federalist creation, it surely embodied
the ideals of the Federalist gentry. Ignoring Jefferson's utilitarian

apostasies at Charlottesville, the trustees drew up an antique menu as the proper mental and moral diet for planter gentlemen, making no concessions to depraved modern tastes. Latin and Greek would face all students as regularly as hominy grits appeared at table for breakfast and rice for dinner. At least a small taste for Latin and Greek would naturally follow as a chief admission requirement and, incidentally, a barrier to most plebeian youth, few of whom could afford preparatory schooling.

When the most recent historian of the college, Daniel Walker Hollis, calls the entrance standards "truly admirable," he does not mean to praise their socially exclusive character. He simply recognizes what bargain-basement educators unwittingly or fatuously deny, that a college is only as good as it is mentally snobbish. That is, if it aims to be more than a "laboratory for living" or a charm school for the proletariat. In setting high admission standards the college trustees served their own class, but they also served the cause of intellect in their state. Poor bright boys who did pass inspection at the gate would at least find more stimulating company than normally gathered at the crossroads store.

That young South Carolinians could meet the college test was due largely to such dominies as Dr. Moses Waddell, whose "log college" at Willington, near Abbeville, sent a bright shower of star pupils into the world: John C. Calhoun, for instance, James Louis Petigru, Hugh Swinton Legaré, and Augustus Baldwin Longstreet. Most of these luminaries testified in later years to the doctor's Calvinistic stringency and gave it generous credit for their rise. In his novel *Master William Mitten* Longstreet quotes a former student as saying, "That school fills my notion of what a boy's school ought to be. Plain dressing, plain eating, hard working, close studying, close watching and when needful good whipping . . . the best school in the United States."

Like the South Carolina College, Willington aimed to form gentlemen but not dandies. It neither cultivated pretty airs nor spared time for the lighter arts and amusements. Waddell taught primarily the Greek and Roman classics, and he taught them unsparingly from morning till night. As Margaret Coit describes the Willington regimen in her life of Calhoun:

*Three times a day fifteen minutes were snatched from study
for [a] pitifully inadequate diet of cornbread and bacon. . . .
In primitive log cabins, lit by pine torches or flickering tapers,
the boys lived in groups, studying from sunrise until nine o'clock
at night. A horn roused them at "first dawn streak," and after
breakfast they gathered in the schoolroom for prayer. They
studied in the woods, each in his own chair, with his name
carved on the back; and on cold days obtained heat and exercise
from chopping trees and building "log-heap fires." Though not
under the teacher's eye, they studied their grammar and syntax,
their Vergil and Homer, with intensity. A hundred and fifty
memorized lines a day would be the quota for the slower pupils;
over a thousand for the brilliant ones.*

Archaic though his methods seem, Dr. Waddell anticipated one
modern ideal: he cut the cloth to fit the boy; but, unlike today's
timorous pedagogue, he made the boy swell out his chest for the
measurement. Dr. Waddell also promoted the democratic ideal, at
least as Jefferson conceived it. He sought as pupils not merely bright
young aristocrats but bright young potential aristocrats. He encouraged the decent poor to send him their brainy offspring, cutting
his fees accordingly. Matching wits with plantation heirs, such youths
went on to the South Carolina College or, like Calhoun, to Yale and
shortly acquired the manors they were fit to grace.

Though Republican board members of the South Carolina College
did not agitate for Jeffersonian studies, some did hold out for a
Jeffersonian president. When the mantle was about to fall on Jonathan Maxcy, a Rhode Island Baptist divine who had presided at
Brown University and at Union College in New York, one member
tried to rally party support for a local product, writing Colonel Wade
Hampton that "We must have a republican at the head of our college or all is lost." The plea did not excite Hampton, who said he
knew of no necessary connection between literature and party politics, nor did many other trustees, for Maxcy was shortly invited to
head the college.

Surprisingly for a man reared on New England's classical fare,
Maxcy cut down on the language staples and introduced such novel

nourishments as chemistry. But neither he nor his ante bellum successors diverted the college from its inceptive aim to purvey the literature culture of gentlemen. Reaffirming the mission in 1854, President James H. Thornwell declared that, while others were "veering to the popular pressure," "let it be our glory to abide by the old landmarks—improving where improvement is desirable—but substituting nothing. Let it be our aim to make *Scholars* and not sappers or miners—apothecaries—doctors or farmers."

Before the college had even begun to convert backwoods youth to slavocracy, the rich promise of cotton was converting their elders into slaveholders. Their scruples gone with the first clank of Eli Whitney's ginning machine, one-time free-labor partisans besieged the slave marts. There they met competition from the parish rice growers, increasing their output to cash in on war-inflated European prices. The joint demand stepped up the Negro market to such a pitch that the legislature voted in 1803 to reopen the slave trade—closed in 1787—for the four years until Congress would doubtless invoke its constitutional right to outlaw importations forever. Slavers lost no time in exploiting the renewed opportunity, and between 1804 and 1807 British, French, New England and Carolina ships unloaded nearly 40,000 Africans from their stinking holds onto the Charleston docks.

Acquiring their first slaves in these years, countless frontiersmen passed the initial test of admission to the Carolina ruling class and inaugurated a process that their heirs, actual and symbolic, would repeat on successive Southern frontiers in the coming fifty years. In *The Mind of the South* W. J. Cash typifies the process in recounting the rise of a "stout young Irishman" who "brought his bride into the Carolina upcountry about 1800." On a winter trip to Charleston to sell his liquid corn and the coarse woolen cloth from the family loom, he had picked up some cotton seed for his wife to plant around the cabin as a flower and a year or so later had picked up the electric notion that he could grow the white lint for cash.

> *Land in his neighborhood was to be had for fifty cents an acre. With twenty dollars, the savings of a lifetime, he bought fifty acres and set himself to clear it. Rising long before day, he toiled deep into the night, with his wife holding a pine*

torch for him to see by. . . . A wandering trader sold him a horse, bony and half-starved, for a knife, a dollar and a gallon of whisky. Every day now—Sundays not excepted . . . he drove the plow into the earth, with uptorn roots bruising his shanks at every step. Behind him came his wife with a hoe. In a few years the land was beginning to yield cotton—richly, for the soil was fecund with the accumulated mold of centuries. Another trip down the river, and he brought home a mangy black slave—an old and lazy fellow reckoned of no account in the rice-lands. . . . Next year the Irishman bought fifty acres more, and the year after another black. Five years more and he had two hundred acres and ten Negroes. Cotton prices swung up and down sharply, but always, whatever the return, it was almost pure velvet. For the fertility of the soil seemed inexhaustible.

Ultimately the hustling frontiersman owned 2,000 acres, 114 slaves and four cotton gins. He lived in a columned "big house," sent his son to the South Carolina College, stood for the legislature and married his pretty daughter to an impecunious Charleston aristocrat. When he died in 1854 the county newspaper spoke of him as a "gentleman of the old school." His wife died ten years later—"by her portrait a beautifully fragile old woman and, as I have heard it said, with lovely hands, knotted and twisted just enough to give them character, and a finely transparent skin through which the blue veins showed most aristocratically."

By 1808 slavery had caught on so well in the back country that the parishes risked conceding a fairer basis of representation in the General Assembly. Knowing their interests would dominate any elected body henceforth, they submitted to "the compromise of 1808," a constitutional amendment that effectually transferred control of both houses to the state's legal "upper division." Sure to be outvoted now, free-labor champions from that division would inevitably decrease as slaves multiplied. By 1860 they would be almost extinct. Slaveless whites continued, of course, to eke out a hand-to-mouth existence, but rarely did a voice speak out for their miseries in the coming half century.

South Carolina's pre-eminent statesman, John Caldwell Calhoun, the tall upcountryman who would lead her with bold and tragic brilliance toward the dead end of Secession, first appeared in public life as a member of the legislature that half buried the sectional hatchet. This entente may not have germinated his later doctrine of the concurrent majority, but he recalled it to instance the theory at work. In the "Fort Hill Address," his 1831 rationale of states'— and minority—rights, often cited as a major contribution to American political theory, he pointed out that such compromises were the lifeblood of the democratic process. Without them democracy would harden into a tyranny of the majority. Compromise alone ensured justice, for it took every interest into account.

At the moment, however, the twenty-six-year-old Calhoun was not bothering his ambitious head about minority rights. Nor was he thinking in that direction when he strode onto the national stage three years later as a U.S. congressman. In fact, he and the other two bright young Carolinians chosen for the House together—the Charleston patrician William Lowndes and the self-made patrician Langdon Cheves—went north with a mutual determination to stiffen the young Republic's spine against a bully-boy Britain. (The King's navy was impressing seamen from American vessels and interfering with trade to Europe.) Joining forces with Kentucky's Henry Clay, who was tired of seeing America "eternally the tail to Britain's kite," they swooped down on the aging Congressional eagles and taunted them into war with England. Known afterwards as the "War Hawks" of the "Second American Revolution," they might bear some discredit for starting a needless fight; but they would also wear a kind of glory for galvanizing a complacent people to the challenge of nationhood.

Showing a combative streak at the outset of his career, Calhoun played true to his Scotch-Irish father, who had picked off many a Cherokee in revenge for the Long Cane Massacre of 1760, in which his mother and a brother were "most inhumanly butchered." But in the careful phrasing and the close logic of his first major address —an appeal for war—he played true to his schooling. For, unlike his father, Calhoun had a school-sharpened mind. In fact, he had whetted it at the best hones the times afforded, Moses Waddell's Academy, Timothy Dwight's Yale College and Judge Topping Reeves's Connecticut law school. He had chosen these institutions himself when his brothers had persuaded him to quit the fields after old Patrick's death. If they wanted him to have an education, he would take only "the best . . . to be had in the United States."

His trained mind resting on frontier self-reliance and Presbyterian morality, Calhoun was admirably equipped for his future role as defense counsel for a hard-pressed Southern economic and social system. In the parish view he further equipped himself for leadership by his marriage to a well-born Charlestonian, Floride Calhoun, back-country Scotch-Irish on her father's side, it was true, but maternally descended from Huguenot Bonneaus. If opportunism figured in this alliance it did not stem, oddly enough, from the aspiring young piedmont lawyer, who was more the chosen than the chooser. Having taken a frontiersman to husband herself, Floride's mother coveted a similar mate for her daughter. "With rare wisdom," as Margaret Coit observes, Floride Bonneau Calhoun "sensed the decadence of the hard-living, inbred young blades of the low-country." Floride's husband must be virile, bright and forceful. Her search began and ended with her husband's distant cousin, apparently, for she kept him in friendly tow from her daughter's twelfth year, when she invited Calhoun from Yale to mend from an illness at her Newport, Rhode Island, summer place. Unlike the usual designing *maman*, Mrs. Calhoun did not have to look out for a wealthy son-in-law: she was rich enough to be driven north every summer by her own liveried British coachman.

Calhoun's fellow War Hawk William Lowndes was the least warlike of men, but he encouraged defiance of England and worked for adequate defenses with an equal regard for the national honor. A near-invalid for most of his life and studious by nature, he spoke with the moderation of one accustomed to suffer and to think. Their mutual friend Langdon Cheves judged Calhoun as "far more brilliant" than Lowndes but apt to "leap to conclusions boldly, perhaps hastily." Lowndes, by contrast, Cheves said, "looked at a subject calmly . . . in every light. . . . I should have preferred his judgment to that of any man; and such, I think was the feeling of their contemporaries."

When the war for "free trade and seamen's right" began in the summer of 1812, William Lowndes's father-in-law, Major Thomas Pinckney, was commissioned a major general and placed in command of the Southeast. The old Federalist did not leap, however, at the chance to win glory in a Republican war, snapping that the Administration's views "could best be executed by those in sympathy with it." Like most of his kind, he regarded England with far less enmity than Napoleon's France, which by President Madison's admission had captured more American vessels since 1807 than Britain. He took the mission only at the urging of his friends, who argued that he should set a patriotic example to the community. His acceptance touched off a rumor in Washington that his son-in-law had converted him to Republicanism. "An amusing idea," Mrs. Ravenel comments in her life of Lowndes, "since Mr. Lowndes used to complain that 'so stubborn were the Pinckneys that he had never been able to convert his own wife,' who remained an unflinching Federalist to the end."

Since the federal government was unable to send troops, South Carolina had to rely on her militia, which proved as unreliable as in the Revolution. More so, perhaps, for they were called on merely to watch and wait, a piddling duty, unworthy of chevaliers. Until the British showed some disposition to attack in force, they could very well wait at home. As soldiers in garrison they could scarcely keep enemy ships from the coastal inlets nor stop their crews from looting a remote plantation now and then. Some militiamen even refused an occasional turn at guarding the Charleston magazines, and their comrades thought them so innocent of offense that they denounced Governor Joseph Alston's court-martial proceedings as a "tyrant's" "unhallowed libel" on the citizen soldiery.

As bold as his father-in-law, Aaron Burr, if not as clever, Alston disbanded the militia when a state judge decided that the law provided no penalty for disobeying orders to defend the state. Shortly afterwards, however, when the British landed on St. Helena Island, he revoked the order and summoned the legislature to obtain adequate powers.

Earlier in the year the rash Governor had touched off a similar furor, jeopardizing the state's Washington seats because five congressmen had not, as the law required, reported their intention to accept election. He was accused of trying to unseat Langdon Cheves, whom he had called a "political Jesuit." Newspaper attacks on the Governor slyly returned the compliment, hinting that the man who had intrigued with the archintriguer Aaron Burr might in better grace hold his tongue. Whether the imputation was just or not, Alston had financially backed the ex-vice-president in the grandiose scheme for which he was brought to trial, a plot, reportedly, to separate the Western states from the Union and set up a government at New Orleans under Spanish protection. Though Burr was acquitted of treason, the evidence left no doubt that he had played fast and loose with his country, flirting along the way with some very shady characters. Alston may not have known what business was afoot any more than did Andrew Jackson, who at one point was ready to campaign south with Burr; but it strains reason to think he never suspected: he and his wife, Burr's only daughter, Theodosia, spent several weeks with the conspirator in Ohio and Kentucky as he gathered forces along the Mississippi in 1806.

But whatever he knew or thought, Alston seems never to have failed of loyalty to the brilliant, suave and visionary Burr. Out of devotion to his wife, if nothing else, for Theodosia and her father idolized each other. They had many qualities in common: wit, gaiety and compelling charm. And her mind was equally trained, for he had insisted that she have a liberal education. In prescribing Latin, Greek and mathematics in addition to French, music and dancing, he had said, "But I yet hope by her to convince the world what neither sex appears to believe—that women have souls." It must have been hard for him to relinquish her at seventeen to the Carolina rice planter Joseph Alston, who was rich enough to suit the spendthrifty Burr—he was the eldest son of Colonel William Alston, of Clifton—but who would carry her off, nonetheless, a week's journey from New York.

Carolina chronicles justly allot Theodosia Burr Alston a line of text and a footnote, but a legendry might well spend a chapter on her story. For no historic figure, certainly none who live along the rice coast, has inspired so many or such enduring tales. Most of these spin variations on the mystery of her disappearance at sea in 1812. Still grieving for her only son, the fourteen-year-old Aaron Burr Alston, who had died of fever in June, she took ship for New York at Georgetown on the last day of December and vanished forever. History surmises that the ship went down in a storm, but romantic fancy, of course, prefers to see her walking the pirate's plank or wandering in sad distraction about Cape Hatteras, a captive in that buccaneer domain.

But many highborn ladies have vanished at sea and left no tales behind. Theodosia's fate survives in romance, by exception, because she was the adored and adoring child of a famous, not to say an infamous, father. His disgrace at the height of what had promised to be a dazzling career lends her death something of the pathos that touches the victims in classic drama. The storytellers have recognized, unconsciously at least, the old pattern of sin and retribution working itself out in the lives of father and daughter. They have appropriated these figures from history, in other words, and installed them in the timeless realm of poetry where they belong, the realm, as Aristotle said, of things not as they are but as they ought to be.

History portrays Aaron Burr as a self-seeking visionary, as something even of a crackpot. Inklings of comic opera attend this would-be Napoleon as he floats down the Mississippi with an army of sixty men to seize an empire and mount a throne. And his stature does not increase as he graciously submits to arrest and trial, insisting like an artful schoolboy that he had no wrong intentions. But legend casts him in the role of tragic hero, a great and prideful man who reaches too high and falls to his ruin at the will of jealous divinity. It invests him with a dark grandeur, suggesting a little the air of Milton's archangelic conspirator.

The historical and poetic conceptions of Theodosia are more in keeping. Though we are told that she was a "vital young woman" rather than the melancholy wraith of legend, very active in raising money for her father while he plotted abortively in exile abroad, she nonetheless seems to have loved and suffered in the old high way of romance. If she loved her father as she said, then she must have shriveled at every imputation. And there's no reason to doubt her sincerity in writing that he appeared "so superior, so elevated above other men," that she viewed him with "such strange mixture of humility, admiration, reverence, love and pride, that very little superstition would be necessary to make me worship you as a superior being. . . . I had rather not live than not be the daughter of such a man." And this after his exposure and trial. It is impossible not to feel, in spite of the facts, that her father's disgrace somehow blighted her life and the life of her son and even at last the life of her husband, for he survived only a few years after she disappeared at sea.

Joseph Alston was succeeded as governor in 1814 by a no less impetuous man, David R. Williams, whose verbal pyrotechnics in the national Congress had won him the byname "Thunder and Lightning Williams." Out of Congress and in service as a brigadier general during the War of 1812, he behaved accordingly, stalking off the Northern front in disgust at the army's inertia and charging south to take the field against the Creek Indians in Georgia.

Williams is better remembered in his native state, however, as the "Carolina Cincinnatus," which commemorates the fact that the gubernatorial summons reached him in the field, happily reminding a Latin-schooled generation of the antique general who was "twice called from the plow" to the dictatorship of Rome. The official messenger actually found him driving a team of oxen, but however yeomanly the circumstance, Williams was a man of large concerns, having a sizable slave corps to work his acres along the Pee Dee River. On another day the emissary might have found him at his cotton mill, one of the first in the state, or at his desk writing an article on the prime utility of the mule, which he claimed to have introduced to Southern farming.

David R. Williams was the second back-countryman to govern the state, but the fact signifies more the region's growing wealth than the extraordinary rise of a clodhopper. Though born outside the zone of coastal refinement—in the Baptist Welsh Neck section —he spent his early years in Charleston, going from school there to Rhode Island College (Brown University).

Williams was chiefly concerned as governor to strengthen the militia and to urge its use as an arm of national as well as state defense. As a congressman and in the field he had faced the peril of making war without anything like an adequate federal army. Militarily the nation stood at the mercy of the not always merciful states: they all could and sometimes did refuse to lend their soldiers. By that refusal, Williams declared, "We . . . saw . . . 'the veil of the temple' of the constitution 'rent in twain.' "

As Williams exhorted the state to a sense of the national welfare, John C. Calhoun and William Lowndes led the fight in Congress for

Henry Clay's "American System," the program states' rights Jeffersonians had necessarily borrowed from the archcentralist Alexander Hamilton. Like Williams, they too had seen the specter of defeat and had reached the inevitable conclusion: in a threatening world national existence depends on national solidarity and strength. And they had no doubt of the threat. As the only considerable nation on earth committed to popular government, the United States was a prime object of European and especially British enmity. As Calhoun said in urging the creation of strong naval and military forces, "the most growing nation on earth" would "have to encounter British jealousy and hostility in every shape."

But defensive strength, as he knew, rests ultimately on economic health. The nation must prosper in all its parts and interests. "Neither agriculture, manufactures, nor commerce, separately is the cause of wealth; it flows from all three combined." No measure could better serve the common welfare, he believed, than a protective tariff. It would seem to favor one interest above the others, but in the long run it would benefit all equally. Under government fosterage industry would grow strong enough to stimulate the demand for farm products and, of course, step up trade. A system of roads and canals would accomplish the same ends. As Calhoun rather eloquently appealed to Congress:

> We are great, and rapidly—I was about to say fearfully—growing. This is our pride and our danger; our weakness and our strength. Little does he deserve to be intrusted with the liberties of this people, who does not raise his mind to these truths. We are under the most imperious obligation to counteract every tendency to disunion. The strongest of all cements is, undoubtedly, the wisdom, justice, and above all, the moderation of this House; yet the great subject on which we are now deliberating, in this respect deserves the most serious consideration. Whatever impedes the intercourse of the extremes with this, the centre of the republic, weakens the union. The more enlarged the sphere of commercial circulation—the more extended that of social intercourse—the more strongly are we bound together—the more inseparable are our destinies. Those who understand the human heart best know how powerfully

> *distance tends to break the sympathies of our nature. Nothing
> —not even dissimilarity of language—tends more to estrange
> man from man. Let us, then, bind the republic together with
> a perfect system of roads and canals. Let us conquer space.*

In the light of his future role as a sectionalist this plea is sharply
ironic. But it does not prove that his mind veered like a weather
vane in the winds of local interest. He did believe in 1816, of course,
that nationalistic measures would benefit the South, just as he later
came to believe they were undermining the Cotton Kingdom. Setting
his mind against them, he did not reject the ideal of union as a
mutually beneficial partnership.

On the whole, South Carolina public opinion assented to the
nationalist program that Calhoun and Lowndes steered through
Congress. Few leaders within the state, of course, shared their vision
of the national destiny, but they did share the vision of prosperity,
being at the moment themselves comfortably fat and unafraid for
the years ahead. No one had seriously questioned their right to
own their labor body and soul, cotton prices were riding the wave
of postwar demand, Charleston was booming as a port.

Like the rest of the nation South Carolina was enjoying what contemporaries called an "era of good feelings." Hindsight shows that
it might better have been called a "moment of good feelings." For
it lasted scarcely a decade, from the signing of the peace with Great
Britain until—it is difficult to set a date, but 1820 perhaps will serve.
In that year murmurings of disunion spread throughout the land as
Congress passed the Missouri Compromise, which in forbidding
slavery to that portion of the Louisiana Territory north of the line
36° 30′ signaled to thoughtful men the beginning of an onslaught
upon the South's peculiar and profitable institution.

Virtually on the eve of this portentous measure—the first of the
long series of tremors that would end in the earth-splitting quake
of the Dred Scott decision in 1857—a proud and affluent Charleston
demonstrated to President Monroe, as she had to Washington, South
Carolina's happy allegiance to the union. The President arrived in
April with a large official party that included his secretary of war,
John C. Calhoun. The bells of St. Michael's rang out in welcome.
They rang out for six days, in fact, as this last scion of the Virginia

dynasty bowed to the applause of his fellow patricians. Whether he or they suspected it or not, the occasion was in the nature of a valediction. It was the last time wellborn ladies and gentlemen would turn out ceremoniously for a president who was truly one of their own. It was almost, in fact, the last time that Charleston could hail even at a distance a president who was to the Southern manor born.

X

God, Old Hickory and cMr. Petigru

In July of 1827, just two days before the annual feasts of bombast and barbecue hallowing America's separation from England, a testy Englishman exhorted South Carolina to separation from the American union. Before an antitariff assemblage in Columbia President Thomas Cooper of the South Carolina College, damning Henry Clay's "American System" as a Northern ruse to pick Southern pockets, doubted whether membership in the United States was worth the unholy price. "We shall before long," he warned, "be compelled to calculate the value of the union."

The first influential South Carolina voice to invoke the demon of disunion, Dr. Cooper left the state aghast. And in succeeding weeks he became a hotly disputed figure—to his private if not open delight. Editors flayed him as a "learned renegade" from abroad preaching treason against his benign foster country. Others vaunted him as an apostle of liberty who had "ever asserted the rights of the people against tyranny and oppression."

The scrap over Dr. Cooper was only the first of the clashes that in the next few years would rend the state, pitting unionists against nullifiers, or as they name-called each other "submissionists" and "fire-eaters." The unionists fought a losing battle, but they never weakened, even when the ingenious Calhoun, sure of his logic but unsure of such ingenuous minds as Andrew Jackson's, led the state close to war. Though federal-state tensions eased with Congress's 1833 compromise tariff, unionists and nullifiers fought on violently within the state for at least two more years. As the decade ended, however, unionists defected under the goad of abolitionism, making South Carolina politics at last a kind of gospel shout to the glory of her peculiar institution.

Actually opinion was fairly united on the issue that prompted Dr. Cooper's warning. By 1828 the state's ruling class was persuaded by and large that the American System had sold the South out to the North. Led to expect equality of profit by their spokesmen Calhoun and Lowndes in 1816, Carolinians understandably grumbled as cotton prices declined and rising tariff schedules boosted the cost of manufactured goods. The whole economy, of course, declined with cotton, so visibly in Charleston that her merchants and bankers built a 136-mile railroad—longest in the world at the time—to divert some of the river trade flowing to Savannah, Georgia. The protective tariff, though it sucked economic blood from the South, was not the vampire that loomed in the nightmares of platform rhetoric. Actually South Carolina was leeching her own blood with cotton. Farmers used up the soil at a reckless rate in their haste to graduate from log cabin to white-columned piazza. When virgin acres sickened from abuse, the old pioneering spirit quickened, and they trekked off to use up the rich black lands of Alabama and Mississippi. Huge crops there in the twenties helped to flood the market and incidentally to enrich Mobile and New Orleans more or less at Charleston's expense. Those who remained behind to suffer hard times saw emigration as a distressing effect at home, failing understandably to see the transplanted emigrant as a cause.

A few wise South Carolinians perceived the true causes of depression. Even Congressman George McDuffie, who was so angry at the tariff in 1828 that he renounced his Northern-made broadcloth coat as "fit only for slaves," admitted in 1825 that the old Southern states were victims of the westward scramble for cheap and fertile lands. And Hugh Swinton Legaré, the young lawyer and classicist, then (in 1831) editing the chauvinistic *Southern Review* in Charleston, could discern only a slight connection between falling prices and the tariff. No apologist for the tariff, however, he scarcely wondered "at the indignation which . . . such a burthen . . . has excited in our people in the present unprosperous state of their affairs."

Legaré shows here the analytic turn that undoubtedly made him oppose nullification as a gross specific for a radical disorder, but he also reveals the emotional bias that drove less philosophic men to unreason. Pampered son of a not too affluent planting family, he could and did feel the sting of having skimpier means than his birth and being ordained. As United States chargé to Belgium, a post he took in 1832 partially to escape the nullification rumpus, he wrote that sending agents abroad with "inadequate compensation" exposed them to "perpetual mortification," making "their whole life a painful struggle to reconcile inevitable expense with necessary, however sordid, parsimony." He further bared his patrician heart by grieving for the English nobility, which had just lost a chip of their monumental privilege to the working class through the Parliamentary Reform Bill. "Imagine, if you can," he wrote his sister, "the *hell* of the haughtiest minds in the world exposed to the mortification of comparative poverty in the midst of their absolute wealth, and haunted with apprehensions of the future. But I *do* like them so, and if I were rich, I should choose one of them for my wife."

When proud Americans as a class feel the chill of poverty they do not normally look to the crack around their doors. They blame the exposure or the cutting wind from north or south. Their impulse is to move—in political terms to remove as far as they can get from Washington. Feeling the chill in the 1820's, South Carolinians obeyed the normal impulse, hitting the old states' rights road and hurling imprecations over their shoulders at those "unconstitutional devices," the protective tariff and "internal improvements."

Though legislative condemnations were adopted in 1824, a hard-headed rationale did not appear until 1827, shortly after Dr. Cooper issued his mutinous invitation. A wealthy Charleston lawyer, Robert J. Turnbull, fulminated in *The Crisis* that the state not only could but should assert its sovereignty and withdraw from the federal compact.

Like Turnbull, John C. Calhoun postulated absolute state sovereignty when he sat down amid his upcountry fields in the summer of 1828 to work out his nullification doctrine. Arguing from a wider frame of reference and to saner effect, he urged the states' right to judge when their agent, the national government, had overstepped its powers. As the immediate organ of sovereignty, a state convention might invalidate any national act and move to block its local enforcement. He conceded only one check on the individual state—a majority vote of the states to amend the Constitution.

Granted his premise, Calhoun's case was eminently plausible. And it may at least be said for his premise that state sovereignty did not appear then so academic a matter as it has since 1865; though the aged former-President Madison could find "not a shadow" of excuse in the Constitution for this "preposterous and anarchical pretension."

Preparing to explain nullification in his *South Carolina Exposition and Protest,* Calhoun no doubt reviewed, among other sources, Dr. Cooper's *Political Economy,* if he didn't consult the old "schoolmaster of state rights" in person. He also advised with numerous nimble politicians, including spokesmen for the state legislature, which would publish his work to plead the state's case before the nation. He surely went over the ground with the eloquent U.S. Senator Hayne, who would expound the doctrine to Congress, and with the quick-tongued and quick-triggered Congressman James Hamilton, Jr.—reported to have fought fourteen duels in his time —who would evangelize the voters: "He who dallies is a dastard; he who doubts is damned."

Whoever came to advise the Carolina prince left instructed by the national politician not to fly the Calhoun name from the *Exposition*: he could not risk souring the North on his candidacy as Andrew Jackson's running mate. A normally forthright man, Calhoun must have chafed at the muzzle, even more at this point than during the last four years as vice-president under John Quincy Adams. For, though he had broken his chairmanly neutrality in the Senate to cast a deciding vote against the wool tariff (1827), South Carolinians were beginning to doubt his sympathies.

Actually he was anything but indifferent, as friends knew. Grasping tariffs had fully restored his birthright faith in human depravity. Protective laws had not bound each to each in loving fellowship— they had set one section to plundering the other. He wanted to avoid sectional feuding, however, and therefore regretted the trigger-snapping disposition in Carolina. It was foolhardy to antagonize the North as Jackson advanced on the White House to bring relief. The old Tennessee slaveholder would rout protectionism, Calhoun had reason to hope, as bravely as he had routed the British at New Orleans.

He may also have thought to inherit Jackson's mantle and ensure permanent safety for Carolina's agrarian elite by uniting the West with the South against the capitalistic East. Such an alliance might in the long run, he predicted, benefit the Eastern capitalists as well. For, as the historian Richard Hofstadter suggests, Calhoun was a rare American specimen, a thinking reactionary, who anticipated Karl Marx in recognizing class tensions as historical moving forces. Northern factory masters might happily plunder Southern planters, but the time would come, Calhoun thought, when they'd welcome allies in saving their wealth from plundering workers.

Before Jackson, much less Calhoun, could even assail the Northern protectionists, hubbub mounted in South Carolina as Congress passed the 1828 "tariff of abominations"—a snare to catch voters for Old Hickory both north and south by keeping duties high on factory goods but making them even higher on raw materials. Drawing first blood in the North, this was only a deepening of the Southern wound, which was already sore past endurance. Calhoun could temporize no longer.

If a single figure might be thought to have smoked Calhoun out, it was the twenty-seven-year-old state legislator Robert Barnwell Smith—he later took the name Rhett in homage to his pirate-fighting great-great-grandfather, Colonel William—who struck fire in a June, 1828, speech in low-country Colleton. Blazing the shibboleths of '76, he incited defiance of the oppressive tax and called on the Governor to alert the legislature. In thus jumping the gun Rhett took the first rash step in his terrifyingly consistent career of dissent. Incorrigible and maddeningly self-righteous (to public associates), he soon won a name as the *enfant terrible* of Carolina politics. In time he would bring his state the name "Rhettsylvania" and acquire a venerable if tattered mantle as the "Father of Secession."

It puzzles a bit to know that Rhett professed Christianity as ardently as disunion, that he counted the Prince of Peace an ally in his lifelong provocations to violence. The irony did not escape the Unionist leader, James Louis Petigru, who wrote (to Legaré in Belgium) during the height of the nullification furor that "religion

never has been more flourishing. In Beaufort and Walterboro its
triumphs have been very signal. Robert Barnwell and Barnwell
Smith have given in their adhesion. It is like Mahomet's faith,
however. They combine war and devotion, and, in fact, it seems
to me that fanaticism of every kind is on the increase."

Petigru, nonetheless, valued Rhett's friendship. The two men
were so close, in fact, that when Rhett took heavy losses in the 1837
financial crash Petigru offered his own credit "to the last dollar."
And though by 1850 Petigru had long since despaired of the public
Rhett, he probably sighed in helpless admiration when the arch
fire-eater stood on the U.S. Senate floor and risked his honor by
refusing on Christian principle to save it in a duel. Perhaps Wallace
is not merely lapsing into late Victorian cant when he calls Rhett
"this most amiable and lovable of friends, the well-nigh perfect
Christian gentleman, a man of the refinement and purity of a
woman."

This "well-nigh perfect Christian gentleman" held slaves, of
course, watched over them with a fondly paternal eye, burned to
increase their kind (by imports from Africa) and slept with an easy
conscience. His equally pious abolitionist cousin Sarah Grimké
once described him as a man of "high passions, great talents, a fair
specimen of the aristocratical despots of the So[uth]." If her fanaticism had not taken the opposite turn from his, she might have
figured him "the noblest flower of Southern manhood," for he stood
six feet tall and flashed blue-gray eyes from a beardless choirboy's
face.

Rhett may not have known that his cousin Sarah thought him a
fair specimen of the South's aristocratical despots, but he did know
that a growing opinion to the north thought slavery a form of
despotism, a noxious weed to be eradicated from American soil.
Almost as early as Calhoun, who admitted by 1830 that "the real
cause of the present unhappy state of things" was the South's
"peculiar domestic institution," Rhett saw in the growing imbal-
ance of Congressional power a thrust at slavery. If the North could
override the South to fasten tariffs on the country, it could and
would in time override her to unfasten the bonds of her black labor.

Sharp-eared slaveholders had actually picked up the abolitionist
drumbeat long before Rhett came on the scene, at least by 1819,

when the Missouri Compromise, as Charles Pinckney foresaw, gave the South a battle but lost her a war by fixing the principle that Congress could exclude slavery from the territories. Before that time antislavery utterances were not uncommon in South Carolina: in 1816, for instance, a Charlestonian had regretted in the newspaper that slavery was not abolished "when British tyranny was expelled from America." After the compromise the state was on the defensive, and few doubted publicly the worth of the institution, at least in Southern practice. Early written defenses, however, were apt to assume the institution "abstractly considered" an evil, pursuing the *tu quoque,* or you're another, line of vindication. As Legaré exclaimed in the *Southern Review*: "They [the finger-pointers of old and New England] talk about the imprescriptable rights of mankind, and question the very *titles* which they became bound to warrant, by selling us the property."

More cogent defenses seemed in order—and did, in fact, appear—when Charleston uncovered in 1822 the most egregious slave conspiracy since 1739. At the beck of Denmark Vesey, a free Negro carpenter who had bought title to himself with a lottery windfall, slaves were to rise in the city and surrounding countryside, kill their masters, burn the mansion houses, rob the banks and seize ships for transport to San Domingo. The plot was bared by a house servant, as a Vesey lieutenant had feared it might be when he warned a co-conspirator, "But take care and don't mention it to those waiting men who receive presents of old coats, &c from their masters, or they'll betray us."

Writing in the wake of Reconstruction, Mrs. Ravenel lays the blame on Northern abolitionists, who she says had poisoned Vesey's mind on his trips to the North. Later and less partisan analysts, however, do not suggest that he had ever been out of Charleston after a boyhood voyage to the West Indies. The contemporary historian of the Negro E. Franklin Frazier concludes that Vesey had some knowledge of French revolutionary principles and the Congressional debates on the Missouri Compromise. At any rate, he believed in equality and used his wide and apparently caustic influence to build up the Negro's confidence. According to the official trial reports:

> *Even whilst walking through the streets in company with*
> *another, he was not idle; for if his companion bowed to a*
> *white person he would rebuke him, and observe that all men*
> *were born equal, and that he was surprised that any one would*
> *degrade himself by such conduct. . . . When answered, We are*
> *slaves, he would sarcastically and indignantly reply, "You de-*
> *serve to remain slaves"; and if he were further asked, What can*
> *we do, he would remark, "Go and buy a spelling book and read*
> *the fable of Hercules and the Waggoner"; which he would*
> *then repeat, and apply it to their situation.*

Tried by a court made up of "the most respected citizens," as
Wallace puts it, who acted with "exemplary fairness," thirty-five of
the conspirators were hanged and thirty-seven deported from the
United States. All were slaves except Vesey. Most seem to have
met their fate courageously. Vesey died without naming his confederates, and on the gallows one of his lieutenants charged the
Negroes waiting for trial: "Do not open your lips! Die silent as you
shall see me do."

Charleston's terror of insubordinate blacks in 1822, or for as long
as slavery persisted, makes common sense, but it seems a strange per-
versity to react at this date from the assumptions and conditions of
1822. It seems a pity, in other words, that South Carolina historians
imply neither regret for the waste of such talent and courage as
Denmark Vesey's nor even a breath of impartial wonder at his
accomplishment. And it was an accomplishment—for good or ill,
as one chooses. Preaching the same doctrine as Barnwell Rhett,
Vesey reached proportionately as many ears and worked ends as
incalculably widespread if not in the long run as bloody.

One result that Vesey perhaps failed to anticipate was tightened
control of the Negro, free and slave. Easygoing Charleston hastened
to enforce winked-at or lapsed regulations, and the state tried to
fence off its black tribes from alien witch doctors, legislating imprisonment of Negro seamen while calling at local ports and their
sale into bondage if employers failed to bear jail costs. Lawmakers
refused a bill cutting off slave traffic with other states, however.
One South Carolina historian, judging this traffic the major source

of pollution, blames Governor Thomas Bennett for wavering, in distraction perhaps at the complicity of his own trusted house servant in the Vesey plot. His legislative message voices neither outrage nor resolution but only a kind of late Roman stoicism in the face of "admitted evil." Learning, ingenuity, and the stores of experience "have been exhausted," he said, "in the fruitless search for a practical remedy . . . we can do no more than steadily to pursue that course indicated by stern necessity and a not less imperious policy."

No psychological palsy afflicted the sixty-four-year-old "schoolmaster of state rights," Dr. Thomas Cooper, who championed the Negro seaman's act when Charleston's federal judge, William Johnson, pronounced it unconstitutional. He not only denied the federal right to meddle with the states in their handling of the slave problem but passed benedictions on slavery itself, forecasting, perhaps even starting, the trend from shame to pride of the institution. This great friend and disciple of Jefferson—touted from Monticello as "the greatest man in America in the powers of his mind and in acquired information"—repudiated in Carolina the rights-of-man creed that had drawn him to America and exerted his boundless pugnacity in teaching young squires logical defenses of plutocratic rule.

A scarred but unscared veteran of many polemic skirmishes when he advanced on Columbia—in his youth he had bearded the old lion of the British Constitution, Edmund Burke, and in maturer years had gone to jail under the Alien and Sedition Laws for insulting President John Adams—Cooper started a row that in the course of ten years exposed almost every vital nerve of South Carolina thought and feeling. His effect might almost be read, in fact, as a sociopolitical graph. His arrival signified to begin with a certain liberal-mindedness in the state's ruling clique, for his notoriety as a freethinker had already cost him appointment as the first professor at Jefferson's university. The clerical yells that soon echoed through the upcountry, however, suggested that fundamentalism was already hardening South Carolina for its coming stand as a Bible Belt fortress. Persuaded that Dr. Cooper was subverting the gospel in the college, the Presbyterian elders howled for and finally got a legislative inquisition in 1831. By that time, happily for the doctor, he had so captivated the slavocrats as a states' right oracle that they rescued him from the bigots.

Religion and politics were so mixed in the wrangle that some of the state's most enlightened voices joined the bigot chorus. James L. Petigru, for instance, as sane and generous a mind as the ante bellum period could show, cried out from Charleston that Cooper sought "to bury in one common ruin the whole Christian Clergy and the institution of religion." A worshipper at mild-mannered St. Michael's, Petigru could scarcely have shared the Presbyterian terror of that "dangerous heretic who was exerting an insidious and pernicious influence" on tender youth. Obviously it was his terror of political heresy that made cause with the Calvinists. After all, he had such reverence for the Union that he not only stood up to nullification but stood bravely facing north as Carolinians swarmed past him on the road to secession. Petigru doubtless felt at heart about Thomas Cooper as did "An Old Farmer," who wondered in a Camden sheet why an Englishman who had spent his life "sewing [sic] discord disunion and revolution" should be harbored "in the bosom of our state." In declining to say that such a villain "deserves the gallows," he implied his readiness to furnish a rope if the occasion should arise.

Dr. Cooper was neither timid nor inept in fending off his traducers. In fact, his disputative skill probably endeared him as much to the argufying gentry as his laissez-faire preachments in the college. But it is no surprise that he met his polemical match in South Carolina. Having rebuked Judge William Johnson for omitting his title in a journalistic debate, he was handed such a scathing apology that he retired from the match: the judge said that he had unintentionally neglected the "Dr." but would never do so again, for he "would not pluck a feather from the cap of an idiot if it afforded solace to his harmless vanity." Cooper could only summon the witless rejoinder that in a contest of vulgarity and scurrility he yielded the palm to a master.

Dr. Cooper also met his match in the campus bloods, who wanted to act like roughneck boys and be treated like Ivanhoes. Disposed to treat them like responsible men, he tried to install a form of student government, but they held out for license and the immunity of their "honor." Feeling free to insult professors, get drunk uptown, rock the windowpanes or flog the college servants, they felt insulted at the mildest rebuke. As Cooper wrote to Jefferson:

> *Every student in College holds himself bound to conceal any offense against the Laws of the Land as well as the Laws of the College: the robbing of henroosts, the nightly prowling about to steal Turkies, from all the houses in the neighborhood are constant practices, among a set of young men who would never forgive you, if you doubted their honor, altho' I know this form of declaration is little else than an insolent cover for falsehood for many of them. . . . Republicanism is good: but the "rights of boys and girls" are the offspring of democracy gone mad.*

Pushing his authority at one point, he was forced to suspend more than half the enrollment.

But Cooper did not waste all his energies in contention. He raised academic standards—refusing thereby to popularize the college among "ignorant people"; and to help mitigate the ignorant clamor for lax requirements, he pleaded for better common schools throughout the state. Off campus he aroused the state to improved care of the insane and spoke so cogently for medical training that shortly afterwards Charleston doctors asked the legislature to empower a college of medicine.

In the final weeks of Dr. Cooper's presidency a student duel—bringing death to one youth and all but fatal wounds to another—vindicated his judgment that Carolina parents disgracefully pampered their young. As the pioneer gynecologist J. Marion Sims remembered it, this affair of honor sounds like a travesty of all such formalistic and deadly quarrels:

> *They were very intimate friends; they sat opposite to each other in the Steward's hall, at table. When the bell rang and the door was opened, the students rushed in, and it was considered a matter of honor, when a man got hold of a dish of butter or bread, or any other dish, it was his. Unfortunately, Roach and Adams sat opposite each other, and both caught hold of a dish of trout at the same moment. Adams did not*

let go; Roach held on to the dish. Presently Roach let go of the dish and glared fiercely in Adams' face, and said: "Sir, I will see you after supper." They sat there all through the supper, both looking like mad bulls, I presume. Roach left the supper-table first, and Adams immediately followed him. Roach waited outside the door for Adams. There were no hard words and no fisticuffs—all was dignity and solemnity. "Sir," said Roach, "what can I do to insult you?" Adams replied, "This is enough, sir, and you will hear from me." Adams immediately went to his room and sent a challenge to Roach.

Young Govan Roach's death from his wounds a few years later, grieving his only sister, would also touch the ante bellum South's emergent mythmaker, her husband-to-be, William Gilmore Simms. Whether the circumstances of the duel itself stirred his imagination —risking one's life for a dish of trout might well have suggested Hamlet's "greatly to find quarrel in a straw"—certainly the attitudes that made it possible infused his novelistic portraiture of the Southern aristocrat. And though he seems never to have sought the dueling grounds himself, Simms often showed a duelist's daring.

In the nullification period, for instance, he had to show more than ordinary nerve to stay in business as editor of a unionist sheet in Charleston, where feeling ran so high from 1830 to 1833 that an unarmed man scarcely walked the streets after dark. Once he stood up to a mob of nullifiers bent on thrashing him for his editorial cheek and perhaps smashing his print shop as a future corrective. By his own rather ponderous account he was "assailed . . . between the hours of two and three [in the morning], while standing on the threshold of his Office by a mob of from two to three hundred persons, armed generally with clubs." When three miscreants "assaulted and collared" him, he might have "lost his life" but for "the use of a weapon of some little potency, and the timely interference of a few friends." Actually the friends were friendly enemies, who came forward in "manliness and gentility" to stop the cowardly assault.

If no one had come forward, Simms would doubtless have gone down fighting, for he was a physical as well as a moral stalwart. Nearly six feet tall, he was powerfully built and stood "erect as a poplar." Having the sort of massive brow that his age acclaimed as noble, he boasted an undershot jaw to match and blue-gray eyes that his poet friend Paul Hamilton Hayne described as flashing like scimitars in moments of excitement.

When Simms became a newspaper editor in 1830 he was already gravitating from the law to his heroically busy career as the South's first professional man of letters, having published five books of verse and survived the first of many hopeful excursions into the miasmic gardens of Southern magazinery. But in aspiring to literature he had not forsworn politics. Except for brief periods he never would. And it is profitless to suppose with Vernon Louis Parrington that he might have renounced the intoxications of public life in his time. The ante bellum Carolinian stood to make his mark on a three legged stool of planting, politics and the law. Inheriting plantations, he would train for the bar and take a ready-marked-out seat in the legislature. Coming to the law empty-handed, he would work to buy plantations and then mark out a seat in the legislature. Born in Charleston to an obscure if respectable and landowning family, the ambitious Simms turned to the law and to public affairs in emulation of such figures as the lawyer-intellectuals Legaré and Petigru and the fabled diplomat, natural scientist, aesthete and bon vivant Joel Roberts Poinsett.

He turned to planting, or at least the planter's way of life, when he married the only child of a widowed landowner and went to live at their place in Barnwell District. Parrington sees the union as luring Simms from the Whitmanesque open road of democracy and realism into the swamplands of Southern fantasy. A "richly endowed" plebeian, cruelly snubbed by the Charleston he adored, so the thesis goes, Simms married his way into "the ranks of the lesser gentry" and embraced their cause in self-vindication. The thesis errs not so much in misconstruing the facts about Simms as in misunderstanding the sources and ends of fiction. Though obviously wrong in assuming a social chasm between Simms and his second wife—they belonged more or less to the same "class"— its worst fault lies in diagnosing his literary work as an aberration. The writer, like any other man, derives from a time and a place. He is a good writer to the extent that he is able to mythicize the spirit of that time and place. When he also creates a universal myth, an image of everyman, we call him great. Simms missed greatness. He was second-rate, because he lacked the powers to be first-rate. To say that he was cheated of his artistic birthright, or cheated himself, is like Gray's lamenting the "mute, inglorious Miltons" of his country churchyard. If they were mute, they were not Miltons.

In the long run Simms may have more importance—certainly more interest—as a reflector of the ante bellum social climate. And for that purpose his five-volume *Letters,* heroically assembled by his granddaughter Mary C. Simms Oliphant, have more importance than his eighty-two works of published prose. We find expressed here, for instance, the feeling that Charleston looked down its nose —but not, as biographical accounts reiterate, in contempt of a stunted family tree. The truth is that Simms' deep longing to be an epic poet was suspect in a culture addicted to the useful and manly forensic arts. Aside from the real or imagined disregard that every proud and poetical young man smarts under, Simms had to endure squirearchic mistrust of the earnest literary pursuit. A verse now and then for a funerary or nuptial occasion—that was a fit indulgence for gentlemen. He wrote his New York literary friend James Lawson just after his clash with the nullification mob that "in Charleston, a literary man is obnoxious—he is decidedly a nuisance. . . . I have been severely abused because—as they phrased it—I was a poetry man." He was only twenty-four at the time, but the same note in one guise or another echoes through his letters almost to the end. It came out in his anger at the South for allowing magazine after magazine to wither and especially in his pathetic yearning to be consulted on state affairs, even to be chosen for high office.

Like most young writers a glutton for applause, Simms was not quite the pariah he figured himself to Lawson. He counted Petigru, for instance, among his partisans—at least he dedicated a book of verse to the eminent lawyer. As a unionist editor, moreover, he undoubtedly frequented the public company, if not the drawing rooms, of such lustrous figures as Poinsett, Chancellor DeSaussure, William Drayton and Henry Middleton.

The sound and fury of the clash between South Carolina and the federal government has obscured the fact that unionism commanded names so eminent as these or that they in turn commanded such wide-flung and vehement support. Drawing much of their strength from the upcountry, where cotton was not yet absolute king, they swung enough weight in the 1830 legislature to block the necessary two-thirds vote for a nullification convention. And though they carried so few districts that they lost out in 1832, they still ran in the popular vote not far behind the nullifiers.

When South Carolina's boyishly handsome Senator Hayne— pointedly homespun-clad—stood up in 1830 to match rhetoric with Daniel Webster on the nature of the federal union, he vastly cheered the nullifiers at home. He scarcely wielded, however, the hypnotic influence of Calhoun, who, it was being said, could make Carolina sneeze by taking a pinch of snuff. The movement did not gather irresistible momentum until Calhoun, at despairing odds with Andrew Jackson, broke his vice-presidential silence and openly expounded the doctrine he had rationalized in the *Exposition*.

With two such bristleheaded antagonists as Calhoun and Jackson stalking about the national stage, electric scenes were bound to occur. They sparked initially over the sometime barmaid and lady of many rumored loves Peggy Eaton, who, having caught a husband in Jackson's cabinet, had snared the old man's frontier gallantry as well. Jackson apparently blamed the Calhouns for the social ban on the tarnished Mrs. Eaton—he pronounced her "chaste as a virgin" and Henry Clay parodied, "Time cannot wither, nor custom stale her infinite virginity"—but whether they had decreed the snub or not, Floride Calhoun had refused to call, and her husband would not, probably could not, change her patrician mind. Jackson is said to have tried it himself and had the chilling luck of being shown to the door by Floride's butler.

The breach widened with Jackson's pistol shot toast at the 1830 Jefferson Day banquet, "Our Federal Union: It must be preserved," and Calhoun's counterfire, "The Union: Next to our liberty most dear. May we all remember that it can only be preserved by respecting the right of the States and distributing equally the benefit and burden of the Union." But the irreparable break came a few weeks later when plotters apprised Jackson of Calhoun's strong inclination as secretary of war to repudiate the General's free and easy conduct in the Seminole campaign. Bitterly the President wrote his one-time "sincere friend" that he never expected to say of him, *Et tu Brute.* "Understanding you now," he concluded, "no further communication with you on this subject is necessary."

In October, 1832, Petigru addressed Legaré in Belgium, "Since you left us things have turned out as fools wished and wise men expected." He meant, of course, that the nullifiers had swamped the unionists, that a convention was assured, that, in his view, "as far as South Carolina has a voice her fate is sealed." It had been the bitterest election campaign the state had ever known, with both parties, at least in Charleston, resorting to such tricks as keeping potential voters under lock and key and plying them with rum for days ahead. Making allowance for Petigru's bias, we get a fair picture from him of the turmoil:

> We were beset at Sayle's [a public meeting hall] night after night by a disorderly mob and obliged to arm ourselves with bludgeons and march out in files. The mob crowded on us with every species of insults. Their leaders entreated us to retire, as their men were perfectly disorderly and would listen to nothing. It was with great difficulty we could persuade our men to do so. Many blows were aimed at me; Drayton and Poinsett were both struck and we drew off our people amidst every species of insult and abuse. We could have cleared the street . . . but doubtless the parties would have met the next time with muskets.
>
> After the city election a treaty took place between the parties to prevent bribery. The Nullifiers construed this compact as they do the Constitution—they gave men money to prevent them from selling their votes . . . the paupers . . . were discharged by Tom Gantt on the day of election, and they voted by the unanimous consent of his brother managers, backed by old Turnbull, who insisted roundly that as they were discharged from the Poor House they had a right. . . . There appears to me a great contempt for justice that seems to go hand in hand with every revolution.

Petigru's quizzical turn of mind was rare in South Carolina public figures of the time. It may partially explain, in fact, why he never sought elective office. He was unable or unwilling apparently to learn what most men of the Carolina master class seem to have been born knowing, that, as Abraham Lincoln said, Americans want

"solemn asses" in high places. During the nullification fracas certainly he sounded almost the only humorous note, though C. G.
Memminger (later Confederate secretary of the treasury) did burlesque the leading "fire-eaters" in a biblical parody. At one point
he figured Governor Hamilton as the prophet James preaching
to the men of Colleton on the knaveries of the people "called
Yankees," who "have despoiled you of your substance and put
chains upon your members." When his hearers doubted, James
called "aloud on the name of George [McDuffie] the Prophet,"
who said that

> *"although your fields are green and your hands free, yet desola-*
> *tion and destruction and famine shall surely come upon you, for*
> *by the spirit of John [C. Calhoun], the Conjuror, I swear*
> *that great and inconceivable are the evils which the tariff of*
> *John of Quincy shall bring to pass.*
>
> *"Wherefore, O men of Colleton, let not your hearts be faint,*
> *but hearken to the words of James and wax stronger in the*
> *faith—for lo! I will show unto you a hidden secret."*
>
> *Then George waved his hand before the eyes of the men of*
> *Colleton, and they beheld in the air a host of Yankees bearing*
> *from the fields of the South "forty of every hundred parts"*
> *of the increase thereof.*
>
> *And he gave them to drink of certain liquor, which James*
> *and his companions had procured from the kingdom beyond*
> *the great waters . . . and they waxed warm, and they felt the*
> *chains and the shackles whereof James had spoken.*

The new legislature promptly voted for a convention and adjourned to the celebrant boom of cannon and—by an appalling
fluke—the jaunty strains of "Yankee Doodle." The convention as
promptly met in an atmosphere of roaring bravado—one speaker
invoked the readiness of sixteen thousand "back-countrymen with
arms in their hands and cockades in their hats" to march to
Columbia's defense—and passed the Ordinance of Nullification. It
declared the 1828 and 1832 tariffs null and void, forbade appeals to
the federal courts, enjoined all officers and jurors to swear enforcement of the ordinance and declared that any Congressional act to
use force or interfere in the state's commerce would be "inconsistent

with the longer continuance of South Carolina in the Union."

Less than a month later Jackson countered with his own Proclamation to the people of South Carolina, a statesmanlike appeal to reason and love of country. In calm, lucid and firm language it denied the right of nullification, brushing aside all the fine-spun theories of constitutional lawyers and resting the case on the common-sense ground that the United States and un-united states could not coexist. It also made plain the federal government's resolve to use force if necessary.

Toward the end of his Proclamation Jackson entreated directly his "Fellow citizens of my native State!" wishing not only to "admonish you as the first magistrate of our common country not to incur the penalty of its laws" but to "use the influence that a father would over his children whom he saw rushing to certain ruin. In that paternal language, with that paternal feeling, let me tell you, my countrymen, that you are deluded by men who are either deceived themselves or wish to deceive you." Portraying America as the glory of the past and the promise of the future, he then concluded:

> *Look on this picture of happiness and honor, and say, we, too, are citizens of America. Carolina is one of those proud States, her arms have defended, her best blood has cemented this happy Union! And then add, if you can without horror and remorse, this happy Union we will dissolve—this picture of peace and prosperity we will deface—this free intercourse we will interrupt—these fertile fields we will deluge with blood —the protection of that glorious blood we renounce—the very name of Americans we discard.*

The private reaction of the nullifiers may be gauged by McDuffie's epistolary reference to Jackson as "the driveling old dotard" in the White House. The official reaction was a legislative threat to "repel force by force" and Governor Hayne's calling the militia to arms. Most unionists shared the elation of one who wrote that "God and Old Hickory are with us," though not all rared to fight with Old Hickory as did the members of an upcountry union society, who resolved that "we have but two words by way of reply to the Nullifiers, which are these: '*Come on.*'" Uneasy at the "roasting ferment," Petigru was a bit dubious of the President's "high federal doctrine, which seems to come from Jackson most oracularly, as if the priest was giving utterance to what the Deity forces from him, without any volition on his part."

Jackson's unofficial South Carolina agent, Joel R. Poinsett, a spy in the enemy camp, so to speak, had raised a patriotic voice no less affecting than the chief's. Addressing his party at Seyle's, he had brought a charge from Lafayette, whom he had visited in Paris the previous year. " 'Tell your countrymen' " he quoted the old Revolutionary hero as saying,

> "[that] if they are so mad . . . as to quarrel among themselves about the mere matter of interest, about five or six per cent more or less for duties . . . they will discredit republican government throughout the world. [Say] we are looking anxiously to them, for if they . . . dissolve the Union, and cause the failure of the great experiment . . . we who are contending for freedom on this side of the Atlantic must lie down in despair and die in our chains."

Poinsett had also drawn for effect on his flag-waving triumph in Mexico, where he had gone in 1825 as the first American minister. When "infuriated soldiery" lunged at the embassy on one occasion— Poinsett had played too open a hand in the nation's politics:

> My only defense was the flag of my country, and it was flung out at the instant that hundreds of muskets were leveled at us. [The secretary] . . . and myself placed ourselves beneath its waving folds and the attack was suspended. We did not blench, for we felt strong in the protecting arm of this mighty republic. We told them that the flag which waved over us was the banner of that nation to whose example they owed their liberties. . . . The scene changed as by enchantment. . . . Fellow-citizens, in such a moment as that, would it have been any protection to me and mine to have proclaimed myself a Carolinian; should I have been here to tell you this tale if I had hung out the palmetto and the single star?

Though he had served the state loyally and well—as chairman of the Board of Public Works he had built a system of roads and canals linking the interior with the coast—Poinsett had less reason than any other Carolinian of his time to nurse parochial animosities. Educated abroad—chiefly in military science—he made a seven-year pilgrimage through Europe and Western Asia, refusing en route a flattering request to serve the Russian Czar Alexander I. Then he had spent nearly as many years representing his own country in South America, indulging his martial and republican ardor by conspiring with native patriots against Spain and campaigning with the Chilean revolutionary army.

After his Mexican adventure, Poinsett had come home to establish an urbane little social court in Charleston, sufficiently cultivated by this time fully to appreciate the wide range of his intellect. As Mrs. Ravenel reports it, his once-a-week breakfasts became "as marked a feature of society as the St. Cecilia itself." Having the courage of his tastes, he banished after a trial invitation women who failed to meet the test of beauty, charm or intelligence and men who did not prove agreeable. No doubt guests were also expected to admire his garden, where he grew among other exotics the famous Christmas flower that he had brought from Mexico and that now bears his name.

In his declining years—after serving with distinction as Martin Van Buren's secretary of war—Poinsett would find himself more and more out of step with his native state, though unembittered. Seeing him in retirement at his wife's plantation near Georgetown (1850), the Swedish writer Frederika Bremer found him the second man she had met with in the South to speak of slavery "in a really candid and impartial spirit." He wished his native land "to free itself from this moral obliquity," but he saw "the difficulties attending any change so great, that he leaves the question to be solved by the future." Far from content with the drift of things in his country and state, he nonetheless forecast the "onward progress of America. . . . He is one of the New World's wise men, who more and more withdraw themselves . . . looking on calmly from his hermitage."

She found this American version of the French *gentilhomme* a benign slavemaster. His Negroes occupied a village of neat white-washed houses shaded with peach trees. Every family kept its own vegetable and flower garden. The old and sick got special care, and nobody worked later than six in the afternoon.

Though seventy-one when Miss Bremer called at the White House plantation, Poinsett still presented a "slender and agile" physique, still recalled the spirited adversary of nullification.

During that crisis Poinsett kept Jackson informed of events in South Carolina, appealing for arms and troops, and at the will of his party took command of the forces to be composed of regular militia in sympathetic districts and secret volunteers in fire-eating bailiwicks. But Poinsett was no Hotspur or General Gates: as a military scientist he knew the unionists would have slim chances in a showdown. He was not satisfied with Jackson's assurance that he *could* send at least 50,000 men to South Carolina within forty days.

Though Poinsett never did have a United States army at his back, he did sufficiently abash the nullifiers. Openly blusterous, they quailed in private at the rumors he sent abroad. Certainly these rumors did not alone precipitate the state's nullification of Nullification in March, but they deepened the sighs of relief backstage when Congress lowered the tariffs. Too relieved at the peaceful resolution of the crisis to gloat, Poinsett must have smiled to himself, if not gritted his teeth, when the nullifiers gloated that by their "courage and high principles" they had "foiled the swaggering giant of the union."

It was undoubtedly such cockcrowing that tempered Petigru's joy. When his "nullifying acquaintances and quondam friends" inquired of his mood, he would "tell them sincerely that though I am glad the evil day is put off, I am not sensible of any great happiness in thinking that instead of happening to me it is reserved to my children, and a devilish evil day it will be." The crowing did not let up in coming months, and Petigru found it increasingly hard to stand. When the dominant party rallied to honor their dead father of nullification Robert J. Turnbull—with Calhoun as chief eulogist—he wrote that he was "sick and weary of all this flummery; I long for a little common sense."

Though Calhoun spoke pacifically, offering a basis on which nullifiers and unionists could unite to oppose the exercise of arbitrary power from Washington, his South Carolina adherents acted with all dictatorial haste to estrange the minority. They added to the State Constitution a "test oath," requiring every official to swear allegiance to South Carolina. That the oath also required defense of the Federal Constitution did not allay unionist alarm and indignation, for the legislature bullied that whoever refused to pledge loyalty to the "mother that has cherished or protected him" ought to be "an outcast and wanderer upon the earth."

To this insolent piety Poinsett retorted that he had been born in Carolina and intended to die there; "the Star-Spangled Banner should be his shroud, pure and spotless he hoped; but if stained with blood, still . . . his shroud." He urged restraint, however, on his reanimated party and advised an appeal to the state courts as a remedy.

Test cases in Charleston brought annulment from the Court of Appeals and ultimately a peacemaking admission from the legislature that the oath imposed no obligation on the citizen at variance with his duty to the United States. However, the Court of Appeals got no thanks for its offices. Instead, after flouting the dogma of state sovereignty again the following year, it was abolished.

A few days later Petigru wrote to Legaré, "All hail to the dawn of a brighter day. The spell of party is broken and Nullification in Carolina is no more than a recollection. We have compromised and buried the tomahawk." And though despairing of the combative Governor McDuffie, who "rails against those spiritless citizens that think of ploughing instead of learning the use of the sword," he found on his visits to Columbia in the ensuing months "nothing but kindness and civility from our late belligerents. Even Dr. Cooper and I," he exclaimed, "have been quite scrumptious."

Yet in darker moments he must have recalled his prediction of the "devilish evil day" ahead. Cheerful by nature, he could vibrate nonetheless to such elegiac sentiments as Legaré posted from Belgium:

> It [the nullification crisis] ends in my not knowing what to think, except that dangers are around and above and below and within our poor little State,—which may God preserve us from! I ask of heaven only that the little circle I am intimate with in Charleston should be kept together while I live,—in health, harmony and competence. . . . We are (I am quite sure) the last of the race of South-Carolina; I see nothing before us but decay and downfall,—but on that very account, I cherish

*its precious relics the more. . . . Yet my heart sinks within me
often when I think of what may too soon be, and I say, in those
touching words, "Why should not my countenance be sad, when
the city, the place of my fathers' sepulchres, lieth waste, and
her gates are burnt with fire."*

But the nullifiers had their dark forebodings as well. James H.
Hammond wrote that the tariff was lowered to remove "the chief
cause of our excitement," but the principle "is to remain untouched,
and after a few years of respiration the assault again to be made
upon our purses and our liberty." And Barnwell Rhett thundered
that the state "had no rights under this government but what she
was prepared to assert in the tented field." The despotism remained
to perpetuate the evil and until the government was limited in its
powers there would be no security for the South.

*A people, owning slaves, are mad, or worse than mad, who do
not hold their destinies in their own hands. Do we not hear the
insolent assumption of our rulers, that slave labour shall not
come into competition with free? Nor is it our Northern brethren alone—the whole world are in arms against your institutions. Every stride of the Government, over your rights, brings
it nearer and nearer to your peculiar policy.*

Between auguries of doom, perhaps, there may be little to choose,
but between the men who prophesy and the remedies they project
there is and there was for South Carolina a sharp distinction. The
state, of course, chose Hammond and Rhett, who joined with Calhoun to lead her in the coming decades straight to the doom all the
prophets foretold.

XI

The Armed Myth

When Charleston endured one of her periodic fires in 1838, James L. Petigru, idling after an all-night battle with the flames, bantered a distant friend, "We all think it was a judgment but disagree for what it was sent." He chose to blame the "insolent convention" then meeting at Augusta, Georgia, which aimed to cut Yankee profits by diverting European trade to Southern ports. Plainly for him the talk at Augusta echoed the old disunion bluster, which no provocation could excuse.

Many of his old party stalwarts, though, were now cooling to the Union as their blood rose against the Northern antislavery crusade. Some crony, in fact, must surely have explained the fire as Charleston's just desert for nurturing that handmaiden of the devil Angelina Grimké.

Nearly all Charleston would have snapped assent. For patrician Angelina, daughter of Judge John Faucheraud Grimké and offshoot of the old Puritan landgrave Thomas Smith, had committed not one but two unforgivable sins: she had befouled the parent nest by attacking the peculiar institution, and she had befouled the name of Carolina womanhood by screeching her libels in public. A week or so after the Charleston fire she would take the final vows of depravity by wedding (in the North, of course) the archabolitionist Theodore Weld, whose *Testimony of a Thousand Witnesses* would be a source-book for *Uncle Tom's Cabin*.

Angelina's betrayal of her caste, her section and her sex broke on Charleston in 1835 when she testified in the abolitionist *Liberator* for the character of its editor, William Lloyd Garrison, whom Southerners accounted the very old Tempter himself. It broke with a double shock, because Angelina was remembered as the quiet Grimké miss, by contrast with her erratic older sister, Sarah, who oscillated in earlier days between merrymaking and nunlike communion with the Scriptures. After all, too, it was Sarah who had led Angelina off to live among the Philadelphia Quakers.

Vilified in the South, Angelina did not bite her tongue. Instead she turned subversive, writing an "Appeal to the Christian Women of the South" to overthrow "this horrible system of oppression and cruelty, licentiousness and wrong." She bade them strike the bonds from their own chattel and persuade "husband, father, brothers and sons that *slavery is a crime against God and man*." She disclaimed, though, any thought of seeking to "overthrow slavery by falsehood, bloodshed and murder":

> *As a Carolinian, I was peculiarly jealous of any movements on this subject; and before I would join an Anti-Slavery Society, I took the precaution of becoming acquainted with some of the leading Abolitionists . . . and it was not until I was fully convinced that their principles were* entirely pacific, *and their efforts* only moral, *that I gave my name as a member.*

Since fanatic virtue seldom apprehends its own nature, often quite naïvely preaches war in the name of peace, it is no surprise that Angelina traipsed across Northern platforms for several years thereafter inciting more hatred of slaveowners than moral aversion to slavery. Along with her fellow evangels she heightened national tension, in the long run helping to bring on the war: goading each other into furies of vituperation, hot-eyed Yankees and hotheaded Southerners at last brought their sections to such a pass that negotiation was futile and compromise impossible.

Angelina's first offense—praising Garrison—was in the Charleston view perhaps her worst. For it was his American Anti-Slavery Society that had caused riot and unrest by flooding the mails with abolitionist propaganda. In the summer of 1835 unionists and nullifiers fraternized in a midnight raid on the post office, seizing a bag of the hated tracts and burning them in the streets. At a later mass meeting, extremists urged taking over the post office, but moderates tempered the hysteria into pleas for a legal brake on the abolition-ists. Washington conceded, as a result, that postmasters were not obliged to deliver what agitators must remain free to send. Those who did not seize that dodge were shortly afterwards under pain of a state law making it felonious to circulate abolitionist witcheries.

The state's resolve to meet the ideological threat head on signified a growing obsession with slavery. The subject would so tyrannize public discussion, in fact, that a native critic vividly though not too aptly figured the South Carolina mind from 1832 to 1860 as a fetus in a bottle. It was more like a robust man in the clutch of a mania. Certainly the shapers of public opinion were brainy and dynamic, but they taxed their brains and hearts for twenty-five years per-suading Southerners to love, honor and defend their peculiar institution.

The energy South Carolina devoted to the cause—and by obvious correlation her leadership in the South—speaks in the choice of three Palmetto prophets (plus one Virginian) to enunciate the definitive 1852 *Pro-Slavery Argument;* William Gilmore Simms, Governor James H. Hammond and Supreme Court Chancellor William Har-per. Together they dredged up every conceivable justification for slavery except the two that really counted—custom and gainful use. Simms discovered that the Founding Fathers "not only recog-nized, but insisted upon inequalities." The laws of American democ-racy guaranteed every man his "place," not any "place" to every man. "Designed as an implement in the hands of civilization," the Negro merely filled his rightfully servile "place." Governor Ham-mond contrasted the British wage earner's sordid lot with the Negro's feathery bed, and Chancellor Harper drew from Hobbes the familiar argument that "a state of nature is a state of war." The Carolinians left scriptural exegesis pretty much to Virginia's pious old Professor Dew, of William and Mary College.

When Calhoun began openly to plead the case for slavery at the national bar, he inevitably assumed the "positive good" theory that infused all these arguments. His logical, Calvinistic mind declining to excuse a "moral and political evil," he represented the South (in 1837) as turning from that "folly" to see slavery "in its true light . . . and the most . . . stable basis for free institutions in the world." In the Senate he reasoned accordingly that the states enjoyed a right to slavery, having reserved control over their own domestic institutions when entering the Union, and that the federal government as their agent should look to its safety.

Since Calhoun frankly spoke for the ruling caste, he would seem to have victimized the slaveless white majority in beatifying slavery. As spokesman of the South at large, perhaps so, but as the voice of Carolina he at least spoke for a larger minority than is commonly supposed. By 1850 nearly half South Carolina's white population belonged to slaveholding families, a larger percentage than any other state could show. Furthermore, whites who did not own Negroes scarcely despised the idea. In fact, when poor men grumbled at "the nigger question" as a rich man's concern they likely expressed more envy of rich men than moral umbrage. Of course some did profess moral scruples, for instance, the overseer of Mulberry plantation (near Camden), whom Mary Boykin Chesnut quotes in her *Diary* as saying that "Slavery is a thing too unjust, too unfair to last." But then so did a few imperial slaveholders like the Hamptons of Columbia, who went to war, as a contemporary remarked, purely for Southern rights and because "they did not want to be understrappers forever for those nasty Yankees."

The Mulberry overseer also claimed to have met in his lifetime only "one or two womenfolk who were not abolitionists in their hearts, and hot ones too. Mrs. Chesnut [the diarist's mother-in-law] is the worst. They have known that of her here for years." (The old lady had come to South Carolina from Quaker country as a bride, though her father had owned slaves in Philadelphia and had left her some in his will.) He was addressing Mary Chesnut in earshot of her father-in-law, the old colonel, who was a bit too deaf to hear, and "I noticed no voice was raised to enable him to hear. He is a Prince of Slaveholders, and so he will die. His forefathers paid their money for them, and they are his by that divine right—he thinks." She judged the colonel "amiable when not crossed" and "courtly in his politeness" but "as absolute a tyrant as the Czar of Russia, the Khan of Tartary, or the Sultan of Turkey."

Mrs. Chesnut exaggerated a bit with "forefathers"—the old colonel could boast only one slaveholding forefather, his immediate sire, John, who had parlayed a village store clerkship into acres broad enough to assure his capturing George Washington for dinner.

Having swelled his patrimony, though, to embrace five square miles of land and built a four-story brick and stone mansion house, the old colonel must have seemed a lord of immemorial lineage. When his coach traveled to Camden or to his summer place three miles from Mulberry, outriders went ahead to clear the road.

Writing as she gazes out on the Mulberry lawn, Mrs. Chesnut limns a scene reminiscent of every dulcet Southern novel from ante bellum *Swallow Barn* to post-Hollywood *Gone with the Wind:*

> *From my window high . . . I see carriages approach. Colonel Chesnut drives a pair of thoroughbreds, beauties, mahogany bays with shining coats and arching necks. Mrs. Chesnut has her carriage horses and a huge family coach for herself, which she never uses. The young ladies have a barouche and their own riding horses. We have a pair, for my carriage; and my husband has several saddle horses. There are always families of the children or grandchildren of the house visiting here, with carriage and horses, nurses and children. The house is crammed from garret to cellar without intermission. As I sit here writing, I see half a dozen carriages under the shade of the trees, coachmen on their boxes, talking, laughing. Some are "hookling," they call it. They have a bone hook, something like a crochet needle, and they hook themselves woolen gloves. Some are reading hymn books or pretending to do so. The small footmen are playing marbles under the trees. A pleasant . . . easy-going life . . .*

But to fragmentize the last sentence is to wrong Mrs. Chesnut, for she wrote, "A pleasant, *empty*, easy-going life, if one's heart is at ease." Her heart was not presently at ease, but she was apt to have said "empty" when her cup was running over. For though she loved the comforts and graces of Mulberry, even the social idea it manifested, she never confused it with Greek temples and academies. She knew that like most of its kind the place was intellectually barren. For she had a nimble and wide-ranging mind. Though a shade too parochial to excuse George Eliot's living in "contended immorality" with her "husband," she was cultivated enough to adore *Adam Bede* and to lend a hand at translating Schiller from the German. She also had compassion enough to declare that "Wherever

there is a cry of pain, I am on the side of the one who cries," and
she was witty enough to write:

> *Today I saw a letter from a girl crossed in love. Her parents
> object to the social position of her fiancé; in point of fact, they
> forbid the banns. She writes: "I am misserable." Her sister she
> calls a "mean retch." For such a speller, a man of any social
> status would do.*

In short, Mary Boykin Chesnut had the makings of a Jane Austen.
Grateful as we have to be for her brilliant journal—"so much more
imaginative and revealing," the critic Edmund Wilson says, "than
any war novel of that generation"—one regrets the fiction she did
not write. If the Carolina aristocracy deserves any blame for Simms'
vagaries, then it merits a stiff rebuke for not locking the gifted lady
in her room until she turned out a Southern *Pride and Prejudice.*

Coming to live at Mulberry in 1840 as James Chesnut's bride of
seventeen, Mary (Miller) Chesnut—daughter of Governor Stephen
D. Miller—had to endure the vexation of life in another woman's
domain and the reproach of childlessness besides. For old Mrs.
Chesnut was not above preening herself on her numerous issue or
the old colonel of pontificating, "Wife, you must feel that you have
not been useless in your day and generation. You have now twenty-
seven great-grandchildren." Revenge of a sort was in order, and it
was only natural that the spirited younger woman should take it
out in irony at the older's expense. Yet the "glaring inconsistencies"
of life at Mulberry were fairly characteristic of slaveholding society:

> *Our Chatelaine [her mother-in-law] locked up Eugène Sue,
> and returned Washington Allston's novel with thanks and a
> decided hint that it should be burned. . . . Bad books are not
> allowed house room . . . but bad women, if they are not white
> . . . may swarm the house unmolested. The ostrich game is
> thought a Christian act.*

What caused her to lash out at a worse anomaly she does not say—
she dares not say, one supposes, even in a private journal:

> *Under slavery we live surrounded by prostitutes, yet an
> abandoned woman is sent out of any decent house. Who thinks*

> *any worse of a Negro or mulatto woman for being a thing we*
> *can't name? God forgive us, but ours is a monstrous system. . . .*
> *Like the patriarchs of old, our men live all in one house with*
> *their wives and their concubines; and the mulattoes one sees in*
> *every family resemble the white children. Any lady is ready to*
> *tell you who is the father of all the mulatto children in every-*
> *body's family but her own. Those, she seems to think, drop*
> *from the clouds.*

Almost alone among ante bellum observers Mrs. Chesnut offers an occasional glimpse into the mind of the slave, who was, of course, not supposed to have a thought in his woolly head. She reports that Maria, while combing her hair one night, voiced a sharp preference for one cleric over another (both white) because "he preaches to black and white just the same. There ain't but one gospel for all." The other by contrast "goes for low life things, hurting peoples' feelings. 'Don't you tell lies! Don't you steal!' Worse things, real indecent. Before God, we are white as he is, and in the pulpit he no need to make us feel we are servants."

Though scarcely mutinous, this remark does imply that slaves pondered their estate, perhaps even suspecting that man's desire had more to do with their bondage than God's will. At least such doubts occurred to house servants, who lived in close quarters with whites, shared their leisure and their luxuries—as well as on occasion their beds—and came often to identify themselves with the master race. Though many house servants remained loyal during and after the war, they were as a privileged class more liable to disaffection than field hands. As Frederick Douglass, the most famous refugee from slavery, testified: "Beat and cuff your slave, keep him hungry and spiritless, and he will follow the chain of his master . . . like a dog; but . . . surround him with physical comfort,— and dreams of freedom intrude." No wonder Mrs. Chesnut agonized when "Cousin Betsy Witherspoon" died at the hands of her "pampered" domestics—so free and easy they had once given a ball fifteen miles away, taking the mistress' linen, china and silver. Why not herself, whose religion consisted mainly in "trying to be good to Negroes, because they are so in our power, and it would be so easy to be the other thing"?

Mrs. Chesnut's predicament attests one of the sharp backlashes of slavery: a kind master dared not indulge his slaves. Often, in fact, he humiliated himself to exact a proper humility of his blacks. Only an eighteenth-century moralist might have presumed to say that gentlehearted masters suffered worse than beaten slaves, but there is no doubt that many smarted cruelly from the moral whip.

Not all, however, were as tender as Mary Chesnut. There were tough kitchen captains who laid about with a valiant hand, the wife of an Abbeville planter, for instance, who prompted her husband to write:

> *"Her house is always neat and her servants always active and busy or she is always scolding or whipping them, for she does not hesitate for a moment to whip her grown negroes when they deserve it."*

Few mistresses, though, practiced such grotesqueries of despotism as Wade Manning's Aunt Camilla at her weekly "Bed of Justice." As Mrs. Chesnut reports it:

> *With her door wide open, she sat in bed with a bundle of switches; and every Monday morning, everybody in the yard was there to give an account of their deeds or misdeeds for the past week. They were mustered in a row and waited. She solemnly rehearsed their misdemeanors. Some were adroit enough to avert their fate. Those whom she condemned stepped up to the bedside and received their punishment, screaming, howling and yelling to the utmost of their ability to soften her heart. She belabored them with her night cap flying, and her gown in horrid disarray. . . . Wade found her dreadful to think of as he fled from the sight and sound. Peace once restored and everybody once more at the daily avocations, they were as jolly as larks, with perspiration streaming.*

One of the company who heard the story with Mrs. Chesnut wondered what Harriet Beecher Stowe might think, and another ventured that she "would feel exactly as we do; but then she would take [a] freak of nature as . . . a common type." He was right, of course. It was the great abolitionist sin. Equally damaging, however, and less often recognized was the abolitionist fault of treating the

Negro as a type, a sore-oppressed inferior. The Negro's Yankee champion actually thought little better of his capacities than his Southern master, often much less. Their dual assumption, that all blacks are alike, if not all inferior, still impairs most discussions of the Negro, slave or free.

It is admittedly hard to find evidence of slaves as distinctive persons; furthermore, the system pressed them to a mold; but neither fact excuses the supposition that they were all as featureless as buckshot. Nor does it excuse a Carolina scholar's using in 1942 the 1842 generic term "wench" for Negro slave women or gagging at the ante bellum practice of suckling white babes at the Negro breast. It may be human to abhor, but it isn't scholarly.

Mrs. Chesnut reports that sixty or seventy blacks were kept "to wait upon this household" at Mulberry, most "too old or too young to be of any use." She does not say how many were kept to work the fields, but the number doubtless ran well into the hundreds. Though we have no evidence as to how they fared, we do know that the overseer had the "good will and respect" of "our small world." If this means the world of cabin as well as "Big House," the Chesnut slaves hoed a joyful row.

Few overseers gratified master or slave. The one who gratified both was almost as rare as a Joseph in Egypt. The odds were always against him. If he plied too biting a tongue and whip, field hands might balk, crops falter, and the master fret. If he abjured the whip altogether, field hands might lag, crops falter, and the master fume. No wonder the overseer became the scapegoat of the system. No wonder the average planter spent half his time either complaining of his present "trifling rascal" or scouring the neighborhood for a paragon. The man he sought was seldom up for hire—he was probably out looking for a paragon of his own.

The class that furnished plantation overseers neither bred managerial wonders nor encouraged the life of stewardship to other white men. Indeed poor whites rued the necessity that forced them into overseeing, since it threatened the sustaining fiction of their lives— equality with their all too obvious betters. Their betters, incidentally, acquiesced in the fiction, for a complex variety of reasons all more or less symbolized by the democratic ballot. When poor whites applied at Mulberry for work—or a handout—they did not rap at the kitchen steps. Mrs. Chesnut complains of having to sit all one afternoon with a company of "heavy-headed louts," for though Mr. Chesnut "was in imminent danger of going mad," he "would never have forgiven me if I had shown impatience." They all stayed to dinner, presumably sharing the family circle at table. At a nearby plantation on another occasion she found "Squire MacDonald, the well-digger" so blatantly at home among the gentry that she "begins to understand the power" the vote gave to "the meanest citizen." Smoking after dinner in the piazza with the gentlemen, the squire was "most at his ease of all. He had his clay pipe in his mouth, he was cooler than the rest, being in his shirt sleeves, and he leaned back luxuriously in his chair tilted on its two hind legs, with his naked feet up on the bannisters."

Atypical in size and splendor, Mulberry typified the way of life South Carolina slaveholders pursued—or fancied—as owners of more or less than the average twenty Negroes. Actually the pattern varied little from that established on the coast in colonial days, except that the pace was easier. Slaves shared after their fashion the blessings of a ripening order. By the 1830's South Carolina had passed the exploitative stage, and most of her planters aimed to match, not to overtop their past yields. Up-and-coming men bought plantations and cleared new fields, but by and large the hustlers and the buccaneers were striking out for the lower South. The slaves they took along, of course—their own or those they bought on the Charleston market to swap for land—were not so fortunate as those who stayed behind with sedentary masters.

A large portion of the 170,000 blacks South Carolina exported to other states in the three prewar decades undoubtedly went along with pioneering masters, for gentlemen decried selling slaves almost as much as they despised the professional slave dealer. Men of good report might sell in emergencies—to clear a pressing debt, for instance—but they hardly savored the transaction. They might even suffer more than pecuniary or ethical grief. For, in the old parishes at least, the embarrassed planter might be shuffling off the fourth or fifth generation progeny of ancestral chattel. Both family pride and conscience would generally move him to seek cousinly buyers; and his own heart would normally forbid his breaking up a slave family even for the better sale. Of all recreants to the slaveholders code, the "negro-splitter" was adjudged the lowest. The code endorsed, however, as a moral right, if not a social duty, selling the worst of all slave miscreants, the troublemaker.

The master's genuine fondness for an occasional slave is borne out in Governor R. F. W. Allston's purchase of Phoebe, "the daughter of my old faithful man Thomas (Head Carpenter) who has no child belonging to me. Hence my willingness to gratify him in his declining years." The Governor does not explain how Thomas' issue had strayed off; but his brother-in-law J. L. Petigru, who handled the purchase in Charleston, does explain having to pay a steep $1,200: another buyer coveted Phoebe and her children, the eldest of whom was shockingly light and fine-featured, "more in conformity with our ideas of an Western Odalisque than of one of the labouring class."

We do not know how the Governor's aunt met a similar appeal to her sympathies, but the appeal itself implies a human bond. Writing from Mobile, Alabama, a former slave asked for his purchase back to South Carolina, though not from dissatisfaction with his master, who "is remarkably kind." He was just homesick. His mind was always "dwelling on home relations and friends which I would give the world to see," and he begged that "you will write me how all my relations are," and remember him "to Sarah, my ma-ma, and Charlotte, my old fellow servant."

By the 1850's few Northerners would credit such evidences of a kindly feeling, as an Allston neighbor complained to the Governor. On a recent stay in Michigan, this planter had found Yankees so appallingly "ignorant" of "our every day" life that he was happy to provide "Statistics of a Rice plantation" for inclusion in a propaganda booklet. Apology though it is, his little monograph gives a fairly good sense of typical practice, among large shareholders, that is, for the Carolina owner of a hundred blacks was one of an even thousand in 1850.

Each slave was given work suitable to his age and condition: a full "task," what an able-bodied man could do in an ordinary day, or a fraction thereof. The winter workday lasted eight hours and the summer "seldom" more than ten. Pregnant women were "appointed to such light work as will insure a proper consideration for the offspring," and after her confinement a woman was allowed thirty days' respite from the fields. "Hands" were fed what this planter regarded as plentiful and varied "rations"—the usual rice, meal and potatoes being supplemented with salt fish, molasses, bacon and occasionally beef. House servants were "dieted from my own table."

His slave quarters were typical in size—18- by 22-foot partitioned boxes—but in other features, such as closely jointed floors and glass windows, they were as superior to most as they would be to many shanties in present use. Most of the wooden-shuttered, crack-floored shanties in present use, however, were built for tenants, whose health and comfort did not much concern the post bellum cotton opportunist.

This apologist for slavery prided himself on buying eggs, chickens and hogs from his slaves and on holiday indulgences:

> On Christmas Day all plantation tools are inspected and a memorandum taken of each, as a check and guide for the overseer and master. . . . To all who are not defaulters in showing their working utensils and who have not been guilty of any grievous offense during the year, an extra Ration of Rice, Peas, Molasses, and Meat, and Tobacco is given. . . . Each woman after taking out her Rations receives a neat handkerchief, and each man a woolen Cap.

Apology may proclaim guilt, but it also proclaims an active conscience. Like Governor Allston himself, this slaveholder was obviously a man of conscience and character, very much aware of his high calling as a rice planter, the prince of all planters. No doubt he had been reared to the kind of solemn charge an old rice-planting queen delivered to a faltering bride:

> It is a very noble life, if a woman does her full duty in it. . . . I grant you it is a life of effort; but, my child, it is our life: the life of those who have the great responsibility of owning human beings. We are responsible before our Maker for not only their bodies, but their souls; and never must we for one moment forget that. To be the wife of a rice-planter is no place for a pleasure-loving, indolent woman, but for an earnest, true-hearted woman it is a great opportunity, a great education. To train others one must first train oneself; it requires method,

power of organization, grasp of detail, perception of character,
power of speech; above all, endless self-control.

As this regal preceptress went abroad in her carriage, by the way, perennially gowned in black silk, she carried a huge reticule from which she flung to curtsying Negroes along the road small useful gifts—a paper of pins, a spool of thread or perhaps a bag of tea.

Though slavery was an overriding concern almost everywhere in the state and the plantation almost every man's vision of glory, town life did flourish mildly in ante bellum Carolina. Aside from the capital city, Columbia, and Charleston, still the trade and cultural center and increasingly the South's guiding oracle, there were such urbane villages as low-country Kingstree and upcountry Yorkville, Newberry and Greenville. All these boasted Greek Revival courthouses designed by the native Robert Mills, the first professionally trained architect in the nation, who left the mark of his eye for chaste symmetry and stateliness in Washington, Baltimore and Philadelphia as well as in Carolina. (His last and crowning commission was the Washington Monument.)

By 1850 Greenville had not only a Mills courthouse but the beginnings of a Baptist college, chartered as the Furman University, a jockey club, four or five small cloth factories and, above all, several hotels cartering to summer exiles from the low-country miasmas. So many coastal gentry had at last discovered the prospects Mr. Woodmason vainly hymned that fashionable strollers began to edge tobacco-spitting rustics off the main streets. An occasional young visitor, like Senator Robert Y. Hayne's Charleston niece Elizabeth McCall, accepted overtures from a mannered young man, like the lawyer Benjamin F. Perry, and settled down to further tone up society as a wife and mother.

Not many miles to the southwest a low-country colony made civilizing ripples from the village of Pendleton. Attracted by the "healthy" climate, they had built manor houses along the Seneca River and sowed the upcountry fields with slaves, cotton and cattle. Along with John C. Calhoun, when he presided at "Fort Hill" during Congressional recesses, they attended meetings of the Pendleton Farmer's Society in a suitably classic little temple on the town square; argued plantation self-sufficiency as a hedge against the tariff in *The Farmer and the Planter;* supported master carriage- and cabinetmakers; and patronized a yearly fair, handing out prizes for the best homespun woolens and ginghams, the lushest fields of grain, and the lustiest bull calves and stallions.

Charlestonians of a different social stratum and persuasion—Ger- man shopkeepers and clerks—had by 1850 laid out the town of Wal- halla, some thirty miles northwest. Pariahs among the planter Brahmin on the coast, they had secured a refuge among the hills for plain people. There they enjoyed a democratic, sober and thrifty life, owning few slaves and showing little disposition to increase the number.

The hill towns were all fundamentalist strongholds—except Pendleton, an Episcopalian retreat—and each tended to fly a single sectarian banner. Walhalla was of course a Lutheran seat; Green- ville was a Baptist Zion; Spartanburg to the east was a Methodist Rome—with its Wofford College in session by 1854; and Due West was the holy city of the Associate Reformed Presbyterians. The last- named sect, by the way, were anything but newfangled or liberal Presbyterians. They claimed, to the contrary, a purer devotion to John Knox's Reformation polity. Zealous to keep their sons from corruption in Columbia, they opened at Due West the state's first four-year denominational college—Erskine—in 1839.

Other than Charleston, the only town aspiring to be a city was Columbia, which had four thousand or so inhabitants by mid- century. Where George Washington had drily noted a few straggling houses among the pines, some rather imposing state buildings and numbers of private mansions in the Greek Revival mode looked out to wide shady avenues, gaslighted by 1853. The town's reigning plan- tation-based society patronized the South Carolina College—gentle- men sat on the board of trustees as a matter of course—worshiped at Gothic-spired Trinity Episcopal Church, and gave family dinners that Mrs. Chesnut thought "the climax of the good things here":

> *They have everything of the best. Silver, glass, china, table linens, damask, etc. The planters live "within themselves" as they call it; from the plantations come mutton, beef, poultry,*

*cream, butter, eggs, fruits and vegetables. It is easy to live here
with a cook who has been sent to the best eating house in
Charleston to be trained.*

Above all Columbians Mrs. Chestnut seems to have admired the
princely Prestons, the Virginia-born brothers William C. and John
S., great-nephews of Patrick Henry. The former stood so well with
the regnant gentry that they made him president of the South
Carolina College when he lost his place in the U.S. Senate by crossing Calhoun on national issues. (At a consolation dinner on his
return from Washington, J. L. Petigru likened the state in her
thralldom to Calhoun to a "lazy old planter" who woke up one day
to find his spry overseer master of the place.) A man of taste and
learning, Preston befriended the American sculptor Hiram Powers
and helped rescue Thomas Cooper from his Calvinist inquisitors.
Undoubtedly he sided with the old disputant to the end and helped
pay for the gravestone "ERECTED BY A PORTION OF HIS FELLOW
CITIZENS."

Equally the man of taste, John S. Preston—"the stateliest cavalier
of them all," Mrs. Chestnut saluted—was rich enough to patronize
the arts, having married Caroline Hampton, daughter of General
Wade I, and having turned whopping profits from a Louisiana sugar
plantation. He afforded Hiram Powers the means to study abroad
and commissioned various works for his Columbia mansion. Not
content with local fish and game, he "sent to the lakes for his salmon,
to Mississippi for his venison, to England for his mutton and grouse."

Mrs. Chestnut found his wife a model of "gentle dignity" and
motherhood. Outwardly mild as a dove, the Hampton heiress was a
true daughter of her masterful sire. Receiving at a ball in her husband's absence—"resplendent in diamonds, point lace, [and] velvet
train"—she descended quietly belowstairs, collared a drunken knife-
wielding servant, led him off to the smokehouse, locked him within,
slipped the key into her bosom and returned to her guests "without
a ripple on her placid face."

Ante bellum Carolina was so enchanted by the Preston manner
that few listened when a retired Columbia jeweler warned of economic and social flaws in the slave and cotton structure beneath it.
Factories were needed to balance the economy, William Gregg urged,

and to salvage the state's derelict poor whites. Though Gregg did attract some Charleston investors, his model factory and village at Graniteville inspired no copies before the war. Gregg breathed not a word against slavery, but he affronted the slavocrats by doubting at least two primary articles of their faith: poor whites were a mongrel breed, scarcely worth the shot it would take to kill them, or at best the inevitable dregs of a healthy body politic; and free labor, if given a foothold, would undermine the peculiar institution. Gregg went ahead nonetheless to prove that a factory located "away from a town" would encourage a wretched people to "develop all the elements of good society."

Using native materials and labor as far as possible and giving his full time and talent to the enterprise, Gregg built the first large, well-equipped cotton factory in the South. He also ran it to the profit of both his investors and the "tackeys" who flocked in from the sandhills to live in the South's first cotton-mill village and to work the looms twelve hours a day six days a week. It may sound as though one profit was real and the other imaginary. But the truth is that his workers prospered beyond their wildest dreams. Some had coin in their jeans and a tight roof over their heads for the first time in their lives. And if Gregg was not quite the savior he imagined himself to be, he was a benefactor. Actually he was more like a Yankee patriarch than the hard-boiled entrepreneur of the Gilded Age. He ruled his shop with a self-righteous but not unkindly hand. He put children from six to twelve in school and supplied the classrooms, the teachers and the books. Frequently he would drive his buggy among the scholars at recess, pass out gingerbread men from his wife's kitchen and, explaining that he never doffed his workman's apron until he was worth $50,000, admonish, "Now go to work, boys." He personally belted truants; and if he caught boy or man trying to sneak a bottle into the Village he smashed it with his cane.

Chartered in 1845, Graniteville soon came to represent half the state's textile investment, indicating both its relative size and the industry's midget proportions. Gregg's success cheered the shippers and money men of Charleston, who welcomed goods for their ailing port from any source. It swayed very few, however, from the Hayne-McDuffie-Calhoun dogma of salvation through free trade and railroads linking Charleston with the West. Hayne had even spent the last four years of his life promoting—though failing to achieve—a line to Cincinnati; and Calhoun had agitated for a line to St. Louis, as more likely to draw the West under a Southern economic and political hegemony.

As Charleston's fortunes declined in the 1840's—partially through competition from Savannah and Wilmington—Gregg feared "another ten years' crusade, to prepare the mind of the people . . . for revolution." Rather than exhort wasteful South Carolinians to Yankee husbandry and factory pursuits, her leaders would screw them up to a second Nullification.

His fears were amply justified. The crusade had already begun. It would take five years longer than he predicted, but it would succeed where Nullification had failed, or, if one chooses, it would fail more catastrophically. It would succeed, because Charleston's politico-intelligentsia were loath to stand alone, as they had in 1832. This is not to say that the Confederate States of America materialized in 1861 as a Carolina stratagem. But it is to say that Nullification had taught a rigorous lesson to the Carolina dissidents and that by 1850 they commanded attention throughout the South.

They were a forceful and persuasive breed, and they had neighbors readier to listen. As South Carolinians gathered to nullify a tariff in 1832, pioneer Mississippians were spreading out to claim virgin soil for cotton and slavery. Now, after twenty years of prodigal harvest, they could recline on their galleries and contemplate the Yankee threat to their splendors.

By 1850, moreover, the Carolinians had begun to proclaim an idea far more persuasive than any rationale of slavery or minority rights —the myth of blood and race. Here was food for the soul of poor and rich alike—Southerners were a chosen people, destined to found a nation among nations. Already convinced of their own matchless worth, Carolinians had only to stretch the parish lines.

Carolina's recent, if not her whole, history conspired to produce the idea of Southern nationalism. Except during the two or three post-Revolution decades, the state had never rejoiced in the American union; and, as that honeymoon ended, her leaders felt Yankee tugs at the mantle of national leadership, just passing from Virginia's failing shoulders. The Carolina social order was certainly distinct from the Northern pattern and, so Carolinians thought, in constant

danger of subversion. For that order her intellect had found sanctifying ideas and myths in the European romantic movement, specifically
in such writers as Walter Scott, Victor Hugo, Thomas Carlyle and
Friedrich Schiller.

They found them especially in Scott, whose romances invited them
to espouse the myth of chivalry. Sir Walter may not have conjured
the Civil War, as Mark Twain suggested, but he did mightily assault
the ante bellum mind, softening it up for the fiction that Southerners
were a noble race and Yankees a base peasant stock. In the two
decades before the Civil War everybody who read at all read the
Waverley Novels. Ivanhoe and Rowena came to the allusive pen
and tongue as readily as the biblical Boaz and Ruth. Mrs. Chesnut,
for instance, described a Columbia matron as a veritable Rowena,
"the purest type of Anglo-Saxon, exquisitely beautiful, cold, quiet,
calm, fair as a lily." The planter gentry diverted themselves with
pseudo-medieval tourneys adapted from *Ivanhoe,* in which the
knights aimed their lances at wooden rings instead of each other.
The newspaper accounts of these affairs fluttered with Scottian
panache: "All the beauty and bravery of the parish" were gathered
on the "lush and spacious greensward" of a Cooper River "castle"
as "the Knights of Rob Roy, Avon and Roderick Dhu" vied for the
honor of crowning "the Queen of Love and Beauty."

J. L. Petigru almost epitomized the Carolina male when he wrote
of a grandson's dividing his time between "outdoor amusements
and the Waverly Novels." Scott's fiction sanctified the outdoor
amusements—hunting, shooting, riding, mustering with the parish
militia. With slaves to command as well as dogs and horses, gentlemen could scarcely help developing a vain and martial spirit.

The two military academies established by the state in 1842 (one
still flourishing in Charleston as The Citadel) reflected this spirit as
well as auguries of a coming fight. Cadets were instructed in the code
of honor, personal and state, and though not urged to settle their
tiffs on the dueling field, they came under tutors who regarded the
code duello as a prime social monitor.

Most gentlemen also admired dueling as a virile pursuit. As the
discerning Northern novelist John W. DeForest judged from South
Carolina observations, the " 'chivalrous Southron' " would "forgive
almost any vice in a man who is manly":

> *If you will fight, if you are strong and skillful enough to kill your antagonist, if you can govern or influence the common herd, if you can ride a dangerous horse over a rough country, if you are a good shot or an expert swordsman, if you stand by your opinions unflinchingly, if you do your level best on whisky, if you are a devil of a fellow with women . . . he will grant you his respect.*

He added that both Southern men and women would regard the pure young Northern male as a "monster of neutral insipidity," quoting a Southern girl's remark that she wouldn't " 'fancy a hen-husband.' "

Another keen observer bears him out—Francis Lieber, a South Carolina College professor who observed the genus chevalier for twenty rueful years. A brilliant German political thinker who endured a long "Exile to South Carolina" waiting for a call to Harvard or Columbia, Lieber complained (in 1851):

> *Every son of a fool here is a great statesman meditating on the relations of State sovereignty to the United States government; but as to roads, common schools, glass in the windows, food besides salt meat, as to cheerily joining in the general chorus of progress, what is that for Don Ranudo de Colobradoes of South Carolina,—out at elbows to be sure; but then, what of that? Does he not belong to the chivāl'ry (do not pronounce chiv'alry; no one here says so, and surely we must know; who else should) of Caarol-i-nar?*

Shortly after joining the faculty he incredulously followed the career of a student expelled for dueling in 1836. By the age of twenty-two the young buck had traveled by a series of quaint and rapid stages to high repute: he had brawled in the Columbia streets, read law, won admission to the bar, gone to prison for two months, married and fathered a daughter and, *mirabile dictu,* mounted to a seat in the legislature. "What a state of society this requires and must produce!" Lieber exclaimed.

This chevalier had probably married a pliant creature whom he would keep in a holy state of pregnancy for twenty-five years and whom he would exalt on the stump, generically, of course, as "those

constant stars in our Southern sky, our angel wives and mothers."
For the code embraced woman worship as a primary article, or at
least obeisance to her role as the vessel of Christian honor and of
white Southern blood. As W. J. Cash says:

> She was the South's Palladium ... the shield-bearing Athena
> gleaming whitely in the clouds ... the mystic symbol of its
> nationality in face of the foe. She was the lily-pure maid of
> Astolat and the hunting goddess of the Boetian hill. And—she
> was the pitiful Mother of God. Merely to mention her was to
> send strong men into tears—or shouts. ... At the last, I verily
> believe, the ranks of the Confederacy went rolling into battle
> in the misty conviction that it was wholly for her that they
> fought.

If Cash seems to lay it on a little thick, listen to a modern South
Carolina historian on the subject (Wallace):

> The unsurpassed virtue of Southern women cannot be dis-
> puted. ... The common explanation that men's easy access to
> slave women protected the white even from temptation is doubt-
> less true as far as it goes; but it must be supplemented by the
> chivalric regard for women fostered by Southern society, and the
> consciousness that trangressions were at the risk of the man's life
> and the woman's social ostracism rather than divorce or damage
> suits. At least two first-class scandals in the highest South Caro-
> lina circles in the generation before 1860 might be cited; but
> the wives were Europeans.

If "chivalry" derived pretty much from the Waverley Novels, it
found vindication at home in William Gilmore Simms' Revolutionary romances. Moved by Scott, Fenimore Cooper and fireside tales of
Marion's men, Simms worked up a kind of prose epic of the demi-
gods who sired the Southern race. He quite consciously essayed the
epic vein, setting out to justify the ways of Carolina to Carolinians
and, not incidentally, to skeptic Yankees. Taking the swamp warfare
against the British as heroic subject, he glamorized the fighting
gentry and the social body of which they formed the head and
crown. Though he shaped a few "realistic" characters, he never
undercut his romantic vision to debase the noble or ennoble the

base. His chevaliers merit their rank, his honest yeoman their yeomanry, his loyal slaves their slavery and his scrubby whites their poverty and debasement.

These works undoubtedly helped propagate Southern nationalism. Though they had more Yankee than Southern readers, as Simms lamented, they did have a faithful audience in the South. As the Charleston *Mercury* avowed:

> *Our children have learned from his Revolutionary stories . . .*
> *their earliest and most impressive lessons of patriotic devotion,*
> *and our Southern statesmen have gathered from his historic*
> *pages their most full and conclusive arguments for the defense*
> *of a people basely and slanderously assailed.*

Simms acted from a sense of mission, surely, in agreeing to edit the *Southern Quarterly Review* in Charleston, for he had groaned repeatedly that literary journals in the South were doomed from birth. Knowing that his voice would carry far and well, he undertook (1848-1854) to awake the South to a consciousness of its distinctive soul and to interpret that soul to the nation. With characteristic élan he importuned almost every writing name in the South, including the Maryland novelist John Pendleton Kennedy, who replied that "Charleston is a very authoritative center of . . . opinion; and wholesome counsels [not overtly political] will be listened to with more deference than from any other quarter."

If one man could be singled out as the author of Southern nationalism, it would have to be Simms. Certainly its germinal forces can be felt beating like a steady pulse beneath his life and work—his passion for his native Carolina country. His identity as a Southerner originated from and fed on that essential piety. In the 1850's he called himself a "Southron"—an archaic form of Southerner borrowed from Sir Walter—but like the colonial Charlestonian in London he felt himself at heart a Carolinian.

On Carolina's behalf Simms underwent in 1856 what was doubtless the worst humiliation of his life. Embarking on a Northern lecture tour, he chose to rebut Massachusetts Senator Charles Sumner's slur on the Palmetto State's role in the Revolution. Though he got a civil hand in three New York towns, unfriendly newspapers hooted him so rudely that his Manhattan sponsors reported a failure even to give tickets away. The roughest of these pictured him as a "stout florid man . . . with coarse wiry gray hair . . . a loud imperious, crackling voice, and manners suited to the overseer of a plantation, where slaves have to be daily cursed and flogged." He appeared "as if conscious that he came from a region superior to this, where greasy 'mechanics' and men and women who do their own work . . . are not permitted to mingle with slaveholders and gentles."

Only a Simms would have been asked to lecture in the North, but only a Carolinian would have broken out his regimental pennons in enemy terrain. Perhaps only a Carolinian also would have felt such crawling shame to find himself "brutally described . . . as a Southern pauper, 'seeking cold charity in Northern lecture rooms.' " No wonder he declined "compensation for anything that I should do in this province" and signed over "to public charities all the money . . . paid me here."

If this incident reflects the passionate Carolinian in Simms, it also indicates the Northern and Southern mind-set after twenty years of passionate and abusive debate. Simms reaped on this occasion a whirling gust of the wind he had helped to sow as a vocal Southern nationalist and slavocrat. But like all who come to reap, he yelped with indignation at his evildoing neighbors, just as they, still broadcasting the winds of hatred, would yelp at the cyclone of war.

XII

Boon for Barnwell Rhett

In the summer of 1850 Calhoun's old fellow "War Hawk" of American nationalism, Langdon Cheves, emerged from plantation retirement to invoke "united secession of the slave-holding states." Representing South Carolina at a Southern protest convention in Nashville, Tennessee, he charged:

> *Unite and you shall form one of the most splendid empires on which the sun ever shone, of the most homogeneous population, all of the same blood and lineage, a soil the most fruitful, and a climate the most lovely. . . . O, Great God, unite us, and a tale of submission shall never be told.*

Whether Calhoun's grim specter nodded in complete accord is a moot question. Certainly his spirit was present, for in his last weeks he had framed the convention as an extralegislative maneuver against the Wilmot Proviso, which would bar slavery from the New Mexico and California territories. It was a kind of last-ditch maneuver in his long campaign—openly conducted after a final bid for the presidency in 1842—to keep a favorable balance of power for the South in Washington. In his last Senate speech (read for him as he sat too ill to speak, "looking like a ghost with burning eyes") he had warned of certain disunion unless the North agreed to slavery in California and New Mexico, restored the South's old-time equality in the Union and called off the abolition hounds. Addressing his Yankee colleagues in national meeting, he could scarcely do more than warn of disunion, but even privately to Southern comrades he never praised it as the great good end. He offered secession as a weapon, not as a prelude to Southern national independence.

When Calhoun died a few weeks after his "disunion" speech (in March, 1850), the bells of St. Michael's in Charleston tolled all day long. All his old colleagues in the Senate eulogized him, all but crusty Thomas Hart Benton, of Missouri, who said that Calhoun's doctrines were treason and he made no distinction between the treason and the traitor. From rites in the Senate chamber his body was borne south in a black-draped steamer, with twenty-five prominent Carolinians aboard. A crepe-hung Charleston received him with mourning bells and minute guns on April 25. Silent crowds followed his hearse through the streets and filed past his City Hall bier from dawn to nightfall. Next morning he was buried in St. Philip's churchyard, his own wish to lie in his native upcountry turned aside by a Charleston knowing better than the great man himself where he truly belonged.

The influence of Calhoun's later career and the effect of his departure at a critical moment are still debated. Some historians believe that Calhoun led the South to war, others that he prophesied in the wilderness against its coming. Some have declared that his death removed the last brake from the wheels rolling downhill; others that he died luckily before events forced him to loose the brake and ride to the smashup. If he counted on militant action at Nashville, his shade must have wept, for the convention merely repeated the old demand for equal rights in the territories. Only nine states sent delegates, moreover, and only South Carolina a full complement. To his own state at least he was the voice of caution: Never secede alone! In that respect Cheves and Governor Hammond spoke his mind at Nashville; while Barnwell Rhett reiterated the advice he had passed out for nearly twenty years at the fluctuation of a tariff: Secede now and let the devil take the hindmost!

There is no doubt as to one result of Calhoun's death: a "desperate [Carolina] struggle for his falling robes," as Simms phrased it. Behind the funerary masks silent tongues thanked heaven that he was gone. (The few surviving unionists agreed openly with William C. Preston that his death was the interposition of God to save the country.) His match, however, was scarcely available—a grievous effect, Simms thought, of his greatness, remarking of Calhoun alive that "His shadow falls heavily upon our young men and darkens all their pathways." Calhoun had brooked no challenge to his mastery.

The chief rivals for Calhoun's Senate place, Governor Hammond and Barnwell Rhett, both rendered full-dress invitational eulogies of the fallen leader, Hammond primed by Simms to eschew the pathetic: "There is nothing to weep for. The man dies in the fullness of his fame . . . foot to the foes, lance in rest, and his enemy quailing;—and he has lived a hero all his life." Though Hammond's bid came from the Charleston potentates, Rhett's emanated from Governor Seabrook, foretelling where legislative favor might lie. Actually there was no contest. Rampant for action, the legislature chose Rhett, the man who had raced home in crimson fury at the white-livered Nashville delegates. ". . . let it be that I am a Traitor," he raved, "The word has no terrors for me. . . . I have been born of Traitors, but thank God, they have ever been Traitors in the great cause of liberty." Better a dead traitor, he cried, than a living slave. Death mattered little,

> whilst duty performed, may remain in its effect to many generations, and a fair fame, live forever, looking to that undying reputation which has ever followed every people who have dared all to preserve their liberties, and have conquered or perished in their defence; instead of shrinking, we might pant for the trial which shall isolate South Carolina in this great conflict.

Rhett could and did sway multitudes with such gusty rant, but, in at least one upcountry lady's opinion, only multitudes of jackasses. Describing a rally at which he spoke, she names him "beast Rhett" and sees him "cheered forward by things in the shape of men . . . and the bellowing of mules":

> he went illustrating the advantage of secession and how we would roll in wealth and the most unheard of arguments. His gaping gang gulped it down and even applauded him for every puke anecdote he told. . . . They went so far as to have a flail to beat the floor of the stand to applaud the villain.

The lady's ridicule by no means implies, however, that she—or the men in her family—opposed slavery or even secession in theory. The state's property-owning electorate was unanimously proslavery, including the hill men who sent three lone unionists to the legislature from Greenville district in 1851. And most were secessionists, divided only on questions of prudence and policy: some wanted to go it alone with Rhett, others to wait for neighboring laggards, and still others to hold back with certain whens and ifs. The feeling against immediate secession did, however, reflect an undercurrent of class discontent. At least the cry that slavery was a rich man's cause was raised loudly enough in some precincts to alarm the oligarchs, who countered by teasing at the poor-white fear of Negro equality.

Divergent class attitudes to slavery also infused a renewal of sectional animosities in the early 1850's. Now far ahead of the low country in white population and nearly abreast in the value of its products, the upcountry started protesting the old constitutional inequities. The pressure was strong enough to gain a few more legislators for the upcountry but not strong enough to budge the aristocratic Constitution, which Governor Adams rejoiced in as a rock of safety in a churning sea of "radicalism."

The hot-blooded 1850 legislature readied for secession and war, voting for both state and Southern conventions, upping taxes 50 per cent to buy arms and audaciously, if legally, asking Washington for public land money declined in an 1841 fit of self-righteousness. But general Southern compliance in the Clay compromise (of the Wilmot Proviso) had so laid tempers by 1852 that the long-deferred state convention resolved that Carolina could secede if she wanted to, that she really ought to considering the provocation, but that she would abstain "from reasons of expediency." Hammond declared these dictums "too pitiful for comment," and Rhett resigned from the U.S. Senate, unable to serve a craven people. In the eyes of his contemporaries, by the way, nothing so became Barnwell Rhett as his abdicating the chair he had coveted all his political life. His personal friend and public enemy, B. F. Perry, hailed it as the "brightest feature in his cap," evincing the "true spirit of the Chevalier and Patriot."

With Rhett in retirement, South Carolina, along with the rest of the nation, enjoyed calm weather until 1854, when the Kansas-Nebraska Act raised, as Stephen A. Douglas had forecast, "a hell of a storm." Breaching the hallowed Missouri Compromise to allow "squatter sovereignty," the right of territorials to vote on slavery, the measure inflamed both North and South. Southerners soon apprehended the eventual cost of this giveaway: crossing the line 36° 30′ with their slaves, they would clear a path for abolition forces straining south. Resolute to give pioneers, as Lincoln said, "a clean bed, with no snakes in it," Northerners were equally distraught. The Kansas-Nebraska Act precipitated months of inflamed debate and in Kansas itself a bloody rehearsal of the war. Of the two—the talking and the shooting war—the first probably did the greater damage.

It also produced on the U.S. Senate floor a spectacle so macabre that Charles Sumner, of Massachusetts, and South Carolina's Preston Brooks won permanent niches in the chamber of American political horrors. One can scarcely say which acted the more baleful part, Sumner in jeering at Senator Butler, of South Carolina, in his "Crime against Kansas" speech or Butler's nephew Brooks in paying back the score with a gutta-percha cane. Hailed as an avatar of chivalry in Carolina, Brooks was showered with votes for re-election— he had resigned from the House after failure of a motion to expel him—gold-headed canes, loving cups and money to pay his assault and battery fine. Brooks's knight-errantry had not always been so admired in his native state. At least South Carolina College authorities had withheld his diploma when he brandished pistols to the rescue of a brother in the Columbia lockup.

While South Carolina was crying Brooks up as a hero, the North was hooting him as a vicious poltroon. The sections, however, diverged characteristically in taking grounds for praise and blame. His own state saw Brooks as personally aggrieved and personally avenging his grievance, while the North interpreted his cane as a symbol of the "bullying" slave power smiting the emblematic brow of twenty-five million free people.

If the Brooks-Sumner affair did not itself quicken the sectional animus, it did sharply focus the bitterness, and it marked the beginning of a newly critical phase in the great national dispute. For the first time in the nation's history parties approached the Mason-Dixon line, the Republicans almost uniting the North and West on an antislavery platform and the Democrats carrying most of the South and portions of the West to elect Buchanan as a Southern rights champion. In South Carolina Rhett and his fire-eating fraternity broke with the Democrats to urge a party that would compel Southern rights or else.

At least one incident vividly reflects the hardening sectional face. As J. L. Petigru reports it, "the gentry of St. Bartholomew's [a low-country parish]" seized a poor Yankee woodchopper, "tied him and carried him to jail, and under the ridiculous pretense that he had stolen a piece of rope, whipped him publicly." Defending the man in a court action, Petigru was up against two bigwigs who "labored hard [but failed] to involve my client and me in the odium of abolitionism."

Committing what Wallace calls the "ugliest retaliatory excess" of the time, extremists tried to reopen the slave trade. Arguing that slavery must end or become the absolute basis of society—to every white man his black—they brought a proposal into the legislature. Though it was rejected, the agitation spurred the illegal traffic, and at least one slave ship boldly sailed into the Charleston harbor. When the crew of another was brought to trial, Federal Judge A. G. Magrath flouted the national piracy laws to throw the case out of court.

Trying to play a strong but patient hand in Washington, Senator Hammond suffered acute embarrassment at these flagrancies. "The South has done nothing but stab herself since October [1858]," he wrote. After Lincoln's prophecy that "A house divided against itself cannot stand," and after the terror of John Brown's raid at Harpers Ferry, however, he despaired of his own or any man's power to allay the madness. As he wrote to Francis Lieber in the spring of 1860:

> So fas as I know, and as I believe, every man in both Houses is armed with a revolver—some with two—and a bowie knife. It is, I fear, in the power of any Red or Black Republican to precipitate at any moment a collision in which the slaughter would be such as to shock the world and dissolve this government.

When the national Democratic convention met in Charleston a few days later, Hammond was missing, but he wired his state's delegation to join the other cotton states in a bolt from the Northern-dominated party. The Southerners wanted a platform of legal protection for slavery in the territories, but the convention swung as expected to Stephen Douglas' doctrine of popular sovereignty. As the Northerners departed for Baltimore to nominate Douglas, the Southern delegates left for Richmond to choose a hopeless candidate. Dividing the Democratic vote, the rift ensured, as Francis Butler Simkins remarks, "the most momentous political defeat the South and the Democratic party have ever suffered." It assured Lincoln's entrance to the White House and the South's exit from the Union.

As Lincoln strode toward the White House in the early fall South Carolinians were swearing never to serve this *"beau ideal* of a . . . dogged, free-soil border-ruffian." His party platform was bad enough, favoring higher tariffs and denying all agencies the right to legalize slavery in the territories. But the man himself, reminding salt-water gentry of a backwoods Bible-thumper, had rasped for all the nation to hear that "this government cannot endure permanently half slave and half free." His election promised "Northern domination" and "continued aggression," but worst of all it threatened the *bête noire* of "negro equality." No one bothered to perceive that, in fact, Lincoln never expounded emancipation, that he scarcely even broached slavery as a moral issue. His diagnosis of slavery, however, as a virulent disease, catching to whites as well as blacks, was possibly counted more dangerous to the South than moral indignation.

Some Carolina paranoiacs even fancied stopping his inauguration at gun-point if the state should funk its messianic obligation to secede. At word of this insanity Senator Hammond wrote that violence of any sort before disunion would properly constitute treason and begged to "be excused the risk of a halter." As a sovereign state, of course, South Carolina could withdraw "without assigning any cause. . . . General incompatibility, the best of all grounds for a divorce, had better be pleaded."

As election day drew near, the radical spirit took the lead, and South Carolina, alone among Southern states, readied for action. Having notified his fellow chief executives throughout the South, Governor William H. Gist summoned the legislature for a special session on November 5 to choose electors and act "for the safety and protection of the State." Meeting at Senator Hammond's home in advance, the ruling clique agreed with Congressman Keitt that the state must set the example. "If we wait for Alabama," he said, "we will wait eternally. . . . Davis in Miss[issippi]. is far more promising. But we must rely on ourselves in moving off."

If many Southern minds turned to second thoughts at the news of Lincoln's triumph, to notions of compromise, few South Carolinians counseled a waiting game. In Charleston, in Columbia and even in the upcountry hills minds were set for independence at any price: the temper was belligerent and the mood optimistic. At Woodlands plantation William Gilmore Simms waited in delirious anticipation, organizing Committees of Vigilance and Safety and dashing off letters to his Northern friends, the pages crackling with bravura and elation, with jaunty threats and, oddly enough, with raptures of fraternal devotion. In one long November effusion to James Lawson in New York he boasts of 20,000 men ready armed, threatens economic ruin to the North and pours out his heart in lyric hospitality.

"Settle here alongside of me, as a Cotton Planter," he invites:

> You shall have a cypress canoe, and Mary & Kate shall be Ladies of the Lake; and we shall eat strawberries daily in the spring, and melons from June till October, and Green Peas at Christmas, and you shall revel here in Roses while the benighted heathen of the North, are shivering from the Snows. . . . I will get or give you a farm, and you shall set my verses to music, and your girls & mine will carol them together under the light & smile of the sweetest moon that ever carried love, or a silver shaft, into the deepest avenues of a tender heart.

He is clearly bewitched, lost in the mazes of romance. Like a knight come triumphant through his last ordeal he stands to claim his lady fair: the day is gold, the trees emerald, and all his tomorrows float by rosy with delight.

Intoxicated Simms may have been, but he was not the only jubilant Carolinian. For many, indeed, this was the golden time, the apocalyptic season, lasting from the autumn of 1860 until the new national flag rose above Fort Sumter. In retrospect, the very time of year seems prophetic. For the mood was as buoyant as a bright

October day, a day of high blue skies and a sun not too warm to leave a promise of winter behind as it set amid the long-leaf Carolina pines.

The Greenville unionist B. F. Perry took the first political defeat of his life in the fall elections. He surmised that his own followers had caused it by staying home from the polls in despair at the inevitable victory for disunion. He also ventured that the majority of South Carolinians opposed secession in their hearts but were afraid or ashamed to own it.

Nonetheless, absolute unanimity prevailed as the legislature met in Columbia to receive the expected news of Lincoln's election. Its arrival prompted an instant vote for a convention to meet December 17. The members also turned their back on Barnwell Rhett and chose as their crisis governor Francis W. Pickens, englamored by his recent service abroad as U.S. minister to Russia.

The convention met on schedule in Columbia's First Baptist Church—appropriately fronted with Greek Revival columns—resolved to secede, and named a committee to draft an ordinance. Then, at reports of smallpox in the capital, the delegates were persuaded to adjourn to Charleston for the signing. Charleston was, of course, the fitting if not the fated scene. Her thinkers and talkers and writers had virtually sorcerized the state to this momentous end, and she deserved what glory there was in the audible scratches of the pen for disunion. She made the most of her good fortune, so much in fact that one wonders if the smallpox scare was not cunningly magnified to the delegates. At any rate, she was ready with bands and bunting and cheering crowds when the secessionists arrived by train from Columbia. Citadel cadets presented arms at the station and military companies marched the delegates to the Mills House.

Next day—December 20—the Ordinance of Secession was unanimously adopted at St. Andrew's Hall—delegates "occupying the gilt velvet-covered chairs sacred to the chaperons of the St. Cecilia"— but the signing took place by night at Institute Hall. There, in the presence of the legislature, Governor Pickens and a throng that filled every seat, overflowed into the aisles and packed the window ledges, the delegates filed across the stage to sign their names, each to receive his tribute of wild applause. A strange hush fell as one tall blue-eyed figure strode to the table where the Ordinance lay, knelt and bowed his head in silent prayer. When Barnwell Rhett then rose to affix his name, handkerchiefs that had fluttered from uplifted arms dabbed at tear-filled eyes all through the house.

At last the names were inscribed—the proudest names from every quarter of the state—and President D. F. Jamison rose to proclaim South Carolina an independent commonwealth.

Amid the bells and the cannon and the shouting that night in Charleston many people must have felt their hearts miss a beat, as Mrs. Chesnut did, confessing "a nervous dread and horror of this break with so great a power as the United States"; and yet like her to have been "ready and willing." "South Carolinians," she added, "had exasperated and heated themselves into a fever that only blood-letting could ever cure. It was the inevitable remedy. So I was a seceder."

If she spoke for many Carolinians, J. L. Petigru, the only un-seceded man in the state, as she put it, spoke for more men and women than he or they could know when he said to a friend on that December night, "I have seen the last happy day of my life."

XIII

"The Gay and Gallant Boys"

As William Gilmore Simms' nation was born at last in Montgomery,
Alabama, his friend Henry Timrod, musing through the February
days in Charleston, hymned the long-awaited consummation. "Hath
not the morning dawned with added light?" he began his natal ode:

> *And shall not evening call another star*
> *Out of the infinite regions of the night,*
> *To mark this day in Heaven? At last, we are*
> *A nation among nations, and the world*
> *Shall soon behold in many a distant port*
> *Another flag unfurled!*

Invoking ghostly aid of the Carolina Revolutionary heroes if "our
foes should fling us down their mortal gage," he imaged a Yankee
tribe of Shylocks and Pharisees crassly affronting a Southern race of
Galahads, theirs the meed of

> *Unblemished honor, truth without a stain,*
> *Faith, justice, reverence, charitable wealth.*

Though Timrod spoke for the South, he sang Carolina affections.
Consciously "national," he was like most Carolinians helplessly
parochial at heart. Natural though it was, this primary devotion to
parish and state—duplicated everywhere in the South—boded no
good for a nation doomed to fight in its swaddling clothes.

Timrod's lyric bravado scarcely promised any better, echoing as it
did the actual Carolina mood in the weeks before the guns erupted

at Fort Sumter. As gold braid and red sashes flashed through the Charleston streets, as the "beauty" gaily folded bandages by day and sipped champagne with the "bravery" by night, no one seemed to doubt that the walls of Jericho had crumbled. There would be no war, for cotton was king, and a mercenary North would soon kneel to its majesty. Normally sane men joined ranters in offering to drink every drop of blood spilled in a North-South collision. For if economic fears did not mute the Yankee bark to a whine, then Southern chevaliers would frighten soldier plowboys and peddlers back to their plows and packs.

Though high Timrodian dedications sounded on the floor of the Provisional Confederate Congress in Montgomery, they cramped no one's political style. The delegates had scarcely renounced all selfish ambitions as they gathered at the cradle of Southern nationhood. On the scene with her delegate husband, Mrs. Chesnut lamented that "intrigue is as rife as in Washington"—an observation recurring time and again as she circulated through rumorous Confederate drawing rooms in Richmond and Columbia. Even the cynics shared her disillusion. They had looked somehow to a purer dispensation, as though in their long wrestle with Northern turpitude they had clean forgot the verity of original sin.

Much of the scheming at Montgomery derived from that Southern master passion—the will to command. Probably no delegate saw Jefferson Davis take the President's oath on February 18, 1861, without a twinge of envy; and many a delegate frankly wondered why the tall Mississippian instead of himself. Certainly Barnwell Rhett wondered and wept. Having goaded and lashed the South to this fulfillment, he stood unregarded as the crowd hailed a latter-day prophet. Though he was allowed to shape the permanent constitution as chairman of a drafting committee, he was denied first the presidency and then every secondary post big enough for his *amour-propre.*

Rhett had good reason to sulk though scant reason to expect more of Montgomery than Columbia, which had preferred as governor a man just back from service abroad under the hated American flag. To Rhett and his disciples Francis W. Pickens was little more than a renegade, having deserted his beleaguered state in 1858 for the gaudy pastime of bowing to the Russian Czar at St. Petersburg. (In taking the ministerial post, Pickens had yearned less for diplomatic pomp than domestic peace, his third wife, the beauteous Texan Lucy Holcombe, being vain, sociable and most persuasive.) To the general legislative mind, however, his experience abroad was all to the good, for the state would need a diplomat to steer it through a term of independent nationhood. Rhett was not the man. The ruling gentry mostly agreed with the botanizing Carolina planter Henry William Ravenel that he was "devoted to his State & to the South" but too injudicious ever to "be relied on for statesmanship as a leader."

While Rhett raged in Montgomery, his Charleston mouthpiece, the *Mercury,* raged at Governor Pickens for allowing the Stars and Stripes to "wave in insolent defiance" above Fort Sumter. Back from Alabama, Rhett himself was said to have demanded an instant barrage. Pickens, a little weary of his trap—cold comforters on the one hand and hot persuaders on the other—is said to have replied, "Certainly, Mr. Rhett, I have no objection! I will furnish you with some men and you can storm the work yourself."

Less the diplomat than supposed, Pickens had wrought his own dilemma—or at least he had brought incipient crisis to a head—by asking what even the friendly President Buchanan could not in conscience grant: South Carolina occupation of Fort Sumter, then standing unmanned in the harbor. All but threatening force to gain this end, Pickens had instead forced the President to renounce his gentleman's agreement with the South Carolina congressmen to maintain the *status quo* in Charleston. Doubtless also his failure to check the Carolina fever gave Major Robert Anderson excuse to shift his puny United States garrison from Sullivan's Island to the harbor fort (on December 26). There he would be free of nightly checkups from a "rebel" boat patrol, indeed, as Anderson put it, somewhat less a tied sheep watching the butcher hone his knife.

Avenging this "secret" and "treacherous" maneuver, Pickens ordered batteries emplaced on Morris and Sullivan's islands to thwart any try at reinforcing Anderson by sea. He thus clinched Buchanan's refusal to send the Federals back to their usual post and so clogged the path of his Washington go-betweens that they might as well have decamped for Charleston.

It is possible to indict Pickens or Buchanan or both for triggering the guns of the Civil War. Pickens blundered, obviously, and Buchanan broke his "pledge," but since the United States had not recognized South Carolina as a fellow nation, Buchanan scarcely had the right to dicker with her agents. Moreover, if Pickens had not given the crucial dare, some Carolina Hotspur or other would have thrown a rash defiance in Buchanan's teeth.

It seems an undisputed fact, however, that a Citadel cadet fired the first shot on January 9, 1861. He aimed it from Morris Island at the merchant steamer *Star of the West,* which Buchanan had sent to drop off men and supplies at Fort Sumter. Though neither the first nor ensuing shots did much harm, they foiled the *Star*'s attempt, and she sailed back up the coast.

Through a special envoy to Washington, Pickens then tried to oust the Federals from Sumter by asserting Carolina's "right of eminent domain." Having small hope of routing the United States government by this maneuver, he might at least divert the rabid *Mercury* for a spell. Meanwhile he could beg Montgomery to relieve him and South Carolina from their murderous exposure.

On March 6 at last Pickens gratefully surrendered his baton to a Confederate commander in chief who seemed heaven-cast for the role, a lithe Creole with grave Napoleonic eyes and a name that sang like a bar of the *Marseillaise*—General Pierre Gustave Toutant Beauregard. Arriving just two days after Abraham Lincoln had pointed a cautionary finger at the South in his inaugural address, Beauregard set about reorganizing the Charleston defenses and curbing Carolina's frolicsome volunteers. His previous training as a U.S. major of engineers made the first job easy; but not even his Creole *politesse* was quite adequate to the second. For half the blooded young cocks of the state were encamped on the islands, allaying the martial itch with pistol shoots and coaxing their patrician appetites with champagne and French *paté.* As the London *Times*' William Howard Russell reported of a visit to Morris Island:

> In one long tent there was a party of roystering young men, opening claret, and mixing "cup" in large buckets, whilst others were helping the servants to set out a table for a banquet to one of their generals. Such heat, tobacco-smoke, clamor, toasts . . . hand-shaking, vows of friendship!

The only hardship they suffered, apparently, was sleeping alone, and sometimes they got around that. Mrs. Chesnut (whose husband had joined Beauregard's staff by the end of March) reveals the confidence of a lady who was "persuaded to stay two days" when she called upon her husband at his island camp. "She had no clothes down there, pushed in that manner under Achilles' tent, but she managed. She tied her petticoat around her neck for a nightgown!"

Though scarcely prone to garrison exactitudes, these holiday soldiers were susceptible to Beauregard, to his Creole punctilio, his proficiency, even his neat black goatee, which they complimented by trimming down their bushy beards. The Charleston ladies were even more susceptible. They fluttered around him wherever he went and stripped their gardens to embower his headquarters at Institute Hall and his suite at the Charleston Hotel.

An idol to the soldiering young squires and the ladies, Beauregard found himself—far less happily, no doubt—a captive host to throngs of stately monitors—senators and ex-senators, judges and ex-judges, governors and ex-governors—from every Southern quarter. Some had joined his staff by appointment, and others awaited the nod from Montgomery.

Beyond all question the most flamboyant of these sages was the Carolina-born and -bred Louis Trezevant Wigfall, late U.S. senator from Texas, who flushed a colonelcy out of Beauregard by the sheer exuberance of his arrival at headquarters. Striding in booted and spurred, a red sash girding his frock coat, he swept off his plainsman's hat and roared for action. Having tarried in Washington through Lincoln's inaugural to pass a funerary benediction on the federal government, he was ready to hold a wild "Irish wake at the grave." He had left it up to the North to choose a "peaceable Protestant burial" instead but had left no doubt as to which would suit his leonine soul. In frenzied Charleston he was, as Mrs. Chesnut reported, "in his glory." "There was no placidity today," she wrote on April 8, "no sleep for anybody last night. The streets were alive with soldiers and other men, shouting, marching, singing. Wigfall, the 'stormy petrel,' was . . . the only thoroughly happy person I saw."

The "stormy petrel"—his wife's appellation—had emigrated to Texas only a dozen years back from his home county of Edgefield, a breeding ground for the species. He had grown up in the same neighborhood as Preston Brooks, and at the South Carolina College he had made a name for insurgency that even Brooks found hard to match. He rarely attended classes, being too busy ventilating student grievances to the faculty and quenching his thirst at local taverns. Graduating to the Edgefield bar and political stump, he had also graduated to the field of honor, where he killed one antagonist and wounded Preston Brooks. On Wigfall's election to the Senate from Texas, Governor Sam Houston reportedly exclaimed, "Thank God this country is so great and strong that it can bear even that!"

When this ripsnorter arrived from Washington, Charleston was breathlessly awaiting the fleet Lincoln had ordered south to provision Fort Sumter, or rather, as most historians believe, to seize the moral advantage by inciting Confederates to strike the first blow. Until a few days before, there had been reason to believe that Lincoln would sue for evacuation instead, but when news came otherwise, the Confederate high command decided to reduce the fort if Anderson failed to vacate on demand. Either Montgomery did not guess Lincoln's strategy or did not care which side fired the opening salvo. If Southern leaders really believed, in fact, that they had wrought an independent nation, then the choice might well have seemed not so much a melancholy fate as a lustrous opportunity.

On April 11, as Mrs. Chesnut's little court was rising from "the merriest, maddest dinner we have had yet"—with "an unspoken foreboding that it was to be our last pleasant meeting"—Colonel Chesnut returned in a grave mood from delivering the Confederate ultimatum to Anderson at Fort Sumter. Then he was off again to get Anderson's reply, having to eject from his boat a young knight-errant who "thought himself ill-used; a likelihood of fighting and he to be left behind." Judging Anderson's reply unsatisfactory, Colonel Chesnut and his negotiating party crossed to James Island in the early hours of April 12 and ordered the Fort Johnson guns fired at 4:30.

Mrs. Chesnut lay in bed sleepless. "I count four by St. Michael's chimes, and I begin to hope. At half past four, the heavy booming of a cannon! I sprang out of bed and on my knees, prostrate, I prayed as I never prayed before." She heard "a stir all over the house, a pattering of feet in the corridor," all hurrying in the same direction.

She threw on "a double-gown and a shawl" and hurried after them to the housetop. "The shells were bursting," and her heart was in her mouth, for "I knew my husband was rowing about in a boat somewhere in that dark bay, and that the shells were roofing it over, bursting toward the Fort." Though few women had her special cause for alarm, they stood everywhere that morning on the Charleston rooftops transfixed at the garish premonitory scene.

Sumter's guns began to answer a few hours later, continuing to duel with Fort Moultrie and Johnson—while Lincoln's fleet stood idle off the bar—until the morning of the 13th, when the barracks inside caught fire and flames tongued the embrasures. About 1:30 the flag was shot down, and Beauregard sent aides to offer assistance. Simultaneously at Cummings Point the fierce Colonel Wigfall, no doubt posted to Morris Island for the sake of headquarters sanity, saw the flag go down and judged that honor had been satisfied all around. Conceiving himself the fated second for his country on this watery field, he leaped into a boat, having collared a brace of Negro oarsmen, and set out through the bursting shells with a handkerchief flying aloft on his sword. Jumping out on the narrow shore beneath the flaming gates, the colonel strode to a side embrasure, vaulted into the fort and roared a cease-fire in the name of his commanding general. When Major Anderson was summoned to treat with this black-maned apparition, he received a courtly commendation for the noble defense of his flag and a civil inquiry of his terms. Anderson then stated and the colonel magnanimously accepted for General Beauregard the very terms Colonel Chesnut had rejected just two days before. Whereupon the white flag of surrender rose above Fort Sumter.

Meanwhile at the Mills House (a Charleston hotel)—"where the sound of those guns makes regular meals impossible"—Colonel Wigfall's native-born wife solaced herself with tea in Mrs. Chesnut's room. The two ladies rather disdained the "anxious hearts" who "lie on their beds and moan in solitary misery," as well as the pious souls who traipsed about crying "God is on our side." Alone together "Mrs. Wigfall and I ask: 'Why?' Answer: 'Of course, He hates the Yankees! You'll think that well of Him.'"

Repudiation of Colonel Wigfall was unthinkable, at least not when the "Lion of Fort Sumter" put in at the docks that afternoon and took the homage of Charleston, parading through the streets and toward evening appearing for a climactic ovation with his wife on the Mills House balcony. The next day Major Anderson retired from Sumter—miraculously leaving no dead behind—as cannon boomed out a fifty-gun salute to the American flag, for him the prime stipulation of his terms and the very one Beauregard had begrudged.

Then as bells rang and a great crowd cheered and wept on the Battery, the Confederate Stars and Bars rose on Sumter's ramparts alongside Carolina's Palmetto ensign. Mrs. Chesnut was undoubtedly there, watching from the supernal height of an Izard or a Pringle piazza, though she failed to note the event. She found little time to write during those last days in Charleston, for "I did not see how one could live such days of excitement."

Like Mrs. Chesnut as she settled down again at Mulberry, Charleston could "bid farewell for a while . . . to all the pomp and circumstance of glorious war, and come down to . . . domestic strifes and troubles." All signs of the enemy had vanished, not to reappear for at least a summer and fall. No thoughtful person, however, imagined that the North would forbear. Accordingly, military units were forming all over the state to meet President Davis' plea for troops. Many volunteer militia companies called to duty before secession enlisted en masse. Though combs drooped a bit in the dog days of that summer, enlistments were heavy enough to put nineteen Carolina regiments into Confederate service by November.

Young chevaliers from all over the state—those who had not already marched off to Virginia with Colonels Maxcy Gregg and Joseph Kershaw—rallied at Columbia in early June as a great planter chieftain, Wade Hampton III, invoked a thousand men to serve in a "Legion" of all arms. Within a few weeks of his clarion, the drilling Hampton Legion was the magnet for all Columbia's *jeunes filles,* who sighed in their mamas' carriages as thoroughbreds galloped across the drill ground bearing their weight of gilt buttons and braid and plumed shakos.

Though most of the Legionnaires were wellborn and few were seedy enough to report without a body servant, none was as lordly rich or perhaps as altruistic as their colonel. Master of many plantations and more than a thousand slaves, he could afford lavish contributions, but opposed as he was to slavery and disunion he might have shunned the fight in all good conscience. Convinced by Fort Sumter, however, that Carolina needed his abilities, his name and his money, he gave all three, partly equipping his Legion out of pocket. He also tendered the Confederate government an estimated million dollars' worth of cotton to swap for arms in Europe. The offer was pigeonholed, by the way, and the cotton burned as Federals approached the Mississippi plantation where it lay in storage.

Hampton was, of course, not the only well-to-do South Carolinian to open his purse. Scores of men and women—Langdon Cheves's daughter, Mrs. David McCord, for example—outfitted companies with uniforms and guns and even with mounts from their stables. And far more reluctant seceders than Hampton backed the war effort. The Greenville unionist B. F. Perry, who had grimly tagged along with his state as it persisted in "going to the devil," urged upon the hill-men of his district—understandably loath to mix in a quarrel they never started—the "dire necessity of self-defence." Having done all he could to keep his country "from going wrong," Perry argued, a man should "go heart and hand *with* his country. . . . Let him sink or fall with her, and never rise upon her ruins." At a Greenville fund-raising rally Perry said:

> As an old Union man, I give to this Brooks Cavalry [a local troop Hampton accepted for his Legion] my son, two horses and a Negro boy, and fifty dollars for the support of necessitous families of soldiers. I hope no secessionist, who wore in peace his blue cockade, ready to march at a moment's warning, will refuse to do less, now that war has come.

Camping near Richmond in late June, the Hampton Legion drilled hard by day, flustered Confederate belles by night, and dazzled a social and senatorial throng with weekly dress parades. Taking the field at Bull Run in July, they maneuvered smartly enough for Beauregard (now chief of the Confederate Army) to liken them to old campaigners. Both Beauregard and President Davis heaped such praises on Hampton that he dared not write what they said "even to my wife, lest I appear vain." Though Hampton could bask in the afterglow of a wondrous victory—so wondrous that too many Confederates thought the war was over—he and his men realized as they counted their dead and wounded that drills and dress parades could have their melancholy price.

Back in Richmond the jubilee was too much for the prescient Carolina historian and diplomat William Henry Trescot, who told Mrs. Chesnut (her colonel was now aide to President Davis) that "this victory will be our ruin. It lulls us into a fool's paradise of conceit at our superior valor, and the shameful force of their [the Yankees'] flight will wake every inch of their manhood." Though Mrs. Chesnut could crackle with male disdain herself—"But we will dilly-dally, and Congress will orate, and generals will parade"—she could and would as often bite her lips from pity and apprehension. Sitting at the hotel one afternoon she heard funeral drums in the street: "The empty saddle and the led war horse; we saw and heard it all. Now it seems we are never out of the sound of the Dead March in Saul. It comes and it comes until I feel inclined to close my ears and scream.

As General McClellan reorganized the Union Army, Hampton sat out the late summer on a quiet Virginia front, impatient as autumn came on "to show how Carolinians should fight on their own soil. We would try to wipe out the stigma left upon our Army by the Port Royal affair." By "the Port Royal affair" he meant the capture on November 7 of Beaufort and the adjacent sea islands, which would remain in the Federals' hands until the end of the war. Confederate forces at Beaufort, powerless to stand off the assaulting Union fleet for more than an hour or so, had retreated to Charleston, leaving the island planters to fend for themselves. Certain that the fleet off Port Royal was shamming, bound, in fact, for Charleston, the planters sat easy through the morning's barrage. When disabusing word arrived by afternoon, they only had time enough to herd their families and a few domestics into boats and row for the mainland, leaving their houses and crops to the dubious care of their "people" and the Yankee soldiery.

As General W. T. Sherman, commanding the "Expeditionary Corps," reported: "The wealthy islands of Saint Helena, Ladies, and most of Port Royal are abandoned by the whites, and the beautiful estates . . . left to the pillage of hordes of apparently disaffected blacks."

Another Federal officer wrote that the Negroes flocked into Beaufort "and held high carnival in the deserted mansions, smashing doors, mirrors, and furniture, and appropriating all that took their fancy. After this loot a common sight was a black wench dressed in silks, or white lace curtains, or a stalwart black field hand resplendent in a complete suit of gaudy carpeting just torn from the floor."

After this debauch they may have "reveled in . . . idleness and luxury," on their home plantations, but surprisingly few looted their masters' homes, that is, not until Yankee soldiers set the example. On remote islands many even kept on at the old routines under the loyally stern sway of their "drivers" (slave foremen).

Though the sea island Negroes were at first badly used, by the earliest version of the carpetbagger—Treasury agents sent to round up contraband cotton—they were gathered to the merciful bosom of social reform by mid-1862. At Sherman's application for mentors to impart the "rudiments of civilization" and guide the blacks' labors until they were ready "to think and provide for themselves," the federal government dispatched a band of missionary superintendents, many fresh out of Harvard and Yale. These earnest greenhorns dispersed to the Sea Island Big Houses and set about raising cotton for their country.

This "experiment" continued until 1863, when the government began to sell the conquered lands at auction for South Carolina's portion of the war tax levied directly on the states. Some acreage was sold to private individuals (Northerners, obviously) and some was bid in by the United States, partly for eventual sale to the Negroes themselves, then free by Congressional Act and Lincoln's 1863 Proclamation.

No South Carolinians paid a more ironic price or an unfairer penalty for their disaffection than the Sea Island planters. To satisfy a tax levied on the state at large they gave up their lands to sustain the very assault that made them liable to the sacrifice. Very few ever reclaimed so much as a silver spoon. The heir to one plantation reported after an exploratory visit in 1865 that "Our Negroes . . . treated me with overflowing affection. They waited on me as before, gave me beautiful breakfasts and splendid dinners; but they firmly and respectfully informed me: 'We own this land now. Put it out of your head that it will ever be yours again.' " The Negroes knew whereof they spoke. A redemption act in 1872 allowed owners to repossess only those lands still held by the government; and even then the price was too steep for most—taxes, costs, interests and penalties.

Though the Yankee "superintendents" were prone to view their charges as a "herd of suspicious savages," they strove conscientiously to groom them for citizenship. Guion Johnson says (in *A Social History of the Sea Islands*) that some failed from lack of skill but none "from lack of purpose or unwillingness to endure hardships. Some even died at their posts . . . victims of the fevers from which the former masters had annually fled to the health-resort towns." Among the earliest to arrive and surely the longest to persevere was Miss Laura M. Towne, of Philadelphia, who with the aid of Miss Ellen Murray founded what was later called Penn School, which until recent years provided the only instruction available to Sea Island Negro children.

During the initial three years they had on their staff a high-minded young Negro woman from Philadelphia, Charlotte L. Forten, afterwards to marry the Rev. Francis Grimké, whom Sarah and Angelina Grimké publicly, though painfully, acknowledged as their Charleston brother's son by a slave woman. Acutely race conscious, Miss Forten labored at Port Royal to free her skin from the world's contempt as much as to free her small pupils from slavish ignorance. Having taught them about "the noble Toussaint [L'Ouverture]," she remarked (in her *Journal*): "It is well that they sh'ld know what one of their own color c'ld do for his race. I long to inspire them with courage and ambition (of a noble sort,) and high purpose." She gloried in the plan to organize a South Carolina "black regiment" for the Union Army and with proprietary ardor watched it muster and drill under Colonel Thomas W. Higginson.

The Federals' capture and occupation of Port Royal dismayed the state and panicked Charleston. As Colonel John S. Preston reported, "Great terror prevailing here, and no preparations. . . . I believe the fort [Sumter] could be taken in six hours." General Robert E. Lee's November 8 arrival to shore up the city's defenses seemed to many like latching the stable door after the horse was out. Fuming at the "incompetence of our Engineering and Generalship" and lashing "the poor imbeciles in office," William Gilmore Simms anticipated the enemy at Woodlands plantation. He would send his family to

Georgia and "blow up my establishment. They shall have nothing that I can destroy." He felt himself a prophet without honor. For the past six months he had preached—in the Charleston *Mercury*—the necessity of better coast defenses. He thought it was "not the Yankee race alone that needs purging and scourging. We too need punishment to destroy the packed jury, & old family systems, the logrolling & the corruption everywhere."

The Port Royal disaster worked a radical change in Columbia. The Secession Convention met and virtually delivered the state to an emergency council of four: the Governor made a fifth but was allowed only one vote. The Council, which Mrs. Chesnut called "a bundle of sticks and crutches for old Pickens," boosted the state's war potential—among other things, declaring state conscription, starting the manufacture of gunpowder and stopping the manufacture of firewater. It also raised hackles. Heading the Council with iron self-possession, Colonel Chesnut sloughed off the abuse, but his wife spent a good many of her social hours in hot rebuttal. She also spoke up for President Davis against his many and mordant critics. When Barnwell Rhett plunged into the "deeps of abuse" one day, she pointed out that all hands would sink if a crew were "mad enough to mutiny" in a storm.

> *After that I contented myself with a mild shake of the head when I disagreed with him, and at last I began to shake so persistently it amounted to incipient palsy. "Jeff Davis," he said, "is conceited, wrong-headed, wranglesome, obstinate—a traitor." "Now I have borne much in silence," said I at last, "but that is pernicious nonsense. Do not let us waste any more time listening to your quotations from the Mercury."*

The Council was dethroned at the end of 1862 and the Convention scolded by the legislature for ever setting it up, but its rule was at least militarily vindicated when Federals attacking from Port Royal in the spring of 1862 were repulsed with sharp losses from the extensive fortifications around Charleston.

Meanwhile in Virginia Wade Hampton got his long-awaited action as a Federal army under McClellan advanced from the coast toward Richmond. Raised to a generalcy, he engaged his Legion in the Seven Days' Battles until he was wounded in the foot and sent home to recuperate. Columbia hailed him as the very incarnation of Southern triumph at arms. To honor his appearance at the Governor's mansion, "the lovely Lucy" had the servants all decked out in their gold-embroidered Russian livery, reserved for the stateliest state occasions. She herself met him at the door, whisked his crutch away and lent her shoulder instead. "That is the way to greet heroes," she cried. Of modest disposition, Hampton was tongue-tied at such floridities.

Among friends, however, he relaxed and spoke with decision and pertinence, warning that "If we mean to play at war as we play at chess . . . we are sure to lose the game. They have every advantage. They can lose pawns to the end of time and never feel it. We will be throwing away all that we had hoped so much from, Southern, hot-headed, reckless gallantry. The spirit of adventure. The readiness to lead forlorn hopes!" Hampton wanted to play more or less Francis Marion's hit-and-run game, and as second-in-command of General J. E. B. Stuart's cavalry in the coming months he found the chance, executing a number of brilliant maneuvers during Lee's second Manassas and Antietam campaigns.

Also conspicuous in those campaigns were General Maxcy Gregg's 1st South Carolina Volunteers, who saved Stonewall Jackson from defeat on August 29 when they held a strategic knoll with the bayonet after exhausting their ammunition. The historian Edward McCrady, an officer in the unit, wrote afterwards:

> I can see him now [General Gregg], as with his drawn sword, that old Revolutionary scimitar we all knew so well, he walked up and down the line, and hear him as he appealed to us to stand by him and die there. "Let us die here, my men, let us die here." And I do not think that I exaggerate when I say that our little band responded to his appeal, and were ready to die, at bay, there if necessary.

But no excesses of gallantry could force a triumph for Lee in the Maryland hills at Antietam, where triumph would almost certainly have guaranteed Confederate independence. Though the Southerners fought off a series of desperate attacks and executed a series of equally desperate counterattacks, they were so bloody and exhausted after a day's fighting that Lee had to withdraw across the Potomac.

His retreat signified ultimate Northern victory, for time, as usual, favored the side that came to the field with the most men and materiel.

If Antietam did not eclipse the sun in South Carolina, it did becloud the fall days of 1862. Simms grumbled in October that Lee's foray into Maryland was "a flash in the pan," and Bragg seems to have "marched up a hill [and]—marched down again." (General Braxton Bragg had failed to take Louisville, Kentucky.) Either there was "something latent in these transactions which I do not fathom, or they are sad failures." In addition he recognized the constant danger of a sea attempt on Charleston. Gunboats were to have been ready to smash the Yankee blockades a month before, and "We hear of their getting christened and all that nonsense."

Worse was to come the following summer. Though South Carolina reinforcements under Colonels States Rights Gist and W. H. T. Walker sped to the rescue of General Pemberton at Vicksburg, that "Confederate Gibraltar" passed into Northern hands on July 4. On the same day Lee escaped from Gettysburg, leaving nearly 4,000 Southerners and the last great hope of the Confederacy dead in the Pennsylvania cornfields. Perhaps unable to endure the double blow, Rhett's *Mercury* cried up Gettysburg as a glossy plume for Lee; but not even Lee himself could believe it anything but an evil portent for the South.

As the dual disaster approached, Mrs. Chesnut set out for Alabama by train to visit her ill mother. She traveled "in a sadly moulting condition. We had come to the end of our good clothes, and now our only resource was to turn them upside down or inside out, mending and darning and patching." Somewhere along the way she heard a fellow passenger read out from a newspaper, "The surrender of Vicksburg." The words struck like "a hard blow . . . on the top of my head, and my heart took one of its queer turns."

The same news so afflicted B. F. Perry in Greenville that he stopped writing in his *Journal.* He told his wife that his heart was broken. His last entry gloomed that "whether restored to the Union . . . or held as conquered Provinces we are a ruined people!" But Perry's was an angry despair. He was indignant for the "poor men from the mountains," drafted to bleed in a hateful cause while the plutocrats who "urged on the contest" were happily profiteering at home. He cried "Shame! Shame! on the farmers & planters . . . now asking four or five dollars per bushel for corn & seven & eight for wheat."

Disaster threatened much closer when the Federals lunged at the Charleston forts in mid-July. After troops failed to storm Battery Wagner on Morris Island, land and naval batteries shelled it almost continuously for fifty days, driving out its defenders in early September. Their real objective, however, was Fort Sumter, which held out against bombardment and kept the Yankee fleet at distant bay. What joy Charleston took of this feat was poisoned by the thought of an enemy garrison now biding its time on Morris Island.

Mrs. Chesnut blamed Beauregard's "supreme negligence" for the chilling prospect. "He is accused of saying that they put him in Charleston [to command the South Carolina and Georgia coastal defenses] because he could make no reputation there. Faith, but he can lose what he has! He never had much brains, and now he's losing heart." She could never abide long, though, in that snappish humor. She turned in a moment to a "strange" and poignant sight (the passage of Longstreet's corps to Georgia):

> What seemed miles of platform cars, and soldiers rolled in their blankets lying in rows with their heads all covered, fast asleep. In their grey blankets packed in regular order, they looked like swathed mummies. One man nearby was writing on his knee. He used his cap for a desk, and he was seated on a rail. I watched him, wondering to whom that letter was to go. To his home, no doubt. Sore hearts for him there!
>
> A feeling of awful depression laid hold of me. All these fine fellows going to kill or be killed, but why? A word took to beating about my head like an old song, "The Unreturning Brave."

At Woodlands Simms could not "divert my thoughts from the crisis in which the country trembles in suspense." He could write only in "a single burst of passion—hope, or scorn, or rage or exultation." The results of these spasms he would post to the *Mercury* with such titles as "Fort Wagner," "Beauregard—A Lyrical Ode," and "The Angel of the Hospital." Otherwise he struggled with reluctant crops and trifling or "peculant" overseers and hunted up makeshifts for scarce necessities. He reported the satisfactory use of peach leaves as a leavening for bread and "common wire grass" for ladies' bonnets.

At the beginning of 1864 Henry William Ravenel prayed (in his *Journal*) that God would give "our rulers" wisdom "in this our hour of need." Having absolute faith in God, he had scant trust in the Confederate Congress. As a result of its bungling, food was scarce and prices so high "as to seriously threaten . . . our cause." Wantonly impressing produce for the army, the government was also busily impressing the necessary growers. If mouths kept increasing as "hands" decreased, then "famine is inevitable."

Ravenel bore hardship manfully, but he liked to choose the hardship. Like most men of his kind and class, he hated to part with a single jot of the personal independence for which supposedly his nation was contending. Any incursion raised the specter of tyranny or incompetence or both in the Richmond leadership. Undoubtedly that specter haunted Governor Hammond when he defied impressment officers to sell his surplus corn at a higher rate to private buyers. He had donated cotton, bought bonds, sold food at cost to his neighbors and put up "refugees" from Charleston; but he would not bend to the presumptions of "an arbitrary, inflated Captain of Quartermasters." He would probably have resisted, however, any agent of the Confederate President, who "could not . . . have acted so effectively for infamous purpose" if he had been "bribed to abort our efforts to achieve our liberties."

But inflation and crop impressments were not the only causes of South Carolina discontent. Planters balked at sending their slaves to work on the coastal defenses, and slaveless whites growled at going into the army while their slaveholding neighbors stayed home to boss the slaves: owners of fifteen hands were exempt from service, and large operators could keep one white man for every twenty blacks. Embittered men were evading the draft or deserting the army in such numbers by 1864 that the northwestern woods were infested with outlaw camps. Marauding bands swooped down on loyal Confederates with their own brand of impressment.

Desertions were not as numerous in South Carolina, native historians are quick to report, as in most other Confederate states. Nor was disaffection as general. South Carolina not only gave a soldiery equal to her 1861 population of males between eighteen and forty-five—she also lent the heroism of her women, who, Wallace says, "evinced a devotion equal to the courage with which they inspired the men."

Led by Sally Hampton (daughter of Wade Hampton) and her cousin Susan Preston, Columbia women founded a wayside hospital that sheltered or fed some 75,000 soldiers before the war was out. Mrs. Chesnut was in regular attendance during the summer and fall of 1864, working often, as she said, like a galley slave from five in the morning, when a trainload of soldiers would arrive, until half past eight, when the last cars would pull out with their awful freight of maimed and battered flesh. On occasion the beauteous "Buck" Preston (Sally Buchanan Campell Preston, whose father, John S., was now a general and head of the Confederate Conscription Bureau) would accompany her, though Mrs. Chesnut hated "for young girls to go to the hospitals." Or at least she chafed to see her beloved Buck pursued by nakedly appraising eyes and irreverent "comments," no doubt the Confederate equivalent of the wolf call.

Columbia women also helped staff the Confederate hospital set up in the South Carolina College buildings. There Louisa Cheves McCord was "dedicating her grief for her son—sanctifying it, one might say—by giving up her soul and body, her days and nights, to the wounded soldiers." Her son, Cheves, had died from wounds incurred at Second Manassas, in spite of her prodigious ministrations. Hearing that he was wounded, she set out for Richmond only to find that he was still at or near Manassas Junction, that the government had seized all trains and no passports were being given to the battle area. "But that very night, I chartered a special train and ran down to Manassas and brought back Cheves in triumph." On his feet again but not fit for duty—"the ball had never been removed from his head"—he "grew restless and insisted on returning to camp," dying a few days later.

That little story could serve as a parable of the Confederacy at war. Such gallantry might have saved the day for France at Orleans, but in 1863 one train more or less could have meant the difference between a battle won or lost.

Though powers and dominions could not hold Mrs. McCord when her son was in danger, she was inclined to exact a disciplined service of her voluntary hospital staff. She expected the beauties to check their beauty at the door, thus avoiding such "insults" as came to one "lovely lady" from a "rough old soldier": When she asked, "Well, my good soul, what can I do for you?" he replied "Kiss me!"

Mrs. McCord's fury was at the woman's telling it. She knew there were women who would boast of an insult, if it ministered to their vanity. She wanted her helpers to come dressed as Sisters of Charity, not as fine ladies. . . . When she saw them coming in angel sleeves, displaying all of their white arms and in their muslin showing all of their beautiful white shoulders and throats, she felt disposed to order them off the premises.

In late July Buck Preston was "breaking her heart for brother Willie," dead in Virginia. Remembering his "bonny blue eyes, shaded like a girl's with the longest, tangled black lashes," Mrs. Chesnut was reminded of

all the true-hearted, the light-hearted, the gay and gallant boys who have come laughing and singing and dancing across my way in the three years past! I have looked into their brave young eyes, and helped them as I could, and then seen them no more forever. They lie stark and cold, dead upon the battlefield or mouldering away in hospitals or prisons. I think if I dared consider the long array of those bright youths and loyal men who have gone to their death almost before my very eyes, my heart might break.

News more portentous than that of Willie's death was to come on September 2: Sherman had taken Atlanta from Buck's impetuous fiancé, General John Bell Hood, her "lame lover," someone named him in Columbia, for he had come courting on a wooden leg. Atlanta's fall, Mrs. Chesnut prophesied, "means fire and swords for us here." Though she nor anyone else knew whether he would strike for Savannah, Charleston or Richmond—or all three in turn—his part in the general Union strategy was fairly clear. Pursuing the advantage won with the previous capture of Chattanooga, Sherman could swing around the Great Smokies and attack any of the easterly strongholds. As Mrs. Chesnut phrased it, "Sherman will catch General Lee by the rear, while Grant holds him by the hand, and while Hood and Thomas [the Union general facing Hood in Tennessee] are performing an Indian war dance on the frontier." This last prediction she made after Sherman had cut loose from Atlanta on his march toward the sea (October 17), first sending Thomas to deal with Hood, whose plan was to break the line of Union communications in Tennessee. The plan misfired, of course, and Hood's army was virtually annihilated at Nashville in December.

President Davis himself was probably none too confident of Hood's success when he approved the campaign on his inspectional and hortative visit to Georgia in September. With Sherman entrenched in Atlanta, however, there was no alternative. Davis recommended the maneuver in public exhortations to the people of Georgia: "Our cause is not lost. Sherman cannot keep up his long line of communication; and retreat sooner or later he must. And when that day comes, the fate that befell the army of the French Empire in its retreat from Moscow will be reënacted."

Columbia was hardly in a gala or acclamatory mood when the President stopped off in October on his way back to Richmond, but a crowd gathered nonetheless at the Chesnut "cottage" on Hampton Street and cheered him out to speak on the piazza. And every notable who could squeeze inside tipped julep glasses in his honor and dined with him on the "eatables" Mrs. Chesnut had garnered from the Confederate commissariat and the delectables conjured up by her loyal women friends.

The President had anticipated a quiet day while his staff conferred with Carolina officials—including General Chesnut, who now commanded the State's military reserve—but as he and Mrs. Chesnut sat on the piazza after breakfast, "Some little boys, strolling by, called out: 'Come here and look! There is a man . . . who looks just like Jeff Davis on a postage stamp.' " When people began to gather, he went inside, but by midday he gave in to the clamor and appeared. Afterwards a throng swarmed in to shake his hand and presumably to offer advice about Georgia and to criticize General Hood, for when he "stood up for her General, Buck said she would kiss him . . . and she did, he all the while smoothing her down the back . . . as if she were a ruffled dove."

Meanwhile, as Mrs. Chesnut was "concocting . . . dessert on the back porch," she gossiped with the President's aide-de-camp General George Washington Custis Lee (General R. E. Lee's eldest son). He perched "on the banister with a segar in his mouth . . . and told me many a hard truth about the Confederacy." More impressive than anything he said, however, was the "unbroken silence he maintained as to that extraordinary move by which Hood expects to entice Sherman away from us."

Shortly after the President's visit Columbia was up in arms at a local legislator's proposal—by open letter to Davis—that the Confederacy sue for immediate peace. A citizens' rally condemned the scheme, and the *Mercury* branded it "the basest treachery or the weakest desperation." The President's stock rose a little by dissociation from the peacemakers, but it dropped lower than ever when he asked Congress' consent to buy slaves for army use and emancipate them at the end of their service. Barnwell Rhett wrote that nothing since the war began had "struck him with such alarm" as the central government's presuming the right of emancipation. Not even the United States government had ever dared that insolence.

Anger at Richmond culminated in the election of a fanatic states'-righter as governor, A. G. Magrath, of Charleston, who promised to maintain "the honor and independence" of South Carolina. Even as he orated to the inaugural crowd, however, Sherman's army paused at Savannah "burning with an insatiable desire to wreak vengeance" on the Palmetto State, the "hell-hole of secession"; and Magrath spent his first gubernatorial weeks plaguing Davis for help. He was so insistent—pounding away at Charleston's importance over Richmond—that General Lee finally asked whether his Excellency imagined it would help the Confederacy to have Grant as well as Sherman in South Carolina.

Magrath had good reason to implore. The available force—less than 30,000 effectives to Sherman's 60,000—was obviously inadequate, as Beauregard, now heading the Military Division of the West, wrote to Davis from Augusta, where he reviewed the situation with his generals. Facing the predicament, the legislature called for duty all white males between sixteen and sixty, and Magrath adjured them to hide their property, then "return to the field. What you cannot carry destroy." "Let all who falter now . . ." he threatened, "be henceforth marked."

At Woodlands the fifty-nine-year-old Simms packed his children off to delusive safety in Columbia and busied himself loading up a railroad car with produce to feed his flock in exile. Pathetically begging excuse from military service—because of numerous ailments and infirmities—he offered to accept "cheerfully" "some bureau occupation in Columbia." Despairing as never before—and perhaps never afterwards—in his life, he wrote to the son of his recently dead friend Governor Hammond that he began "to congratulate those fortunates [the dead] who have escaped this crisis, and whom we still, perhaps unwisely, deplore." Hammond, by the way, had in pointing out his burial place to another son the day before his death enjoined, "But mind, if we are subjugated, run a plow over my grave."

At his farm near Aiken—directly in Sherman's probable path— the methodical Henry William Ravenel buried his "silver & valuable papers in the garden after dark," charged his slaves to hide out from the enemy and departed with his flock for St. John's Parish. Passing through Charleston he was "astonished to see so much less damage than I expected from the constant shelling for near 18 months," though he was saddened at the emptiness and the desolation. "In Broad St & all the lower part of the town grass & weeds are growing in the streets."

While Confederate generals talked, Sherman marched and burned his way to mid-South Carolina. By February 7 he was encamped along the Charleston-Augusta railroad, and all opportunity for effective concentration against him had passed.

As foot troops uprooted the rails and the ties, horsemen fanned out to forage, pillage and to light up the night skies. Sherman's General Kilpatrick had boasted on the eve of the campaign that "In after years when travelers passing through South Carolina shall see chimney stacks without houses, and the country desolate, and shall ask 'who did this?' some Yankee will answer 'Kilpatrick's Cavalry.' " The boast was carried out with a vengeance. Whole towns were put to the torch, and for miles along the route of march scarcely a house or a barn escaped. Stragglers roamed far enough afield to burn Woodlands, including Simms' 10,000-volume library, "the most valuable library, to a literary man," he believed, "to be found in the Confederacy."

Sherman so misled Carolinians as to his route north from the Edisto that refugees crowded into Columbia with their baggage and treasure. By February people were virtually camping in the streets, and the town's bank vaults were bursting with jewels and silver plate. Though General Chesnut was uneasy enough to send his wife to Mulberry—giving in to her greater anxiety, however, and letting her go to North Carolina—many people shared the optimism of the sprightly young widow Malvina Black Gist, who wrote: "This wild talk about the Federal Army and what it's going to do is all nonsense. Coming here! Sherman! Why not say he's going to Paramibo? One is about as likely as the other, notwithstanding that papa shakes his head so solemnly over it, and mamma looks so grave."

On February 11, however, she felt "the dawning of a doubt." "Is he coming," she asked herself, "that terrible Sherman, with all his legions?" Then she added, "Well, and if he does, Beauregard is coming too, and Hampton [is] already here." (She meant General Wade Hampton, detached from Lee's command to oppose Sherman.)

On the 14th evacuation orders came for the Treasury Note Department, where she worked signing bills, and in the afternoon she "could distinctly hear firing in the distance, and at this writing (8:30 P.M.) we can see the sky arched with fire in the direction of the Saluda factory. Yearning to stay and have "a taste of danger" and complaining of her "frightfully monotonous" woman's fate, she gave in to her parents and boarded a train with the other "Treasury girls." As she waited in "the cars" she wrote:

> *A reign of terror prevails in the city.* . . . *Government employees are hastening to and fro, military stores are being packed, troops in motion, aids-de-camp flying hither and thither, and anxious fugitives crowding about the train, begging for transportation. All kinds of rumors are afloat.* . . . *I am strangely laden.* . . . *Six gold watches are secreted about my person, and more miscellaneous articles of jewelry than would fill a small jewelry shop.* . . . *Shelling has begun from the Lexington heights [across the river to the south].* . . . *We catch now and again, peculiar whizzing sounds—shells, they say. Sherman has come; he is knocking at the gate. Oh, God! turn him back! Fight on our side, and turn Sherman back!*

On the morning of February 17 General Hampton withdrew the last Confederate troops, first sending Mayor Goodwyn off to hand over the city to the incoming Yankees. Though Sherman's pyrotechnic fame did not promise well for Columbia, Goodwyn might have surrendered a less inflammable town, and he knew it. The place was stored with enough wine and whisky to float the population—much of it sent from Charleston for safekeeping—a fact that he had pointed out to Generals Beauregard and Hampton, who declined to meddle with private property.

Having no such scruples, Columbia Negroes had taken advantage of the confusion to help themselves, and they welcomed their "liberators" with potent draughts. A Yankee colonel reported that his troops marched through a gauntlet of extended bottles, cups and dippers. "Here was an old white-wooled man, who, with 'Lord bless you, Massa; Try some dis',' offered brandy from a gourd that had been filled from the bucket in his hand."

Charged with firewater, Sherman's touring arsonists required no orders to set about the ruin of Columbia. They would doubtless have hooted any order to the contrary. Stacking arms in the heart of town, the troops broke ranks and sprinted to grogshops, stores and public buildings. By midmorning, as the sixteen-year-old Emma LeConte reported in her *Journal*, the family servants had all vanished uptown (from the South Carolina College campus) "to see what they could get in the general pillage . . . in some parts of Main Street corn and flour and sugar cover the ground." Frenzied soldiers were tearing through the State House smashing "the many trophies and mementoes" of Carolina's "not inglorious past" when Emma ran upstairs in time to see the Stars and Stripes go up on the roof. "O what a horrid sight!" she moaned. "What a degradation! After four long bitter years of bloodshed and hatred, now to float there at last!"

Understandably nervous, the mayor called on Sherman toward sundown and received assurance that "your city will be as safe in my hands as if you had controlled it." He planned to burn several public buildings but, not wishing to endanger private property, would wait until the present gale-like winds subsided.

Nonetheless, red, white and blue rockets flared above the State House shortly after nightfall, and a minister heard a soldier exclaim, "Now you will catch hell—that is the signal for a general setting fire to the city." No sooner said than done. Simultaneously, in different parts of the city flames leaped from the rooftops. They were set, as innumerable witnesses could testify, by blue-clad soldiers dashing through the streets with oil-soaked cotton balls and pockets full of matches.

"The wind blew a fearful gale," Emma LeConte observed, "wafting the flames from house to house with frightful rapidity." She watched "night turning into noonday, only with a blazing, scorching glare that was horrible—a copper colored sky across which swept columns of black rolling smoke glittering with sparks and flying embers."

Next door the college library "seemed framed by the gushing flames and smoke, while through the windows gleamed the liquid fire." Fires soon broke out on the adjacent roofs, and as doctors and nurses rushed up to put them out, the wounded soldiers within crawled out to the Commons or waited helplessly in their beds. The staff managed to save the buildings, but they had to fight not only falling sparks and debris but drunken pyromaniacs.

When dawn came at last the "drunken devils" vanished like ghosts at cockcrowing. Their work was done. The greater part of Columbia lay in ashes. From the center of town as far as the eye could reach Emma LeConte could see nothing "but heaps of rubbish, tall dreary chimneys, and shattered brick walls." The fire consumed 84 of the city's 124 blocks.

Four days later Emma reported:

> A heavy curse has fallen on this town—from a beautiful city it is turned into a desert. How desolated and dreary we feel— how completely cut off from the world. No longer the shrill whistle of the engine—no daily mail—the morning brings no paper with news from the outside—there are no lights—no going to and fro. . . . One feels awed if by chance the dreary stillness is broken by a laugh or too loud a voice.

Sherman never officially admitted that he burned Columbia. Technically perhaps he didn't, since he gave no orders to set the blaze. But as head of an earth-scorching legion he was indubitably responsible. Though refusing ultimate blame, he "never shed any tears over the event, because I believe that it hastened what we all fought for, the end of the war."

Sherman's army resumed its march toward Winnsboro on February 20, leaving to the hisses and boos of watching Columbians and trailing behind it a procession of whites and blacks who wanted Federal protection or provender. Following the troops in a battered carriage, which she "exchanged" for a shining equipage on the outskirts of town, was the notorious Mary Boozer, whom General Preston had once called "the most beautiful piece of flesh and blood" he had ever seen. Suspect for her ministrations to Federal prisoners—she helped one escape and concealed him until Sherman arrived—she got out while the getting was good. Another carriage in the Yankee van bore an old Negro woman garbed in castoff finery and waving an ostrich-feather fan. Recognized by a lady on the sidelines and asked, "Why, Aunt Sallie, where are you going?" the delirious traveler replied, "Law, honey! I'se gwine right back into de Union!"

On the night Columbia burned, Confederate troops evacuated Charleston, firing vast stores of cotton as they left. Incoming Federal soldiers put out the flames, sequestered what was left, along with other stores, and stripped unoccupied dwellings. These depredations galled Charleston far less, however, than the bone-picking that took place in April when two boatloads of pious Yankee patriots landed to raise the American flag at Fort Sumter. Gathering within the crumbling ramparts on the 14th they cheered as the officer who had surrendered there in 1861 (now Major General Anderson) pulled the halyards, restoring to "its proper place this dear flag which floated here . . . before the first act of this cruel Rebellion." Then they listened to the Rev. Henry Ward Beecher (Harriet Beecher Stowe's brother) excoriate the South at merciless length and adjourned to scrounge all over Charleston for souvenirs. The Rev. Mr. Beecher's wife, for instance, fancied a panel from the pulpit of St. Michael's Church (which she later restored).

As Federal troops fanned out in the low country, plantation slaves celebrated their "freedom" by ransacking the homes of their absent masters. Roaming the roads by day and carousing by night, they were in such a frenzy that Adele Petigru Allston's overseer advised against her return to Chicora Wood plantation, near Georgetown:

> *I do think if you had been on the Plantation that you would have been hurt by the People I have been Compeld by them on the Place to give up the Barn Key or to suffer from theare hands . . . on Sunday the 5 of march two yankeys come up & turnd*

the People loose to distribet the house which they did, taking out every thing & then to the smoke hous and Store Room doing the same as in the house & took the Plough oxen and Kild some of them . . . the Pore mules has been Road to death all most.

A few days later he reported that "the yankeys has been up and have taken all the Cotton. Thay are to be up shortly & divide the Stock to the People thay tell the yankeys every thing all the yonge men & boys have gone down to them to go in the army."

Some of their kind, if not some of these very "yonge men and boys," marched with General Edward E. Potter when he moved north from Georgetown on April 9 to deliver the killing blow to crippled South Carolina. Riding upstate to Camden, he destroyed railroads and cotton gins and fired some homes along the way, easily brushing off opponent reserves—striplings and graybeards for the most part. Halfway back to the coast he halted the destruction with the news of General Johnston's surrender to Sherman in North Carolina. By that time, of course, Lee had already bowed to Grant at Appomattox.

In the small hours of April 29 General Wade Hampton galloped into upcountry Yorkville, trying to overtake the fleeing Confederate President, who had passed through the day before. Nearly alone of Johnston's army Hampton had not surrendered—absent from duty at the time, he judged himself exempt from the terms—and now he planned to rescue Davis from his pursuers, join the Western troops and continue the fight in Texas. It was a characteristic gesture. It was equally characteristic, however, that he bent to his wife's persuasion—she had sheltered in Yorkville since the burning of the Hampton plantation homes—that he stand by his own family and the beaten South.

War's end found the Southern laureate, Henry Timrod, penning letters for the Governor in a Columbia basement. His trifling wage could not sustain a household of six or eight, but he wrote his poet friend Paul Hamilton Hayne rather gaily that "We have eaten two silver pitchers, one or two dozen forks, several sofas, innumerable chairs, and a huge bedstead."

Though he would soon be on his feet and begging help for Timrod, William Gilmore Simms fared no better as the spring of despair passed in the summer of distraction. Lodging in a Columbia garret, his only resource "a few dollars per week" from squibs for "a petty County Court Newspaper," he was kept from wiring his New York friends "by sheer inability to pay for the telegrams." Writing in June, he asked the New York editor Evert Duyckinck to arrange a publisher's advance as soon as possible "as I wish to escape the humbling necessity of incurring petty debts at the shops of strangers." All he wanted now was to "get home, & go to work in solitude and quiet, if not in peace & happiness. . . . My hair & beard are quite white . . . but I am healthy, comparatively vigorous, & with my children present ever to my eyes, I feel that I have many years of good work in me yet."

In Chester, where she had stopped on her way back from North Carolina, Mrs. Chesnut spent weeks of "madness, sadness . . . [and] turmoil" as the Confederacy "double-quicked down hill," then gathered up her belongings and set out for Mulberry. "For your sentence is pronounced," the General said. "Camden for life!" She must have envied the Prestons, who were off to Europe: "Burnside in New Orleans owed [them] some money and will pay it."

("The Hood melodrama" was ended. The wooden-legged cavalier had galloped into Chester and lost his last campaign—to Buck's iron-willed Hampton mamma.) She might even have envied the Wigfalls, who "passed through on their way to Texas . . . bound for the Rio Grande," aiming, so their daughter told General Hood, "to shake hands with Maximilian, Emperor of Mexico." But her "heart was like lead" when the fleeing Varina Howell Davis (the President's wife) stopped off with her children and then flew on again, "calm and smiling as ever." She also turned a pitying eye as "our soldiers" trudged through the town: "Yesterday those poor fellows were heroes, today they are only rebels, to be hung or shot at the Yankee's pleasure."

Finally on May 2 she left with General Chesnut for Camden, passing on Sherman's track, where "nothing but tall, blackened chimneys" showed "that any man has ever trod this road before us." It was hard not to curse the ravager. "I wept incessantly at first. 'The roses of the gardens are already hiding the ruins,' said Mr. Chesnut, trying to say something. Then I made a vow. If we are a crushed people, I will never be a whimpering, pining slave."

XIV

A Dark Interregnum

One day soon after the war a small Negro boy stood outside a low-country plantation office tooting a little tin horn for all he was worth. "Finally the overseer could stand it no longer," as Governor Duncan Clinch Heyward tells it in *Seed from Madagascar*, and ordered him to stop the noise or move on. "Wudduh use fuh be free," the boy whined, "ef can't blow tin horn?"

The boy voiced almost literally what freedom meant to a great many former slaves—the right to make a racket. Like children out of school they wanted to kick up their heels and shout. As the Freedmen's Bureau officer John W. DeForest says in his Reconstruction memoirs:

> What with trapping rabbits by day and treeing 'possums by nights, dances which lasted till morning, and prayer-meetings which were little better than frolics, they contrived to be happier than they had "any call to be," considering their chances of starving to death.

"Free as a frog"—so they put it in a song—they scarcely imagined being free to make their own bread, much less make laws for the state.

Too many one-time masters also failed to imagine such prodigious freedoms. Like sage parents and pedagogues they held their tongues, knowing that high spirits do collapse and truants invariably return.

Both frolicsome blacks and knowing whites were living in a fool's paradise. Blacks had yet to learn the economic facts of life, whites to recognize the punitive Northern mood and the severity of revolutionary infections along the coast. If neither were quite to blame for their ignorance, both were to suffer by it, whites bitterly through a dark interregnum and blacks—well, they have yet to enter the promised land. They still, in fact, suffer the consequences of their old dependency and their sudden release from bondage.

Slave conduct throughout the war had encouraged white complacency. Except at Beaufort, blacks had generally hoed their usual rows, and though some had traipsed off behind Sherman in the spring of 1865 and others had vied with their deliverers in looting the Big House, few had shown a gory disposition. They often stood poker-faced to hear the news of their emancipation and drifted back to the fields. At "Goodwill" plantation near Columbia, Governor Heyward reports, the Negroes listened quietly as a Federal officer explained—standing up in the Heyward buggy—that they could now go and come as they pleased. They loafed the rest of the day "talking among themselves and probably speculating as to when they would return to Combahee," that is, to the Heyward rice lands from which they had "refugeed" with their master in 1862. Next day they shouldered their hoes again on promise of division when the season's crop was in. In the fall they sold their portion and "returned to Combahee, all in one body as they had left it," traveling unescorted by train to Charleston and thence down the coast by water. As they left Goodwill for the station, they filed by the Big House piazza to tell the old master good-bye. They were "going home," they murmured, "and would look for him soon."

It was probably a blessing that the old master—Governor Heyward's grandfather—died shortly at Goodwill, for as his son wrote a year later on returning to Combahee, the Negro disaffection "would have killed my father and worries me more than I expected." He found them very evidently "disappointed at my coming here; they were in hopes of getting off again this year and having the place to themselves. They received me very coldly; in fact it was some time before they came out of their houses to speak to me. . . . They are as familiar as possible and surprise me in their newly acquired 'Beaufort manner.' They are constantly in Beaufort, quite too much for their own good."

The "Beaufort manner" had flaunted itself to the state at large in

November of 1865 when a Colored People's Convention met in
Charleston to protest the Negro's menial status under the first postwar constitution, drawn up the previous month. Fully aware of its
import as the first gathering of the kind in South Carolina, the convention scored state authorities for denying Negroes "the rights of
the meanest profligate in the country" and asked Congress to impose
martial law, grant "equal suffrage" and abolish the "black code."

Translating the Negro from slavery to serfdom, the Black Code
exemplified South Carolina's quaint conception of what took place
at Appomattox. In many hallucinated minds, apparently, Lee had
stilled the guns as Grant knelt at his feet and a chorus of black mam-
mies sang hallelujahs for "Marse Robert." The ante bellum unionist
B. F. Perry surely had a like image at the back of his head when he
undertook South Carolina's "reconstruction" in the summer of 1865.
For as provisional governor he guided a constitutional convention
in framing the "black code."

Chosen for the job by the Southern (if not chivalric) President
Johnson, Perry went about it in a sort of willful oblivion to ill-bred
Yankee howls for vengeance on the rebel South. A gentleman and
a lawyer, he would restore his state to legal good grace in the
federal union. In effect he counseled the gentlemen delegates to
renounce slavery first and then shape a government to suit themselves. He disclaimed state sovereignty, but neither he nor such
ex-fire-eaters as old Governor Pickens quite believed the disclaimer.
The Constitution, after all, forbade meddling in local matters.

A Northern observer's thumbnail description suggests Perry's
ineptitude. A "tall, large, straight man," carrying a gold-headed
cane and wearing gold-bowed spectacles, he had "a very long,
large nose . . . a very long, large . . . chin" and "wears a wig."
Looking "like a man of power," he had "an inoffensively self-satis-
fied appearance." Obviously the very incarnation of an upright,
stubborn and pompous Jeffersonian lawgiver. If he ever made a
joke in his life he never committed the indiscretion in public.

What the state needed, by contrast, was a bit of a knave, or at
least somebody with a subtler mind and a mealier mouth than
Perry's. The occasion demanded both a canny reading of Northern
blood pressure and a willingness to nurse it along. As Francis B.
Simkins and Robert H. Woody suggest in their *South Carolina*

During Reconstruction a weathercock might have saved the state a good deal of pain.

Perry advocated a stern paternalism as the only workable substitute for slavery. By a just and kindly treatment of "your 'freedmen,'" he told the convention, "you may attach them to you as strongly . . . as they were whilst your slaves." He warned the delegates to expect idleness and discontent but promised eventual "order and system": "The 'freedman' will soon find out that he must work or perish."

Though Perry never dreamed of raising the Negro to full citizenship, he did faintly perceive the wisdom of a gesture. Like Wade Hampton and others, he thought whites might welcome a few blacks to the polls and dissuade the rest with a small property qualification. But the only "black rascal" most delegates expected to welcome at the polls would sidle in to empty the cuspidors. Close to that persuasion himself, Perry kept quiet about token voters.

Virtually all South Carolinians agreed with Perry that to enfranchise the Negro in his "present ignorant . . . condition, would be little less than . . . madness." Few would admit with Henry William Ravenel that when "qualified to . . . exercise the rights of a citizen," the Negro should have "all the rights." And even fewer shared Ravenel's wish to see him so "elevated in the scale of life" as to deserve the ballot.

Closing doors to the Negro, Perry held them ajar to bottom-rail whites. He urged the delegates to seize the chance of reforming a constitution "less popular and republican . . . than that of any other State in the Union." Scarcely leaping to the charge, they did finally agree to shift the balance of power from the coast to the upcountry —by abolishing the parishes as election districts—and to transfer the Governor's election from the legislature to the people.

The Northern reporter Sidney Andrews says that after "this great victory" he heard "—and for the first time since the Convention met— . . . in the rooms of the up-country delegates, a lively and long-continued fire of champagne corks. Peace to the ashes of the parish system!"

Undoubtedly first among the cork-poppers was George Dionysius Tillman, "untiring . . . enemy of the parish system, or, to use his

own phrase, 'the Chinese conservatism of Charleston.'" Older
brother and mentor of Benjamin Ryan (Pitchfork Ben) Tillman,
George D. was a "genuine Red Republican," Andrews declares, "in
his disregard of what are called 'ancient rights and privileges.'"
He may have been, but as the touchy kingpin of a touchy slave-holding clan, he was surely not averse to privilege per se. Andrews turns
a neat but misleading phrase when he says that Tillman had
"served six years in the State Legislature for honor, and two years
in the State Penitentiary for manslaughter." He had done time in
jail all right but in the Edgefield jail and on such cushy terms that
he courted his future wife, kept up his law practice, and often had
his brother Ben in for overnight company. Though remorseful
enough to help support the daughters of his victim—a lowly by-
stander at a faro game—Tillman was not sufficiently humble to
forgive his Edgefield peers their sending him to jail. Like his mettle-
some mother, he had resented the suggestion that he leave the
state in return for a pardon.

Northern critics nipped Perry at every turn. Editors joined with
such Washington inquisitors as Senators Charles Sumner and Thad-
deus Stevens to execrate his "doctrine" as a libel on American
democracy. The New York Nation found it "monstrous" to have
"this theory . . . of our government boldly thrust in our faces . . .
by men who have come red-handed from the battle field" and
equally shameful that a president so indebted to "the valor . . . of
colored troops" should yield to the heresy. Even sharper teeth
nipped at James L. Orr, who took over from Perry as elected governor
in November, for he effected the Black Code, which went so far in
proscribing the new citizen as to create special law courts and a
separate—and harsher—scale of punishment. Though the black
could own property, sue and be sued, he could not, except by state
permission, leave the farm or the kitchen. As plow hand or domestic
he would have a status not unlike that of the eighteenth-century
indentured servant.

Governor Orr had more to contend with than rhetorical abuse.
Within the state U.S. General Daniel E. Sickles, commanding a
large occupation force, interfered to check white "disloyalty" and
to guard blacks from harm. Defying the local courts, he sometimes
clapped "brutal" whites into jail and rescued "innocent" Negroes

from it. In January, 1866, he decreed the Black Code null and void.

Meanwhile Congress had signified its displeasure by refusing to seat the members-elect from South Carolina (and other Southern states). Thus flying in Johnson's face, it made itself the arbiter of "reconstruction" by naming a joint committee to weigh the Dixie states' fitness to sit in national meeting. This action persuaded even die-hard legalists that Carolina would have to walk a Congressional chalk line, since she would hardly exist without a voice in Washington.

In spite of his slippery hold on the reins, Orr managed to drive the state government to reasonably firm fiscal ground. He had small luck, however, in relieving the misery that accrued from Sherman's charring march and two bad crop years thereafter. Though the Freedmen's Bureau, intended mainly to safeguard the Negro's claim to confiscated land, fed starving whites and blacks, distress was still so general in the spring of 1867 that Orr could report thousands going hungry.

Conditions were worst in the larger towns, crowded, as Simms wrote, with Negroes come to "quarter themselves for rations on the Government" and in the absence of restraint and succor to die "of exposure, drunkenness, [and] starvation." Outside the towns large plantations suffered most from the confusions and disruptions, their owners standing helpless without labor. Often lone women, bereft of their men, they could do little but trail the Negroes to town and live on their silver and diamonds if they had been lucky enough to save these from thieves and fire. Veteran male planters themselves, however, often failed to cope with the harsh anomalies. Too proud to parley with the "uppity niggers," they were also far too vain to bend their backs to the plow.

Applying at a Freedmen's Bureau office on behalf of a destitute gentle family, a former slave explained:

> *"They's mighty bad off. He's in bed, sick—ha'n't been able to git about this six weeks—and his chil'n's begging food of my chil'n. They used to own three or four thous'n acres; they was great folks befo' the war. It's no use tellin' them kind to work; they don't know how to work, and can't work; somebody's got to help 'em. Sir."*

If bankrupt gentry could stoop neither to work nor to beggary, their ante bellum hangers-on, the "po'-white trash," were unwilling to rise from their beggary and go to work. Having compassion for the first class, the New England DeForest had little patience with the second, who badgered him for handouts from the Freedmen's Bureau stores, legally intended for Negroes and destitute white unionists. Day after day he "took an unwilling part" in such dialogues as this:

> "*Mornin'. How you git'n long? Got anything for the poor folks?*"
> "*Nothing at all. Not a solitary thing.*"
> "*Got any corn?*"
> "*No.*"
> "*Got any shoes?*"
> "*No.*"
> "*Got any close?*"
> "*No.*"
> "*Ha'n't got anythin'?*"
> "*No. I told you so at first.*"
> "*Didn't know but you had* somethin! *I thought I'd name it to you.*"

Before the war, he surmised, this tribe had lived off the Negro's labor, begging from the slaveholder and trading moonshine to the slave for stolen chickens, pigs and corn. The war had impeded if not dried up both sources of livelihood. "Reduced to his last crust" the planter had nothing to spare to mendicancy and little for the Negro to steal.

Obviously small farmers, who had least to lose by the war, suffered least. Laying down their rifles, they picked up their hoes, and if they struck no gold they at least turned up cowpeas and corn. Adding a little shrewdness to their brawn, they did sometimes make a relative "killing." Rounding up a couple of "loose" mules that first spring, they could grow corn enough to sell at a fancy price and buy or rent nearby idle acres. Rural Carolina still affords countless tales of postwar opportunism. When envies smart a bit at the sight of present riches or affectations, the envious console each other with tales of how "Old Man Wash" got his start, rounding up "homeless" stock by night, stringing "niggers" up by the thumbs

—"the kind of 'pay' they get when they come bellyachin' to me for pay."

Suffering was acutest on the coast, where much valuable rice and cotton land had been appropriated to the former slaves. Charleston was especially hard pressed. Trade was totally disrupted, and the flow resumed very slowly in the immediate postwar years. Its normal population barely able to feed itself, the city was packed with indigent patrician exiles from the surrounding parishes. Six years after the war a visitor described it as a

> city, first, of idle, ragged Negroes . . . second, of small dealers . . . starving on the rebel custom; third, of widows and children of planters keeping respectable boarding-houses, or pining in hopeless and unspeakable penury; fourth, of young men loafing in the saloons on the proceeds of their mothers' boarding-houses; fifth, Jews and Massachusetts merchants doing well on the semi-legal Negro custom; sixth, of utterly worthless and accursed political adventurers from the North.

Casting about for decent occupation, many gentlewomen gave lessons or fitted up their homes as boarding schools, too many, so Adele Petigru Allston complained as fewer and fewer young ladies knocked at her door. Asking ex-Governor Pickens to recommend her school in the Edgefield district, she got his gloomy promise to do so, "for I know . . . it is just such a place as a genteel young girl ought to go, but then my dear madam, there is no one who can afford to go any where." The outlook was so bad (the autumn of 1867) that "if a man . . . can have potatoes, and grits and meat and keep out of the hands of the Military and the negroes, he is doing well this winter."

Mrs. Allston was more fortunate than many women of her class. She was getting supplies from the family plantations on the Waccamaw, one of which at least she would keep as her dower when the other five went on the block for her husband's wartime debts. Nonetheless, she wrote her niece, James Louis Petigru's secession-hating daughter Caroline Carson, that she now saw "how wise you were" to have left "this country" and gone north early in the war.

Mrs. Allston had written Caroline Carson, incidentally, to praise the "beautiful inscription for your Father's monument," which represented, as she may not have known, prodigious labors of hand and spirit. Unable to come home when Petigru died—in 1863— Mrs. Carson spent the next few years scrimping to buy a marker for his grave in St. Michael's churchyard. Feeling that "her father would like best to be honored by the work of his daughter's hands," according to Petigru's biographer, she refused aid from his admirers and for two years "painted, and when too ill to paint . . . lay on her back knitting overshoes" sometimes "twelve hours a day." Then with journalistic aid, she produced the epitaph that Jonathan Daniels calls "the best statement I know of the aristocratic ideal, which remains as important as it has always been rare in the South as on the earth."

The main body reads:

> *Future times will hardly know how great a life*
> *This simple stone commemorates—*
> *The tradition of his Eloquence, his*
> *Wisdom and his Wit may fade:*
> *But he lived for ends more durable than fame,*
> *His Eloquence was the protection of the poor and wronged;*
> *His learning illuminated the principles of Law—*
> *In the admiration of his Peers,*
> *In the respect of his People,*
> *In the affection of his Family,*
> *His was the highest place;*
> *The just meed*
> *Of his kindness and forebearance*
> *His dignity and simplicity*
> *His brilliant genius and his unwearied industry*
> *Unawed by Opinion*
> *Unseduced by Flattery,*
> *Undismayed by Disaster,*
> *He confronted Life with antique Courage*
> *And Death with Christian Hope.*

The clouds seemed to lift in the spring of 1866 when President Johnson declared the rebellion ended, acting partially on the strength of South Carolina's modifying the Black Code to give the Negro legal equality. He presumably thought this concession would soothe the radical element in Congress. Whether it would or no, South Carolina was not disposed to take another step along the road of social and political reform.

In the summer of 1866, accordingly, the legislature rejected the Fourteenth Amendment to the Federal Constitution, which aimed to enfranchise the Negro and bar from office every man who had held a post under the Confederacy. Exhorting the legislature against it, Governor Orr said that any Northern state would deny the vote to blacks if, like South Carolina, it counted forty-one to every thirty whites. Let others pass the amendment, he advised, but "let us preserve our self-respect . . . by refusing to be the mean instrument of our shame."

Righteous as he may have sounded in Columbia, Orr impressed the North as brazenly rebellious. Congressional moderates were so aroused that they fell into line under the Sumner-Stevens whip and helped pass (in the spring of 1867) the acts that delivered Carolina up to her former slaves. Putting the army in control, these acts set unqualified male suffrage (except disfranchised ex-Confederates) and passage of a new constitution and the Fourteenth Amendment as conditions for the state's return to the Union.

The military commanders—General Sickles and his successor General E. R. S. Canby—laid on a firm but not a merciless hand. During the summer Canby directed voter registration under boards from which nearly all native whites were excluded: appointees had to swear what only a woman or an infant male could truthfully avow, that they had never fought against the United States or held office under a hostile power. By November the completed rolls showed almost twice as many black as white names.

The large black registration indicated a surge of political interest that was not due to Canby or his troops. The army gave the Negro access to the rolls, but a different kind of army marched him forward to make his cross-mark on the books, an ill-assorted band of rascals, renegades and reformers. Most were "carpetbaggers," that is, Yankees who had descended on the South for both mean and lofty purposes. Though South Carolinians have always reviled the class as a flock of buzzards come to feed on the mortally wounded body politic, many figured themselves eagles of a righteous retribution. Greed may have been the dominant motive, but crusading zeal played its part. Among the "scalawags," however—native or at least long-resident whites—venality and chicane ran unalloyed. The few Negroes who assisted in the campaign, whatever their motives, can be judged as neither rascals nor meddling reformers. They were simply indulging, after all, the normal human urge for recognition.

As they hustled to the registration places, Negroes had very little idea of what the fuss was about. "Quite a number brought along bags and baskets 'to put it in,'" a New York *Herald* correspondent reported, "and in nearly every instance there was a great rush for fear we would not have registration 'enough to go around.' Some thought . . . it was something to eat; others thought it was something to wear; and quite a number thought it was a distribution of confiscated land under a new name."

The instigative army used a variety of stratagems to arouse and bamboozle the illiterate blacks. Initially the most effective was the Union League, a secret society that bound the Negro through an awesome hocus-pocus to vote the Republican ticket. The League was shrewdly contrived to appease every longing of a naïve and status-hungry people. Initiation rites and weekly oath-takings fed their sense of importance, and campfire singing opened the pores of jubilee and fellowship. As meetings ended the brothers all rose to manifest the secret signs, the four "L's": Liberty, Lincoln, Loyal and League.

During the campaigns of 1867, "disorganizers," as a local newspaper called them, supplemented their League incitements with huge political rallies, enjoining crowds to vote for the party "that has led you out of the Wilderness into the Promised Land." Gospel shouts punctuated the appeals, often to the consternation of earnest young carpetbaggers. Observers reported revivalistic fervor running so high that shouts of "Hallelujah! Ain't it so! Glory be to God!" drowned out the speakers. When promises were made "to take away the land of the white rebels and traitors and give it to you—forty acres and a mule and a $100 for every man," audiences would sway and moan and clap their hands in a frenzy of delight. Ecstatic sisters not infrequently had to be carried out and brought to their senses with dippers of water in the face.

Kept in a state of "camp-meeting excitement" for weeks in advance, Negroes trooped to the polls in November (1867) to elect an almost unanimously Republican delegacy, forty-eight whites and seventy-six blacks.

The mysteries of voting, however, had baffled as many Negro heads as the rites of registration. A Freedmen's Bureau agent on the coast reported, for example, this plea for light, "Lord, mars'r! do for Lord's sake tell me what dis yere's all about." When he explained that "the election was to put the state back into the union and make it stay there in peace," the grateful black petitioner exclaimed, "Lord bless you, Mars'r! I'se might' glad to un'erstan' it. I'se the only nigger in this yere districk now that knows what hes up ter." Relaying the story, DeForest judges that most Negroes in his upcountry Greenville quarter had by contrast "a sufficiently intelligent sense" of what they were about. "The stupidest . . . understood that he was acting 'agin de Rebs,' and 'for de freedom.'"

At Wade Hampton's lead, white moderates also courted the Negro, urging him to stick with his "old white friends." They assailed the Yankee organizers as false prophets, seducing the black man from his ancient protectors. Lavish helpings of barbecued shoat and catfish stew enforced the message, but to no avail—League promises were too seductive. At last native whites despaired and renounced all blandishments. Meeting in convention at Columbia —with ex-General Chestnut in the chair—they declared the Reconstruction Acts illegal and pledged "never to acquiesce in Negro equality or supremacy."

The old planter oligarchs brooded at home as a company of their one-time slaves gathered in Charleston (January, 1868) with a crew of scalawags and carpetbaggers to inject South Carolina, as W. W. Ball phrased it, with "the deadly and foreign poison of democracy." The first of their race to darken official chambers, the Negro delegates were actually too self-conscious to have much part in the operation. They kept a bashful silence, speaking only to vote as white voices bade—such crisp white voices, for instance, as that of Daniel Henry Chamberlain, of Massachusetts, Harvard graduate and Union officer who had set up as a Carolina planter after the war. The only Negro to play a central role, Francis Louis Cardozo, was neither an ex-slave nor black nor tongue-tied. Free-born in Charleston, of a Negro-Indian woman by a prosperous Jew, he had graduated from the University of Glasgow, studied theology in London and held a Presbyterian pulpit in New Haven, Connecticut.

The constitution that men like Chamberlain and Cardozo wrote was not radical by Northern standards. It prescribed universal male suffrage, junked property qualifications for office and fixed population as the sole basis for lower house seats. It also decreed the popular vote for nearly all state and county functionaries. On the Negro's behalf it forbade distinctions "on account of race or color." Going to the Jeffersonian root of the matter, it also projected a system of free public schools. Delegates toyed with a scheme to ensure economic as well as political democracy but dropped it when Washington telegraphed that money would not be forthcoming to buy lands for the landless.

Roused from their "lethargy" by such militants as Perry, white South Carolinians organized Democratic clubs and nominated a slate to oppose the framers of "The Yankee Negro Constitution." If the people would not "exert themselves," Perry said, "to prevent this vile and putrid patchwork of a government being saddled on them, then they . . . are worthy of being the slaves of negroes and the outcasts of Northern society." But neither invective nor exertion served to prevent the inevitable. Protected by the U.S. Army, the virgin black citizens went to the polls, ratified the new constitution and voted a Republican state and Congressional ticket. The Democrats won six of the thirty-one Senate and fourteen of the 124 House seats.

The Negro legislators who gathered at Columbia in July, outnumbering whites by ten to one, might have come all gravely conscious of their symbolic role as redemptors and vindicators of their race. And they might have walked a godly way for the coming nine years. It wouldn't have mattered in the least. In the mind of white South Carolina they were tools of a hellish revenge. Such tools might humiliate but would never humble and subdue the master race. The white temper was such that the very fact of Negro rule guaranteed its end. And more tragically for the Negro, as well as the white, in South Carolina, it promised years of violence and still more years of mutual suspicion.

Negroes would have been inhumanly virtuous, of course, if they had not enjoyed their supremacy, or at least their tenancy of the offices and taverns of Columbia. As the Northern observer James S. Pike wrote in *The Prostrate State:*

> *[A few] years ago these men were raising corn and cotton under the whip of the overseer. To-day they are raising points of order and questions of privilege. They find they can raise one as well as the other. They prefer the latter. It is easier, and better paid. Then, it is the evidence of an accomplished result. It means escape and defense from the old oppressors. It means liberty. It means the destruction of prison-walls only too real to them. It is the sunshine of their lives. It is their day of jubilee. It is their long-promised vision of the Lord God Almighty.*

Though sympathetic to the Negro, Pike judiciously scored the abuses and corruptions to which the Reconstruction government was inherently liable. White Carolinians, however, rarely heard or wished to hear a moderate word. They preferred and got such unholy skirls as the Fairfield *Herald* raised against

> *the hell-born policy which has trampled the fairest and noblest States of our great sisterhood beneath the unholy hoofs of African savages and shoulder-strapped brigands—the policy which has given up millions of our free-born, high-souled brethren and sisters, countrymen and countrywomen of Washington, Rutledge, Marion and Lee, to the rule of gibbering louse eaten, devil worshipping barbarians, from the jungles of Dahomey, and peripatetic buccaneers from Cape Cod, Memphremagog, Hell, and Boston.*

However, such billingsgate did not and was apparently not meant to inflame white Carolinians against the Negro per se. Evoking a nightmarish vision of apes raising pandemonium in the State House, it scarcely troubled the daily sight of a crooning Dulcy at the washtub or a solemn "Uncle" Lige in the bean patch. Since most Negroes were somebody's Dulcy or Uncle Lige, relations continued pretty much as before, at least in the sphere of house and barnyard. Whites continued to regard blacks as more or less the human mules of their world—dear, perverse and inescapable. Except at the polls, most Negroes in turn retained the old attachment to "us white folks," or resumed it after flapping about the country a bit to try the wings of liberation. They did not forget in a day or two the old dispensers of cornmeal, fatback—and the whiplash —having failed in their rovings to spy out that milk-and-honey land called "freedom."

In *The Black Border* (Gullah Stories of the Carolina Coast) Ambrose Gonzales tells of a militia company's "touching their little monkey caps" and scraping their feet in deference as a party of white deer hunters trotted past. One soldier even ran out to beg and receive a pipeful of tobacco from his former master, grinning proudly as he returned to his fellows, "Da' duh my massuh [That there's my master]." Angry at this slavish inclination, the drillmaster ordered the company to attention and lectured, "Don' look at de buckruh [the white men], look at yo' officer!" Then to the pipe smoker he added, "Me yent hab no massuh. Uh free ez uh buzzut [buzzard]!" Unrebuked, the soldier replied, "Yaas bubbuh. Buzzut free and buzzut black, but buzzut ent free 'nuf fuh light 'puntop nutt'n 'cep'n' 'e dead, en' nigguh ent free 'nuf fuh mek buckruh fuh bex [the buzzard aint free enough to light on anything unless its dead, and the nigger aint free enough to vex the buckra]!"

Even militant Negro politicians reverted on occasion to their former servility. The six-foot black senator, Beverly Nash, for instance, whom a colleague admired for his ability to "handle" "the white chivalry, as they call themselves," often dropped in to pay an old butler's respects on "Miss Isabella." Quite in keeping with this impulse, Nash is supposed to have rebuked obstreperous legislators on occasion by rising to a point of personal privilege: "Mr. Speaker, when *real* gentlemen used to occupy these seats befo' de wah, dey nevah used no sich language as dat widout somebody got shot or else got der heads knocked off wif a gov'ment inkstand!"

Like Nash, a Heyward nursemaid who had married high in politics, retained a menial passion for her old "white family." Arrayed in "neat cap and apron," she would "stop her carriage around the corner from her former mistress' home, and alighting would walk to the house and beg to take the children" for a drive. Those "who had seen her gala attire in the middle of the day would behold the

strange spectacle of the same Nancy, as demure as a novice, seated
in the front seat of her landau" while the Heyward children rode
grandly behind.

We don't know that Nancy took the Heyward name with emancipation, but it's likely. Slaves commonly adopted their master's name
when they liked the master. Otherwise, they assumed a neighboring
patronymic or chose one from afar that suited their fancy.

Carpetbaggers rather than Negroes held most key offices, at least
early in the game, such men as the first Reconstruction governor,
Robert Kingston Scott. A Pennsylvanian who had prospected for
California gold and practiced medicine in Ohio, Scott achieved
general's rank in the Union Army and after the war got appointed
second-in-command of the Freedmen's Bureau for South Carolina.

Not unsympathetic to the old ruling class, Scott possibly coveted
their acceptance as a fellow officer and gentleman. He is supposed
at any rate to have bidden a dozen leading Confederates, including
General Hampton, to dine with him and other state officers shortly
after his inauguration. When the company sat down with a dozen
vacant chairs (so Dr. Ball reports in *The State That Forgot*), Scott
addressed the court fool of Reconstruction, a Yankee Irishman who
had published a Charleston Negro newspaper:

> "*Mr. Hurley . . . I think we have a beautiful entertainment
> . . . the foods are delicious, so are the wines, the decorations are
> beautiful and we have a good orchestra—but are you not
> surprised, Mr. Hurley, that so few of the gentlemen of Columbia
> have responded to our invitation?*"
>
> *Mr. Hurley looked at his chief and his smile was of motherly
> tenderness. "Governor," he said, "I think if I were a gentleman
> I wouldn't be here myself."*

Snubbed or not, Scott tried to mollify the evicted masters of
Carolina, failing, so Simkins and Woody judge, because he lacked
the courage and the skill to handle the foxy characters slinking
around his office. With the legislature he was utterly helpless. Blacks
joined white members in denouncing him, and in 1871 the House
voted impeachment for a large overissue of bonds. The Governor
was described as "subject alike to alcoholic and female allurements":

at one point wily officials seduced him to sign a bond issue through the proxy wiles of a vaudeville queen.

The first draughts from the public tap seem to have raised an unholy thirst in Scott's legislature, and vote-money was soon flowing as freely as liquor in the State House bar or tobacco juice on the floor of the House. A carpetbagger lobbyist testified that he paid some twenty to twenty-five thousand dollars through Speaker Moses for a bill granting a Charleston company phosphate-mining rights in the state's navigable rivers. The wholesale marketing of votes prompted Governor Scott to observe that Jesus Christ could recommend a bill to the legislature and suffer crucifixion for his pains if he failed to bribe the members.

A Southern observer—whose finding the legislature "as good as a circus" does not necessarily impugn his veracity—reports seeing an ex-Union general lobbying a bill through the House by passing from seat to seat with a wad of greenbacks in his hand:

> . . . suddenly a negro jumped to his feet and claimed . . . recognition . . . on a question of privilege. When asked to state it, he said he had just been informed that [the general] had just given another member twenty-five dollars for his vote on the bill, and he had only given him, the protestor, five dollars. He wanted that "white man" to understand that his vote was worth as much as that of any ricefield nigger from Santee.

Scott bribed himself and a few cohorts into ownership of a railroad, buying its stock from the state at a fraction of its cost to the treasury. He also lined his pockets and tripled the state's printing bill by organizing a print shop. No wonder the state's debt increased thirteen million dollars in a couple of years.

The Governor faced such a restive electorate—some blacks among the whites—that he girded his 1870 campaign with a Negro running mate and a Winchester-armed black militia. The second effrontery—and perhaps the first as well—inspired whites to arm themselves with shotguns and in a few northern counties with the ghostly robes of the Ku Klux Klan. In the nature of things, somebody was bound to get hurt. Violence did not break out, however, until after Scott's re-election, as swaggering militia increasingly toyed with their triggers. The worst eruption came in Union County, where Klansmen snatched ten black troopers from jail and shot them in rather generous revenge for the murder of a white man who had declined to surrender his wagonload of whisky to a thirsty black detachment.

Violence bred violence as usual, and soon lawless blacks and whites were venting personal grudges with ropes, knives and bullets. Finally lawful citizens appealed to Columbia, and Scott disbanded his militia in the stricken counties. Then, as Negroes quieted down and whites put away their Klan regalia, President Grant moved to put down the "rebellion," and federal soldiers crowded the jails with suspected Klansmen.

One of the men caught in the roundup was ex-Confederate Major J. A. Leland, president of the Female College at Laurens, who claims (in his *A Voice from South Carolina*) that he had done nothing more heinous than offer neighborly aid to the wife of the Laurens scalawag chieftain after a postelection riot—her husband had taken up quarters in a hollow log. Perhaps Leland was a victim of scalawag malice, but he must have brought suspicion on himself when he called on the President in Washington (as one of a committee) to explain that his townsmen had abjured the Klan and ought to be exempt from the pending measures against it. He found Grant as granitic as a statue and the Capitol, with its "rings and cliques, and 'wheels within wheels' . . . perplexing . . . to plain, blunt men."

Arrested and jailed in Columbia not too long thereafter, Major Leland found himself and his fellow suspects "transformed from Ku-Klux prisoners, ordered about by dirty little turn-keys, or dirtier little Lieutenants, into something like moral heroes . . . in the eyes of those whose opinions we most valued." He means men and women "of the old regime"—LeContes, Boatwrights, Prestons, for instance—who spread such enfolding wings that in four weeks "we never ate one morsel of jail rations." The ladies organized along army lines. Some collected, some cooked, and others fetched and carried. A few good souls, their "nerves" shrinking from "such a jail," sent prayers.

Countless doctors of divinity brought their prayers in person. Having different notions of *"spiritual* comfort," General Preston sent a *"keg of lager beer,"* calling first with the message that "we are all in jail in South Carolina; the only difference is, you are under shelter, and those of us . . . on the outside, have to dodge the storm as best we can."

The General did, however, escape—to his native Virginia—in 1873, selling his wife's patrimonial mansion to Scott's scalawag successor Franklin J. Moses, Jr. Whether or not Columbians resented the sale, some must have wished the old place had died honorably by fire in 1865. Better consuming flames, they must have felt, than defilement by cakewalking "nigger gals and bucks." Catholic nuns had saved the house for this fate, by the way, begging Federals to spare it to them after their convent had burned.

By his own testimony Moses made a $15,000 down payment on the Preston home with a bribe he got for signing an appropriations bill. Undoubtedly he extracted the $25,000 balance from the state by hook or crook, for by all accounts he was the grandest grand rascal of Carolina, perhaps Southern, Reconstruction. This is not to say he was the biggest thief, or even a very big thief by the standards of U. S. Grant's larcenous cronies. His special infamy lay in the treasons he committed for a brief turn at the public trough. He betrayed not only the state, but his class, his college, the Negroes who voted him to office, and himself.

Unlike most scalawags, who had no status to lose by their rogueries, Moses belonged to the lesser gentry. He was Jewish, but in a state where substantial Jews had mixed freely and united with good Gentile families, that fact did not count against him. It did not prevent, for instance, his marrying a "good" Carolina name or being chosen private secretary to Governor Pickens. In the thick of things, as Charleston led the South to war, he very well might, as he claimed, have raised the Confederate and Palmetto flags over Sumter.

As a Sumter editor after the war he pitied the poor Negro his enthrallment to the carpetbaggers, those "wretches" "with their high-crowned hats, their closely buttoned . . . coats, their Uriah Heepish hands and their saturnine smiles prowling through the country with the keen scented rapacity of wild beasts." Soon, however, his yearning to prowl with the carpetbaggers made it wise for him to lay down his indignant pen.

Running with the foxes for the next decade, he turned in 1877 to run with the hounds, telling tales on his accomplices to Wade Hampton's investigators. This final treachery, however, brought him no profit. Anathema everywhere in the state, scared to show his face in his native Sumter, he wandered north, where he fell into drug addiction and petty crime. Interviewed in a Chicago jail at one point, he said, "I wanted to be Governor. It was pride—a personal and family pride. I saw there was but one way—make myself popular with the niggers. I did it. I flattered some, associated with others, but bought a great many more. It was all wrong I know."

Not the least of Moses' crimes—to South Carolinians—was his complicity in opening the State University (South Carolina College before the war) to Negro students in 1873. Even his election to the board in 1868 had so agitated the campus that members of his old literary society declared his name a "black stain" on their rolls.

University admission came as a bid for the Negro's vote after a split developed in Republican ranks. If native whites regarded this as a prostitution of hallowed halls to dirty politics, Negroes themselves had every right to feel that dirty politics had given them rightful entry to the hallowed halls. Their presence may have crippled the university, since it drove away virtually all white students and most of the old professors—the first Negro graduate of Harvard, Richard T. Greener, supplanted one—but it did not breech any rights. Negroes had every theoretic and legal right to attend the university, and since they had no state college of their own, they had a practical right as well. The wonder is that they waited so long. The fact that so few of their race were qualified for collegiate study no doubt had something to do with their patience. A good many of the students who did enroll, incidentally, were legislators and officials eager to secure the innovation.

Negroes were so grateful to Moses for opening doors—outward from the state prison as well as inward to the university and the Preston mansion—that legislators made him a judge *after* he had departed the governorship under indictment for stealing. They were most grateful, perhaps, for his social condescension. For instance, one observer reported seeing the Governor emerge one afternoon from a Main Street saloon, followed by a waiter with champagne and glasses, to engage in "a perfect orgy" with a quartet of bejeweled "Negro wenches" seated in a "handsome landau drawn by . . . high-stepping Kentucky horses." Though some Negroes would have been as scandalized at this indecorum as the white observer, most would have felt at least an inward surge of gratification. They would have been less than human not to breathe that great biblical paean of the envious heart, "How are the mighty fallen!" or perhaps its complement, "How are the lowly risen!" At this remove one can spare a sympathetic nod for the Negroes, and, if the Governor had not been revealed as a monstrous hypocrite, one might almost admire his courage.

Mrs. Chesnut had prefigured the Moses career in 1862, or at least she had discerned an aspect of the diabolic in his look and manner. Bending over Mrs. Pickens' chair at an evening party, he suggested "the Devil whispering in Eve's ear." The blunt General Chesnut simply pronounced him "a liar" and "a sneak." As Moses lied and cheated his way up the Reconstruction ladder of disrepute, they must have consoled themselves at Mulberry now and then with the one consolation always left to the wise—the memory of their sage predictions. Though even that must have been a poor and bitter comfort for Mrs. Chesnut, for whom war's end had meant not only the withering of the Southern dream and of personal resources but the end of glamour, the death of romance. Reading about the Moses carousals at the Preston mansion, she must have wept for that departed time when, as she had once said, all the brilliant and beautiful people in the South foregathered in Charleston, in Richmond or in Columbia. If she wept, however, she did not write. Whatever she felt, she had no heart to record. She made her last journal entry in August of 1865. Copying out a sprightly letter from a young woman friend which closes, "Your last letters have been of the meagerest. What is the matter?" she comments bleakly, "What is the matter? Enough! I will write no more!"

Succeeding Moses as governor, Daniel Henry Chamberlain also patronized and championed the Negro, but more in high-minded resolution than high-spirited fraud. He also threatened a holy war on legislative jobbers and treasury buccaneers, losing by this determination what favor he stood to gain by the first.

Though Chamberlain rode close herd on the lawmaking tricksters and kept them reasonably straight for a year, they got the best of him at last. Taking advantage of his one-day absence from Columbia in December, 1875, they stabbed his administration in the back by investing Moses and an equally scurvy Negro with judicial robes. Chamberlain won his fight to keep these two off the state bench, but the damage had been done. He himself declared this action a "calamity . . . greater . . . than any which had yet fallen on this State, or I might add, upon any part of the South."

The Governor's lamentation was partisan as well as patriotic. He rightfully guessed that the harm done his administration would in the long run advantage the Democrats. Initially, however, he appeared so much the image of wronged virtue that Democrats espoused his bid for re-election. Standing for honesty, he also had a claim on the Negro vote, which the old Confederates were powerless to dislodge. Just as he had feared, though, a countercurrent set in, and before his term was up the too long dishonored prophets of old had risen to scourge him from office—and the Republican party from mastery in South Carolina forevermore. (At least the state has not gone Republican since.)

The campaign against Chamberlain started ironically at the height of his popularity with native bigwigs. At a Charleston banquet culminating the Fort Moultrie centennial (June, 1876), they alternated in toasting him and Wade Hampton, grand marshal of the day's parade. Perhaps honestly respecting Chamberlain, they did not confuse him with Hampton, whom they loved, not less because, having risked so much for his "country," he had borne his losses with such Roman equanimity. Reduced to outright poverty, the one-time millionaire had lately rejoiced to get $118.85 from the sale of personal effects at the courthouse door in Columbia.

Hampton had not actually committed himself to Chamberlain. Nor had another ex-general, Martin Witherspoon Gary, as stormy a petrel as Colonel Wigfall and hatched in the same Edgefield breeding ground. Gary had, in fact, already urged that the Democrats "put a straightout ticket in the field." As the old Confederates rocked along together by train from Charleston, Gary drafted Hampton to lead a campaign in which he would be Democratic nominee for governor. "With Butler [General Matthew C.] and myself on your flanks," he promised, "we can win the battle as we won others in the war."

Gary initiated his flank maneuver at Edgefield in August before Hampton was actually nominated. Advancing at the head of a 600-man cavalry formation, he and Butler pre-empted "dividing-time" —an equal chance to speak—from Governor Chamberlain and his Republican cohorts. Verbally lashing the Governor before his own party faithful, he vaulted back into the saddle and galloped away, leaving all chances of "co-operation" dead on the platform and 1,500 Negro voters sweating cold in the August sun.

The fright was intensified by the aggressors' red flannel shirts, making their first appearance here and worn afterwards at every Hampton rally. Edgefieldians themselves had first put on "the bloody shirt" at nearby Aiken, where a good many were indicted for murderous roles in the July Hamburg Riot. Though it symbolized defiance of their Northern critics, it accurately represented their bloody temper. They had shot five blacks in a row they started by design in the "nigger-town" of Hamburg. As Pitchfork Ben Tillman remembered, Edgefieldians had wanted "to teach the Negroes a lesson; as it was generally believed that nothing but bloodshed and a good deal of it could answer the purpose of redeeming the state."

Martin Gary conceived the election campaign as a war to the death against the Negro. If Hampton had not damped his fire at intervals, the casualty list might well have grown to sickening lengths. (It is remarkable that only twenty-three Negroes and nine whites lost their lives in possibly the most excited months South Carolina has ever known.) Hampton's notion was to lure Negroes to his party as well as to scare them out of their Republican loyalties. He ordered his ranks, accordingly, to break no heads open when they broke up a meeting. The magic of his voice and name ensured a fairly general obedience. Armed "clubs" marched on Republican rallies to shout, jeer, and sing—the favored tune was "John Brown's Body"—or rear up their mounts under candidates' noses, but they did not rake the black voters with buckshot.

At the start of the campaign Hampton received a letter addressed "Dear Marse Wade" and signed "Your friend and former slave, Rev. Francis Davie." It began:

Seeing you are nominated for governor by the white people and hearing you have promised the black man all the rights he now has, and knowing you were always a good and kind man to me when your slave and knowing you are a good and kind man who will do what he promises I write to say that I will vote for you and will get all the black men I can to do the same.

Perhaps as eloquent a testimonial as Hampton ever received, the letter suggested why Hampton curbed his rabid followers and also why thousands of Negroes pledged to vote the Democratic ticket. Not all blacks who made that vow, however, actually kept it. Considered renegades by their own race, they were in constant peril of a thrashing, if not a blade in the back. Women turned on them often as fiercely as men. One man had his clothes stripped off by an outraged hen-flock for shouting "Hurrah for Hampton!" Another was locked out by his wife—"said she wouldn't have any Democratic nigger sleep with her as long as she lived."

No one could tell how many Negroes voted for Hampton, but many observers were pretty certain of the kind. Dr. Ball judged the few dozen black Democrats in his native Laurens "trifling, lazy, and careless fellows, who lived by tips from their white friends." He reports that only one of six black well diggers took his mother's proffered bribe of a five-dollar gold piece to loaf around her premises all through election day, and the one vote-seller even bargained a little. "Miss Lizer," he said, "if you will give me, beside the five dollars, all the sweet 'tater custards I can eat . . . I'll come."

The great event of the campaign was Hampton's heroic 60-day oratorical progress through the state. "Heroic" is the only word, as anyone knows who has worn out his voice, his right hand and his taste for barbecue on that 46-county pilgrimage. For Hampton it was ten times more grueling than for his modern political heirs, who ride swiftly in their Buicks and suffer a good deal less adulation. Rattling from town to town by rail, Hampton daily climbed into a flower-decked carriage and led a mounted and band-blaring procession through miles of swirling dust and jubilant Carolinians. Daily he delivered the "message" and daily consumed slabs of "the finest 'cue in the State of South Carolina" and "the lightest pound cake."

Only a man of Hampton's tough body, massive self-possession and iron stomach could have borne it.

In one upcountry town, 3,000 mounted Redshirts escorted Hampton to a platform where "South Carolina" awaited him posed against a bank of laurel and roses—"a bowed figure draped in robes of dense black and wrapped with chains." As her promised deliverer ascended the steps, chains and mourning robes fell aside and "a young woman in pure white stood tall and stately, head uplifted and eyes shining like stars."

Never an eloquent speaker, Hampton addressed the crowds with simple force, varying his phrases but reiterating a few basic tenets. He spoke to the Negro as much as to the white, promising that "they shall be equals under the law of any man in South Carolina." Though Hampton normally made this pledge to well-disposed Negroes, he carried it once to a hostile audience in the "black bailiwick" of Beaufort. Wisely declining an armed escort for this excursion, he commanded a silent respect for his own voice but could not still the derisive uproar that met every other candidate.

Enough violence erupted during the campaign to justify Chamberlain's disbanding the Democratic "rifle clubs" and to give excuse for President Grant's ordering army troops in to police the election. Though Redshirts fumed and even hostile Northern editors denounced the action, Hampton ordered "Keep the peace," and Hampton's word was close to law.

The peace was pretty well kept even on November 7, the tensest election day South Carolina has ever known—kept in part because the regulative U.S. troops did not perform their mission with missionary zeal. Many detachments spent the day in camp as Redshirts scared enough Negroes from the polls to win the election. At Laurens, according to Dr. Ball's memory of the day, two Redshirts started the intimidation by staging a mock row, cursing, milling about and waving their pistols. To the Negroes, he said, "it looked to be a white man's bloody riot—and the ruse drove many . . . from the scene. To vote was not worth the risk of a stray shot."

Peace was restored slowly, the minutes wore on—only the minutes—and then the clatter of hoofs from the northeast corner of the Square. Then the splitting yell as thirty Redshirts galloped almost to the polls, pulling up their foam-flecked horses. They galloped around the court-house, watered their mounts at the two public wells. They hurt nobody, but six-shooters were strapped to their waists.

These sudden, terrifying "assaults" on the crowded public square were repeated at intervals throughout the day, "never harming anyone, but by ten o'clock the Radicals had gone home."

Edgefieldians, according to Francis B. Simkins, delivered a county Democratic victory—probably the crucial factor in Hampton's election—by a "flagrant use of fraud and violence." General Gary helped bring it off by forcing all Negroes to place their ballots in a single schoolhouse box, which was so inadequate that the closing polls left hundreds unvoted. When the cheated throng marched toward the courthouse box, Gary not only ordered his men to pack the steps and corridors but stood off interference from U.S. General Ruger.

Final returns on November 10 showed Hampton the winner by roughly a thousand votes and his party the House winner by a small majority. The news touched off wild celebrations throughout the state, none wilder than in Columbia, where Hampton was paraded through the streets on Negro Democrat shoulders while cannon boomed and flags waved from windows and housetops.

The joy was premature. No sooner had the votes been tallied than Chamberlain decided to contest the results or simply to overturn them in his favor, taking advantage of an election law he had once condemned as "scandalous." Since a board made up of state officials —his own at present—could rule votes in or out as they chose, the means were not hard to find. With some justice, perhaps, the board promptly invalidated the elections at Laurens and Edgefield, thus readmitting the Republicans to office.

Refusing to give in or up, Democrats gathered at the State House on November 28 and, when Union troops barred their way, adjourned to a nearby hall to organize their own House. Two days later the Democratic House slipped by the doorkeeper at the State House, and their speaker took his seat. When Republicans arrived with their speaker, the Democrats stood pat—as did the troop commander—and for four days and nights all hands remained, eating and sleeping together. Finally the Democratic speaker led his cohorts away to avert a general throat-slitting.

When Chamberlain was inaugurated in December, Hampton told a rival gathering that "The people have elected me Governor, and, by the Eternal God, I will be Governor or we shall have a military Governor." Though he continued to restrain his restive followers, he held bravely to that pledge, at last wringing from President Hayes a promise to call off the army on April 10, which was tantamount to seating him in the governor's chair. His accession was anticlimactic. He simply walked into the office after Chamberlain had gathered up his papers and left, having denounced the President's action futilely in an address to "the people."

If dramatically the counterrevolution thus ended in anticlimax, it nonetheless ended in triumph. For white South Carolinians it was as though the filth had been swept from the Holy Place and the Holy Place resanctified to the Fathers.

Biblical metaphor does not falsify the mood. Simms' literary son, Paul Hamilton Hayne, exclaimed to a Northern friend with prayerful ardor, "Oh, if you could only appreciate what this means!" Now at last his own Charleston might cast off the aspect of savage Africa and stand forth again "a Christian city in a Christian land!"

If Hampton's rise signified the restoration of a faith, Chamberlain's fall equally marked the failure of a great mission to scourge it from the land. W. J. Cash says the Yankee had to leave the South almost as he had found it:

> a world in which the first social principle of the old was preserved virtually intact; a world in which the Negro was still "mud-sill," and in which a white man, any white man, was in some sense a master. And so far from having reconstructed the Southern mind . . . in its essential character, it was [his] fate to have strengthened it almost beyond reckoning . . . to have made it . . . one of the least reconstructible ever developed.

XV

Boss of the Wool Hat Boys

As legislators readied to choose a United States senator in December, 1890, the gray-bearded old soldier who had sat in Washington for twelve years waited at his pinewoods cottage near Columbia to hear that his day was done. It was a cruel pass for General Wade Hampton and for thousands of Carolinians who had devoutly wished him to keep the place for life. Neither he nor they quite understood why the blow was to fall, how so false a prophet as Ben Tillman could have risen to bid this infamy.

Bewildered at the killing judgment on his public life, Hampton met it with patrician calm. When friends begged him to go and walk through the State House corridors—like Napoleon landing from Elba to win his forgetful people back to loyalty—he refused. "The Senatorship," he said, "is a place to be bestowed and not to be sought . . . if the people do not . . . consider me worthy to remain as their representative, I will accept defeat without a murmur."

Actually many lawmakers who voted for another man thought Hampton as worthy as ever. Desolate before their apostasy, some came to swear undying affection. They would do anything for him, they promised, anything in the world but vote him back into the Senate. That they could not do, because the "Agricultural Moses" who had led them to Columbia had set his hard, thin mouth and his one glittering eye against it.

Even the one-eyed man himself, now governor after a ripsnorting campaign against the "broken-down aristocrats" suckling "the public teat," admitted a twinge of distress as he shoved Hampton aside.

He knew the old hero had only the public teat for sustenance, but his rankling memory of recent platform encounters easily got the best of his sympathies. His only apology was to blame the senator for his own political death. The high and mighty Hampton, he said in effect, should have thought twice before sneering at a Tillman.

Like most men who hack away at the feelings of others, Tillman was often very tender of his own. Throughout the long county-to-county debate—which he had exacted of the Democratic party as a warm-up for the primary—he freely taunted his stately opponents and by silence at least egged his raucous following on to hoots and barnyard brays. But he yelled persecution when the indignant old guard drummed up a hostile crowd to face him in Columbia and accused him on the stand of the blackest sin in the Southern decalogue—dodging service to the Confederacy. His rival for the governorship, Colonel Alexander C. Haskell, whose empty left eye socket testified to his battlefield valor, sprang the charge. "What age were you," he demanded, "when the war ended; honest now, true age?"

"Seventeen," Tillman replied.

"The law called him at sixteen," Haskell sneered, "and patriotism put thousands in the army at fifteen."

Thus impaled before a gloating audience, Tillman sweated and squirmed. Shaking his finger at Haskell, he frantically explained about the youthful illness that had cost him an eye and kept him honorably from the colors. Then, with the inspiration of political genius, he fixed attention on the dignitaries banked across the stand like a jury hand-picked to find him guilty. Calling on "a better general than you, Haskell, to tell what part the Tillman family took in the War," he held out appealing arms to General Ellison Capers, rector of Columbia's Trinity Episcopal Church.

Though his presence on the stand had been calculated rather to daunt a bully than to rescue a perishing sinner, the old soldier could not refuse. Deserting class loyalties for Christian duty, he threw the lifeline. When asked to bear witness "to the heroic gallantry of one of my brave men who followed the standard of the Twenty-Fourth South Carolina, God forbid that I should keep silent. Jim Tillman of Edgefield [Ben's brother] was the oriflamme of my regiment."

The old veterans in the crowd, many bearing guns to intimidate the Edgefield braggart, wagged their beards in helpless commiseration. Loyal clansmen themselves, how could they doubt the honor of a hero's brother?

Safe behind a borrowed shield, Tillman could now risk a jab at Hampton, who had scolded the Tillmanites for such outrages on the chivalric code as the "howling down of honored gentlemen": "When I saw that a South Carolina audience could insult [General] John Bratton," he had thought, "good God! have the memories of '61, of '65, have they been obliterated?"

Leaving the platform Tillman jeered at Hampton, "The grand mogul here who ruled supremely and grandly cannot terrify me. I do not come from any such blood as that." Then to Haskell he snarled, "When any man comes here and talks about my record, I simply spew him out of the mouth."

Though Tillman had not decisively won the skirmish, he had maneuvered his ambushers onto open ground and made a nervy stand. From the howls that went up in the aristocratic camp, however, it would seem that he had ranged over the field slashing the wounded and dying. A Columbia lawyer cried, for instance, "In the very presence of Hampton I have heard this man strike with poisoned tongue at the vitals of our civilization. [We must] take [him] by the throat and choke him until his lips are livid and . . . he retracts his infamous insinuations."

The "poisoned tongue" half explains Tillman's rise to infamy and office, though it was not so venomous as it was naturally blunt and designedly reckless. On the stump, for example, he would regret that he must follow "the silver-tongued Governor, whose glowing words in praising South Carolina have stirred my heart," then blurt out that he was "nothing but a barnyard rooster . . . I am chock full of rocks and want to chunk some." Working up momentum, he might then image a newspaper critic as "some buzzard who had escaped from the market house in Charleston and gone into the *News and Courier* office, where it was spewing its slime all over me." In other words, barnyard figures came unbidden, but he used them to deliberate effect.

For if the tongue crackled with churlish envy, it articulated, nonetheless, the thoughts of a keen and prideful mind. Harboring no doubt of his gifts and no false modesty, Tillman had apprised the Democratic convention when he stood for the governorship that "you will have at your head the only man who has the brain, the nerve and the ability to organize the common people against the aristocracy."

For both his crudities and his self-assurance "the common people" loved him, that is, the one-horse farmers to whom he pitched his suit. The first marked him as a brother, though he scarcely trusted to mere implication. "You don't have to vote for those pot-gutted blue-bloods," he would yell. "Vote for me. I'm one of you boys and proud to own it." (After Tillman, fraternal oaths became so routine on the stump that at least one vote seeker varied the formula with notable success. "I'm still one of you boys," he would crackle, "even though I have moved up with a better class of people.") If he thus tickled the Wool Hat Boys—so called from the badge of their class, rusty black felt hats—he equally regaled them by daring to sass the bigwigs to their faces.

In his drive to unseat the aristocracy—more properly a ruling clique of the educated and blooded in cahoots with the prosperous —Tillman had more than class envy to exploit and more to offer than a turnover at the public trough. Though envy was a strong motive, so was poverty and so was the notion that Bourbon office-holders preferred the champagne-supper pleasantries of merchants and bankers to the groans of tax- and price-squeezed farmers. The poverty no doubt resulted chiefly from growing too much cotton and too little foodstuff, but it was real. Between 1875 and 1885, for instance, cotton dropped six cents a pound, which meant for many a family going shoeless through the winter. (On a higher plane it might signify only a difference in the quality of a bride's wedding silver: fingering a thin, battered spoon, a bride of the eighties once explained, "Your poor old aunt was married the year the bottom fell out of the cotton market.")

By 1887 so many Carolina landowners were unable to scratch up a few dollars for taxes that over a million acres had reverted to the state for resale.

Meanwhile their betters seemed to manage the state government as though its sole function were to keep ex-Confederate colonels in senatorial frock coats and maintain a platform for their ritual discourses on the Lost Cause. Loyal sons of the fathers who had listened to Thomas Cooper's laissez-faire sermons in the twentys and thirtys, they equated political virtue with forbearance—from lining one's own pockets, naturally; from doing for the people what the people ought to do for themselves; and from plaguing merchants and factory owners with high taxes and labor laws. Hand in hand with these restraints went the duty of chiding the federal government for its lack of restraint, in the matter of tariffs, for instance—still, as Dr. Cooper had fumed, a Northern ruse to pick Southern pockets.

Tillman hinted none too subtly that the state afforded these aristocratic gentlemen more than frock coats and a platform. In short, he all but called them swindlers. Decidedly, they were not, and he very well knew it, but the imputation delighted the sorehead Wool Hat Boys, who craved scapegoats to blame for their want.

Tillman was closer to the truth when he charged the oligarchs with licking industrial and mercantile boots. They called it "encouraging industry and trade," however, with equal truth. For if they looked to the past, they also looked to Henry W. Grady's "New South" future, believing rightly that their section needed factories to get along in a manufacturing nation.

To most of Tillman's backwoods congregation their "bloated aristocratic rulers" were fairy-tale fiends, pursuing vague if monstrous iniquities "in them fancy hotels down to Columby." They came upon flesh-and-blood villains, however, crouching over the ledgers at the crossroads stores. Supply merchants these were, who staked them to guano, fatback and "overhalls" until the season's crop was gathered.

The supply merchant, as W. J. Cash writes, was an ugly though serviceable child of postwar need. Skinflint and profiteer, he nonetheless supplied essential credit to the farmer, credit available from no other source. A victim of harsh Yankee terms himself, he "fastened upon the . . . cotton grower terms which are almost without a parallel for rigor." In return for credit he exacted a lien on the crop, interest rates of 40 to 80 per cent, and sometimes a mortgage on the lands as well.

When prices fell and crops sickened in the eighties, Ben Tillman vented some of his abundant spleen on these credit merchants, who always picked "a large crop of cotton whether they grew it or not." Owning more than a thousand acres, however, and carefully growing

his own meat and foodstuffs, he was able to withstand reverses better
than the average farmer. His analytic mind told him, furthermore,
that farm distress was due as much to ignorance as to the merchant's
greedy hand. "We are land butchers . . ." he informed a farmers'
gathering; "the negroes are eating us out of house and home, while
we follow the old ante-bellum system, and strive after money to
buy a living, instead of *making* [it] at home. Our lands, too, are
going down the rivers."

Disclaiming any thirst for the public teat, Farmer Tillman set
forth in 1885 on an evangelistic mission that would land him the
governorship in 1890 and keep him in the frock-coated ranks until
his death twenty-eight years later. He sounded off at a state farmers'
convention, regaling his audience and enraging the "demagogues,"
who connived with merchant robbers, he said, while they bribed the
watchdog farmer with sops. The paltriest of these sops was the agricultural department of the South Carolina College, an institution
that "marched backward when [it] marched at all." Its very atmosphere "tainted with contempt for farming," it went about its antique
business of propagating lawyers and scholars, half of them mere
"drones and vagabonds."

No state hireling or officeholder, he shouted, cared a rap for the
dirt grubber. Even the man who plodded up the State House steps
with a pitchfork in his hand emerged at the end of the legislative
session twirling a gold-headed cane:

> *He went there to do something for the people. After breathing
> the polluted atmosphere for thirty days he returned home intent
> on doing something for himself. The contact with General
> This and Judge That and Colonel Something Else, who have
> shaken him by the hand . . . has debauched him. He likes this
> being a somebody; and his first resolution, offered and passed in
> his own mind, is that he will remain something if he can.*

Tillman advocated a separate agricultural college as a starting
remedy. In full accord, John C. Calhoun's son-in-law, Thomas G.
Clemson, willed to the state for this end the old Calhoun place near
Pendleton and a cash endowment, naming Tillman and six other
men life trustees with power to choose their successors. Though
legislators could vote additional trustees, they were inclined to look

a Tillman-bitted gift horse squarely in the mouth. They pleaded in opposition, however, the future welfare of the existing state colleges and the well-being of Clemson's granddaughter—"the only living descendant of John C. Calhoun's favorite child"—who they said was being cheated of her "patrimony."

Badgering the legislature to accept the bequest, Tillman exalted his name as the founder of Clemson College and the great benefactor of higher education in South Carolina. Ironically, though, his nettling agitations stalled a proposal that might otherwise have gone through without a murmur. As governor, moreover, Tillman's rank partisanship for his cowbarn academy cost the university sacrifices from which it has scarcely yet recovered. Division of the small appropriational loaf, in fact, may partially explain why South Carolina has yet to afford a first-rate college, even by Southern standards.

Having a devout body of converts under his spell by 1888, Tillman was ready to accept their votes for the governorship. But Democratic party bosses, somewhat less devoted, refused him the nomination. They were forced to grant his request for stump debates between candidates, however, and thereby to ensure his ultimate triumph. For both he and his rough-and-ready disciples were more than a match for such gallants as Wade Hampton.

Though platform debates were made to order for Tillman, they did have a useful social and civic function. They relieved the petrifying monotony of rural life, bringing men—and less squeamish women—together for a sort of educational cockfight. Trading accusations—and sometimes blows—the candidates ventilated the issues as they exercised their tongues and fists. If personalities got a stronger play than issues, nonetheless candidates had to expose their minds to the ordinary voter for the first time in South Carolina history.

Though not running for office in 1888, Tillman campaigned mightily for Tillmanism, invading even Charleston, the very sanctum of a "broken-down aristocracy" that seemed, judging from the fury of his attack, in pretty good health after all. He chastised the plebeian voters as "the most arrant set of cowards that ever drew the free air of heaven. You submit to a tyranny that is degrading to you as white men. . . . God have mercy on your pusillanimous souls. . . . If anybody was to attempt that thing in Edgefield, I swear before Almighty God we'd lynch him."

Thus defaming holy precincts—he had spoken in the very shadow of St. Michael's—Tillman alienated Charleston for good. By his daring, however, he delighted the upcountry, where men inherited their aversion to Charleston along with the belief that Episcopalians were only a shade less blackhearted than Roman Catholics.

Two years later Tillman cashed in on his five-year incitement of "the common people" against the Bourbons, survivals of the past, he said, in all but "patriotism and honor." His close disciples finagled a Democratic party endorsement, and he whooped up the voters to hand him a 4-to-1 majority over Colonel A. C. Haskell, leading an intra-party revolt. In despairing fury the Haskell faction committed the sin against the Holy Ghost—in the Tillman gospel— of courting the Negro vote. They claimed Republican blessings by the gesture but received little Negro support: they offered blacks nothing but "fair play" at the polls, and Tillmanites nullified even this come-on by threatening to pepper them with buckshot if they dared seek it.

Tillman's Negrophobia was a major key to his popularity with the Wool Hat Boys. Though born to a slaveholding clan, Tillman seems to have hated the Negro with underdog venom. Leading the underdog to power, he enthroned a proclivity that future vote seekers would eagerly exploit, some with Tillmanic conviction, others with opportunistic zeal. Ellison DuRant ("Cotton Ed") Smith, for example, a gentleman born, went to the U.S. Senate in 1908 swearing a raw deal to the Negro as loudly as he pledged a fair deal to the cotton farmer. From that time forth he taxed neither his brain nor the voters with a new issue, being of a mind with the man who declined to purchase a book because he already owned one. For six terms he rode back to Washington on a wagonload of cotton waving the banner of white supremacy.

On the Negro issue, Tillman claimed he had the guts to say in national meeting what Hampton era Bourbons cravenly kept under their hats. Once when the U.S. Senate was discussing the appointment of a black man to office, he cried out, "You can keep up that kind of thing until you compel the people of the South to use shotguns and kill every man you appoint." To a shocked Yankee colleague, who declared that his predecessors never avowed such gory intentions, he rejoined, "Maybe not, but if they didn't, they concealed the facts. We do not intend to submit to negro domination and all the Yankees from Cape Cod to hell can't make us."

It may be true that all Carolina whites were equally determined not to "submit to negro domination." But it is also true that Hamptonites had not pressed schemes to drive the Negro into civic limbo—as Tillman did—nor had they proposed Jim Crowism for the railroads. (When Tillman came to office, incidentally, the state had one black congressman and several blacks sitting in the legislature at Columbia.) Certainly no Bourbon governor had ever invited a lynching bee, as Tillman did in his second administration, publicly hoping on one occasion that a Negro rapist be dispatched "before the officers of the law get possession of him." In all fairness it must be said that he urged the rope for one crime alone, but "Governor as I am, I would lead a mob to lynch the negro who ravishes a white woman."

Though as governor Tillman failed to disfranchise the Negro, he did rouse the voters to ask for a new constitution as a means to that soul-satisfying end. Already translated to the empyrean of the U.S. Senate when the convention met in 1895, he nonetheless bestrode the deliberations, helping contrive a Machiavellian suffrage principle, tricky enough to bar a Negro college head from the polls while admitting any white man smart enough to tell his right hand from his left. Tillman's Negrophobia did not, however, blind him to Carolina social fact. Always the realist, he insisted on a fairly literal bar to the marriage of blacks and whites. Opposing the zealous metaphysicians, who claimed that "one drop of nigger blood made a nigger," he defined a Negro as a person having one eighth or more of the Negro taint. Otherwise, as he agreed with his brother George, "respectable families in Aiken, Barnwell, Colleton and Orangeburg would be denied the right to intermarry among the people with whom they are now associated."

A handful of Negroes attending the convention as elected delegates ably but futilely protested the political emasculation of their race. It is ironic that even Tillman lent a courteous ear to their arguments, since his influence guaranteed their performance as the Negro's farewell to public life in the state. Perhaps the shutout was inevitable, but it is possible that gentry rulers might have spared the

Negro at least a dissenting voice in civic counsels. Certainly if such a voice had spoken down through the years it might have softened the pain whites now feel at the militant threats to white supremacy.

If Tillman's "nigger"-baiting spiel endeared him to the rubes, it also deepened antipathies among the gentry. In their view it signified, as nothing else could, a "po'-buckra" raising. The "chivalric" code had always demanded mercy to the slave. Postwar heirs of the code, bereft of all but toothless old Molly, still remembered nonetheless to be nobly obliging, whether they paid her anything or not. They could imagine Governor Tillman, by contrast, bawling at the Mansion butler, "Spill that coffee on me, nigger, and I'll knock your teeth down your damned black throat." No wonder Columbia's dowagers neither called on Mrs. Tillman nor sent cards for their receptions.

Outside of Columbia the gentry seldom had the chance to administer the snub direct, but they snubbed all the same, if only by swapping tales of his gaucheries. Common people, on the other hand, piously christened the latest male towhead Ben Tillman. Both sides were so passionate, and the sides were so inclusive that John Rice, toddling about the Methodist parsonages of his Carolina childhood, thought everybody in the world was either a "Tillmanite" or an "Anti-Tillmanite."

A man's persuasion so invariably fitted his social and economic status that a Columbia livery stable keeper, John Rice reports, took bets on one occasion that he could tell "fer's" on sight from "agin's":

> *Presently a well-dressed stranger came down the street and Gus said, "He's a Anti." When the stranger reached the crowd of loafers and was asked, "Are you for Tillman?" he replied indignantly, "Certainly not," and Gus collected his dollar. Another of the same looks gave the same answer and Gus collected another dollar. Then a broga021ned blue-jeaned unwashed customer came along; Gus put him down as a Tillmanite and won again. At last he grew so confident that when another man came in sight, unkempt and unshaven and dressed in a suit that had once been decent but was now spotted and caked with mud, Gus varied his question and said to him, "You're for*

*Tillman, ain't you?" The man gave him a cur-dog look and said,
"No, pardner, I ain't. The reason I look this way I bin drunk
three days."*

Men of good if not lustrous name did, of course, support and
accept office from Tillman, some because he had offices to give,
others because they admired his championship of the disinherited
white farmer. Even the patriciate, in fact, supplied an occasional
Tillmanite whose peers would label him a crank, connoting thereby
a "common streak" or a brain too restless for a gentlemanly skull.
On the whole, however, gentlefolk, the new-risen as well as the
fallen-from-ante-bellum-grandeur, viewed with such alarm that
down to the present day "Tillmanite" can be used as a social
weapon. A young Carolina couple, for instance, do not boast to
every guest indiscriminately of their "historic" dining-room table
and chairs—relics from the estate of Pitchfork Ben.

John Rice says that his Methodist preacher father, having grown
up in genteel poverty, was the only person on either side of the
family to have a kind word for Tillman. When the elder Rice
described Tillman's fending off a savage display of patrician contempt on the speaking stand, he would become in sympathetic
identification "the proud poor boy from Colleton County." When,
on the other hand, he had put himself at a social disadvantage—
by wearing his newly acquired dinner jacket to tea, for instance—he
was apt to sigh and wish he had been born a gentleman. The conflict was scarcely peculiar to John Rice's father. Nor has it been
uncommon since his day. It is manifested so often, rather, that it
might be thought of as the Carolina neurosis.

No one has better described the soil that produces this conflict
than John Rice in his chapter on "Grandmother Rice's Plantation,"
in the low country, where "you were best or you were nothing." The
Rices were not best, except in their own Colleton precinct. They
were "county as distinguished from state gentry, and very distinguished from Charlestonian." Socially submerged, they were also
"sunk in the double poverty that comes of having seen better days."

The original plantation house had burned down years before
John came along, and its story-and-a-half replacement was indis-
tinguishable from the homes of their plain farmer, or "cracker,"

neighbors. It was not easy to look down socially from an economic swamp, but the Rices did by exertion of will, associating on equal terms with one family alone, a mother and daughter, the last of an aristocratic tribe living "in splendid squalor, in a great house that was falling to pieces." The cost was ruinous, including, among other things, a houseful of old maids. Living nineteen miles from the nearest hamlet, the girls scarcely had a chance. One "had held out until her middle years" and then eloped with a neighboring small farmer who soon realized that he had "stolen more woe than joy; his wife had used up all her courage in one act and now felt the weight of her guilt increasing with the years." She could not bear her role as the family outcast, who could never "darken this door again," according to the fiat of her matriarchal elder sister. Another had "leapt into marriage with a man who was in some way —I never learned just how—connected with the liquor traffic." Also banished "to live in outer darkness," she "had the fortune to bury her husband" in time, "sue successfully for grace, and return to her home."

These poor ladies endured, however, far worse than maidenhood or exile with unworthy mates: they labored in the fields. Able to hire only one Negro "hand," they sank during July and August into a literal and metaphysical hell. Hoeing corn and picking cotton, they performed, as a Carolina farm woman once observed, "the hardest work that God Almighty ever devised for a man to do." But they also suffered a degradation that only a Southern lady could fully apprehend, for not working in the fields was—and is—the rock-bottom condition of ladyhood.

For the cruel task of picking cotton the Rice women wore "mittens, cut from lengths of discarded stockings," but these left the fingers exposed, and John Rice reports seeing his aunts "drag their bodies up the front steps—Jake had gone to the back, as Negroes must—too weary to have removed their mittens, beyond which their fingers stuck out streaked with blood:

> But swollen fingers and aching back were forgotten as their feet touched the bottom step, merged in a greater ignominy from which there was no escape, for the same law that sent Jake to the back forced them to the front. Above them Aunt Mollie

[who stayed in to do the cooking], now the lady, dressed in a clean apron smelling of the sun, with hair slicked back and freshly washed face, stood by her mother's side waiting to receive them. Throughout the picking season this daily ritual of contempt was repeated. It was field nigger and house nigger all over again. . . .

The Negro field hand hoped he was as good as the white by whose side he worked, while his fellow laborer, with only the color of his skin to mark the difference, was afraid that he was no better than the Negro. These were the wellsprings of their natures, making the one gay and free, as hope will, the other sullen, angry and bound. During the summer season my aunts became truculent poor white trash, and their sister's contempt only poured salt on a wound that was already there.

The necessitous decline from station made them despise even more the station to which they sank. Another Jake or two would have allowed a gracious, at least a tactful, condescension to their neighbors. As things were they wore their resentment on their sleeves, and the neighbors did not fail to notice. Once when the Rices decided to clear a piece of new ground, they issued a general invitation to a logrolling and cooked piles of food for the hungry workers. When the day came "no one showed up except a few impelled by sheepish curiosity to see how the snub would be taken. The rest sent word that 'if the Rices wanted their logs rolled, let 'em send for their high-toned friends.' " This had occurred sometime before John Rice went to live with his grandmother, and he "got the story only bit by bit; but the memory still blistered."

If not all landed families were as poor as the Rices, they were nearly all ruled by women. The South became a matriarchy when the men went off to war, and it remained one thereafter partly because so many never came back and partly because the women had acquired the pleasant habit of command. John Rice says that he used to hear "old ladies talking about the terrible war, how they had 'worked their fingers to the bone,' pinching and saving . . . only to see their little all go up in flames set by the invader; but through all their talk ran the sweet memory of happy days, with just enough sad experience to sharpen their delight." The worst they had against

Sherman was "not that he had robbed them of sons and lovers, but that he had stolen the family silver."

In this regard Charleston impressed the touring expatriate novelist Henry James around the turn of the century as "a city of gardens and absolutely no men—or of so few that . . . the war might still have been raging and all the manhood at the front." The wraiths he glimpsed in the gardens, however, did not suggest the masterful ladies of John Rice's memory—"rare, discreet, flitting figures that brushed the . . . walls with noiseless skirts in the little melancholy streets of interspaced, over-tangled abodes—clad in the rigour of mourning that was like the garb of a conspiracy."

Ben Tillman had a Ricean matriarch for mother, "the strongest minded, best balanced woman I ever met," whom he always credited with "whatever ability and judgment I have in life." Her husband had died before the war, leaving some 1,800 acres, fifty slaves and seven sons in her able hands. She managed so well that by 1860 she had nearly doubled both land- and slaveholdings. The richest farmer in the neighborhood, she spent not a penny more than needful, hitching her horse on the Carolina side of the river and walking across the bridge to avoid the toll when she had business in Augusta, Georgia.

Sophia Tillman must have had a queenly heart to match the queenly figure and carriage that Ben recalled, for she never broke in health or spirit as she buried a husband and five sons and suffered George's going to jail for murder. When two of her wild-blooded brood were killed in manly scrapes, she inscribed this defiant dirge on their tomb:

> *Now is done thy long day's work*
> *Fold thy palms across thy breast,*
> *Fold thine arms, turn to thy rest.*
> *Let them rave.*

Hearing that James had been wounded in the Hood-Johnson campaign of 1864, she rushed to Atlanta, searched the hospitals until she found him and nursed him back to health, only to get him home at war's end a shattered wreck.

Sophia Tillman lived well but plainly. Like most ante bellum planters, she imported Yankee schoolmarms for her children, but unlike families even on the ragged edge of gentry, she sold her hospitality to passengers on the stage between Edgefield Courthouse and Augusta. This in itself may not have disjointed the high Edgefield noses, but it was symptomatic of an alienating grubbiness. Edgefield never really accepted the Tillmans, and in a sense Ben Tillman spent his mature life proving that Tillmans were, by God, as good as any Pickens or Brooks or Butler.

Half the time, of course, he didn't care what anybody thought, as when, more or less in emulation of his frugal mother, he invited U.S. Senate clerks to spend the summer recess in his corn and cotton fields on pain of losing their jobs if they declined. He would rouse them from bed at ungodly hours and drive them through the long hot days "with stick in hand and curses on his lips," so his biographer reports.

If Tillman often got the best of Edgefield and even Washington on occasion, Edgefield got the best of him in one supreme instance. He tried to stave off the humiliation but failed, as did Edgefield in its way. Tillman warned his son and namesake—known as B.R.— against marrying the most patrician young lady in the district, granddaughter of Governor Pickens and "the lovely Lucy," daughter of the almost legendary Douschka, whose name recalled her birth during the Pickens ministry to Russia. Tillman thought glamour a poor substitute for the farmyard virtues. Edgefield, in turn, thought a roughneck, cow-college (Clemson) graduate no substitute at all for a man of blood and breeding. Both were at least justified in their fears. The couple separated after a few years, B.R. walking off with their two little girls and deeding them to his parents under an old Carolina statute giving a father arbitrary power over his offspring. Charging her in-laws with kidnaping, the mother brought and won a suit to repossess her children. The old man battled her in the courts with such apoplectic fury that he suffered a stroke two days after the decision. Though he won the right to have the children for two months in the year, he did not win their disposition to stay when dutifully sent. In despair he confessed to the state's chief justice that the little girls would probably always hate him. He was right. They never softened.

On the mother's behalf many Carolinians scored their blackest marks against Tillman. Even those who had forgiven his previous breaches of Carolina decorum boggled at this affront to motherhood. If Tillman did overreach himself in this affair, he only acted from the same willfulness that half prompted every act of his career. Like many figures who have inspired intensities of love and hate—Andrew Jackson, for instance, or Franklin D. Roosevelt—Tillman was profoundly self-centered. He would have his own way come hell or high water.

Since he was also a thinking man, his way was often the intelligent way. In the matter of liquor control, for example, he showed a good deal more sense than the Carolina electorate, which returned him as governor in 1892 with a clear mandate for prohibition. Convinced that no law could pry men loose from the bottle and deciding that the state could ill afford to stanch a healthy flow of revenue, Tillman sidestepped the mandate and put South Carolina in the liquor business. Imposing his own will on the state, he managed at one stroke to infuriate almost everybody, the forces of Methodist aridity as well as the saloonkeeping and moonshining votaries of private enterprise. The opposition was violent and long-sustained and, as usual in such cases, brought bitter enemies to a common bed. Tillman wryly noted that "wet" editors and liquor sellers lay down in loving embrace with temperance "cranks" and preachers.

Tillman's Dispensary Act, closing barrooms and entrusting liquor sales to public boards, created the first state alcohol monopoly in the country. Though a few towns had already pre-empted the liquor traffic, no one had dared propose what on a larger scale would smack of foreign radicalism. The device was, of course, socialistic, but it derived from no more radical theoretic source than common sense. Tillman figured reasonably that if the grogshops of the day were a nuisance a back-alley trade in rotgut would scarcely improve the moral tone. Beyond that he merely exploited in a new way the hoary truth that man's appetite for anodynes always turns a handsome profit. He almost had to exploit it, for office had quickly taught him the equally hoary truth that one promised "reform"—lowered taxes—would negate all the others. Essentially no more radical than the Bourbons, Tillman had promised more and was hell-bent on delivering.

Opposition so raised his gorge that he "haunted" the dispensary warehouse in Columbia, where liquor was bottled for distribution, "watched everything . . . organized the whole machine, and . . . didn't go away until I got it running." When the initial purchase fund ran out, he journeyed up to the bourbon country and finally induced a Cincinnati distiller to let him have supplies on credit. Asked what kind he wanted, he said he hadn't drunk enough booze "to get my tongue educated," but with his usual self-confidence he laid down a formula on the spot: ship three kinds, he ordered, one-, two- and three-year-old whisky, each mixed half and half with cologne spirits (ethyl alcohol), and mark the barrels X, XX and XXX. He then closed the deal by admonishing, "If I catch you monkeying with your agreement, I will quit you, and won't buy a gallon." Thus was decreed the kind of whisky law-abiding South Carolinians would drink for nearly fourteen years.

Plenty were so incensed by Tillman, however, that they would drink anything else but his one-, two- or three-X whisky. In Darlington, for example, topers refused by common agreement to patronize the local dispensary and ganged up on the agents that a furious Tillman dispatched to spy out blind tigers. Guns were drawn, and the constables fled to the swamps leaving one of their number and two Darlingtonians dead in the streets and exposing the Governor to a verbal fusillade from every quarter of the state. Tillman also faced a mutinous militia: Columbia and Charleston units defied his order to put down the "insurrection." Seldom at a loss, however, Tillman cried havoc through the backwoods, and the Wool Hat Boys came running with their shotguns, five hundred strong. They hung around for two or three days, feeling perhaps a bit cheated as the fugitive constables reported back safe and sound to the Governor and the crisis fizzled out.

After this fracas the national press welcomed Tillman to the side of the angels for the first time in his career. Normally deplored as a prophet of the unenlightened, the unwashed and the unruly, he was now hailed as a bulwark of law and order. The "civilized" classes had behaved no better than Yahoos. Tillman could be pardoned for gloating that "My enemies . . . are now confessing failure and defeat and are sorely chagrined over their blunders."

When Tillman graduated from the governorship to the U.S. Senate in 1894, he left the dispensary firmly established and paying good returns to the state. Though it would ultimately become something of a paradise for grafters, it continued to afford the treasury several times more annually than saloons had ever yielded in taxes. Whether the social effects were as happy depended on one's point of view. If drunkenness had not declined—Tillman sold booze cheaper than the barkeeps had—public hangouts for drunkards had sharply diminished.

Only once in his four years as governor did Tillman manage to please everybody—when he fostered a state college for women. Laying the cornerstone at upcountry Rock Hill toward the end of his second term, he said that the building of Winthrop College was "the one thing and the only thing upon which the men of South Carolina are at present united." If he enjoyed that fact, he rejoiced even more in the school's primary mission, which was, as he saw it, to furnish trained helpmeets for the graduates of his farmers' college to the west. Though it was also to furnish schoolmarms for the state, it was close to Tillman's heart as a female auxiliary to Clemson, a sort of kitchen academy, where plain poor girls would learn how to sew and cook and tend the chickens.

The college did attract plain poor girls eager to learn the industrial arts, but since poverty in South Carolina was not restricted to the common orders, it also attracted a great many young ladies more eager to learn Latin, French and the fashionable abstrusities of Robert Browning. As a result the college was inclined to borrow its tone from bluestocking Smith in Massachusetts. Its successive changes in name reflect a steady progress from the educational back yard to the parlor. Starting out as the South Carolina Industrial and Winthrop Normal College, it evoluted to the Winthrop Normal and Industrial College and finally to Winthrop College, the South Carolina College for Women. "Winthrop" derives, by the way, from Robert C. Winthrop, the Bostonian who for many years administered the George Peabody Fund. Through his auspices an annual subsidy was given to the college's parent institution, a training school for teachers in Columbia.

Tillman's sympathies did not follow the plain people of South Carolina who in the eighties and nineties exchanged their hungry servitude in the cotton fields for a better-fed servitude in the cotton mills. He referred to them, in fact, as "the damned factory class," and when a measure came up to limit their working hours to sixty a week, he gave it his blessing chiefly to spite the Bourbons, who joined with millowners to howl that "a ten-hour day would ruin every mill in the State." Some of Tillman's disciples, however, were already eyeing the vote potential gathering in the upcountry textile villages, Representative Cole L. Blease, for instance, who exhorted the factory bosses, "If you have to buy any capital by murdering women and children, for God's sake let it go, let it go!"

Factory bosses were not merely crying wolf at this point. Many were hard-pressed for capital, or at least they were hard-pressed to meet the interest on capital they had begged from the North or borrowed from their fellow townsmen. They were, in fact, more a class of entrepreneurs than of owners. If they were also exploiters of Southern poverty, they did not regard themselves in this light. To the contrary, they believed themselves pioneering the salvation of a blighted Carolina. For the state to meddle, therefore, was to bite the hand that fed.

They were not alone in this view. Almost everyone across the upcountry looked to them as economic saviors, from the merchants, bankers and lawyers, who owned a few shares of stock, to the workers, who owned nothing in this world but a "passel o' chaps [children]." The operator was not infrequently a local banker or lawyer, even a preacher, who had started a mill at the prayers of his fellow citizens to "save our poor country people from ruin, bring us Progress and Prosperity." Petitions of this kind were so urgent that the number of cotton mills increased by 300 per cent in the eighties and by 400 per cent in the nineties, from 14 plants in 1880 to nearly 150 in 1900.

The cotton-mill movement swept through Carolina—through the whole South, indeed—with all the electric force of the great Methodist revivals in the early nineteenth century. The impulse leaped from town to town, sweeping the citizens into mass assembly, rousing local patriotism as it had not been roused since 1860. In one town, for example, a Presbyterian minister implored his congregation to start a cotton mill as an earnest of Christian charity, and they almost literally rushed from the church to do his bidding.

Like the sand tackeys who had traipsed in to William Gregg's Graniteville before the war, the hill grubbers flocked to the upcountry mills, sometimes from worn-out hereditary acres, more often from a landlord's forty acres they had cropped on shares. If they could scare up a wagon and a mule, they piled it full of towheaded children and rattled off; if not, they shouldered their corn-shuck mattresses and walked. At the mill they would find a four-room house to live in at 50 cents a room per month—sometimes they camped out while the carpenters nailed the clapboarding on the studs—and they would find work for every grown man and woman and every towhead over twelve. Wages varied from 50 cents a day for a childish beginner to $1.50 for experienced adults. Since most families could provide half a dozen loom tenders, the living was fairly good. Compared to the living they had been scratching from the ground, it was princely.

Multiplying factories soon exhausted local fields, and the bosses sought recruits in the North Carolina mountains. They had not long or far to seek. Starving to death on their stony corn and "baccy" patches, the mountaineers eagerly enlisted, whole families boarding the trains at company expense. Descendants of a proud, tough Anglo-Saxon breed, they were still tough, but too weary to hold out any longer on the old ancestral ridges of independence. Retracing the path their forebears had taken into the high green country of the Cherokees, they embraced the great new American opportunity—industrial wage slavery.

Theirs might be a healthier bondage than the Pennsylvania coal fields were fixing on a similar breed, though cotton lint was no kinder to the lungs than coal dust. Doubtless, too, rations bought from a company store would do better than no rations at all. But debasement, nonetheless, awaited them at the mills. The Carolina social climate and William Gregg's plantation pattern saw to that. Cotton-mill workers were the first great body of Southern whites to rise to a boss's whistle and stretch out their hands on payday. More significant, they were the first to live in rows of identical cottages on the boss's demesne, very much like "niggers" on the old plantation. Enforcing the analogy, the boss not infrequently set his "Big House" on an overtopping hill nearby.

Long deprived, the early millworkers tended to spend their wages like children at the circus, thereby encouraging the paternalism that ran in the blood of their bosses, who were old Confederate captains by inheritance if not in fact. As the large-scale planter kept store to "carry" his tenants from one harvest to the next, the mill boss kept store to "carry" his spendthrift hands from one pay-day to the next. If the system was inherently vicious, the average boss did not suspect it. Far from setting out to bleed a captive trade, he construed the enterprise as guarding his filial workers from merchant sharks. He sold fatback and snuff on credit from much the same motive that prompted him to assemble his villagers around a lighted cedar at Christmastime and pass out apples and tin horns and firecrackers.

Isolated in their villages, despised as creatures of an overlord and sentenced to the looms for life, millworkers rapidly acquired both physical and psychological stigmas. Scrawny poor-white to begin with, they degenerated into sorrier specimens than the parent breed —pasty-faced, sunken-chested and stoop-shouldered. As W. J. Cash says:

> Chinless faces, microcephalic foreheads, rabbit teeth, goggling dead-fish eyes, rickety limbs, and stunted bodies abounded. . . . The women were characteristically stringy-haired and limp of breast at twenty and shrunken hags at thirty or forty. And the incidence of tuberculosis, of insanity and epilepsy, and, above all, of pellagra, the curious vitamin-deficiency disease which is nearly peculiar to the South, was increasing.

They wore a caste uniform, blue denim overalls for the men and poke bonnets and shapeless ginghams for the women. Both male and female were addicted to snuff, which they "dipped" rather than sniffed. That is, they inserted a pinch between gum and cheek, chewing a twig to induce saliva. The practice gave a muffled sound to their harsh, twanging speech, a dialect fairly general in the mountains but in most of upcountry Carolina peculiar to mill villagers and backwoods poor whites. (To this day an unrounded "i" in words like "wife" can raise a social doubt in certain Carolina ears.)

The first generation in the mills scarcely knew their A B C's, and the second and third by custom and necessity rarely advanced beyond the first three or four grades of school. For amusement they liked to hear some nasal troubadour whine their Elizabethan bal-lads, parent types of all the "country" or "hillbilly music that now wails across the land. In church they liked to raise joyful noises to the Lord, the joyfuller the better. Temperamentally, if not actually, they were all "wash-foot" Baptists, relishing the hell-fire exhortations that stood a woman's hair on end and made strong men sweat for their devilment. They would have fetched a deeply sympathetic sigh for the old lady who complained of a Presbyterian divine that he could "go down the deepest, stay down the longest and come up the driest of any preacher ever stood in the pulpit."

Profoundly caste conscious after thirty years' stigmatizing bondage to the looms, factory men were ripe for manipulation at the polls. Tillman could have had them for the asking, but he neither wanted nor required their votes, having little opposition as a U.S. senator after 1896. (When a favorite Carolina son goes up at last to the Senate, he virtually puts on the mantle of immortality: who, after all, could wish to vote a saint out of heaven?) One of his early disciples, however, Cole Blease, stooped to court the pariah "lintheads" and thereby wrenched the governorship from the resurgent Bourbons in 1910.

Unlike Tillman, he offered the groundlings nothing but identification. Though middle-class by origin—his father kept an upcountry village hotel and livery stable—Blease embodied and voiced for the millworkers all their apprehensions and animosities. If he now and then promised to enforce child-labor laws, he normally keyed his pitch to no aspiration higher than envy and no qualm more reasonable than fear of lecherous "nigger bucks." He denounced almost every social measure the poor and oppressed—that is, the organized poor and oppressed speaking through their organizers—have yearned for: protective labor laws, for instance, and compulsory education. As governor he threatened to quash any bill to improve adult working conditions on the ground that men and women were free to labor where and as they pleased. On the question of rounding up the young at schooltime he said that favoring arguments usually came from "those who expect to receive higher salaries by it . . . or else from some narrow-minded bigot who has made a failure in raising his own children . . . and now wants to attempt to raise somebody else's."

His following actually rejoiced at such churlish talk. They were far less enamored of learning than of the weekly pay envelope from their twelve- and thirteen-year-olds, and besides they mistrusted the

do-gooder's meddling hand. By the same token, most have held out
against labor organizers right down to the last scrap of fatback on
the table.

They stuck with Blease because he felt as they felt or said what
they felt. They would have stuck, however, regardless of what he
said, so long as he wallowed verbally with the underdog. That he
never failed to do. On one occasion he wallowed so fervidly that a
blue-shirted clodhopper interrupted him to avow, "Coley, I'd vote
for you even if you was to steal my mule tonight"; and a mill hand
shouted in rapturous affirmation, "I'd put my vote in for Coley if I
was a-standin' knee-deep in Hell."

If the Bourbons had despised the Edgefield Moses for rousing up
the Wool Hat Boys, they loathed Coley Blease for inciting the lintheads. Their bitterness was vividly exemplified by a Columbia *State*
cartoon a few days before his election as governor. It portrayed him
as a buzzard swooping down on a berobed female "South Carolina"
wielding the sword of "The Ballot." His pinions were inscribed with
all the sins of bigotry and guile in the book. Such malignancies did
not chasten Coley; indeed, they probably dared him to such lengths
as opening the state prison gates to 1,700 thieves, murderers and
lesser offenders during his double term. His record in this and other
departments alienated even Pitchfork Ben, who claimed that the
Bleasite vote in 1916 included "all the tin horn gamblers, all the
blind tigers, all the red light habitués, all the criminals and near
criminals—those who have been pardoned and those not yet caught
and convicted."

Tillman might justifiably disavow Blease on certain grounds, but
in lunatic scorn and fear of a black face the younger man was blood
of his blood. From Tillman's arrival in Washington until illness cut
short his extracurricular crusade, Pitchfork Ben carried the gospel
of racial antagonism wherever he could find a willing audience. In
Senate recesses he followed the lyceum trail—east and west as well
as south—preaching Negro inferiority and urging social, economic
and political sanctions against the race. Barely admitting the Negro
to the human family, he insisted that "it took something else besides having the shape of a man to make a man" and that some
Negroes were "so near akin to the monkey that scientists are yet
looking for the missing link."

He treated his Washington colleagues to similar lessons in out-house anthropology, boasting on one occasion that "as governor of South Carolina I proclaimed that, although I had taken the oath of office to support the law . . . I would lead a mob to lynch any man, black or white, who ravished a woman, black or white." Note the discretionary additive "black." Impetuous he may have been, but he cared for his reputation. In South Carolina, of course, he scarcely needed to weep public tears over ravaged black virtue.

When Blease finally got to Washington in 1924 he took up where Tillman had left off at his death in 1918. In fact, one Carolina critic thinks he outdid the master, claiming that since he "first appeared in the public eye . . . he has been the most ardent defender of the divine right of the Caucasian race to dispose of the offending blackamoor without benefit of jury." While governor, for instance, he posted the following congratulation to the organizers of a triple lynching: "You did like men and defended your neighbors and put their black bodies under the ground."

Among his heroic exertions for his constituency, he could count U.S. Senate bills to prohibit mixed marriages and to require separate seating on the District of Columbia streetcars. If he labored in vain, he could at least report back home that he poured it to those "nigger-loving Yankees" hot and heavy. It was not his fault that a black man could ride the trains "in the very berth beneath, or above, or next to, the berth occupied by a white lady" or that in some towns blackamoors handed U.S. mail "to the white ladies at their doors."

In South Carolina Cole L. Blease is a forgotten man, memorialized only in the names of countless now aging men born under his dispensation. His political methods, however, his single-minded appeal to bigotry, are memorialized on the Carolina hustings, in fact, since the Supreme Court ruling on the schools, almost every time many Carolina politicians open their mouths.

If the gospel of white supremacy also echoes the memory of Pitchfork Ben Tillman, worthier memorials do survive—the colleges for men and women he founded and perhaps the conviction that government is every man's proper business. The evil he did was incalculable—his biographer Francis B. Simkins says he fostered in the nation at large the modern reaction against the Negro—but the good he wrought "is written in heroic terms; he was the founder of the sort of democracy his state cherishes":

> *It is fitting that his statue stands on the State House grounds as a complement to Wade Hampton's. Inevitably, the form and features of Pitchfork Ben are not as classical as those of the Great Aristocrat. But there is determination in the expressive face and the rugged strength of a leader of the common people in the lineaments.*

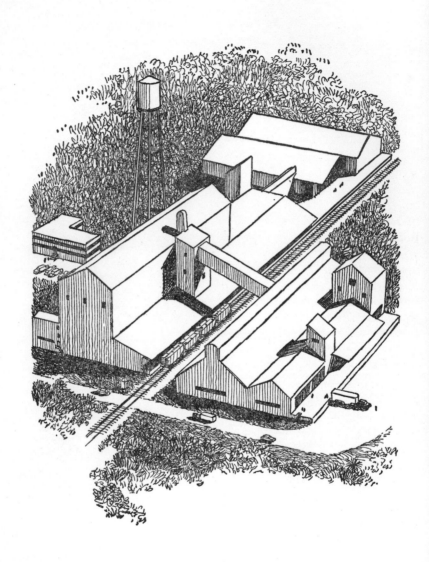

XVI

"Music in Their Shuffling Feet"

In 1929 a novel of plantation Negro life—Scarlet Sister Mary, by Julia Peterkin—brought South Carolina her first and only Pulitzer prize for literature. Two years earlier, a drama of Charleston Negro life—*Porgy*, which DuBose Heyward (with his wife, Dorothy) adapted from his novel of that name—had given spry notice of South Carolina to Broadway. If these two events proclaimed a resurrection of the state's ante bellum muse—and they were hailed in such terms—they must at least have murmured to the Carolina Negro that history had no end of sportive uses for him. Having served Carolina politicians as a bogeyman for half a century—Cole Blease's Negrophobic blather still plagued the U.S. Senate at this juncture—the black man, it now appeared, would do a rakish turn for her writers at the national literary fair.

The two writers in question, however, were scarcely purveyors of the scandalous. Though both offered glimpses of the Negro in the raw, so to speak, neither sidled up to the reader with a verbal leer. In approach they were as far removed from the dirty-picture hucksterism of an Erskine Caldwell as, say, Wade Hampton was removed from Pitchfork Ben Tillman. Respect for their subject, in fact, was accounted the measure of their success. For the first time in American letters, it was said, the Negro acted out a truly human role, free at last from the matrices of charade, à la Thomas Nelson Page or Harriet Beecher Stowe.

Nevertheless, it is rather a crashing irony that a state so wed to the gospel of white superiority has to rest its modern literary claims on explorations of the black underside of its culture. It has to, because Heyward and Mrs. Peterkin, modest as their achievements may seem in the national perspective, have written the only works in our time very much noticed as serious art. Before they set to work in the early twenties, South Carolina was all of a barren piece with the region H. L. Mencken hooted as the Sahara of the Bozart. They made an oasis—as Mencken himself acknowledged in cheering Mrs. Peterkin—the first in their stretch of desert and still the greenest.

Certainly no Carolina novels, with the possible exception of William Gilmore Simms' *Yemassee,* have had a wider circulation than *Porgy* and *Scarlet Sister Mary.* In its operatic form, moreover—as *Porgy and Bess,* with score by George Gershwin—Heyward's tale of the crippled beggar and his summertime mate has found as large an audience as almost any other American work one could name. It has been seen and heard in virtually every large city of the two Americas and of Europe, including Moscow. Now Goldwynized for the movie screen, it will undoubtedly show for years to come all over the world.

Along with Simms these two writers uphold the Carolina novelistic reputation. Like Simms, they have perhaps more interest—in this context, anyway—as cultural mirrors than as artists. Like Simms as well, they essentially work the romantic vein, for all contemporary reviewers had to say about the "stark realism" of their portrayals. As Simms mythicized a fading manorial Carolina, so they glorified the "primitive" Negro as he stood on the threshold of his passage to social-casedom.

In a brief poetic essay of 1923 DuBose Heyward reveals his essential attitude to the Negroes of his native Charleston. With their casual attachments, he wonders whether morally they forge ahead or lag behind the white man ("free love" was much in the air those days of flinging off the corsets of late Victorianism):

> *Who knows? But one thing is certain: the reformer will have them in the fullness of time. They will surely be cleaned, married, conventionalized. They will be taken from the fields, and given to machines, their instinctive feeling for the way that leads to happiness, saved as it is from selfishness, by humor and*

genuine kindness of heart, will be supplanted by a stifling moral strait-jacket. They will languish, but they will submit. . . . And my stevedore, there out of the window. I look at him again. I cannot see him as a joke. Most certainly I cannot contort him into a menace. I can only be profoundly sorry for him, for there he sits in the sunshine unconsciously awaiting his supreme tragedy. He is about to be saved.

Virtually the same idea informs a sonnet he called "Modern Philosopher":

> *They fight your battles for you every day,*
> *The zealous ones, who sorrow in your life.*
> *Undaunted by a century of strife,*
> *With urgent fingers still they point the way*
> *To drawing rooms, in decorous array,*
> *And moral Heavens where no casual wife*
> *May share your lot; where dice and ready knife*
> *Are barred; your feet are silent when you pray.*
> *But you have music in your shuffling feet,*
> *And spirituals for a lenient Lord,*
> *Who lets you sing your promises away.*
> *You hold your sunny corner of the street,*
> *And pluck deep beauty from a banjo chord:*
> *Philosopher whose future is today!*

Heyward's first novel, *Porgy*, opens on a correspondingly reflective note, invoking the halcyon past of authorial childhood and directing a gentle irony at the meddling reformist spirit abroad in the prosier time of his maturity. "Porgy lived in the Golden Age," he begins, "when men, not yet old, were boys in an ancient beautiful city that time had forgotten before it destroyed." It was also the Golden Age of beggary:

> *In those days the profession was one with a tradition. A man begged, presumably because he was hungry. . . . His plea for help produced the simple reactions of a generous impulse, a movement of the hand and the gift of a coin, instead of the elaborate and terrifying processes of organized philanthropy.*

*His antecedents and his mental age were his own affair, and, in
the majority of cases, he was as happily oblivious of one as the
other.*

Setting his characters in motion, Heyward never quite sets them
free. By his tone as a narrator he constantly and perhaps unconsciously reminds the reader of the Negro as a type and of himself as a
Charleston aristocrat, an unusually sensitive and compassionate
scion of the great rice-planting squirearchy. As such he regrets every
show of inhumanity or unfeeling exercise of justice, construing the
skull-breaking nightsticks and the stifling jails that threaten his
Porgies and Besses as plebeian lapses from *noblesse oblige*. The real
menace in *Porgy* is not the "villain" of the tale, the dope-pushing
Harlem dude, Sportin' Life, who lures Bess away from the crippled
Porgy. It is rather those snarling white cops who periodically invade
Catfish Row, their entrance to the courtyard a signal for dispersal,
silence and a feigned oblivion to all but the fact of being in the
room where one belongs. Opposing this menace is the figure of the
lawyer Alan Archdale—the name bespeaks birth and breeding—who
in rueful good humor concedes Porgy and his stinking goat the
shade of his office walls and pays the beggar's friend out of jail.
While the friend languishes behind bars, his furniture is repossessed
by Archdale's antitype, "a vile-mouthed, bearded Teuton," who
"swore so fiercely that no one dared to protest."

Identifying the economic oppressor as a German, Heyward reflects
a Charleston actuality: its small tradesmen were and still generally
are of German descent. By his more or less whimsical choice of the
word "Teuton," however, he does suggest the traditional bias of his
Anglo-French planter class against the late-arriving mercantile Germans. Heyward's parochial mind-set is implicit in the reference. He
could never forget that he was a Heyward, portraying the life of a
city where the name sounded of ducal altitudes. Doubtless, though,
his becoming a writer at all owed something to reduced family circumstances, if we accept the view that some form of psychological
displacement as well as inborn talent is required to make an
artist.

When DuBose Heyward came along—in 1885—his branch of the
family had come down in the world to a rented Charleston house.

His father worked in a rice mill, having lost the patrimonial rice-lands, which had descended from Signer of the Declaration Thomas Heyward. Dying of an accident when the writer was an infant, he left his wife such scanty means that she had to permit her son's going on the street as a newsboy. By this necessitous lapse, however, the family did not vacate the Charleston social heaven. Heywards may stoop, but they do not fall. When a New York scribbler assumed —more or less on the evidence of his career as a newsboy—that the author of *Mamba's Daughters* was a self-made man, a Charles-tonian promptly scoffed at the notion that a Heyward could pull himself up by the bootstraps: however low his fortunes to begin with, he was essentially up before he started.

In the usual American view, however, DuBose Heyward was a self-made man. Unable to afford a college education, he worked at various clerical jobs around the city—he was timekeeper at a dock-side warehouse for a spell—and eventually cofounded an insurance firm that made him a very decent income.

If the shell of caste enfolded Heyward as a youth, material want must have formed a pearl-making grain of sand. Poverty does make a difference. It might have hurt less acutely in name-conscious Charleston than almost anywhere else in America, but it could have hurt more insidiously. It takes money to live in peace with pride. It takes a certain visible weight and shine of things to uphold the supposition of rank. Daily reminders of a lustrous past—a lost grandfatherly mansion or a grandmotherly tale by the fire—might as reasonably prick as lave a tender ego.

The intent is not to explain Heyward's art as a simple response to a simple irritant but only to suggest the grounds of a conflict usual enough in South Carolina to make him seem an epitomizing figure. A sensitive nature cannot live undisturbed among the ruins of his heritage. Loving what has been, he is bound to hate it a little as well, if only for its failure to last or for the cruel light it throws on the present.

Increasingly apparent in his work, the ambivalence seems to Frank Durham, Heyward's Carolina biographer, a result of mature experiences in the world beyond Charleston. Fame and success broadened his vision

> *as early poverty had deepened his knowledge of the many-*
> *faceted life of his city. From the comforting security of an*
> *inherited position he made forays into worlds where achieve-*
> *ment, not inherited position, was the criterion of acceptance,*
> *where the color of a man's skin mattered less than his skill in*
> *the arts, where he began to question intellectually the things*
> *he still cherished in his heart.*

Doubtless the head did increasingly quarrel with the heart as Heyward consorted with Negro actors on Broadway, but doubtless also the quarrel had begun when the patrician youth was forced to earn his daily bread—and not too much of it at that—from his social inferiors. Working among dockside Negroes, he responded with a poet's eye and ear to their bold physical rhythms and to the haunting minors of their songs, but as a trifling functionary he must have taken a little to heart their deep-grained hatred of the everlastingly omnipotent boss. His own predicament, in other words, enabled him to feel the black predicament as he might never have felt it otherwise.

The black predicament is the overt subject of *Mamba's Daughters,* published in 1928, or rather it is one of the subjects. For the novel deals with the varied relations of white to black, white to white and black to black in Charleston. The result is by turns sharply dramatic, gently amusing or sociologically informative, if not satisfying as a novel. Heyward gave it a specious unity by entwining the lives of a white and a Negro family, more specifically the rise of a poor and dreamy young aristocrat to business success and the progress of a talented Negro girl from the Charleston slums to the "New Metropolitan Opera House stage. A double rags-to-riches tale, so to speak. But the trouble is that neither of these stories is really dramatic, because neither of the characters grapples with anything much beyond the question of what it all means. They both seem moved by forces they dimly understand but in no sense control: Saint Julien de Chatigny Wentworth is shaped by the iron hand in the velvet glove that is Charleston and family tradition; and Lissa Atkinson is thrust upward by the iron will and the fanatic aspiration of her grandmother, the crafty old Mamba. If no reader is apt to care very much about the maundering Saint Wentworth or to credit very deeply the "artistic" Lissa, surely no Southern reader could withstand Mamba, the sly old crone who adopts the Wentworths as her white folks and works them to the far, improbable glory of her infant granddaughter. She works herself equally hard, as she points out to her drunken daughter, Hagar, whose child is at stake:

> "*Here yo' ain't gots nuttin' tuh do, 'cep' meet de steamer an' wash fuh de sailor. Yo' gots yo' own house tuh lib in, an yo' frien' roun' yo', an' yo' gots yo' baby fuh pet and handle. An' all Ah ax is dat yo' keep sobuh an' don't git lock in jail. T'ink on dat, dem 'membuh what Ah' doin' fuh yo' baby so she kin hab chance in de worl'. Leabe my frien', an' de talk an' all, an' put up wid de damn quality w'ite folks. . . . Ah swear tuh Gawd my belly fair ache from de pure polite. Some time Ah t'ink dat ef it ain't fuh dat boy, Saint, Ah'd hab tuh gib up tryin' an' tell 'em all tuh go tuh hell.*"

Of all the characters in the book only Mamba and Hagar, who is finally bent to her mother's fanatic will, have energy enough to carry a novel, but unfortunately they get only half the chance they deserve.

If somewhat sprawling and thematically inconclusive as a novel, *Mamba's Daughters* is highly pertinent as a revelation of what Frank Durham calls "the dilemma of the liberal but nonrevolutionary Southern aristocrat confronted by a world he never made." Sympathetic to the Negro as a person, he brakes the wheels of an often careless, often cruel system, occasionally at great expense of time, money and anguish. Saint Wentworth, for instance, is after a fashion as much responsible for Lissa's New York apotheosis as Mamba. Furthermore, he feels an exalted pride in her triumph, in Mamba's selfless endurance and in a race that could produce these wonders after ages of subjection. He would never have stood up, however, and demanded Lissa's right to realize her talent, even her full human potentialities, in Charleston. Heyward evokes the character definitively—and not a little of himself—as Saint waits for the curtain to go up on Lissa's debut:

> *Already while only in the middle thirties, his figure was commencing to show the comfortable outlines of one who appreciates the pleasant things of life at their full value and who has learned to meet the unpleasant ones with an amiable*

*acquiescence. Yet the face, with its high forehead and thoughtful
slate-coloured eyes, showed evidences of having passed through
some spiritual conflict. The strong lines of the chin indicated
sufficient courage for an individual course of action, but the
sensitive mouth suggested that when this course violated the
standard of good taste of his class its pursuit would be at a cost
that would amount to a minor heroism.*

Quite in keeping with Saint Wentworth's patronage of Lissa,
DuBose and Dorothy Heyward insisted that Ethel Waters have her
first chance as a dramatic actress in the play they made of *Mamba's
Daughters* (produced in New York, 1939). In doing so they honored
a promise given two years before when Miss Waters, then known
only as a blues singer, told them of her strong personal response to
the novel. Hagar was her own mother to the life, she said, "fighting
on in a world that had wounded her so deeply"; but Hagar was also
"all Negro women lost and lonely in the white man's antagonistic
world." The play marked not only Miss Waters' debut on the legiti-
mate stage but also the Negro actor's coming of age in America. "I
was the first colored woman," she puts it, "the first actress of my
race, ever to be starred on Broadway in a dramatic play."

Ruling out the Saint Wentworth story in their dramatization of
Mamba's Daughters, the Heywards gained the kind of unity Julia
Peterkin had achieved in her novels by inventing a plausibly dis-
crete Negro world and by setting her characters free of authorial
interpretation. She knew by instinct apparently that man's contest
with woman and their common battle with disease, death and the
elements were as much to the point for a novelist as caste antagon-
isms. Or perhaps she discerned her limitations. One might suspect
as well that she departed the "real" world for a never-never land
where she could sentimentalize the Negro to her heart's content,
figure him as child of earth and sky, unaware and unwary of the
ruling white caste. If moved by such an impulse, she could at least
make him believable as a primitive isolate, having known him somewhat in that character on Lang Syne plantation, at Fort Motte
(thirty-odd miles south of Columbia), where she went to live as a
bride around the turn of the century. In summer vacations on the
coast north of Georgetown, moreover, she had observed an even

"purer" form of Negro life on the moribund rice plantations of the Waccamaw Neck. In the early 1900's she saw here Negro settlements that time had almost forgotten, scratching at lands the owners seldom cared whether they owned or not till rich Yankees invaded the district hunting quail and glamour.

Whatever the actuality, she makes us believe that her characters at any rate were engaged "in a patient struggle with fate," not a restive struggle with social misfortune. (Her skill, if not the "truth" of her portraiture, was attested by Northern Negro "realists" as well as by white Southern "romantics." A famous Negro singer, in fact, racked by the anomaly of his position in American life, was so taken in that he begged to come and live among the undivided black souls at Lang Syne—begged in vain, for Mrs. Peterkin was too wise to indulge such risky make-believe.) Her coastal Gullahs battle the perversities of nature—animal, vegetable and human; they do not contend with arbitrary white justice or bourgeois morality. *Black April,* for instance, her first novel, contains one white figure, a purely incidental storekeeper.

The Bluebrook people manage without any apparent white assistance or pay, working the crops under the stern foremanship of April, a giant-bodied man who walks lonely and proud as a god among the hinds. In effect he is a kind of god, a phallic god, who possesses with a look and for whose look the Quarters women all invoke their love charms. Subject to no law but that of his own nature, he would not even yield to the spirit of the Lord God Almighty as it descended upon the congregation at Heaven's Gate church. As the "tide of prayer rolled into a flood" it swept everyone along but April: "He sat upright. Unmoved. Passionless. When the preacher's ranting halted to give out a hymn, [he] got up and walked down the aisle, and on out of the door." Later his gorge rises so high at the "jackass" preacher—the squeamish "servant of Gawd" refuses a drink from the lemonade barrel, where April's wife had dropped her false teeth as she poured in the "sweetenin' "—that he vises the man's head between his hands and bites off a mouthful of cheek. His fury spent, he spits and grumbles, "Dat meat taste too sickenin',," then squares his shoulders and walks away: "Cool. Master of himself. Alone."

At last fate strikes the proud man down in the form of gangrene that rots his feet—his toes detach themselves and float off in a tub of water—and sends him finally to the hospital in "town," where his legs are amputated at the hips. Back home, he loses all heart at the realization that his young wife, Joy, cannot love him any longer as a man; that his own son, in fact—by another wife—will lie in her bed while he thrashes about like a baby in the adjoining room. This is death for the phallic essence. Inevitably the body sickens and dies. But just before the end April's old spirit revives to give one last command:

> *Outside the black trees sounded restless. An uneasy pattering and rustling ran through the dry lips of the leaves. Flying insects buzzed into the room and beat against the walls with noisy humming wings.*
>
> *"Uncle—"* [the old man who is watching at his bedside through the night] *April's breath stifled, his eyes widened with the strain, but he forced his lips to twist out the words he wanted to say.*
>
> *"Bury me in a man-size box—You un'erstan'?—A man—size— box—I—been—six—feet—fo'—Uncle—Six feet—fo'."*

It is a wonderfully moving climax to which the novel does not really build. Until the last few chapters Mrs. Peterkin allows no identification with her central character. Perhaps she conceived *Black April* less as a novel than as a fictionalized account of plantation Negro life, or so the chapter headings would imply: "Duck-Hunting," "Hog-Killing," "Church," "Quilting," and so on. If it fails, consequently, as a work of art, it doubtless has some permanent value as descriptive sociology. It is also a beguiling evocation of the coastal scene.

Happily in *Scarlet Sister Mary* Mrs. Peterkin tells a straight-forward tale with hardly a single excursus into folklore or the poetry of woods and waters. At the risk of minimizing her access of craft, one suspects that *Black April* had pretty well exhausted her store of the merely curious and macabre. At the further risk of probing a Southern lady's psyche, one also guesses that in the truimphantly free-spirited Si May-e she had found a subject congenial to her own nature. Having dared so far, one might as well impute to "Miss Julia" the kind of identification Flaubert admitted in the phrase, *"Madame Bovary c'est moi."* (She is still very much alive there at

Lang Syne, a figure of queenly charm and self-possession, with the deep blue gaze of a sibyl.)

In *Black April* the dominant figure is a man, as seen, however, through the eyes of women and children, his subjects, really, who hate him as much as they love him. It is not surprising that the old ram should undergo symbolic emasculation nor that the point of observation should move to his side at this juncture and the mood shift to pathos. In *Scarlet Sister Mary*, by contrast, a woman dominates the scene, and the point of view is hers throughout. Perhaps needless to say, she is triumphantly alive at the close. If April is a phallic god, Si May-e is the deathless mother of phallic gods.

To be done with Freudian meddling—and none too soon—*Scarlet Sister Mary* is pre-eminently a comic work if we think of comedy as a celebration of life. Superficially it is also a kind of Pilgrim's Progress, in which Si May-e falls from Baptist grace by conceiving a child before her marriage and returns at last to the waters of purification some twenty years and a houseful of sin-born children later. But resuming her vows does not mean taking the veil: at least it does not mean forsaking the spirit that has pleasured itself in the flesh and all its abundant fruit. As she receives "the hand of fellowship" at the novel's close, there is little doubt that Si May-e's eye has not done roving yet:

> Old Daddy Cudjoe [*the conjure man*] came last. . . . *He took Mary's hand and shook it, then he cut his eyes all around to be certain Maum Hannah could not hear him when he whispered:*
> "*If you gwine to quit wid mens now, Si May-e, do gi me you conjure rag. E's de best charm I ever made.*"
> *Mary looked straight into his eyes and smiled as she shook her head.*
> "*I'll lend em to you when you need em, Daddy, but I couldn' gi way my love-charm. E's all I got now to keep me young.*"

Si May-e is an irresistible character—gay, loving, generous and clear-sighted—a bit too clear-sighted perhaps for the male reader, for after her heart-love and only husband, July, deserts her in the first year of their marriage, she concludes as she takes man after man into her bed that "not one of them is worth a drop of water that drains out of a woman's eye." Though she grieves herself to skin and bones for July, she points him straight to the door when he comes whining back after a twenty-year absence from Bluebrook. An unforgiving wife, she is all forbearance and compassion as a mother. When her first-born, Unex, comes home from his wanderings to die of some nameless disease, she enfolds him in her arms and rocks him off to "sleep." Brave as she is, his going brings her to the lowest ebb of her life, for "God knew he was the only heart-child she had. The others were the fruit of eye-love, the children of her flesh, yet they were strong and hearty; and her joy-child, her first-born, her jewel, July's son, was gone."

Publicly South Carolina rejoiced in the Pulitzer award to *Scarlet Sister Mary*. The Columbia *State*, for instance, was "particularly gratified," because "It confirms our judgment. We had tried to shout our acclaim of Julia Peterkin from her first rosy dawn on our Southern horizon—'knew her and named a Star.' " Admitting that some native works had been fragmentary and disordered, the editorialist commended Mrs. Peterkin for her superior craft, for a story "thoroughly planned and brilliantly and restrainedly told. It would live as a portrait gallery of certain interesting types of Negroes, and a presentation of a certain kind of Negro life, even if it had no enduring vitality as story. But happily it possesses both." Sharing the *State*'s complacency, Mrs. Peterkin's college, Converse at Spartanburg, gave her an honorary degree.

Privately, however, many custodians of culture were a bit chagrined, if not downright mortified, at the cause of recognition. Literary laurels accorded ill with the sordid amours of a Negro wench. Indeed, such high Carolina talents as Mrs. Peterkin and Heyward accorded ill with the couplings and clashes of a servant race. Professor Yates Snowden, of the University of South Carolina, typified this reaction in saying (to the Charleston writer John Bennett, one of DuBose Heyward's literary mentors) that he hated *Porgy* for its very brilliance. Pronouncing it a "wonderful . . . book of prose . . . true to the last item, and startlingly understanding," he inquired, "Don't he dare write of our WHITE FOLKS . . . HIS white folks . . . he'd make a permanent contribution to the story of the French-English civilization of the South." Confederate Daughters shared his repugnance but found no compensating merits. Often, in fact, they rated without reading, possibly taking their cue from such intrepid souls as the Charleston lady who threw *Porgy* aside feeling "dirty."

Even approving Carolina readers, however—and there were many, especially among the shockproof younger generation—failed in general to see the Heyward and Peterkin fictions as images of universal life. They took them, rather, as pictures of the Negro "life" that everyone knew and sniggered about but that no one had ever before thought to write about. The Columbia *State* reflected this viewpoint in reporting a few days after the Pulitzer award the "rumor" that

> ". . . *Scarlet Sister Mary*" herself is in Columbia, gracing some fortunate kitchen. Further, they say, that now that her flaming youth is past and she can turn her talents to quieter arts, she turns out waffles, gravies, and fried chicken that are if possible richer in flavor than some of the old plantation episodes. Also, though, she is living incognita, of course, it drifted to her ears that she was in a book.
>
> "Oh, my Gawd!" she is said to have exclaimed, when informed of her fame, "What hab Miss Julia did to me?"

On some juvenile Carolinians of the time the Heyward and Peterkin works had an effect quite beyond their interest as candid reportage or their debated value as cultural ornaments. For youngsters trying to express themselves in words—and finding so distressingly little to express—the new Carolina writers and their books served as a pattern and a promise. They announced a subject and they gave reason to hope that the sleek, steel doors of New York might open for South Carolina talents to come. When they saw the names of DuBose Heyward and Julia Peterkin exalted in the *New York Times,* they felt a leap of mingled pride and triumph, an emotion the like of which only an aspiring young Dubliner might have felt to read that Bernard Shaw had jarred rich and supercilious London.

DuBose Heyward did more than symbolize possibilities. He assisted many young writers in finding a voice and an audience through the Poetry Society of South Carolina, which he founded in 1920 with two adoptive Charlestonians: John Bennett, author of the children's classic *Master Skylark;* and Hervey Allen, then a teacher and avocational poet, later to inaugurate—with *Anthony Adverse*—the modern vogue for sheer poundage in the historical fiction market.

Editing the society's *Yearbook* from 1921 through 1924, Heyward helped forward the careers of several fellow Charlestonians, notably Beatrice Ravenel and Josephine Pinckney, both of whom achieved some national recognition as poets. Turning later to fiction, Miss Pinckney wrote several novels—*Three O'Clock Dinner* among them —that skillfully and not unhumorously exploited the theme of individuals in conflict with the orthodoxies and dictates of class as these survive in modern Charleston. The list of writers at least stimulated in varying degrees by Heyward's activities would also include Drayton Mayrant (Katherine Drayton Mayrant Simons), who has published historical novels; Herbert Ravenel Sass, who claimed chief attention for his magazine stories of coastal wild life but also tried his hand at historical fiction; and Samuel Gaillard Stoney, who has written lovingly accurate and graceful surveys of the architecture of Charleston and the surrounding plantation country.

After a fashion the Poetry Society refurbished Charleston's ante bellum literary lamp and for a brief spell upraised it as a light to wanderers on the dark Dixie plain. By example it encouraged lonely versifiers and talespinners to band together for mutual consolation and the propagation of "little" magazines. Through its annual competitions it also helped apprize the nation of such talents as Robert Penn Warren, John Crowe Ransom and Donald Davidson, all of whom would join with Allen Tate and others to take a famous agrarian "stand" at Nashville, Tennessee, in 1930.

Though they issued no manifestoes, the South Carolina writers shared more or less the Agrarians' reverence for the South's old land-rooted and caste-structured social order, or, as they were in the habit of phrasing it, "our traditional way of life." Since the plantation system flourished even less in the environs of Charleston than of Nashville, Tennessee, they were at least equally in thrall to a dying faith or a faith dead at heart before they were born. (This is not to imply that the South Carolinians longed backward into literary inconsequence: William Faulkner as novelist and Allen Tate as poet, to cite only two examples, give ample proof that an obsessive remembrance of things past may breed dynamic works of art as well as nostalgic tales and bitter-sweet verses). The timing of the Nashville declaration suggests a tacit awareness that agrarianism was dead, in fact, that the South had made the decision—reluctantly in some quarters but inescapably—to unhitch its economic wagon from the burnt-out star of cotton. By the same token the South Carolina writers admitted that the "unspoiled" Negro's initiation into the rights-conscious American working class was close at hand.

What must have been plain to naïve and sophisticated mythicizers alike by 1930 was that South Carolina must have new sources of livelihood to keep body and soul together. Industrialism might be the death of hereditary loyalties and obligations, it might mean selling the last vestige of the ante bellum soul to the moneygrubbing North; but clinging to the *status quo* would be as surely a living death for most Carolinians. By the late twenties a glutted world market, exhausted lands and the boll weevil (the "boll-evil," in Negro parlance) had virtually killed the money crop on which the state's economy had continued to rest after the Civil war (despite the turn-of-the-century textile fever). The bottom had fallen out of the market in the early twenties, plunging banks and merchants along with farmers into a pit deeper than the crevasse that would open to Wall Streeters in 1929. By the advent of Franklin Roosevelt mortgage was so universal that it was scarcely a joke to say that the Federal Land Bank owned the state of South Carolina lock, stock and barrel.

The Depression came, in other words, nearly a decade earlier than to the rest of the nation. The 1929 crash, therefore, only worsened disaster, throwing the textile industry out of joint and reducing the factory worker to the pauperism from which his fathers had fled half a century before. If anything, the jobless mill hand faced a bleaker day than the plowhand, the tenant farmer or even the urban Negro. The first two could at least scrounge their usual hog and hominy from the land, and even the town black could hire out for "totin' privileges" or beg a bellyful at kitchen doors. Though even beggary failed at times, and, as one old castaway summed up the not uncommon plight with a defiant and life-loving cackle, "Things got so bad here lately us had to fall back on de cooter, but leastways we ain't had to mess up wid de rat." (By "cooter" she meant the small land turtle, not the sea turtle prized for the coastal stewpot.)

By those who look to economic criteria the Depression might be judged as a boon to South Carolina, as perhaps in lesser degree to the nation at large. It focused attention on and through New Deal ministrations brought help in solving problems the state could not cope with unassisted. In its wake came measures that at least one acute and public-minded Carolinian—David R. Coker—had urged for nearly a lifetime at Hartsville in the rich Pee Dee River basin, where his Pennsylvania Baptist ancestors had settled in the mid-eighteenth century. Pioneering in the breeding of pedigreed seed, which he sold, and in gathering scientific data, which he passed out gratis, he joined with his partners in the Coker family combine to advocate for South Carolina and to effect at Hartsville a marriage of agriculture and industry. The Cokers started with textiles in the 1880's, and in the 1890's worked out a method of extracting paper pulp from Southern pine, a method they had since parlayed into one of the largest enterprises in the state, almost unique for its local ownership and control and for its branch operations outside the state (in Canada and Mexico as well as in the North). The reverse is depressingly normal in South Carolina: most factories, that is, are tentacles of a Northern octopus.

Agricultural patterns have so changed and industry has grown at such a rate since the mid-thirties that South Carolina may now claim a near approach to the Coker vision of economic health. New crops, new techniques, and new machines (not to mention federal price supports) have converted large-scale farming into a sanguine pursuit instead of a yearly plunge from gray hope to black despair. Simultaneously, new-risen factories have given a lift to the sharecroppers and 40-acre independents, for whom the land had never meant—perhaps never could mean—anything but unrelieved despair.

So far, however, only the white man can escape to the factories. The Negro stays behind as usual, except as he is needed to sweep the floors and lift the heavy loads. Here custom maintains fences that state law (though one exists) was scarcely needed to keep in good repair. The white man hugs the right to serve the industrial machine: he will not work side by side with the black man. Blacks would doubtless work cheaper than whites—who themselves work cheaper than Northerners at identical jobs—but they are denied the chance to put themselves in competition. Northern entrepreneurs find the white labor cheap enough presumably not to mind what they might otherwise deplore as a brake on free enterprise.

DuBose Heyward's rueful prophecy has not then come wholly to pass. Though the Negro shares—at least at second hand—in the new industrial prosperity, he has yet to be thoroughly "saved," if salvation means full admission to the body politic and economic as well as submission to middle-class morality. Perhaps no living white South Carolinian will have to face the Negro's accession to equality, though he may have to face some Black Monday of token integration in the public schools. Meanwhile, through motives of fear and nostalgia, white Carolinians will hang on to certain troubling stereotypes of the black man. Some, for instance, harboring the image of a servile buffoon, are bound to chafe at the increasing numbers who do not correspond. Others, obsessed with the image of a drunken satyr, will refuse to see the increasing number of sober citizens with their noses to the middle-class family grindstone. So long as these and other fixed ideas prevail, so long as the white denies the black his claim to the normal human virtues and capacities (as well as vices and ineptitudes), just so long will the black darken Carolina nights and disquiet the days.

It would be folly to predict what South Carolina will do in the face of pressures of which the integration drive is only the beginning. It is even folly to predict what course she will take when, like Virginia, she is driven to the wall on the school issue. Her past history of reckless dissent would suggest more than a grudging nod to the inevitable, but one doubts that even a Barnwell Rhett could raise a squad these days to storm the U.S. Marine base on Parris Island or the Air Force hangars at Greenville.

One thing is fairly certain, however. For a long time to come South Carolina will talk—angrily and fondly and constantly—about the Negro, or, as Carolinians say according to their raising, "the colored people" or "the niggers." They will keep on giving point to an anecdote about the cooks from neighboring kitchens heard discussing a "high company" dinner of the night before. "What that high company talk about?" one asked. "Now you know, Jennie Mae, good as I do," the other replied. "Us!"

It seems barely stretching the truth to say that she compressed in a single word half the burden of South Carolina history.

Bibliography

The most recent and comprehensive description of the South Carolina record is Robert J. Turnbull's five-volume *A Bibliography of South Carolina* (Charlottesville, 1956). Of likelier value to the general reader, however, would be J. H. Easterby's *Guide to the Study and Reading of South Carolina History* (Columbia, 1949), a 56-page pamphlet citing pertinent general references and source materials for some thirty aspects of the state's culture and phases of her history.

These works, especially the latter, have not only assisted me in my researches but have made it seem rather pointless to affix a bibliography. Nonetheless, I have incurred debts that I wish to acknowledge, and perhaps by doing so I will encourage the reader's exploration of some fascinating source books and commentaries.

Under the heading "Of General Significance" below I list works that I have consulted most frequently and quoted most freely in shaping and buttressing my story. Some, like Wallace's *History,* have served as factual guidelines; others, likes Cash's well-known *Mind,* have lit perspectives; and still others, like the Simms *Letters,* Mrs. Chesnut's *Diary* and Mr. Petigru's *Letters,* have provided the marvelously informing drama of acute and archetypal minds at grips with crucial experience. Chapter listings include works of especial value but of limited application. No work appears twice: the text generally names or at least implies reliance on "general" works not given as chapter references or on works previously cited as chapter references.

OF GENERAL SIGNIFICANCE

Wallace, David Duncan, *South Carolina, A Short History* (Chapel Hill, 1951.)

A condensation of the author's four-volume *A History of South Carolina* (New York, 1934), this is the handiest, the most up-to-date and probably the most reliable work on the subject. I have found it an indispensable resource. Wallace devoted his life to the study of native annals, and for a long time to come his name will stand as *the* historian of South Carolina.

BALL, W. W. *The State That Forgot* (Indianapolis, 1932).

CARSON, JAMES PETIGRU. *Life, Letters and Speeches of James Louis Petigru* (Washington, 1920).

CASH, W. J. *The Mind of the South* (New York, 1941).

CHESNUT, MARY BOYKIN. *A Diary from Dixie.* Ben Ames Williams, ed. (Boston, 1949).

DABBS, JAMES MCBRIDE. *The Southern Heritage* (New York, 1958).

HEYWARD, DUNCAN CLINCH. *Seed from Madagascar* (Chapel Hill, 1937).

HOLLIS, DANIEL WALKER. *The University of South Carolina,* 2 vols. (Columbia, 1951).

RAVENEL, MRS. ST. JULIEN. *Charleston, the Place and the People* (New York, 1906).

RICE, JOHN A. *I Came Out of the Eighteenth Century* (New York, 1942).

ROBERTSON, BEN. *Red Hills and Cotton* (New York, 1942).

SIMKINS, FRANCIS B. *The South, Old and New* (New York, 1947).

———. *Pitchfork Ben Tillman* (Baton Rouge, 1944).

SIMMS, WILLIAM GILMORE. *The Letters of William Gilmore Simms.* 5 vols. Mary C. Simms Oliphant, Anfred Taylor Odell, T. C. Duncan Eaves, eds. (Columbia, 1952).

South Carolina Writers' Project. *South Carolina, A Guide to the Palmetto State* (New York, 1941).

CHAPTER II

CHILDS, ST. JULIEN RAVENEL. "Cavaliers and Burghers in the Carolina Low Country," *Historiography and Urbanization.* Eric F. Goldman, ed. (Baltimore, 1941).

CHAPTER III

HIRSCH, ARTHUR HENRY. *The Huguenots of Colonial South Carolina* (Durham, 1928).

MCCRADY, EDWARD. *The History of South Carolina under the Proprietary Government* (New York, 1901).

STONEY, SAMUEL GAILLARD. *Plantations of the Carolina Low Country* (Charleston, 1938).

CHAPTER IV

CRANE, VERNER W. *The Southern Frontier* (Durham, 1928).
RAVENEL, HARRIOTT HORRY RUTLEDGE. *Eliza Pinckney* (New York, 1896).

CHAPTER V

MERIWETHER, ROBERT L. *The Expansion of South Carolina* (Kingsport, 1940).
WOODMASON, CHARLES. *The South Carolina Backcountry on the Eve of the Revolution.* Richard J. Hooker, ed. (Chapel Hill, 1953).

CHAPTER VI

BOWES, FREDERICK P. *The Culture of Early Charleston* (Chapel Hill, 1942).
BRIDENBAUGH, CARL. *Myths and Realities* (Baton Rouge, 1952).
SIMONS, ALBERT, AND LAPHAM, SAMUEL JR. *Charleston, South Carolina* (New York, 1927).
SMITH, ALICE R. HUGER, AND HUGER, D. E. *The Dwelling Houses of Charleston* (Philadelphia, 1917).

CHAPTER VII

BARRY, RICHARD. *Mr. Rutledge of South Carolina* (New York, 1942).
McCRADY, EDWARD. *The History of South Carolina under the Royal Government* (New York, 1901).
WALLACE, DAVID DUNCAN. *The Life of Henry Laurens* (New York, 1915).

CHAPTER VIII

GREGORIE, ANNE KING. *Thomas Sumter* (Columbia, 1931).
JAMES, WILLIAM DOBEIN. *A Sketch of the Life of Brig. Gen. Francis Marion* (Marietta, Ga., 1948).
McCRADY, EDWARD. *The History of South Carolina in the Revolution* (New York, 1902).
SCHEER, GEORGE F., AND RANKIN, HUGH F. *Rebels and Redcoats* (Cleveland, 1957).
WARD, CHRISTOPHER. *The War of the Revolution;* Vols. I and II (New York, 1952).

CHAPTER IX

COIT, MARGARET L. *John C. Calhoun* (Boston, 1950).
FREEMAN, DOUGLAS SOUTHALL. *George Washington,* Vol. VI (New York, 1954).

RAVENEL, MRS. ST. JULIEN. *The Life and Times of William Lowndes of South Carolina* (Boston, 1901).
WILTSE, CHARLES M. *John C. Calhoun, Nationalist* (Indianapolis, 1944).

CHAPTER X

LEGARE, HUGH SWINTON. *Writings of Hugh Swinton Legaré*. Mary S. Legaré, ed. (New York, 1846).
MALONE, DUMAS. *The Public Life of Thomas Cooper* (New Haven, 1926).
RHEA, LINDA. *Hugh Swinton Legaré* (Chapel Hill, 1934).
RIPPY, J. FRED. *Joel R. Poinsett, Versatile American* (Durham, 1935).
WHITE, LAURA A. *Robert Barnwell Rhett, Father of Secession* (New York, 1931).
WILTSE, CHARLES M. *John C. Calhoun, Nullifier* (Indianapolis, 1949).

CHAPTERS XI AND XII

ALLSTON, ROBERT F. W. *The South Carolina Rice Plantation: As Revealed in the Papers of R. F. W. Allston.* J. H. Easterby, ed. (Chicago, 1947).
MERRITT, ELIZABETH. *James Henry Hammond* (Baltimore, 1923).
MITCHELL, BROADUS. *William Gregg, Factory Master of the Old South* (Chapel Hill, 1928).
OSTERWEIS, ROLLIN G. *Romanticism and Nationalism in the Old South* (New Haven, 1949).
TAYLOR, ROSSER H. *Ante-Bellum South Carolina: A Social and Cultural History* (Chapel Hill, 1942).
WILTSE, CHARLES M. *John C. Calhoun, Sectionalist* (Indianapolis, 1951).

CHAPTER XIII

BARRETT, JOHN G. *Sherman's March through the Carolinas* (Chapel Hill, 1956).
CAUTHEN, CHARLES EDWARD. *South Carolina Goes to War* (Chapel Hill, 1950).
COULTER, E. MERTON. *The Confederate States of America, 1861-1865* (Baton Rouge, 1950).
JOHNSON, GUION GRIFFIS. *A Social History of the Sea Islands* (Chapel Hill, 1930).
JONES, KATHERINE M. *Heroines of Dixie* (Indianapolis, 1955).
KIBLER, LILLIAN A. *Benjamin F. Perry: South Carolina Unionist* (Durham, 1946).
RAVENEL, WILLIAM HENRY. *The Private Journal of William Henry Ravenel.* Arney Robinson Childs, ed. (Columbia, 1947).
SWANBERG, W. A. *First Blood, The Story of Fort Sumter* (New York, 1957).

WELLMAN, MANLY WADE. *Giant in Gray, A Biography of Wade Hampton of South Carolina* (New York, 1949).

CHAPTER XIV

ANDREWS, SIDNEY. *The South since the War* (Boston, 1866).
DEFOREST, JOHN W. *A Union Officer in the Reconstruction* (New Haven, 1948).
GONZALES, AMBROSE E. *The Black Border* (Columbia, 1922).
LELAND, JOHN A. *A Voice from South Carolina* (Charleston, 1879).
PRINGLE, ELIZABETH W. ALLSTON. *Chronicles of Chicora Wood* (New York, 1922).
SIMKINS, FRANCIS B., AND WOODY, ROBERT H. *South Carolina during Reconstruction* (New York, 1915).

CHAPTER XV

JARRELL, HAMPTON M. *Wade Hampton and the Negro* (Columbia, 1949).
KOHN, AUGUST. *The Cotton Mills of South Carolina* (Charleston, 1907).
MITCHELL, BROADUS. *Industrial Revolution in the South* (Baltimore, 1930).

CHAPTER XVI

DURHAM, FRANK. *DuBose Heyward, The Man Who Wrote "Porgy"* (Columbia, 1954).
HEYWARD, DUBOSE. *Porgy* (New York, 1925).
———. *Mamba's Daughters* (New York, 1929).
PETERKIN, JULIA. *Black April* (Indianapolis, 1927).
———. *Scarlet Sister Mary* (Indianapolis, 1928).
SIMPSON, GEORGE LEE. *The Cokers of Carolina: A Social Biography of a Family* (Chapel Hill, 1956).

Index

Set in Baskerville
Format by Jacqueline Wilsdon
Manufactured by The Haddon Craftsmen, Inc.
Published by HARPER & BROTHERS, *New York*

27-102

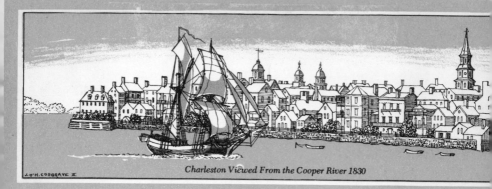

Charleston Viewed From the Cooper River 1830

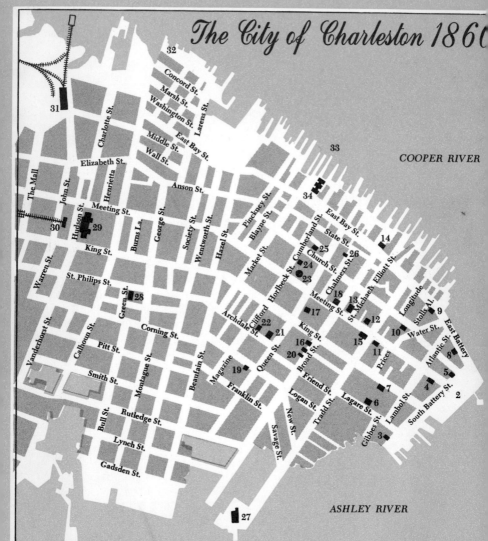